10/19

D1027303

CRUISE PORTS
EUROPEAN
RIVERS

A GUIDE TO PERFECT DAYS ON SHORE

Andy Symington, Mark Baker, Oliver Berry, Kerry Christiani, Gregor C
Marc Di Duca, Steve Fallon, Damian Harper, Catherine Le Nevez, Leo
Ragozin, Kevin Raub, Simon Richmond, Brendan Sainsbury, Andre
Schulte-Peevers, Regis St Louis, Benedict Walker, Nicola Williams

Contents

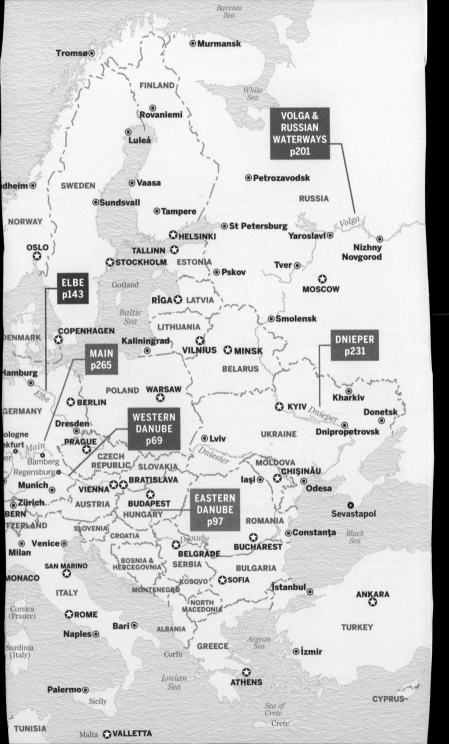

Welcome to European Rivers

Sip your wine while watching picture-perfect European scenery breeze past – castles, medieval villages and fields of flowers. European river cruises are elegantly casual affairs, perfect for exploring the arts and culture that beckon ashore.

Active travellers, nature and culture aficionados, as well as families of all sizes, have discovered that cruising down a quiet, traffic-free river, surrounded by scenic riverfront views, is an ideal way to see Europe. This change in European travel is unfolding in real time, as each year more and more cruise lines offer immersive learning experiences such as cooking classes and home visits, or activities like bicycle trips and long hikes. In fact, a river cruise is often the best way to experience destinations for the first time.

And, of course, there's the food. Many cruise lines offer a regional menu or serve almost solely local cuisine. They know their guests are keen to indulge and cook accordingly. Look for cruises offering cooking classes with the chef as an added bonus.

By necessity, European riverboats are far smaller than the vessels that cruise the Mediterranean and Baltic Seas. Passenger numbers are usually fewer than 200, making these cruises a far more social and intimate experience. More frequent stops mean much more onshore activity.

Additionally, there are no inside cabins on a European river cruise. Cabins come with a large window at the very least, and a great many have their own balcony or floor-to-ceiling panoramic views. You might even forego the ship's entertainment just to watch the scenery breeze past.

picture-perfect European scenery: castles, medieval villages and fields of flowers

Passau, Germany (p88)

Schwarzwälder kirschtorte (Black Forest cherry cake)
ANNA_PUSTYNNIKOVA/SHUTTERSTOCK ©

European Rivers' Top 12

Northern Rhine, Germany

Gorgeous meanders and noble German cities

The stretch of the Rhine south of Koblenz contains Germany's most majestic scenery, winding through picture-perfect villages and craggy landscapes. Beyond, the river grows large as it courses through major cities like Cologne (pictured above), many of which were founded by the Romans. Cultural travellers will be rewarded with such sightseeing gems as the magnificent cathedrals of Cologne and Speyer, plus some richly endowed art galleries.

Above right: Stained-glass windows, Kölner Dom (p38)

TRABANTOS/SHUTTERSTOCK ©

Southern Rhine, France, Germany & Switzerland

Explore intriguing towns in this borderland

Running between Germany's famed Black Forest on one side and the glorious French wine region of Alsace (pictured top) on the other, the southern stretch of the Rhine features a fascinating blend of cultures. Landscapes range from picturesque to more industrial, with cities such as Strasbourg (pictured bottom) and Basel offering brilliant attractions.

PETER UNGER/GETTY IMAGES ©

Western Danube, Austria & Germany

Romantic landscapes in the heart of Europe

Coursing through Bavaria, the western Danube is dotted with postcard-perfect towns and picturesque stretches of riverbank – a golden example of European river cruising. There's plenty to keep you interested on the way, from the culture of Vienna to the intriguing history of Nuremberg (pictured above).

3

Eastern Danube, Hungary & Serbia

A cross-section of Europe's lesser-known east

The eastern Danube begins with one of the river's major highlights, magnificent Budapest, the capital of Hungary and home to bathhouses and intriguing cuisine. Beyond here, the river traces a circuitous path through Eastern Europe, taking in intriguing post-communist locales, as well as some of Europe's lesser-known cultures. Parts of this section of the Danube are a bit off-the-beaten-track and are all the better for it. Right: Széchenyi Baths (p103), Budapest

Seine, France

Cruise plus city-break in northern France

Known as the river that runs through one of the world's most alluring metropolises, the Seine is the perfect choice for a holiday that combines cruising with a city break. Paris alone could hold your attention for days; from here, the river passes through gorgeous French countryside and the historic city of Rouen (pictured right), before arriving at the coast of Normandy, with all its wartime associations.

Elbe, Czech Republic & Germany

Little-cruised but worthwhile stretch of Central Europe

Running across the Czech Republic and eastern Germany, the Elbe is an under-the-radar cruising river that is well worth investigating. The towns of east Germany – from little Wittenberg to reconstructed Dresden – are intriguing. Cruises often begin or end in alluring Prague; Berlin is also sometimes added to the trip. Above: Lutherstadt Wittenberg, Germany (p154)

Moselle, Germany

Intimate stretch of the wine-producing German river

Wending between vertiginous vine-covered slopes, the Moselle (in German, Mosel) has an intimate charm. The German section flows for 195km from Trier to Koblenz on a slow, winding course, with entrancing scenery around every hairpin bend, from brightly coloured, half-timbered medieval villages to crumbling hilltop castles, elegant *Jugendstil* (art nouveau) villas, and ancient wine warehouses.

Douro, Portugal

Spectacular terraced vineyards, the home of port wine

Douro cruises begin at lively Porto, an enticing Portuguese city with bags of soul, whose old town cascades steeply down to the riverfront. Cruises then head upriver through scenery that becomes more and more majestic. Each curve of the river yields a new panorama of steep hills with tiered vineyard terraces. Here the grapes are grown for port wine, aged back in Porto in venerable company lodges. Most cruises end up with a taste of Spain, too.

JAN JERMAN/SHUTTERSTOCK ©

LOU ARMOR/
SHUTTERSTOCK ©

Volga & Russian Waterways, Russia

Jewels of Russia linked by sparkling waterways

A Moscow to St Petersburg cruise on the Volga River and associated waterways not only allows you to take in the two crown-jewel cities of Russia, but also stops in smaller historic towns, offering a slice of Russian life in the countryside that provides a counterbalance to these grand urban centres. The route takes in the picturesque Lake Onega (pictured far left) and impressive Lake Ladoga over the course of two weeks' cruising. Left: Church of the Saviour on the Spilled Blood (p226), St Petersburg

VLADA PHOTO/SHUTTERSTOCK ©

RUSLAN LYTVYN/SHUTTERSTOCK ©

KATATONIA82/SHUTTERSTOCK ©
SCULPTOR: ALEXANDER TOKAREV

Dnieper, Ukraine

Across the Ukraine to the Black Sea

Starting in the capital, Kyiv, traverse the Ukraine from north to south along the wide Dnieper, taking in pretty, historic towns along the way. Emerging into the Black Sea, cruises track west to Odesa, whose turbulent history belies its status as a popular beach resort. Most trips include several days in each city, with around five days of actual cruising. Clockwise from top: Kyevo-Pecherska Lavra (p234), Kyiv; Odesa harbour (p244); St Michael's Golden-Domed Moastery (p239), Kyiv

10

BONCHAN/SHUTTERSTOCK ©

Rhône, France

Gourmet experiences cruising the south of France

The Rhône is definitely one for gourmets, with Lyon's superb food culture a highlight, and the marvellous wines of the river's valley as you cruise south. The aromatic towns of Provence await, with historic Avignon a particular highlight. Add-ons to the route can include the Alpine stretches of the Rhône above Lyon or the Saône, which offers yet more wine in Burgundy. Above: Andouillette (sausage made from pigs' intestines; p253)

AUGUSTIN LAZAROIU/SHUTTERSTOCK ©

Main, Germany

Seductive German river connected to the Rhine and Danube

A tributary of the Rhine, the Main is a German-only affair that is also connected by canal to the Danube, allowing for plenty of flexibility for cruise itineraries. It winds through fascinating Bavarian landscapes and into southwestern Germany, taking in both charming historic villages and the financial centre of Frankfurt (pictured above). Its principal section runs from Bamberg to Mainz, where it joins the Rhine.

Plan Your Trip
Need to Know

When to Go

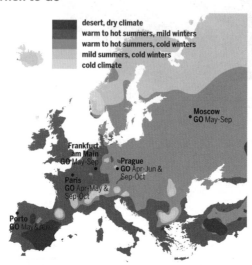

desert, dry climate
warm to hot summers, mild winters
warm to hot summers, cold winters
mild summers, cold winters
cold climate

Moscow
• GO May-Sep

Frankfurt
am Main
GO May-Sep
Prague
• GO Apr-Jun &
Sep-Oct
Paris
GO Apr-May &
Sep-Oct
Porto
GO May & Jun

High Season (Jun–Aug)

○ Everyone comes to Europe and all of Europe hits the road.

○ Hotel prices and temperatures are at their highest.

○ Expect all the major attractions to be very busy.

Shoulder (Apr–May & Sep–Oct)

○ Crowds and prices drop: this is the best time to visit.

○ Temperatures are comfortable but southern Europe can be hot.

Low Season (Nov–Mar)

○ Hotels drop their prices or close down.

○ The weather can be cold and days short, especially in northern Europe.

○ Winter attractions pop up in Central Europe.

Currencies

Austria, France, Germany, Portugal: Euro (€)
Czech Republic: Koruna
česká (Kč)
Hungary: Forint (Ft)
Russia: Rouble (R)
Serbia: Serbian dinar (RSD)
Switzerland: Swiss franc (Sfr)
Ukraine: Hryvnia (uah)

Languages

Czech, French, German, Hungarian, Portuguese, Russian, Serbian, Ukrainian. English is widely spoken on cruise liners and in many port towns.

Visas

The Schengen Agreement allows travellers from many nations entry into EU countries for stays of up to 90 days; if travelling to Russia or Ukraine, you may need to obtain a separate tourist visa.

Money

ATMs are common; credit and debit cards are widely accepted.

Mobile Phones

Roaming charges within the EU no longer exist, so it's worth buying a prepaid local SIM at your first EU stop, then using it throughout your travels.

Useful Websites

Hidden Europe (www.hiddeneurope. co.uk) Fascinating magazine and online dispatches from all the continent's corners.

Visit Europe (www.visiteurope.com) Information about travel in 33 member countries.

Spotted by Locals (www.spottedby locals.com) Insider tips for cities across Europe.

Lonely Planet (www.lonelyplanet.com/ europe) Destination information, hotel bookings, traveller forum and more.

Pre-Departure Checklist

o Ensure your passport is valid for six months past arrival.

o Check you have the required visas.

o Check the airline baggage restrictions.

o Inform your debit-/credit-card company you're heading away.

o Organise appropriate travel insurance.

o Check whether your mobile phone will work in Europe.

Opening Hours

Opening times vary significantly between countries. The following is a general overview.

Banks 9am to between 3pm and 5pm Monday to Friday. Occasionally shut for lunch.

Bars 6pm to midnight or later.

Museums closed Monday or (less commonly) Tuesday

Restaurants noon to midnight.

Shops & businesses 9am to 6pm Monday to Friday, to 1pm or 5pm Saturday. In smaller towns there may be a one- to two-hour closure for lunch. Some shops close on Sunday. Businesses also close on national holidays and local feast days.

Time

From March to October, many European countries observe daylight savings time. The European Parliament proposed to scrap daylight savings time in 2018, but the proposal has yet to be approved by the EU.

o Portugal (GMT)

o Central Europe (GMT plus one hour)

o Eastern Europe (GMT plus two hours)

o Russia (GMT plus three hours)

Wi-Fi Access

o Internet cafes are a thing of the past. Wi-fi is the main way people connect on the road.

o Some cities have free wi-fi zones, and you can usually find paid wi-fi in public areas such as train stations.

o All European river cruises offer wi-fi access and this is increasingly free, though you may have to pay for better speeds.

o By far the easiest way to keep connected is to buy a local SIM card and a cheap data package and pop it in your phone.

Getting Around Ashore

o Most European cities have excellent public transport systems, which comprise some combination of metros (subways), trains, trams and buses. Service is usually comprehensive.

o The centres of these cities are usually surprisingly walkable, so make sure you pack a pair of sturdy shoes for your cruise.

o In smaller locations, river cruises often dock right in the heart of town.

For more on **getting around**, see p307 ➡

Plan Your Trip
Hotspots For...

Castles & Palaces

Defence was long a priority in Europe's heartland, where stony fortresses dominate riverside hills. During times of peace, ruling families expanded ornate palaces.

SAIKO3P/SHUTTERSTOCK ©

Eastern Danube (p97)
The palace complex of Budapest and Belgrade's sprawling fortress contain interesting museums.

Royal Palace (p100)
Budapest's enormous palace complex.

Moselle (p167)
Numerous impressive castles and fortresses dot the banks of this river.

Reichsburg (p179)
The precarious-looking cragtop castle of Cochem (pictured).

Main (p267)
Germany is richly endowed with castles and stately palaces – a trip along the Main reveals plenty.

Würzburg Residenz (p268)
This amazing 18th-century baroque extravaganza is a must-see.

Religious Buildings

Christianity, Judaism and Islam have all influenced Europe. Impressive cathedrals and sacred sites are scattered around the towns and landscape.

MAZIARZ/SHUTTERSTOCK ©

Northern Rhine (p37)
Two of Europe's most incredible cathedrals, at Cologne and Speyer, dignify this stretch of river.

Kaiserdom (p50)
Speyer's magnificent cathedral lives long in the memory.

Elbe (p143)
Home to a rich religious history from early Protestantism to Prague's synagogues (pictured).

Frauenkirche, Dresden (p152)
This reconstructed church is a symbol of renewal.

Dnieper (p231)
The Orthodox churches and monasteries of the Ukraine are sumptuous and atmospheric.

Kyevo-Pecherska Lavra (p234)
The holiest site in Ukraine is this intriguing cave monastery.

Art & Design

From ancient artefacts to creations that defy comprehension, Europe's art is continually evolving. There's an unbelievable array exhibited across the region's towns and cities.

YARYGIN/GETTY IMAGES ©

Volga (p201)
Imperial Russia amassed an extraordinary trove of paintings and sculptures.

State Hermitage Museum (p210)
Perhaps the world's most stupendous art collection (pictured).

Seine (p115)
Paris is stocked with so many quality art galleries, you'll be in serious danger of missing the boat...

Musée Rodin (p131)
Get to grips with the 20th-century's greatest sculptor.

Southern Rhine (p53)
From overflowing galleries to cutting-edge design, this tri-nation area has plenty to offer.

Vitra Campus (p65)
Amazing design exhibitions and installations in Basel.

Gourmet Experiences

Europe's stunning diversity of cuisines and rich heritage of brewing and winemaking means gastronomic experiences are an essential pleasure of a river cruise.

ANASTASIA TURSHINA/SHUTTERSTOCK ©

Douro (p181)
Pair delicious seafood and pork dishes with fabulous wines and ports from the vineyards along the river.

Graham's (p186)
Taste the range at this venerable port lodge.

Rhône (p249)
Luxuriate in the bistro culture of Lyon, then cruise through vineyards producing classic French wines.

Le Musée (p256)
Savour local dishes at this glorious Lyon *bouchon*.

Western Danube (p69)
Cruise from bratwurst and local *Landbier* in Bavaria to schnitzel and strudel in Vienna.

Bratwursthäusle (p93)
Try world-famous bratwurst at this Nuremberg tavern.

Plan Your Trip
Month by Month

January

It's cold but most towns are relatively tourist-free and hotel prices are rock bottom.

✣ Orthodox Christmas, Eastern Europe

Christmas is celebrated in different ways in Eastern Europe: many countries celebrate on Christmas Eve (24 December), with an evening meal and midnight Mass. In Russia, Ukraine and Serbia, Christmas falls in January, as per the Julian calendar.

February

Carnival in all its manic glory sweeps the Catholic regions. Cold temperatures are forgotten amid masquerades, street festivals and general bacchanalia. Expect to be kissed by a stranger.

✣ Fasching, Germany

Germany doesn't leave the pre-Lent season solely to its neighbours. Fasching (or Karneval) is celebrated with abandon in the traditional Catholic regions, including Bavaria, along the Rhine and particularly vibrantly in Cologne.

March

Spring arrives in southern Europe. Further north the rest of the continent continues to freeze, though days are often bright.

April

Spring arrives with a burst of colour. On the most southern beaches, it's time to shake the sand out of the umbrellas. Easter is celebrated in distinct ways across the region, with the Orthodox Easter often on a different date.

✗ Spargelzeit, Germany

No period ranks higher on the German culinary calendar than *Spargelzeit* (asparagus season), when Germans devour great quantities of (mostly) white asparagus. You'll find restaurants with asparagus menus and whole books devoted to the subject, while many towns go so far as to hold asparagus festivals in May and June.

DE VISU/SHUTTERSTOCK ©

☆ Budapest Spring Festival, Hungary

This two-week festival in early April is one of Europe's top classical-music events (www.springfestival.hu). Concerts are held in a number of beautiful venues, including stunning churches, the opera house and the national theatre.

★ Best Festivals
Budapest Spring Festival, April
White Nights, June
Bastille Day, July
Oktoberfest, September
Christmas Markets, December

May

May is usually sunny and warm and full of things to do – an excellent time to visit. It's not too hot or too crowded, though you can still expect the big destinations to feel busy.

♟ Beer Festival, Czech Republic

An event dear to many travellers' hearts, this Prague beer festival (www.ceskypivni festival.cz) offers lots of food, music and – most importantly – around 70 beers from around the country from mid- to late May.

June

The huge summer travel season hasn't started yet, but the sun has broken through the clouds and the weather is generally gorgeous across the continent.

♨ Festa de São João, Portugal

Elaborate processions, live music on Porto's plazas and merrymaking all across Portugal's second city. Squeaky plastic hammers (for sale everywhere) come out for the unusual custom of whacking one

Above left: Fasching, Cologne. Above right: Festa de São João, Portugal

another. Everyone is fair game – expect no mercy.

✤ White Nights, Russia

By mid-June the Baltic sun just sinks behind the horizon at night, leaving the sky a grey-white colour and encouraging locals to forget routines and party hard. The best place to join the fun is St Petersburg, where balls, classical-music concerts and other summer events keep spirits high.

July

One of the busiest months for travel across the continent with outdoor cafes, beer gardens and beach clubs all hopping. Expect beautiful – even steamy – weather anywhere you go.

✤ Bastille Day, France

Fireworks, balls, processions, and – of course – good food and wine, for France's national day on 14 July, celebrated in every French town and city. Go to the heart of town and get caught up in this patriotic festival.

☆ Festival d'Avignon, France

Rouse your inner thespian with Avignon's legendary performing-arts festival. Street acts in its fringe fest are as inspired as those on official stages.

August

Everybody's going someplace as half of Europe shuts down to enjoy the traditional month of holiday with the other half. If you're anywhere near the beach, it will be mobbed and the temperatures are hot, hot, hot!

Sziget Music Festival, Hungary

A weeklong, great-value world-music festival (www.sziget.hu) held all over Budapest. Sziget features bands from around the world playing at more than 60 venues.

September

It's cooling off in every sense, and this might be the best time to visit: the weather's still good but the crowds have thinned.

🍷 Oktoberfest, Germany

Despite its name, Germany's legendary beer-swilling party (www.oktoberfest.de) starts mid-September in Munich and finishes a week into October. Millions descend for litres of beer and carousing that has no equal.

October

Another good month to visit – almost everything is still open, while prices and visitor numbers are way down. Weather can be unpredictable, though, and even cold in northern Europe.

November

Leaves have fallen and snow is about in much of Europe. Even in the temperate zones around the Med it can get chilly, rainy and blustery. Most seasonal attractions have closed for the year.

December

Despite freezing temperatures this is a magical time to visit Europe, with Christmas decorations brightening the dark streets. Prices remain surprisingly low provided you avoid Christmas and New Year's Eve.

🔒 Christmas Markets

In December, Christmas markets (www.christmasmarkets.com) are held across Europe, with particularly good ones in Germany, Austria and Czech Republic. The most famous are in Nuremberg (the Christkindlmarkt) and Vienna. Warm your hands through your mittens holding a hot mug of mulled wine and find that special (or kitsch) present.

Plan Your Trip
Get Inspired

PICTURE ALLIANCE/CONTRIBUTOR/GETTY IMAGES ©

Read

Life & Fate (Vasily Grossman; 1960) WWII, the Holocaust and revolutionary Russia in one of the century's greatest novels.

The Unbearable Lightness of Being (Milan Kundera; 1984) Masterpiece set in Prague in the uncertain days before the 1968 Warsaw Pact invasion.

The Age of Genius: The Seventeenth Century & the Birth of the Modern Mind (AC Grayling; 2016) Very readable background on the Thirty Years' War and the key figures of the European Enlightenment.

Watch

Goodbye Lenin (2003) Comedy set in East Berlin; when a girl awakes from a coma post-communism, her family pretends the Wall never fell.

Schindler's List (1993) One of a number of impressive films to see about the Holocaust.

The Grand Budapest Hotel (2014) The Danubius Hotel Gellért was the inspiration (but not the actual location) for this film.

The Third Man (1949) Trying to find some remnants of post-WWII Vienna will become an obsession after this great film noir by Carol Reed.

Listen

Kraftwerk Based at Düsseldorf on the Rhine, this group created the musical foundations for techno, the club sound that would sweep across the world from the late '80s.

Brahms The Elbe city of Hamburg brought forth Johannes Brahms (1833–97) and his influential symphonies, chamber and piano works. Try to listen to the second movement of *Ein Deutsches Requiem* without air-conducting.

Johann Strauss II, An der schönen, blauen Donau Better known in English as the *Blue Danube Waltz*; what better to listen to when cruising that river towards Vienna?

Above: Kraftwerk in concert, Dresden

Plan Your Trip
Choose Your Cruise

Matching your expectations, budget and travel style to the right cruise is the most important decision of the trip, so it pays to think carefully about what's important to you. Though in general European river cruises are far more intimate experiences than the larger seagoing ships and there isn't a huge variety in ship size, different cruise lines and ships offer significantly different experiences.

Budget

Think about how much you want to spend. Would you prefer a cheaper cabin on a longer trip or a more luxurious cabin on a shorter one? Are all-inclusive trips going to save you money? Plenty of river cruises include generous food and beverage packages, but if you aren't going to be sipping something at the bar during happy hour, you might prefer to pay your own way. Remember to factor onshore time into your calculations, as well as on-board services like laundry, wi-fi and compulsory gratuities for staff.

Look for ways you can save money; buying a local SIM card and popping it in your phone may give you much cheaper, faster internet service than paying to use on-board wi-fi, for example.

You may want to arrive at your cruise's departure city a day early to reduce the risk of missed connections. Budget for a night's sleep in a hotel or rental accommodation plus two or three meals. Cruise companies have partnerships with local lodging, though it can be more cost-efficient to square that away on your own if you don't mind the extra legwork.

Unless you have a port in your own city, you'll have to fly to embark on the cruise of your dreams. Check that airfares are reasonable for the dates you are considering before getting swept away in a cruise bargain. Then, don't forget to factor in the costs of on-the-ground transportation. That includes transfers to and from your hometown airport and the costs of reaching the pier from your arrival airport.

Cruise lines can take care of your transfer costs at a premium; it's also possible to arrange your own taxi or rideshare or even to take public transit. Just triple check your departure and arrival times so you don't miss the boat.

When it comes to souvenir shopping, setting a budget with your spending is crucial. Try allotting yourself one special purchase as a memento of your trip. Do your shopping away from the strip of real estate right by the port, where tourist traps proliferate.

Size & Demographics

Most European cruise boats are of a similar size and hold between 100 and 200 passengers. With smaller passenger numbers, you'll likely have far more contact with your fellow cruisers than on the larger, more anonymous ocean-going ships. This makes it important to consider who a particular cruise is aimed at. Historically, European

★ Best Online Resources

Cruise Critic (www.cruisecritic.com)

Cruise Line (www.cruiseline.com)

River Cruise Advisor (www.rivercruiseadvisor.com)

river cruises have attracted mostly active seniors, but today more and more are catering to multigenerational families, honeymooners and young solo travellers. A few cruise lines – including CroisiEurope, Tauck and Disney – run designated family-friendly cruises with fast-paced itineraries that teach kids totally nonboring history lessons. For the liveliest boatmates, look for an 'active' cruise that comes with bicycles, adventure sports or interactive cultural experiences.

Above: River-cruise boat in Dresden, Germany (p162)

Plan Your Trip

MAPICS/SHUTTERSTOCK ©

Seasons

Cruises on European rivers tend to begin in the spring, around March, and go through to October. Some cruises operating in areas where Christmas markets are a feature run right through December.

Choosing your season is very much a matter of personal preference, and there are pros and cons for each season. Summer cruises offer the most spectacular scenery, the longest daylight hours and the best weather, but the towns you visit will be far busier and you won't be alone in port; in some smaller places, you may have to scramble across the decks of other boats to reach shore.

Spring and autumn mean less time around the pool on the top deck, but quieter times ashore. Expect rains in spring, but also blooming flowers. Autumn is a great time to cruise the Douro, with grapes being picked and clement temperatures, but will be chillier on the Volga.

Winter cruises tend to focus on places where Christmas experiences are on offer.

Shorter daylight hours mean you'll see less scenery, but the charm of the festive season has its own appeal.

Cabin Types

On European river cruises, all of the cabins are exterior, meaning you are guaranteed a great view. Large windows are the norm, and a great many cabins have their own balcony or floor-to-ceiling outlook. Think about which side of the boat you want to be on, both in terms of the scenery and the sunshine.

With fewer cabins, European river cruises tend to offer less options for single travellers than their ocean-going equivalents, but there are exceptions. Don't be afraid to try to bargain down the single supplement, particularly if you are going out of season and the cruise might not reach capacity.

Food & Drink

Your on-board dining choices are more restricted on river cruises, so it pays to study what each company offers in detail. Some

will have only one restaurant, while others offer more options. However, the quality tends to be much higher than on ocean-going cruises, due to the smaller number of passengers and the fact that river cruisers are often keen foodies. Service in general is much more personal on river cruises, so it pays to get onside with the waiters and bartenders. Some cruises will have on-board sommeliers.

Study the drinks packages in detail. What wines are included? What others are available at extra cost? Are drinks included at mealtimes only or around the clock?

Route Options

The two major rivers for European cruises are the Rhine and the Danube. Together, they were once the northern boundary of the Roman Empire. Rhine cruises often run from Amsterdam to Basel, following the course of the river through Germany. Danube cruises start in southern Germany, wend their way through Bratislava, Slovakia; Linz and Vienna, Austria; and

Belgrade, Serbia; then skirt the Bulgarian and Romanian border to reach the Black Sea. While many first-time European river cruisers stick to these two rivers, there are many other options available. In Western Europe, you can cruise through the French countryside on the Rhône and Seine, or check out the vineyards of Portugal on the Douro. Beyond the Danube in Eastern Europe, riverboats visit the remnants of Tsarist Russia on the Volga, while in Ukraine you can cruise along the Dnieper River to the seaport of Odesa, with its statuesque opera house and famed Potemkin Stairs.

Even on the same river, distinct routes can be offered. One company might zip up the Rhine, allowing you to see the highlights in a few days; another might take longer, exploring smaller places along the way and offering more time for onshore experiences. In the time you've got, decide whether

From left: Christmas market, Frankfurt am Main (p270); View from the Potemkin Steps (p245), Odesa

Plan Your Trip

you'd like to get a feel for more places, or more of a feel for fewer places.

Cruise Companies

River cruise lines include, but are not limited to:

- AmaWaterways (www.amawaterways.com)

- Avalon Waterways (www.avalonwaterways.com)

- CroisiEurope (www.croisieurope.travel)

- Crystal Cruises (www.crystalcruises.com)

- Disney Cruises (www.adventuresbydisney.com)

- Emerald Waterways (www.emeraldwaterways.com)

- Riviera Travel (www.rivieratravel.co.uk)

- Scenic (www.scenic.com.au)

- Tauck (www.tauck.com)

- Uniworld River Cruises (www.uniworld.com)

- Viking River Cruises (www.vikingrivercruises.com)

Solo Travellers

Ten years ago, the notion of a cruise catering to the individual was virtually nonexistent. Today, many new ships from brands like Crystal Cruises, AmaWaterways, Tauck and Viking River Cruises come equipped with a small supply of studio rooms – often interior cabins – designed with the solo sailor in mind. It's an overdue development after years of charging solo travellers a 'single supplement' when they booked a cabin for only themselves, a policy that meant they'd pay a premium of 125% to 175%.

Make sure to shop around when selecting a cruise, as each line has a different policy regarding solo travellers and their solo 'tax' can vary. Some travel companies will play matchmaker and link solo cruisers up with one another as roommates to avoid

the dreaded supplement charge, while other groups organise specific singles cruises.

Sociable travellers will have no problem making new connections on small boat tours, especially journeys arranged around common interests, like scuba diving or wine.

Accessibility

When it comes to accessible travel for the differently abled, the cruise industry has some key advantages over land-based travel for tourists needing a wheelchair or vacationers with limited mobility. Cabins may sometimes be smaller than hotel rooms, but staying in one room for the course of a trip smooths out transport issues. Helpful staff can assist at any time while sailing.

That said, vessels and ports vary, and due diligence is required. Cruise companies list the accessible features of each boat, and often have a dedicated phone line for special-needs queries. On board, wheelchairs are provided by the ports for

> ★ **Top Tip**
>
> Many European river cruises have their own fleet of passenger bicycles. Take one out for a bike trip in the French countryside during a stop on your cruise down the Seine.

entering and exiting the vessel, but most cruises will expect that you provide your own mobility aid during your time on board. Service animals are given a pass by most large cruises, but emotional support or therapy animals are strictly forbidden. Some cruises are better equipped than others to host passengers with special needs, and it's imperative to seek out the most accessible option before booking. Do your research and you'll have a stress-free trip tailored to your specifications.

From left: Pasengers above an Eastern Danube cruise near Budapest (p106)

Plan Your Trip
Sustainable Cruising

From air and water pollution to the overcrowding of popular destinations, travelling on cruise ships is not without significant impacts – choose your cruise line carefully.

Environmental Issues

Although the smaller size and footprint of river cruise ships generally means a lower environmental impact than ocean-going giants, river ecosystems are sensitive and the proximity of the banks means that any pollution emitted from a vessel can quickly cause harm.

River cruise ships can generate large amounts of sewage, solid waste and grey water. As consumer pressure grows, more and more ships are being equipped with new wastewater treatment facilities, LED lighting and solar panels. In many river ports, 'cold-ironing' allows ships to plug into local power supplies and avoid leaving generators or the engine running while in port.

There are also the cultural impacts to consider. Though cruise lines can generate money for their ports of call, large groups of people arriving at once can change the character of a town and seem overwhelming to locals and noncruising travellers. There is an increasing perception among locals that cruise passengers are unwilling to spend money ashore, so consider choosing an operator that includes meals in local restaurants and onshore activities.

What You Can Do

Do some research. Email the cruise lines and ask about their environmental policies: wastewater treatment, recycling initiatives and whether they use alternative energy sources. Knowing that customers care about these things has an impact. Treadright has developed a handbook on sustainable river cruising for companies, with examples of best

practice (www.treadright.org/projects/
the-sustainable-river-cruise-project).

Sustainable Exploring Ashore

When you get off the ship, you can do your
part and make a difference. Here are a few
tips to help minimise your impact on the
environment.

Skip bottled water The water in Europe is safe
to drink, so pack a reusable water bottle.

Ride the bus or tram Most cities in the region
have excellent public transport networks.

Hire a bike There's an excellent network of cycle
paths and easy hiring in many of the cities you
will visit.

Say no to plastic Bring your own reusable bags
to carry anything you buy. Plastic straws are also
best avoided.

Don't litter Almost everything discarded on land
makes its way to the sea, where it can wreak
havoc on marine life.

★ Best Online Resources

The following organisations review the
environmental records of cruise lines
and ships:

Friends of the Earth (https://foe.org/
cruisereportcard) Letter grades given to
cruise lines and ships for environmental
and human health impacts.

World Travel Awards (www.worldtravel
awards.com) Annual awards for the
'World's Leading Green Cruise Line'.

Responsible Tourism Awards
(https://responsibletourism.wtm.com/
awards/) Have a cruise category.

Make a positive impact Support independently-
owned businesses and look for opportunities to
interact with local culture.

From left: Filling water bottles from a city water fountain; Bicycle riding along the Danube, Vienna (p80)

Plan Your Trip
Family Time Ashore

HACKENBERG PHOTO-COLOGNE/ALAMY STOCK PHOTO ©

More and more European river cruise lines are catering to families. A few – including CroisiEurope, Tauck and Disney – run designated family-friendly cruises with fast-paced itineraries that incorporate engaging history lessons. While some companies ban very small children, many now have kid-friendly activities for kids ages six and up. On board there may only be a small playroom, but kids will forgive you when they realise how much freedom they have to explore on shore each day. Ashore, there are tonnes of things that will appeal to kids, youths and teenagers.

The Basics

• Europe is very family-orientated. Expect waitstaff to ruffle your kid's hair and bank on seeing young children sitting around at family meals in restaurants until late.

• Nappies (diapers) are widely available; baby-changing facilities vary from country to country but are generally fairly comprehensive.

• Baby formula and baby food are widely available in all European countries, but brands do differ. You might want to bring your own stash as a backup.

• For cheap rooms before and after your cruise, check out Europe's hostels, many of which have at least one family room.

• Don't write off the less obvious sights. Many of Europe's art galleries and iconic monuments give out kids' activity books that include interactive itineraries for children.

• Most European countries have a pretty relaxed attitude to breastfeeding in public.

• Restaurants are rarely equipped with nappy-changing facilities, but some fast-food places have a fold-down change table in the women's toilet.

• For more information, check the Lonely Planet website and search the specific countries you will be visiting, as well as the Family Holidays section (www.lonelyplanet.com/family-holidays), which has regularly

DAVID DAVIES/ALAMY STOCK PHOTO ©

updated information, articles and advice, plus numerous kids' books including *My Family Travel Map: Europe*.

Discounts

Many museums, monuments and attractions are free to anyone under 18 years, but the cut-off age varies. In general, you can assume kids under five don't pay at all. Most places also offer family tickets.

Children qualify for discounts on public transport and tours, where they usually pay half price, sometimes less. Some hotels, including many international chains, have discounted rates for kids or don't charge extra if they're under a certain age (varying from three to 16) and stay in their parents' room without extra bedding.

Eating Out

As long as they're not running wild, children are generally welcome in restaurants, especially in informal cafes, bistros, pizzerias and pubs. High chairs are common and

★ Best Spots for Kids

Deutsche Bahn Museum, Nuremberg (p92)

Le Bonbon au Palais, Paris (p134)

Schokoladenmuseum, Cologne (p45)

Spielzeug Welten Museum, Basel (www.spielzeug-welten-museum-basel.ch; adult/senior/child Sfr7/5/free; ⊙10am-6pm Tues-Sun, daily in Dec)

the server may even bring a damp cloth at the end of your meal to wipe sticky fingers. Many casual restaurants offer a children's menu with popular dishes such as pasta, hamburgers, and chicken and chips.

From left: Schokoladenmuseum (p45), Cologne; Deutsche Bahn Museum (p92), Nuremberg

NORTHERN RHINE, GERMANY

Northern Rhine, Germany

The northern section of the Rhine features dramatic landscapes and a host of interesting towns. Cologne (Köln), Germany's fourth-largest city, offers numerous attractions, led by its famous cathedral, while Koblenz, at the confluence of the Rhine and Moselle Rivers, is a park- and flower-filled delight. Heading south, the Rhine meanders between hillside castles and steep fields of wine-producing grapes. Idyllic villages appear around each bend, their half-timbered houses and Gothic steeples seemingly plucked from a fairy tale. Scarcely damaged during WWII, handsome Speyer is crowned by a magnificent Romanesque cathedral.

With One Day in Cologne

With a day in Cologne, say hello to the gargoyles as you huff and puff up the south tower of the majestic **Kölner Dom** (p39) for a full-on city panorama. Lower your pulse over your first *Kölsch* of the day at a nearby beer hall, then amble down to the **Wallraf-Richartz-Museum** (p42) to have your mind blown by six centuries of European art. After lunch at the riverside **Fischmarkt**, stroll down to the irresistible **Schokoladenmuseum** (p45).

Best Places for...

Gothic Architecture Kölner Dom, Cologne (p39)

Contemporary Art Museum Ludwig, Cologne (p43)

Beer Brauerei zur Malzmühle, Cologne (p46)

Wine Rabennest, Speyer (p51)

Getting from the Ports

Cologne Boats dock along a stretch of the Rhine alongside the Altstadt, meaning it's an easy stroll to most of the sights.

Koblenz Has various berths across its two rivers, but it's a compact place so nothing is far away.

Speyer The historic centre is a short stroll west of the river docks, across pleasant parkland.

Fast Facts

Currency Euro (€)

Language German

Free Wi-fi Most bars and cafes offer free networks. There's also free public wi-fi around the centre of Cologne.

Money ATMs and banks are plentiful, particularly around Cologne's cathedral, Koblenz' Altstadt and in the streets west of Speyer's cathedral.

Tourist Information Cologne's and Speyer's tourist offices are conveniently located near their respective cathedrals; Koblenz' is in the Forum Confluentes.

Central nave

Kölner Dom, Cologne

Cologne's geographical and spiritual heart – and its single-biggest tourist draw – is the magnificent Kölner Dom. With its soaring twin spires, this is the Mt Everest of cathedrals, jam-packed with art and treasures.

Great For...

☑ **Don't Miss**

The underground Domforum visitor centre is a good source of info and tickets.

Germany's largest cathedral, the Dom must be circled to appreciate its dimensions. Note how its lacy spires and flying buttresses create a sensation of lightness and fragility despite its mass and height.

Inside, a phalanx of pillars and arches supports the lofty nave. Soft light filters through the medieval stained-glass windows, while in the transept, a much-lauded recent example by contemporary artist Gerhard Richter is a kaleidoscope of 11,500 squares in 72 colours. Richter's abstract design has been called a 'symphony of light' and in the afternoon, when the sun hits it just so, it's easy to see why.

History

Construction began in 1248 in the French Gothic style but proceeded slowly and was eventually halted in 1560 when funds ran

ALLAN BAXTER/GETTY IMAGES ©

⚓

Explore Ashore

Cruises dock along the old town's river frontage, so it should be a maximum 10-minute stroll to the cathedral from your berth. Depending on crowds and queuing time, allow one to two hours to see the cathedral. Guided tours (p45) take 75 minutes.

❶ Need to Know

📞0221-9258 4720; www.koelner-dom.de; Domkloster 4; tower adult/concession €4/2; ⏰6am-9pm May-Oct, to 7.30pm Nov-Apr, tower 9am-6pm May-Sep, to 5pm Mar, Apr & Oct, to 4pm Nov-Feb; 🚊5, 16, 18 Dom/Hauptbahnhof

out. The half-built church lingered for nearly 300 years and suffered a stint as a horse stable and prison when Napoleon occupied the town. A few decades later, a generous cash infusion from Prussian King Friedrich Wilhelm IV finally led to its completion in 1880, 632 years after it started. Luckily, it escaped WWII bombing raids with nary a shrapnel wound and has been a Unesco World Heritage Site since 1996.

Shrine of the Magi

The *pièce de résistance* among the cathedral's bevy of treasures is the Shrine of the Magi behind the main altar, a richly bejewelled and gilded sarcophagus said to hold the remains of the magi who followed the star to Bethlehem. The bones were spirited out of Milan in 1164 by Emperor Barbarossa's chancellor and instantly turned Cologne into a major pilgrimage site.

South Tower

For an exercise fix, climb the 533 steps up the Dom's south tower to the base of the steeple that dwarfed all buildings in Europe until Gustave Eiffel built a certain tower in Paris. During your climb up to the 95m-high viewing platform, take a breather and admire the 24-tonne Peter Bell (1923), the largest free-swinging working bell in the world.

Other Highlights

Other highlights include the Gero Crucifix (970), notable for its monumental size and an emotional intensity rarely achieved in those early medieval days; the choir stalls from 1310, richly carved from oak; and the altar painting (c 1450) by Cologne artist Stefan Lochner.

Explore Cologne Walk

Cologne's history is everywhere, as you'll see on this walk, which circles through the heart of the bustling city. You can view Roman or medieval ruins.

Start Kölner Dom
Distance 2km
Duration Three hours

7 The **Kölnisches Stadtmuseum** (www.koelnisches-stadtmuseum.de), in the former medieval armoury, explores all facets of Cologne history.

6 Cologne's Third Reich history is poignantly documented in the **NS Documentation Centre** (p43), housed in the former Gestapo headquarters.

5 Home to a wide array of religious treasures, **Kolumba** (www.kolumba. de) also contains the ruins of the late-Gothic church of St Kolumba and has Roman foundations.

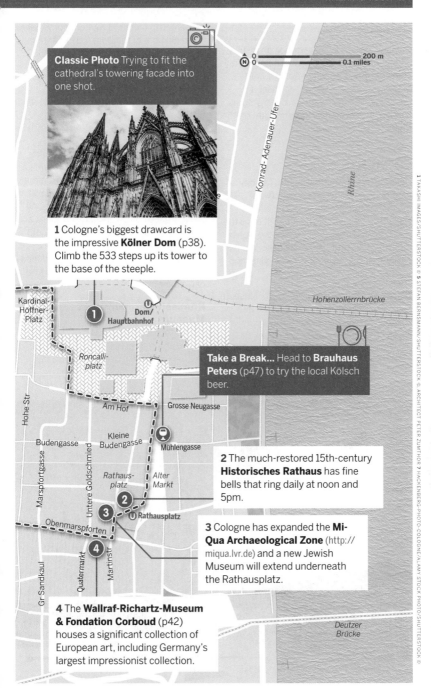

Classic Photo Trying to fit the cathedral's towering facade into one shot.

200 m
0.1 miles

1 Cologne's biggest drawcard is the impressive **Kölner Dom** (p38). Climb the 533 steps up its tower to the base of the steeple.

Kardinal-Höffner-Platz

Dom/Hauptbahnhof

Roncalli-platz

Hohenzollernbrücke

Rhine

Konrad-Adenauer-Ufer

Take a Break... Head to **Brauhaus Peters** (p47) to try the local Kölsch beer.

Am Hof

Grosse Neugasse

Hohe Str

Budengasse

Kleine Budengasse

Mühlengasse

Marspfortgasse

Untere Goldschmied

Rathaus-platz

Alter Markt

2 The much-restored 15th-century **Historisches Rathaus** has fine bells that ring daily at noon and 5pm.

Obenmarspforten

Rathausplatz

3 Cologne has expanded the **Mi-Qua Archaeological Zone** (http://miqua.lvr.de) and a new Jewish Museum will extend underneath the Rathausplatz.

Gr Sandkaul

Quatermarkt

Martinstr

4 The **Wallraf-Richartz-Museum & Fondation Corboud** (p42) houses a significant collection of European art, including Germany's largest impressionist collection.

Deutzer Brücke

1 TAKASHI IMAGES/SHUTTERSTOCK © 5 STEFAN BEERNSMANN/SHUTTERSTOCK © ARCHITECT PETER ZUMTHOR 7 HACKENBERG-PHOTO-COLOGNE/ALAMY STOCK PHOTO/SHUTTERSTOCK ©

Cologne

Cologne is like a living textbook on history and architecture: drifting about town you'll stumble upon an ancient Roman wall, medieval churches galore, nondescript postwar buildings, avant-garde structures and a new postmodern quarter right on the Rhine.

◉ SIGHTS

Cologne has a wealth of sights. The city maintains an excellent website (www.museenkoeln.de) with info on most of Cologne's museums. The Altstadt hugs the riverbank between two bridges, the Hohenzollernbrücke and Deutzer Brücke. You can easily spend a few hours just strolling and soaking it all in.

Domschatzkammer   Museum
(Cathedral Treasury; ☎0221-1794 0530; www.dombau-koeln.de; Domkloster 4; adult/concession €6/3; ⊙10am-6pm; 🚋5, 16, 18 Dom/Hauptbahnhof) Reliquaries, robes, sculptures and liturgical objects are handsomely presented in medieval vaulted rooms below the main floor of the Dom (p39). Standouts include a Gothic bishop's staff from 1322 and a 15th-century sword.

Wallraf-Richartz-Museum & Fondation Corboud   Museum
(☎0221-2212 1119; www.wallraf.museum; Obenmarspforten; adult/concession €9/5.50; ⊙10am-6pm Tue-Sun; 🚋1, 7, 9 Heumarkt, 🚋5 Rathaus) One of Germany's finest art museums, the Wallraf-Richartz presents a primo collection of European art from the 13th to the 19th centuries in a minimalist cube designed by the late OM Ungers. All the marquee names are here – Rubens and Rembrandt to Manet and Monet – along with a prized sampling of medieval art, most famously Stefan Lochner's *Madonna in Rose Bower,* nicknamed the 'Mona Lisa of Cologne'.

Römisch-Germanisches Museum   Museum
(Roman Germanic Museum; ☎0221-2212 4438; www.roemisch-germanisches-museum.de; Roncalliplatz 4; adult/concession/under 18yr

Museum Ludwig

€6.50/3.50/free; ⊙10am-5pm Tue-Sun; 🚊5, 16, 18 Dom/Hauptbahnhof) Sculptures and ruins displayed outside the entrance are merely the overture to a full symphony of Roman artefacts found along the Rhine. Highlights include the giant Poblicius tomb (AD 30–40), the magnificent 3rd-century Dionysus mosaic, and astonishingly well-preserved glass items. Insight into daily Roman life is gained from toys, tweezers, lamps and jewellery, the designs of which have changed surprisingly little since Roman times.

Museum Ludwig   Museum

(✐0221-2212 6165; www.museum-ludwig.de; Heinrich-Böll-Platz; adult/concession €12/8, more during special exhibits; ⊙10am-6pm Tue-Sun; 🚊5, 16, 18 Dom/Hauptbahnhof) A mecca of modern art, Museum Ludwig presents a tantalising mix of works from all major genres. Fans of German expressionism (Beckmann, Dix, Kirchner) will get their fill here as much as those with a penchant for Picasso, American pop art (Warhol, Lichtenstein) and Russian avant-garde painter Alexander Rodchenko. Rothko and Pollock are highlights of the abstract collection, while Gursky and Tillmanns are among the reasons the photography section is a must-see.

NS-Dokumentationszentrum   Museum

(NS-DOK; ✐0221-2212 6332; www.museenkoeln. de/ns-dokumentationszentrum; Appellhofplatz 23-25; adult/concession €4.50/2; ⊙10am-6pm Tue-Fri, 11am-6pm Sat & Sun; 🚊3, 4, 5, 16, 18 Appellhofplatz) Cologne's Third Reich history is poignantly and exhaustively documented in the NS Documentation Centre housed in the very building that served as the headquarters of the local Gestapo (Nazi secret police). The basement prison, where scores of people were interrogated, tortured and killed, is now a memorial site.

Museum für Angewandte Kunst   Museum

(MAKK, Museum of Applied Arts; ✐0221-2212 6714; www.makk.de; An der Rechtschule; adult/concession €5/2.50; ⊙11am-6pm Tue-Sun; 🚊5,

🏛 Cologne's Romanesque Churches

Cologne's medieval heyday is reflected in its wealth of Romanesque churches, which were constructed between 1150 and 1250, and survived largely intact until WWII. About a dozen have been rebuilt since and offer many unique architectural and artistic features. Even if you're pushed for time, try seeing at least a couple, such as **St Gereon** (✐0221-474 5070; www.stgereon.de; Gereonshof 2; ⊙10am-6pm Mon-Fri, to 5.30pm Sat, 1-6pm Sun; 🚊12, 15 Christophstrasse/Mediapark), **St Ursula** (✐0221-788 0750; Ursulaplatz; treasury adult/concession €2/1; ⊙10am-noon & 3-5pm Mon-Sat, 3-4.30pm Sun; 🚊Dom/Hauptbahnhof, Hansaring) or **St Maria im Kapitol** (✐0221-214 615; www.maria-im-kapitol.de; Kasinostrasse 6; ⊙10am-6pm Mon-Sat, 1-6pm Sun; 🚊1, 5, 7, 9 Heumarkt). The website www.romanische-kirchen-koeln.de has good info on all of them.

Vaulted dome, St Gereon church

16, 18 Appellhofplatz, Dom/Hauptbahnhof) If Aalto, Eames and Olivetti are music to your ears, you should swing by the Museum of Applied Arts, which displays a prestigious and extensive collection of classic and innovative objects in its newly reopened Design section. The historical collection upstairs, meanwhile, remains closed for restoration for the foreseeable future.

Museum Schnütgen   Museum

(✐0221-2212 2310; www.museum-schnuetgen. de; Cäcilienstrasse 29; adult/concession

Cologne

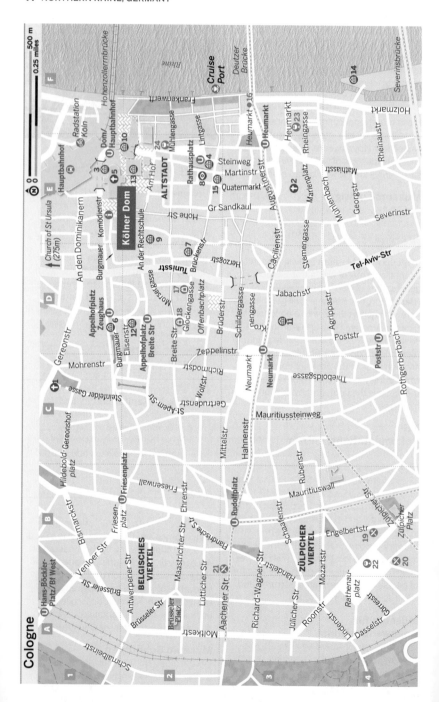

0.25 miles
500 m

Church of St Ursula (275m)

Radstation Köln

Hohenzollernbrücke

Rhine

Cruise Port

Deutzer Brücke

Hauptbahnhof

Dom/ Hauptbahnhof

An den Dominikanern

Komödienstr

Burgmauer

An der Rechtschule

Am Hof

Frankenwerft

Mühlengasse

Lintgasse

Rheingasse

Severinsbrücke

Holzmarkt

Heumarkt

Heumarkt

ALTSTADT

Rathausplatz

Steinweg

Martinstr

Quatermarkt

Gr Sandkaul

Hohe Str

Marienplatz

Mühlenbach

Matthiasstr

Georgstr

Severinstr

Augustinerstr

Cäcilienstr

Sternengasse

Tel-Aviv-Str

Kölner Dom

Herzogstr

Brückenstr

Tunisstr

Morsergasse

Glockengasse

Offenbachplatz

Bruderstr

Schildergasse

Jabachstr

nengasse

Kro

Agrippastr

Poststr

Rothgerberbach

Poststr

Thieboldsgasse

Neumarkt

Neumarkt

Zeppelinstr

Richmodstr

Wolfstr

Gertrudenstr

St-Apern-Str

Breite Str

Elisenstr

Burgmauer

Appellhofplatz

Appellhofplatz Breite Str

Zeughaus

Gereonstr

Mohrenstr

Steinfelder Gasse

Hildebold-Gereonshof platz

Bismarckstr

Venloer Str

Brüsseler Str

Friesen- platz **Friesenplatz**

Friesenwall

Ehrenstr

Mauritiussteinweg

Mittelstr

Hahnenstr

Rudolfplatz

Mauritiuswall

Rubenstr

ZÜLPICHER VIERTEL

Engelbertstr

Zülpicher Str

Zülpicher Platz

Schaafenstr

Handelstr

Mozartstr

Rathenau- platz

Göthestr

BELGISCHES VIERTEL

Antwerpener Str

Maastrichter Str

Flandrische Str

Lütticher Str

Aachener Str

Richard-Wagner-Str

Jülicher Str

Roonstr

Lindenstr

Dasselstr

Brüsseler Platz

Molkerstr

Schmalbeinstr

Hans-Böckler- Platz/Bf West

Brüsseler Str

Hauptbahnhof

Tourist info symbols and numbered points: 1, 2, 3, 4, 5, 6, 7, 8, 9, 10, 11, 12, 13, 14, 15, 16, 17, 18, 19, 20, 21, 22, 23, 24

Cologne

€6/3.50; ⊙10am-6pm Tue, Wed & Fri-Sun, to 8pm Thu; P; UNeumarkt) The Museum Schnütgen is an exquisite repository of medieval religious art and sculpture from the Rhineland region presented within the serene ambience of the Romanesque Cäcilienkirche, one of Cologne's oldest churches. Outstanding works include the Parler Bust, a crucifix from St George and the ivory Comb of St Heribert.

Schokoladenmuseum
Museum

(Chocolate Museum; ☑0221-931 8880; www.schokoladenmuseum.de; Am Schokoladenmuseum 1a; adult/student/child €11.50/9/7.50; ⊙10am-6pm Tue-Fri, 11am-7pm Sat & Sun, last entry 1hr before closing; ☐133 Schokoladenmuseum) This boat-shaped, high-tech temple to the art of chocolate making has plenty of engaging exhibits on the 5000-year cultural history of the 'elixir of the gods' (as the Aztecs called it) as well as on the cocoa-growing process. The walk-through tropical forest is a highlight, although most visitors are more enthralled by the glass-walled miniature production facility and a sample at the chocolate fountain.

 ACTIVITIES

Cologne's dense network of bike routes along the Rhine and throughout the city make it a fine place to cycle. Pick up a bike map at the tourist office (p47).

Radstation Köln
Bicycle Rental

(☑0221-139 7190; www.radstationkoeln.de; Breslauer Platz; bikes from three hours/day €6/11; ⊙5.30am-10.30pm Mon-Fri, 6.30am-8pm Sat, 8am-8pm Sun; UKöln Dom/Hbf) This bike rental outfit behind the train station also offers excellent 3hr tours in English. The website has details.

 TOURS

Dom Guided Tour
Tours

(☑0221-9258 4730; www.koelner-dom.de; Kardinal-Höffner-Platz; adult/concession €8/6; ⊙tours in English 10.30am & 2.30pm Mon-Sat, 2.30pm Sun Apr-Oct, less often rest of year; ☐5, 16, 18 Dom/Hauptbahnhof) Join a guided tour to get more out of your visit to Kölner Dom. Tours meet inside the main portal. No reservations are needed.

Radstation Tours
Cycling

(☑0221-139 7190; www.radstationkoeln.de; Marksmannsgasse, Deutzer Brücke; tours incl bike rental €22.50; ⊙1.30pm Apr-Oct; ☐1, 5, 7, 9 Heumarkt) This bike rental place also runs German/English three-hour bicycle tours that tick off Cologne's main sights on a 15km route.

🔒 SHOPPING

Cologne is a popular shopping destination with a fun mix of eccentric boutiques, designer and vintage stores, plus the usual selection of chain and department stores. And, of course, there are classic outlets for its famous eau de cologne.

Kauf Dich Glücklich
Fashion & Accessories

(📞0221-2774 8020; www.kaufdichgluecklich -shop.de; Neue Langgasse 2; ⏰10.30am-8pm Mon-Sat; Ⓤ Appellhofplatz) With a branch in Berlin, this small indie boutique chain now supplies the same quality threads, accessories and jewellery to Cologne's fashion-forward men and women. Look for its own KDG label alongside brands from around Germany and Europe with particular emphasis on Scandinavia.

4711 House of Fragrances
Perfume

(📞0221-2709 9910; www.4711.com; Glockengasse 4; ⏰9.30am-6.30pm Mon-Fri, to 6pm Sat; Ⓤ Appellhofplatz) A classic gift for Grandma is a bottle of eau de cologne, invented in, yes, Cologne in the late 18th century. The most famous is 4711, named after the address where it was first created. The building now houses a flagship store and a museum where you can marvel at a giant Gobelin tapestry and stop by the Fragrance Fountain.

✕ EATING

Multicultural Cologne offers culinary journeys around the world. Make tasty discoveries in Belgisches Viertal and the streets in and around Zülpicher Platz and Ehrenstrasse. Sample traditional Rhenish dishes including *Himmel un Ääd* (mashed potato with blood sausage and apple) at atmospheric beer halls.

Engelbät
European €

(📞0221-246 914; www.engelbaet.de; Engelbertstrasse 7; crêpes €5.50-9; ⏰11am-midnight Mon-Thu, to 1am Fri & Sat; 📷; 🚋9, 12, 15 Zülpicher Platz) This cosy restaurant-pub is famous for its habit-forming crêpes, which come in 50 varieties – sweet or savoury, meat or vegetarian and vegan. Also popular for its breakfasts (served until 3pm) and salads with homemade dressing.

Salon Schmitz
European €€

(📞0221-139 5577; www.salonschmitz.com; Aachener Strasse 28-34; mains from €10; ⏰9am-1am Sun-Thu, open end Fri & Sat; 🚋1, 7, 12, 15 Rudolfplatz) Spread over three historical row houses, the Schmitz empire is your one-stop shop for excellent food and drink. Greet the day with a lavish breakfast in the retro-hip 1950s and '60s setting of the Salon; order cake, quiche or a hot dish in the Metzgerei, a historical butcher's shop turned deli; or indulge in a fine brasserie-style dinner in the art nouveau–styled Bar.

Feynsinn
International €€

(📞0221-240 9210; www.cafe-feynsinn.de; Rathenauplatz 7; dinner mains €10-23; ⏰9am-1am Mon-Thu, to 2am Fri, 9.30am-2am Sat, 10am-1am Sun; 🚋9, 12, 15 Zülpicher Platz) This well-respected Zülpicher Viertel restaurant is an excellent pit stop at any time of the day. Come for extravagant breakfasts, light lunches and creative cakes or a dinner menu that weaves organic seasonal ingredients into sharp-flavoured dishes. Get a table overlooking the park for a meal or just a drink.

🍷 DRINKING & NIGHTLIFE

Biergarten Rathenauplatz
Beer Garden

(📞0221-801 7349; www.rathenauplatz.de/ biergarten; Rathenauplatz 30; ⏰noon-11.30pm Apr-Sep; 🚋9, 12, 15 Zülpicher Platz) A large, leafy park has one of Cologne's best places for a drink: a community-run beer garden. Tables sprawl under huge old trees, while simple snacks such as salads and very good *Frikadelle* (spiced hamburger) issue forth from a cute little hut.

Brauerei zur Malzmühle
Beer Hall

(📞0221-9216 0613; https://brauereizurmalz muehle.de; Heumarkt 6; ⏰11.30am-midnight

Mon-Thu, to 1.30am Fri, noon-1am Sat, 11am-11pm Sun; 🚋1, 5, 7, 9 Heumarkt) Expect plenty of local colour at this convivial, family-run beer hall attached to a brewery in business since 1858. It serves the popular *Mühlen Kölsch* which has a robust, malty taste. If you prefer a less potent brew, try the *Koch'sches Malzbier* (malt beer; 2% alcohol). Good menu of traditional Cologne brewpub fare (mains €10 to €22.50).

Brauhaus Peters Beer Hall

(☎0221-257 3950; www.peters-brauhaus.de; Mühlengasse 1; ⏱11am-12.30am; 🚋5 Rathaus) This beautifully restored 19th-century pub draws a crowd knocking back their *Kölsch* in a web of highly individualistic nooks, including a little 'chapel' and a room lidded by a kaleidoscopic stained-glass ceiling. On Tuesdays after 5pm, insiders invade for the freshly made potato pancakes (*Rievkooche* in the local dialect; €5.60 to €12.20).

 INFORMATION

Cologne Tourist Office (☎0221-346 430; www.cologne-tourism.com; Kardinal-Höffner-Platz 1; ⏱9am-8pm Mon-Sat, 10am-5pm Sun; Ⓤ Köln Dom/Hauptbahnhof)

 GETTING AROUND

Cologne's mix of buses, trams *(Stadtbahn)*, U-Bahn and S-Bahn trains is operated by **KVB** (Kölner Verkehrsbetriebe; ☎01806-50 40 30; www.kvb.koeln) in cooperation with Bonn's system. Short trips (up to four stops) cost €1.90, longer ones €2.40. Day passes are €7.10 for one person and €10 for up to five people travelling together. Buy your tickets from the machines at stations and aboard trams; be sure to validate them. KVB's website has a journey planner.

Cologne is a very bicycle-friendly city, with clearly marked bike lanes. The Nextbike bike-sharing system (www.nextbike.de/en) makes hiring a bike for a day easy. Alternatively, Cologne is compact enough to be seen on foot, and central sights are all walking distance from the river cruise berths.

 Kölsch Beer

Cologne has its own style of beer, *Kölsch,* which is light, hoppy, slightly sweet and served cool in *Stangen* (skinny, straight glasses that only hold 0.2L). In traditional Cologne beer halls and pubs you don't order beer so much as subscribe; the constantly prowling waiters will keep dropping off the little glasses of beer until you indicate you've had enough by placing a beer mat on top of your glass.

A ceaseless flow of *Stangen* filled with *Kölsch,* along with earthy humour and platters of meaty local foods, are the hallmarks of Cologne's iconic beer halls. Look for the days when each place serves glorious potato pancakes (*Rievkooche* or *Reibekuchen*).

Kölsch beer in *Stangen*
BJOERN WYLEZICH/SHUTTERSTOCK ©

Koblenz

At the confluence of the Rhine and Moselle Rivers, Koblenz is a park- and flower-filled city that serves as both the northern gateway to the Romantic Rhine Valley and the northeastern gateway to the Moselle Valley.

 SIGHTS

Koblenz' Altstadt, most of it rebuilt after WWII, surrounds the northern end of **Löhrstrasse**, the city's main pedestrian-only shopping street. Its intersection with Altengraben is known as **Vier Türme** (Four Towers) because each of the 17th-century corner buildings sports an ornately carved and painted oriel.

Festung Ehrenbreitstein · Fortress
(📞0261-6675 4000; www.tor-zum-welterbe.de; adult/child €7/3.50, incl cable car €13.80/6.20, audio guide €2; ⊙10am-6pm Apr-Oct, to 5pm Nov-Mar) On the right bank of the Rhine, 118m above the river, this fortress proved indestructible to all but Napoleonic troops, who levelled it in 1801. To prove a point, the Prussians rebuilt it as one of Europe's mightiest fortifications. There are fabulous views from its ramparts and viewing platform. Inside are several museums, including an excellent regional museum, photography museum and archaeological museum, as well as restaurants, bars and cafes. It's accessible by car, on foot or by cable car.

Mittelrhein-Museum · Museum
(www.mittelrhein-museum.de; Zentralplatz 1; adult/child €12/free; ⊙10am-6pm Tue-Sun) Spread over 1700 sq metres of the striking glass Forum Confluentes building, Koblenz' Mittelrhein-Museum's displays span 2000 years of the region's history, including artworks, coins, ceramics, porcelain, furniture, miniature art, textiles, militaria and more. Don't miss the collection of 19th-century landscape paintings of the Romantic Rhine by German and British artists.

Liebfrauenkirche · Church
(www.liebfrauen-koblenz.de; An der Liebfrauenkirche 16; ⊙8am-6pm Mon-Sat, from 8.30am Sun) In the Altstadt, the arched walkway at Am Plan square's northeastern corner leads to the Catholic Liebfrauenkirche, built in a harmonious hotchpotch of styles. Of Romanesque origin, it has a Gothic choir (check out the stained glass), painted vaulting above the central nave, and baroque onion-domed turrets. It was destroyed in 1944 and rebuilt in 1955.

🏃 ACTIVITIES
Romantic Old Town Walking Tour · Walking
(📞0261-194 33; www.koblenz-touristik.de; adult/child €7/3.50; ⊙English tours 3pm Sat Apr-Oct) Departing from the tourist office, this two-

Cable car to Festung Ehrenbreitstein

SAIKO3P/SHUTTERSTOCK ©

hour tour takes you through the Altstadt, stopping at sights such as the Basilika St Kastor and Liebfrauenkirche, as well as Deutsches Eck. Tours in German run more frequently.

Seilbahn
Cable Car

(☑0261-2016 5850; www.seilbahn-koblenz.de; Rheinstrasse 6; adult/child return €9.90/4.40, incl Festung Ehrenbreitstein €13.80/6.20; ☺9.30am-7pm Jul-Sep, to 6pm Easter-Jun & Oct, 10am-5pm Nov-Easter) This modern cable car swings above the Rhine River, linking Koblenz with the mighty Ehrenbreitstein fortress. If you have a head for heights, cabin 17 has a glass floor.

🍴 EATING

Winninger Weinstube
German €

(☑0261-387 07; www.winninger-weinstube.de; Rheinzollstrasse 2; mains €7-14.50; ☺4pm-midnight Tue-Thu, from noon Fri-Sun May-Sep, 4-11pm Tue-Sun Oct-Apr; ☎) A cavernous stone building that once housed a museum is now a restaurant and wine bar serving local specialities such as *Koblenzer Saumagen* (stuffed pig's stomach), Riesling-marinated pork knuckle, liver and potato dumplings and *Flammkuchen* (Alsatian pizza) with both sweet and savoury topping options. Wines come from its own vineyard in Winningen just upstream along the Moselle.

Look out for its *Eiswein* ('ice wine'), made from grapes harvested after the first frost.

Einstein
Cafe €€

(☑0261-914 4999; www.einstein-koblenz.de; Firmungstrasse 30; mains €9.50-24, Sun brunch €21.90; ☺9am-10pm Mon-Sat, from 10am Sun, bar to midnight Sun-Thu, to 2am Fri & Sat) Grilled calf's liver with masala jus; gilthead, tiger prawn and lime risotto; ribbon noodles with feta, spinach and tomatoes; and chocolate cannelloni with almond mascarpone and orange sorbet are among the choices at this elegant crimson-toned cafe/bar. It also has lighter bites like soups and salads. Book ahead for Sunday's brunch buffet. Live music often plays on weekends.

🍷 DRINKING & NIGHTLIFE

Alte Weinstube
Zum Hubertus
Wine Bar

(www.weinhaus-hubertus.de; Florinsmarkt 6; ☺3.30-11pm Mon, Wed & Thu, noon-midnight Fri-Sun) Specialising in Rhine and Moselle wines by the glass and/or bottle, rustic Alte Weinstube Zum Hubertus occupies a half-timbered house dating from 1689, with an open fireplace, antique furniture and dark-wood panelling. In summer, seating spills onto the square. Classic German dishes include braised pork.

ℹ️ INFORMATION

Tourist Office (☑0261-194 33; www.koblenz -touristik.de; Zentralplatz 1; ☺10am-6pm) In the Forum Confluentes.

ℹ️ GETTING AROUND

Many central sights are just a few minutes away on foot from the city's main docking berths. Alternatively, the cute Altstadtexpress train (www. altstadtexpress.de/altstadt-express-koblenz; adult/child €6/€2) takes visitors on a 45-minute tour around the centre of the city.

Fahrrad Zangmeister (☑0261-323 63; www. fahrrad-zangmeister.de; Stegemannstrasse 33; standard/electric bike per day €10/25; ☺10am-6.30pm Mon, Tue, Thu & Fri, to 4pm Sat) One of Germany's oldest bike shops was founded, unbelievably, way back in 1898. Bikes can be picked up or delivered within a 15km radius for an additional €10.

Speyer

Scarcely damaged during WWII, the handsome town of Speyer is crowned by a magnificent Romanesque cathedral. Its centre is home to some outstanding museums and the remains of a medieval synagogue, and is easily explored on foot.

SERGEY DZYUBA/SHUTTERSTOCK ©

Altpörtel

⊙ SIGHTS

Kaiserdom Cathedral

(www.dom-zu-speyer.de; Domplatz; crypt adult/
child €3.50/1, tower €6/3; ⊙cathedral & crypt
9am-7pm Mon-Sat, 11.30am-5.30pm Sun Apr-Oct,
9am-5pm Mon-Sat, 11.30am-5.30pm Sun Nov-
Mar, tower 10am-5pm Mon-Sat, noon-5pm Sun
Apr-Oct) Begun in 1030 by Emperor Konrad
II of the Salian dynasty, this extraordinary
Romanesque cathedral has been a Unesco
World Heritage Site since 1981. Its square
red towers and green copper dome float
majestically above Speyer's rooftops; you
can climb the 304 steps of the southwest
tower to reach the 60m-high viewing platform for a spectacular panorama. Other
highlights include the fascinating crypt and
19th-century paintings in the Kaisersaal.

Atmospheric organ concerts (adult/child
€10/5) often take place here.

The cathedral's interior is startling for its
awesome dimensions (it's an astonishing
134m long); walk up the side aisles to the
elevated altar area to get a true sense of its
vastness.

To the right of the altar, steps lead down
to the crypt, whose candy-striped Romanesque arches – like those on the west
front – recall Moorish architecture (ask for
an English-language brochure). Stuffed
into a side room, up some stairs, are the
sandstone sarcophagi of eight emperors
and kings, along with some of their queens.
Tours (adult/child including crypt entry
€7.50/4) of the cathedral and crypt take
place in English by online reservation from
April to October.

Behind the Dom, the large **Domgarten**
(cathedral park) stretches towards the
Rhine.

Altpörtel Gate

(Maximilianstrasse 55; adult/child €3/2;
⊙10am-noon & 2-4pm Mon-Fri, 10am-5pm Sat
& Sun Apr-Oct) The 55m-high, 13th-century
Altpörtel, the city's western gate, is the
only remaining part of the town wall. Its
clock dates from 1761. Climbing 154 steps
to the top of the Altpörtel rewards you with
breathtaking views on a clear day. On the
2nd floor, a permanent exhibition covers
the history of Speyer.

Judenhof   Ruins

(Jews' Courtyard; www.verkehrsverein-speyer.
de; Kleine Pfaffengasse 21; ruins adult/child €3/
free, museum €3/1; ⊙10am-5pm Apr-Oct, 10am-
4pm Tue-Sun Nov-Mar) A block south of the
Rathaus, the 'Jews' Courtyard' is one of the
most important medieval Jewish sites in
Germany: the remains of a Romanesque-
style synagogue that was consecrated in
1104 and used until 1450. Highlights include
the 13th-century women's section, a *Mikwe*
(ritual bath) from the early 1100s – the oldest, largest and best preserved north of the
Alps – and a small museum covering the
city's medieval Jewish community. Signs
are in English and German.

Technik Museum   Museum

(⊘06232-670 80; www.technik-museum.de;
Am Technik Museum 1; adult/child museum
€16/13, IMAX €12/8, both €21/17; ⊙9am-6pm
Mon-Fri, to 7pm Sat & Sun) At this technology
extravaganza, 1km south of the Kaiserdom,
you can climb aboard a Lufthansa Boeing
747-230 mounted 20m off the ground
(and walk out on its wing), a 1960s U-boat
that's claustrophobic even on dry land, and
a mammoth Antonov An-22 cargo plane
with an all-analogue cockpit and a nose
cone you can peer out of. Other highlights
include the Soviet space shuttle *Buran.* Its
IMAX cinema with a domed screen shows
science-related films.

✖ EATING

Domhof-Hausbrauerei   German €€

(⊘06232-674 40; www.domhof.de; Grosse Him-
melsgasse 6; mains €12-24.50; ⊙11.30am-10pm
Mon-Fri, from 11am Sat & Sun; 🛜🚼) Just beside
the Kaiserdom, this historic brewery has a
courtyard beer garden shaded by chestnut
trees. Regional specialities, some prepared
using the three beers brewed on the premises (light, dark and wheat), include fried
local sausages with sauerkraut cooked in
light beer, and liver dumplings in dark-beer-
and-beef broth.

Rabennest   German €€

(⊘06232-623 857; www.weinstube-rabennest.
de; Korngasse 5; mains €8-19; ⊙11am-11pm
Mon-Sat, to 9pm Sun) A half-timbered, green-
shuttered building houses this timber-
panelled, two-storey winery, which serves
Palatinate vintages and specialities such as
Leberknödel (liver meatballs in beef broth)
and *Pfälzer Bauernsteak* (pork steak with
mushrooms, onions and bacon). In summer, tables set up on the cobblestones out
front. Reservations are recommended.

🍷 DRINKING & NIGHTLIFE

Alter Hammer   Wine Bar

(www.alter-hammer.de; Leinpfad 1c; ⊙11.30am-
9.30pm; 🛜) On the grassy banks of the
Rhine, this half-timbered manor house has
a sprawling, 360-seat summer beer garden
canopied by linden trees. Its lengthy local
wine list includes housemade *Glühwein* in
winter. Traditional German fare, vegetarian
options and a kids' menu make it a perfect
place to while away a few hours. Cash only.

ℹ INFORMATION

Tourist Office (⊘06232-142 392; www.speyer.
de; Maximilianstrasse 13; ⊙9am-5pm Mon-Fri,
10am-3pm Sat, 10am-2pm Sun Apr-Oct, 9am-5pm
Mon-Fri, 10am-noon Sat Nov-Mar) Situated 200m
west of the Kaiserdom, next to the historic
Rathaus.

ℹ GETTING AROUND

The bike-share scheme **VRNnextbike** (www.vrn
nextbike.de; per 30min €1; ⊙24hr) has bicyces
at docking stations around town. Sign up via the
app or at a station using your credit card.

Radsport Stiller (⊘06232-759 66; www.stiller-
radsport.de; Gilgenstrasse 24; standard/electric
bike hire per day €15/25; ⊙9.30am-12.30pm
& 2-6.30pm Mon-Fri, 9am-3pm Sat, 1-5pm Sun)
Hires bikes and can provide maps and touring
advice. Speyer is compact, and its main sights
are all easily explored on foot.

SOUTHERN RHINE, FRANCE, GERMANY & SWITZERLAND

Southern Rhine, France, Germany & Switzerland

The Southern Rhine forms the border between Germany and France before becoming Switzerland's northern frontier. Strasbourg is the perfect overture to all that is idiosyncratic about Alsace – walking a fine tightrope between France and Germany, between a medieval past and a progressive future. Further south, the Black Forest spills into Alsace in the German town of Breisach. Unsurprisingly, given its geographical and cultural proximity to France, the locals here have a passion for a good bottle of plonk. Basel, at the juncture of the French, German and Swiss borders, is perhaps where Switzerland's Franco-Germanic roots are most evident.

With One Day in Strasbourg

With a day in Strasbourg, start by wandering the winding streets of **Grand Île** (p58), taking in the atmosphere and stopping off to try a *tarte flambée* (Alsatian-style pizza). Make sure you visit the magnificent cathedral and nearby **Palais Rohan** (p58). Then head west to canalside **Petite France** (p58), and admire the views and atmosphere.

Best Places for...

Cheese La Cloche à Fromage, Strasbourg (p62)

Tea Sthélline, Strasbourg (p62)

Fine Dining Cheval Blanc, Basel (p67)

Design Vitra Campus, Basel (p65)

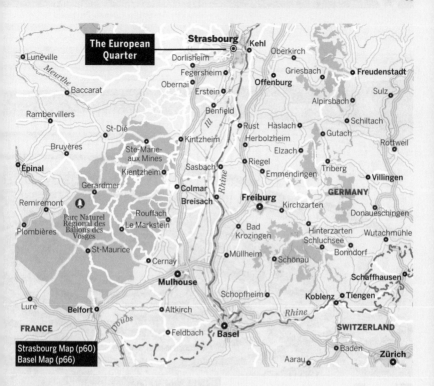

Getting from the Ports

Strasbourg Most cruises dock at Quai des Belges, a couple of kilometres east of the old centre of Strasbourg. There's a tram stop within a short walk, and many companies offer a shuttle into the centre.

Breisach Breisach's dock is very central, and it's just a short walk into the centre.

Basel Most boats dock near the trination border, with trams and buses nearby for the 4km journey to the centre.

Fast Facts

Currency Euro (€) in France and Germany; Swiss franc (Sfr) in Switzerland

Languages French in Strasbourg; German in Breisach; Swiss-German in Basel

Free Wi-fi Nearly every hotel, bar and cafe offers free wi-fi.

Money ATMs are common, especially around Strasbourg's cathedral, in Breisach's Neuf-Brisach and in Basel's old town.

Tourist Information Strasbourg's most convenient tourist office is right by the cathedral; Breisach and Basel both have centrally located offices.

Hemicycle Plenary Hall, European Parliament

LEONID ANDRONOV/SHUTTERSTOCK ©

The European Quarter, Strasbourg

Strasbourg's prominent place in Europe's heart was confirmed when it became the seat of the Council of Europe in 1949 and of the European Parliament in 1992. Head out to the European Quarter to investigate these institutions.

Great For...

☑ Don't Miss

The 'hemicycle' parliamentary chamber at the European Parliament.

European Parliament

The futuristic glass sweep of the **Parlement Européen** (www.europarl.europa.eu; rue Lucien Fèbvre; ◙Parlement Européen) building is a striking sight from the river. Should the inner workings of the EU intrigue you, you can sit in on debates ranging from lively to yawn-a-minute. Sessions alternate between Strasbourg and Brussels; sitting dates are available from the tourist office or on the website. For individuals it's first come, first served (bring ID). Outside of sitting times, 60- to 90-minute tours of the parliament building run regularly in various languages; check the website for times.

⚓

Explore Ashore

The European buildings sit 2km north-east of Grande Île (central Strasbourg), close to Parc de l'Orangerie. From Quai des Belges, walk to 10 to 15 minutes to Esplanade and catch tram route E to Parlement Européen (13 minutes). Allow a few hours at least to wander this area before heading back into the centre of town.

ℹ Need to Know

Take photo ID with you for access to some of the buildings.

Palace of Europe

The headquarters of the Council of Europe, found in the solid square **Palais de l'Europe** (📞03 88 41 20 29; www.coe.int; av de l'Europe; 🚊Droits de l'Homme) across the River Ill, can be visited on free one-hour weekday tours; phone ahead for times and reservations.

European Court of Human Rights

It's just a hop across the Canal de la Marne to the swirly silver **Palais des Droits de l'Homme** (www.echr.coe.int; allée des Droits de l'Homme; 🚊Droits de l'Homme), the most eye-catching of all the European institutional buildings. It houses the European Court of Human Rights, an organ of the Council of Europe (not the EU) charged since the 1950s with upholding the European Convention on Human Rights.

Parc de l'Orangerie

Across from the Council of Europe's Palais de l'Europe is this flowery **park** (🚊Droits de l'Homme), designed in the 17th century by Le Nôtre, of Versailles fame. It's a family magnet with playgrounds, a swan-dotted lake and a free mini-zoo, where kids can get up close to storks and goats. In summer you can rent rowboats on Lac de l'Orangerie.

Strasbourg, France

Strasbourg is the perfect overture to all that is idiosyncratic about Alsace – walking a fine tightrope between France and Germany and between a medieval past and a progressive future, it pulls off its act in inimitable Alsatian style.

◎ SIGHTS

Grande Île   Historic Site

(🏠Grand'Rue) History seeps through the twisting lanes and cafe-rimmed plazas of Grande Île, Strasbourg's Unesco World Heritage–listed island bordered by the River Ill. These streets – with their photogenic line-up of wonky, timber-framed houses in sherbet colours – are made for aimless ambling. They cower beneath the soaring magnificence of the cathedral and its sidekick, the gingerbready 15th-century **Maison Kammerzell** (rue des Hallebardes), with its ornate carvings and leaded windows. The alleys are at their most atmospheric when lantern-lit at night.

Cathédrale Notre-Dame   Cathedral

(www.cathedrale-strasbourg.fr; place de la Cathédrale; adult/child astronomical clock €3/2, platform €5/3; ⊙9.30-11.15am & 2-5.45pm, astronomical clock noon-12.45pm, platform 9am-7.15pm; 🏠Grand'Rue) Nothing prepares you for your first glimpse of Strasbourg's Cathédrale Notre-Dame, completed in all its Gothic grandeur in 1439. The lace-fine facade lifts the gaze little by little to flying buttresses, leering gargoyles and a 142m spire. The interior is exquisitely lit by 12th- to 14th-century stained-glass windows, including the western portal's jewel-like rose window. The Gothic-meets-Renaissance astronomical clock strikes solar noon at 12.30pm with a parade of figures portraying the different stages of life and Jesus with his apostles.

Palais Rohan   Historic Building

(2 place du Château; adult/child per museum €6.50/free, all 3 museums €12/free; ⊙10am-6pm Wed-Mon; 🏠Grand'Rue) Hailed as a 'Versailles in miniature', this opulent 18th-century

residence is loaded with treasures. The basement **Musée Archéologique** takes you from the Palaeolithic period to AD 800. On the ground floor is the **Musée des Arts Décoratifs**, where rooms adorned with Hannong ceramics and gleaming silverware evoke the lavish lifestyle of the nobility in the 18th century. On the 1st floor, the **Musée des Beaux-Arts'** collection of 14th- to 19th-century art includes El Greco, Botticelli and Flemish Primitive works.

Petite France   Area

(🏠Grand'Rue) Criss-crossed by narrow lanes, canals and locks, Petite France is where artisans plied their trades in the Middle Ages. The half-timbered houses, sprouting veritable thickets of scarlet geraniums in summer, and the riverside parks attract the masses, but the area still manages to retain its Alsatian charm, especially in the early morning and late evening. Drink in views of the River Ill and the Barrage Vauban from the much-photographed **Ponts Couverts** (Covered Bridges; 🏠Musée d'Art Moderne) and their trio of 13th-century towers.

Musée de l'Œuvre Notre-Dame   Museum

(www.musees.strasbourg.eu; 3 place du Château; adult/child €6.50/free; ⊙10am-6pm Tue-Sun; 🏠Grand'Rue) Occupying a cluster of sublime 14th- and 16th-century buildings, this museum harbours one of Europe's premier collections of Romanesque, Gothic and Renaissance sculpture (including many originals from the cathedral), plus 15th-century paintings and stained glass. *Christ de Wissembourg* (c 1060) is the oldest work of stained glass in France.

Musée d'Art Moderne et Contemporain   Gallery

(MAMCS; www.musees.strasbourg.eu; 1 place Hans Jean Arp; adult/child €10/free; ⊙10am-6pm Tue-Sun; 🏠Musée d'Art Moderne) This striking glass-and-steel cube showcases an outstanding fine-art, graphic-art and photography collection. Besides modern and contemporary works of the Kandinsky, Picasso, Magritte,

Cathédrale Notre-Dame, Strasbourg

Monet and Rodin ilk, you'll encounter pieces by Strasbourg-born artists, including the curvaceous creations of Hans Jean Arp and the evocative 19th-century works of Gustave Doré. The 1st-floor **Art Café** is graced by bold frescoes by Japanese artist Aki Kuroda and has a terrace overlooking the River Ill and Petite France.

Barrage Vauban   Viewpoint

(Vauban Dam; ⊙viewing terrace 7.15am-9pm, shorter hours winter; 🚇Faubourg National) **FREE**
A triumph of 17th-century engineering, the Barrage Vauban bears the architectural imprint of the leading French military engineer of the age – Sébastien Le Prestre de Vauban. The dam has been restored to its former glory and is now free to visit. Ascend to the terrace for a tremendously photogenic view that reaches across the canal-woven Petite France district to the Ponts Couverts and cathedral spire beyond.

Grande Mosquée
de Strasbourg   Mosque

(Strasbourg Grand Mosque; 6 rue Averroès; 🚇Laiterie) Designed by Italian architect Paolo Portoghesi and opened in September 2012, France's biggest mosque (accommodating 1500 worshippers) sits on a bend in the River Ill and is topped by a copper dome and flanked by wings resembling a flower in bud. More than just another landmark, it took 20 years of political toing and froing for this project to come to fruition and its completion is considered the beginning of a new era for Muslims and religious tolerance in France.

Place de la République   Square

(🚇République) Many of Strasbourg's grandest public buildings, constructed when the city was ruled by the German Reich, huddle northeast of the Grande Île area in the so-called imperial quarter of Neustadt, part of the city's Unesco World Heritage status since 2017. The neighbourhood centres on this stately square, bounded by the **Théâtre National de Strasbourg** (TNS; 📞03 88 24 88 24; www.tns.fr; 1 av de la Marseillaise; ⊙box office 1-7pm Mon-Sat). It stretches eastwards to Parc de l'Orangerie (p57) and is dominated by sturdy neo-Renaissance

Strasbourg

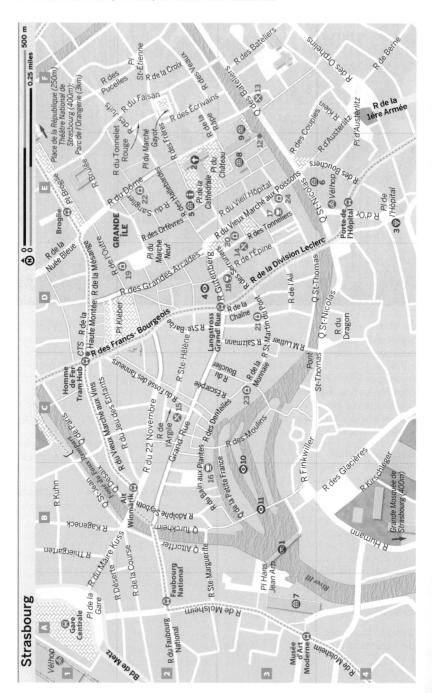

Strasbourg

buildings inspired by late-19th-century Prussian tastes.

Cave des Hospices de Strasbourg
Winery

(www.vins-des-hospices-de-strasbourg.fr; 1 place de l'Hôpital; ☺8.30am-noon & 1.30-5.30pm Mon-Fri, 9am-12.30pm Sat; 🚊Porte de l'Hôpital) **FREE** Founded in 1395, this brick-vaulted wine cellar nestles deep in the bowels of Strasbourg's hospital. A hospice back in the days when wine was considered a cure for all ills, today the cellar bottles first-rate Alsatian wines from Rieslings to sweet muscats. One of its historic barrels is filled with a 1472 vintage. Take tram A or D to Porte de l'Hôpital. From here it is a three-minute walk south on rue d'Or.

😊 ACTIVITIES

Take a DIY spin of Strasbourg's cathedral and the old city with one of the tourist office's (p63) 1½-hour audio guides (adult/child €5.50/2.75), available in five languages.

Batorama
Boating

(www.batorama.fr; rue de Rohan; adult/child €13/7.50; ☺tours half-hourly 9.45am-9.15pm, shorter hours winter; 🚊Grand'Rue) This outfit runs scenic 70-minute boat trips, which glide along the storybook canals of Petite

France, taking in the Barrage Vauban (p59) and the glinting EU institutions. Tours depart from rue de Rohan, the quay behind Palais Rohan (p58).

🔒 SHOPPING

Le Goût du Terroir
Food

(3 rue des Serruriers; ☺10am-7pm; 🚊Grand'Rue) Just try to resist this little shop, where cheese whiz Willy Leproust will tempt you in with his impeccable selection of regional *fromage* and *saucisson sec* (salami). Try some before you buy.

Mon Oncle Malker de Munster
Food & Drinks

(www.malker.fr; 4 place de la Grande Boucherie; ☺10am-7pm; 🚊Porte de l'Hôpital) A modern-day *épicerie* (grocery store) with a nod to top-quality Alsatian products, this is a cracking place to bag everything from prettily decorated ceramic *Kougelhopf* forms to strong-flavoured Munster and Tomme cheeses, *choucroute,* quirkily labelled craft beers, regional wines and schnapps.

EATING

Restaurants abound on Grande Île: try canalside Petite France for Alsatian fare and half-timbered romance; Grand'Rue for curbside kebabs and *tarte flambée* (thin Alsatian-

Pass the Chocolate

Strasbourg is now sweeter than ever, as it's one of the main stops on **La Route du Chocolat et des Douceurs d'Alsace** (Alsace Chocolate and Sweets Road), stretching 80km north to Bad Bergzabern and 125km south to Heimsbrunn near Mulhouse. Pick up a map at the tourist office to pinpoint Alsace's finest patisseries, chocolateries, macaron shops and confectioners. The following are three sweet Strasbourg favourites to get you started:

Mireille Oster (www.mireille-oster.com; 14 rue des Dentelles; ⊙10am-7pm Mon & Sun, 9am-7pm Tue-Sat; ▣Grand'Rue) Cherubs adorn this heavenly shop where Strasbourg's *pain d'épices* (gingerbread) fairy Mireille Oster tempts with handmade varieties featuring figs, amaretto, cinnamon and chocolate. Have a nibble before you buy.

Christian (www.christian.fr; 12 rue de l'Outre; ⊙7am-6.30pm Mon-Sat; ▣Broglie) Sumptuous truffles and pralines, weightless macarons and edible Strasbourg landmarks – renowned chocolatier Christian's creations are mini works of art.

Maison Alsacienne de Biscuiterie (www.maison-alsacienne-biscuiterie.com; 16 rue du Dôme; ⊙10am-7pm Mon, 9am-7pm Tue-Sat, 10am-6pm Sun; ▣Broglie) Bakes scrumptious Alsatian gingerbread, macarons, raisin-stuffed *Kougelhopf* and *sablés* (butter cookies) flavoured with nuts and spices.

Mireille Oster

style pizza topped with crème fraîche, onions and lardons); and rue des Veaux or rue des Pucelles for hole-in-the-wall eateries serving the world on a plate. Stepping across the river, pedestrianised rue d'Austerlitz is lined with patisseries and bistros.

Winstub S'Kaechele — French €
(☏03 88 22 62 36; www.skaechele.fr; 8 rue de l'Argile; mains €12.50-18.50; ⊙7-9.30pm Mon, 11.45am-1.30pm & 7-9.30pm Tue-Fri; ▣Grand'Rue) Traditional French and Alsatian grub doesn't come more authentic than at this snug, amiable *Winstub* (wine tavern), run with love by couple Karine and Daniel. Cue wonderfully cosy evenings spent in stone-walled, lamp-lit, wood-beamed surrounds, huddled over dishes such as escargots oozing Roquefort, fat pork knuckles braised in pinot noir, and *choucroute garnie* (sauerkraut garnished with meats).

La Cloche à Fromage — Cheese €€
(☏03 88 23 13 19; www.fromagerie-tourrette.com; 27 rue des Tonneliers; fondue €25-28; ⊙noon-2.30pm & 7-11pm; ▣Grand'Rue) *Au revoir* diet. Loosen a belt notch or three for Strasbourg's gooiest fondues and *raclette* at this temple to *fromage*, saving an inch for the 200-variety cheese board of *Guinness Book of World Records* fame.

1741 — Gastronomy €€€
(☏03 88 35 50 50; www.1741.fr; 22 quai des Bateliers; 3-course lunch menus €42, 3-/5-course dinner menus €95/129; ⊙noon-2pm & 7-10pm Thu-Mon; ▣Porte de l'Hôpital) A team of profoundly passionate chefs runs the show at this Michelin-starred number facing the River Ill. Murals, playful fabrics and splashes of colour add warmth to the dining room, where waiters bring well-executed, unfussy dishes, such as sea bass with Jerusalem artichoke and Alsatian venison with root vegetables, to the table. Service is excellent, as is the wine list.

🍷 DRINKING & NIGHTLIFE

Sthélline — Teahouse
(http://sthelline.fr; 10 rue des Tonneliers; ⊙9am-6.30pm Tue-Sat; ▣Porte de l'Hôpital) A little

cocoon of warmth and bonhomie bang in the heart of Strasbourg, this literary cafe and tearoom is lined with novels (feel free to browse) and does a fine line in fragrant speciality teas, from green and Darjeeling to rooibos and rare yellow tea – all served ceremonially in pretty pots and with mini-timers.

Café Bretelles   Cafe
(http://suspenders.fr; 36 rue du Bain aux Plantes; ⏱9am-6pm Mon-Sat, to 5pm Sun; ⛙Alt Winmärik) Huddled away in Petite France, this chilled-out haunt has Italian coffee worth raving about – served with an artistic flourish – relaxed vibes and good music. The baristas know their stuff when it comes to speciality coffees, which are best enjoyed with a slice of cake or breakfast (€5.50 to €7.50).

Terres à Vin   Wine Bar
(☏03 88 51 37 20; www.terresavin.com; 1 rue du Miroir; ⏱3-11pm Mon & Tue, 10am-11pm Wed-Sat, 11am-10pm Sun; ⛙Grand'Rue) Snuggled away in a courtyard, this bottle-lined, softly lit wine bar doubles as a deli – with some excellent cheeses, pâtés, gourmet oils, preserves, vinegars and, *naturellement*, wines. See the website for details on tastings.

ℹ INFORMATION

The extremely helpful **main tourist office** (☏03 88 52 28 28; www.otstrasbourg.fr; 17 place de la Cathédrale; ⏱9am-7pm; ⛙Grand'Rue) should be your first port of call. A city-centre walking map with English text costs €1.50; bus/tram and cycling maps are free. You can pick up the money-saving Strasbourg Pass here.

ℹ GETTING AROUND

Strasbourg's centre is easy to get around on foot and largely vehicle-free.

BICYCLE

A world leader in bicycle-friendly planning, Strasbourg has an extensive and ever-expanding *réseau cyclable* (cycling network). The tourist office stocks free maps.

The city's 24-hour, self-rental **Vélhop** (https://velhop.strasbourg.eu; per hr/day €1/5) system

can supply you with a bike. Pay by card and receive a code to unlock your bike. There's a refundable deposit of €150 per bike. Helmets are not available. There are 20 automatic rental points, plus outlets including the following:

City Centre (3 rue d'Or; ⏱8am-7pm Mon-Fri, 9.30am-12.30pm & 2-5.30pm Sat; ⛙Porte de l'Hôpital)

Rotonde (rue de la Rotonde; ⏱24hr; ⛙Rotonde)

Train Station (⏱9am-12.30pm & 1-6.30pm Mon-Fri, 9.30am-12.30pm & 2-5.30pm Sat; ⛙Gare Centrale) Situated on Level -1. Adjacent is an 820-place bicycle parking lot (€1 for 24 hours).

PUBLIC TRANSPORT

Six super-efficient tram lines, A through F, form the backbone of Strasbourg's outstanding public transport network, run by **CTS** (www.cts-strasbourg.fr). The main tram hub is Homme de Fer. Trams generally operate until 12.30am; buses – few of which pass through Grande Île – run until about 11pm. Night buses operate from 11.30pm to 5.30am on Friday and Saturday, stopping at nightlife hotspots.

Tickets, valid on both buses and trams, are sold by bus drivers and ticket machines at tram stops and cost €1.70 (€3.30 return). The 24-hour Individuel (for one person €4.30) and Trio (for two to three people €6.80) tickets, valid for 24 hours from the moment they are stamped, are sold at tourist offices and tram stops.

Breisach, Germany

Rising above vineyards and the Rhine, Breisach is where the Black Forest spills into Alsace. From the cobbled streets lined with pastel-painted houses you'd never guess that 85% of the town was flattened in WWII, so successful has been the reconstruction.

◎ SIGHTS

Neuf-Brisach   Fortress
Vauban's French fortified town of Neuf-Brisach (New Breisach), a Unesco World Heritage Site, sits 4km west of Breisach. Shaped like an eight-pointed star, the town was commissioned by Louis XIV in 1697 to

strengthen French defences and prevent the area from falling to the Habsburgs. It was conceived by Sébastien Le Prestre de Vauban (1633–1707). Take bus 1076 from Breisach station to get here.

St Stephansmünster   Church

(Münsterplatz; ⊙9am-5pm Mon-Sat) `FREE`
Plonked on a hill above the centre for all to behold in wonder, the Romanesque and Gothic St Stephansmünster shelters a faded fresco cycle, Martin Schongauer's *The Last Judgment* (1491), and a magnificent altar triptych (1526) carved from linden wood. From the tree-shaded square outside, the Schänzletreppe steps lead down to the Gutgesellentor, the gate where Pope John XXIII was scandalously caught fleeing the Council of Constance in 1415.

✖ EATING

Pizzerias, cafes and German taverns dishing up hale and hearty meals are all in the mix in Breisach. Marktplatz and the riverfront tend to be safe bets for a simple meal.

ℹ INFORMATION

Breisach Tourist Office (☎07667-940 155; http://tourismus.breisach.de; Marktplatz 16; ⊙9am-12.30pm & 1.30-6pm Mon-Fri, 10am-3pm Sat) The tourist office can advise on wine tasting and private rooms in the area.

ℹ GETTING AROUND

Hire an e-bike from the centrally located **Fahrradverleih Breisach** (☎07667-287 1183; http://fahrradverleih-breisach.de; Fischerhalde 5a; per half-/full day €25/30; ⊙10am-2pm & 5-7pm Mon-Sat).

Briesach is small and easily navigable on foot. To get to Neuf-Brisach, take bus 1076 from Briesach train station.

Basel, Switzerland

Historically, Basel's position astride the mighty Rhine has contributed to its growth as a key trade and transport hub, and its position at the juncture of the French,

German and Swiss borders adds to its multicultural appeal.

◎ SIGHTS

Marktplatz   Square

Begin exploring Basel's delightful medieval Old Town in the Marktplatz, dominated by the astonishingly vivid red facade of the 16th-century **Rathaus** (Town Hall; ☎061 267 81 81; Marktplatz 9; ⊙8am-5pm Mon-Fri) `FREE`. From here, climb 400m west along Spalenberg through the former artisans' district to the 600-year-old **Spalentor** city gate, one of only three to survive the walls' demolition in 1866. Along the way, linger in captivating lanes such as Spalenberg, Heuberg and Leonhardsberg, lined by impeccably maintained, centuries-old houses.

Münster   Cathedral

(☎061 272 91 57; www.baslermuenster.ch; Münsterplatz 9; ⊙10am-5pm Mon-Fri, to 4pm Sat, 11.30am-5pm Sun; P) Blending Gothic exteriors with Romanesque interiors, this 13th-century cathedral was largely rebuilt after an earthquake in 1356. Renaissance humanist Erasmus of Rotterdam (1466–1536), who lived in Basel, lies buried in the northern aisle. Groups of two or more can climb the soaring Gothic towers (Sfr5 per person). Behind the church, leafy **Münster Pfalz** offers sublime Rhine views.

Mittlere Brücke   Bridge

It's hard to believe that this bridge, the symbol of Basel, has been spanning the rushing Rhine, connecting lofty Grossbasel with lowly Kleinbasel, since 1226. Strolling across it when in town is an essential activity.

Museum Jean Tinguely   Museum

(☎061 681 93 20; www.tinguely.ch; Paul Sacher-Anlage 2; adult/student/child Sfr18/12/free; ⊙11am-6pm Tue-Sun; P) Designed by leading Ticino architect Mario Botta, this museum showcases the playful, mischievous and downright wacky artistic concoctions of sculptor-turned-mad-scientist Jean Tinguely. Buttons next to some of Tinguely's 'kinetic' sculptures allow visitors to set them in motion. It's great fun to watch them rattle,

Marktplatz, Basel

shake and twirl, with springs, feathers and wheels radiating at every angle, or to hear the haunting musical sounds produced by the gigantic *Méta-Harmonies* on the upper floor. Catch bus 31 or 36 from Claraplatz.

Fondation Beyeler   Museum

(☏061 645 97 00; www.fondationbeyeler.ch; Baselstrasse 101, Riehen; adult/under 25yr Sfr25/ free; ☻10am-6pm Thu-Tue, to 8pm Wed; P) This astounding private-turned-public collection, assembled by former art dealers Hildy and Ernst Beyeler, is housed in a long, low, light-filled, open-plan building designed by Italian architect Renzo Piano. The varied exhibits juxtapose 19th- and 20th-century works by Picasso and Rothko against sculptures by Miró and Max Ernst and tribal figures from Oceania; there are also regular visiting exhibitions. Take tram 6 to Riehen from Barfüsserplatz or Marktplatz.

Vitra Campus   Museum

(☏+49 7621 702 3500; www.vitra.com/en-hu/ campus; Charles-Eames-Strasse 2, Weil am Rhein; adult/child Vitra Campus €17/15, Design Museum only €11/9, architecture tour €14/10; ☻10am-6pm) Showcasing the works of the adjoining, eponymous high-end furniture manufacturer, Vitra Campus comprises the dazzling **Vitra Design Museum** (of Guggenheim Bilbao architect Frank Gehry fame), the **Vitra Haus**, the **Vitra Schaudepot** (both by Herzog & de Meuron) and an ever-expanding bevy of installations by cutting-edge architects and designers, including Carsten Höller's whimsical, corkscrewing 30m-high *Vitra Slide*. Visiting is a must for serious lovers of architecture and industrial and interior design. Save your pennies and suitcase space for ubercool souvenirs.

Two-hour architecture tours run at 11.30am and 1pm. The campus is located just across the German border, in Weil am Rhein. To get here, take tram 8 from SBB Basel station, Barfüsserplatz or Claraplatz to the terminus at Weil am Rhein Bahnhof/ Zentrum, or walk the Rehberger-Weg (p67).

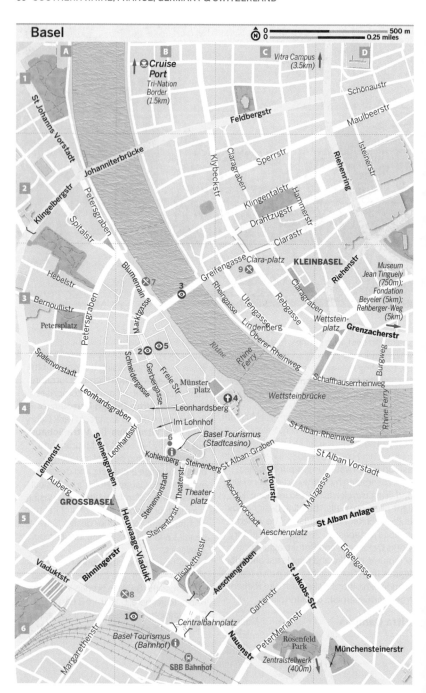

Basel

0   500 m
0   0.25 miles

☉ Cruise Port
Tri-Nation Border (1.5km)

Vitra Campus (3.5km)

Feldbergstr

Schönaustr

Maulbeerstr

St Johanns Vorstadt

Johanniterbrücke

Petersgraben

Klybeckstr

Claragraben

Sperrstr

Isteinerstr

Riehenring

Klingentalstr

Hammerstr

Klingelbergstr

Spitalstr

Drahtzugstr

Clarastr

Hebelstr

Blumenrain

Marktgasse

Greifengasse

Clara-platz

9 ⊗

KLEINBASEL

Riehenstr

Museum Jean Tinguely (750m); Fondation Beyeler (5km); Rehberger-Weg (5km)

Bernoullistr

Petersplatz

Petersgraben

7 ⊕

3 ◉

Rheingasse

Utengasse

Rebgasse

Claragraben

Lindenberg

Oberer Rheinweg

Wettstein-platz

Grenzacherstr

Spalenvorstadt

Schneidergasse

2 ◉ ◉ 5

Gerbergasse

Freie Str

Rhine

Rhine Ferry

Burgweg

Leonhardsgraben

Leonhardstr

Münster-platz

Schaffhauserrheinweg

Rhine Ferry

Leimenstr

Steinengraben

Leonhardsberg

⊕ 4

Wettsteinbrücke

Auberg

Im Lohnhof

St Alban-Rheinweg

GROSSBASEL

Steinenvorstadt

Theaterstr

6 ⊙
ⓘ

Basel Tourismus (Stadtcasino)

Kohlenberg

Steinenberg

St Alban-Graben

St Alban Vorstadt

Theater-platz

Aeschenvorstadt

Dufourstr

Malzgasse

Heuwaage-Viadukt

Binningerstr

Viaduktstr

Elisabethenstr

Aeschengraben

Aeschenplatz

St Alban Anlage

Engelgasse

St Jakobs-Str

⊗ 8

Gartenstr

1 ◉

Centralbahnplatz

Basel Tourismus (Bahnhof) ⓘ

Margarethenstr

Nauenstr

Peter Merianstr

Rosenfeld Park

Zentralstellwerk (400m)

Münchensteinerstr

SBB Bahnhof

Basel

 ACTIVITIES

Rehberger-Weg   Walking

If you've got a smartphone, download the app for this excellent 5km walking path between the Fondation Beyeler (p65) and Vitra Campus (p65) galleries. The walk features 24 colourful and unique public-art installations, designed by artist Tobias Rehberger, as waypoints/stops along the route, which ambles through countryside and crosses the Swiss border into Germany.

Artstübli Urban Art Tours   Walking

(www.artstuebli.ch; Barfüsserplatz; Sfr29) There's more to Basel's dynamic art scene than galleries. These edgy tours take a closer look at the city's emerging urban art, with walks of 1½ to two hours around the city centre, railway line and harbour area. See the website or email Philipp for dates and bookings. The meeting point is on Barfüsserplatz.

 EATING

Markthalle   Food Hall €

(www.markthalle-basel.ch; Steinentorberg 20; dishes Sfr10-25; ⊙8am-7pm Mon, to midnight Tue-Sat, 10am-5pm Sun; ☑🏃) Around the corner from Basel SBB station you'll find this large indoor market/food hall, which is a popular spot for a cheap lunch on the go. Vendors are always changing and feature Swiss specialities and world flavours. Worth a look in.

Volkshaus Basel   Brasserie €€

(☑061 690 93 00; www.volkshaus-basel.ch/en; Rebgasse 12-14; mains Sfr32-46; ⊙restaurant 11.30am-2pm & 6-10pm Mon-Fri, 6-10pm Sat, bar 10am-midnight Mon-Wed, to 1am Thu-Sat) This stylish Herzog & de Meuron–designed venue is part resto-bar, part gallery and part performance space. For relaxed dining, head for the atmospheric beer garden in a cobblestoned courtyard decorated with columns, vine-clad walls and light-draped rows of trees. The menu ranges from brasserie classics (steak frites) to more innovative offerings (salmon tartare with citrus fruits and gin cucumber).

Cheval Blanc   Gastronomy €€€

(☑061 260 50 07; www.chevalblancbasel.com; Blumenrain 8, Les Trois Rois; 5-/6-course menu Sfr220/250; ⊙noon-2pm & 7-10pm Tue-Sat) Shining with the near-unattainable Holy Grail of three Michelin stars, this incredibly sophisticated restaurant ranks as one of the world's best. Head chef Peter Knogl elevates French haute cuisine with a dash of Asian spice and Mediterranean aromas in dishes from filet of red mullet with saffron and black garlic to egg yolk ravioli with white Alba truffle – all totally divine.

ℹ **INFORMATION**

Pop into **Basel Tourismus – Bahnhof** (☑061 268 68 68; www.basel.com; Centralbahnstrasse 10; ⊙8-6pm Mon-Fri, 9am-5pm Sat, 9am-3pm Sun) or **Basel Tourismus – Stadtcasino** (Barfüsserplatz; ⊙9am-6.30pm Mon-Fri, to 5pm Sat, 10am-3pm Sun) for information and maps on the city and its surrounds.

ℹ **GETTING AROUND**

The centre is compact for walking on foot, but reliable buses and trams are helpful for exploring more in a day. Tram and bus tickets cost Sfr2.30 for short trips (maximum four stops), Sfr3.80 for longer trips within Basel and Sfr9.90 for a day pass.

WESTERN DANUBE, AUSTRIA & GERMANY

In This Chapter

Western Danube, Austria & Germany

The baroque streetscapes and imperial palaces set the stage for Vienna's artistic and musical masterpieces alongside its coffee-house culture and vibrant epicurean and design scenes. Moving into Germany, the Danube gently winds its way to the Italianate city of Passau. Top billing in eastern Bavaria goes to Regensburg, a former capital and one of Germany's prettiest and liveliest cities. Nuremberg (Nürnberg), Bavaria's second-largest city and the unofficial capital of Franconia, is an energetic place with a history that ranges from undeclared capital of the Holy Roman Empire to Nazi rallies and the trials that judged their war crimes.

With One Day in Vienna

With a day in Vienna, start at the **Stephansdom** (p81), being awed by the cathedral's cavernous interior, Gothic stone pulpit and baroque high altar. Spend the rest of the morning strolling the atmospheric narrow streets around the cathedral. After lunch, make your way to the **Hofburg** (p80), where one of the ultimate pleasures is simply to wander through and soak up the grandeur of this Habsburg architectural masterpiece. Narrow it down to one or two of the museums here, such as the **Kaiserappartements** (p80).

Best Places for...

Palaces Hofburg, Vienna (p80)

Castles Kaiserburg, Nuremberg (p80)

Sausages Historische Wurstkuchl, Regensberg (p90)

Entertainment Staatsoper, Vienna (p87)

Museums MuseumsQuartier, Vienna (p80)

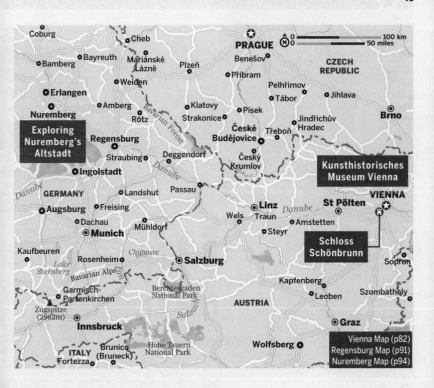

Getting from the Ports

Vienna The principal dock in Vienna is by the Reichsbrücke, 3km northeast of the centre, which is easily accessible by U-Bahn from Vorgartenstraße.

Passau & Regensburg Most cruises in Passau dock within a 10-minute stroll of the centre of the old town, as they do in Regensburg.

Nuremberg River cruises dock 5km south of Nuremberg's centre. It's easiest to use the cruise line's transport service, though you can also walk, bus or U-Bahn it to downtown.

Fast Facts

Currency Euro (€)

Language German

Free Wi-fi Many cafes, restaurants and bars offer free wi-fi and several cities have free hotspots around the centre.

Money ATMs and banks are plentiful, particularly near key tourist attractions.

Tourist Information There are centrally located tourist offices in Hauptmarkt, Nuremberg; the historic Altes Rathaus, Regensburg; the Altstadt, Passau; and near the Hofburg, Vienna.

Mirror Room

DE AGOSTINI/A. DAGLI ORTI/GETTY IMAGES ©

Schloss Schönbrunn, Vienna

The Habsburg Empire is revealed in all its frescoed, gilded, chandelier-lit glory in the wondrously ornate apartments of Schloss Schönbrunn, which are among Europe's best-preserved baroque interiors.

Great For...

☑ **Don't Miss**

The Great Gallery, Neptunbrunnen, Gloriette and Wagenburg.

State Apartments

The **Blue Staircase** makes a regal ascent to the palace's upper level. First up are the 19th-century apartments of Emperor Franz Josef I and his beloved wife, Elisabeth. The tour whisks through lavishly stuccoed, chandelier-lit apartments such as the **Billiard Room**, where army officials would pot balls while waiting to attend an audience, and Franz Josef's **study**, where the emperor worked tirelessly from 5am.

In the exquisite white-and-gold **Mirror Room**, a six-year-old Mozart performed for a rapturous Maria Theresia in 1762. Fairest of all, however, is the 40m-long **Great Gallery**, where the Habsburgs threw balls and banquets, a frothy vision of stucco and chandeliers, topped with a fresco by Italian artist Gregorio Guglielmi showing the glorification of Maria Theresia's reign. Decor

Schloss Schönbrunn gardens

Explore Ashore

Take the U-Bahn from Vorgartenstraße to Schwedenplatz, then change to line 4 in the direction of Hütteldorf. Schönnbrunn station is nine stops along this line (26 minutes). Leave three hours to fully explore the palace and grounds.

❶ Need to Know

www.schoenbrunn.at; 13, Schönbrunner Schlossstrasse 47; adult/child Imperial Tour €14.20/10.50, Grand Tour €17.50/11.50, Grand Tour with guide €20.50/13; ⊘8am-6.30pm Jul & Aug, to 5.30pm Apr-Jun, Sep & Oct, to 5pm Nov-Mar; ⓊHietzing

aside, this was where the historic meeting between John F Kennedy and Soviet leader Nikita Khrushchev took place in 1961.

If you have a Grand Tour ticket, you can continue through to the palace's **east wing**. Franz Stephan's apartments begin in the sublime **Blue Chinese Salon**, where the intricate floral wall paintings are done on Chinese rice paper. The negotiations that led to the collapse of the Austro-Hungarian Empire in 1918 were held here.

Schloss Schönbrunn Gardens

The beautifully tended formal **gardens** (www.schoenbrunn.at; 13, Schloss Schönbrunn; ⊘6.30am-dusk; ⓊHietzing) **FREE** of the palace, arranged in the French style, are appealing whatever the season: a symphony of colour in the summer and a wash of greys and browns in winter. The grounds, which were opened to the

public by Joseph II in 1779, hide a number of attractions in the tree-lined avenues, including the 1781 **Neptunbrunnen** (Neptune Fountain; ⊘8.30am-6.30pm Jul & Aug, to 5.30pm Apr-Jun, Sep & Oct, to 5pm Nov-Mar), a riotous ensemble from Greek mythology, and the crowning glory, the 1775 **Gloriette** (adult/child €3.80/3; ⊘9am-6pm, closed early Nov–mid-Mar).

Wagenburg

The **Wagenburg** (Imperial Coach Collection; www.kaiserliche-wagenburg.at; 13, Schloss Schönbrunn; adult/child €8/free; ⊘9am-5pm mid-Mar–Nov, 10am-4pm Dec–mid-Mar) is *Pimp My Ride* imperial style. On display is a vast array of carriages, including Emperor Franz Stephan's coronation carriage, with its ornate gold plating, Venetian glass panes and painted cherubs. The whole thing weighs an astonishing 4000kg.

Picture Gallery

SYLVAIN SONNET/GETTY IMAGES ©

Kunsthistorisches Museum Vienna

Occupying a neoclassical building as sumptuous as the art it contains, this museum takes you on a time-travel treasure hunt – from classical Rome to Egypt and the Renaissance.

Great For...

☑ **Don't Miss**

Dutch Golden Age paintings, the Kunstkammer and the Offering Chapel of Ka-ni-nisut.

Picture Gallery

The vast Picture Gallery is the most impressive of the museum's collections. First up is the German Renaissance, where the focus is the Dürer collection, followed by the Flemish baroque, epitomised by Rubens, Van Dyck and Pieter Bruegel the Elder.

In the 16th- and 17th-century Dutch Golden Age paintings, the desire to faithfully represent reality is captured in works by Rembrandt, Ruisdael and Vermeer. In the 16th-century Venetian rooms, don't miss Titian's *Nymph and Shepherd* (1570), Veronese's *Lucretia* (1583) and Tintoretto's *Susanna at her Bath* (1556).

Devotion is central to Raphael's *Madonna of the Meadow* (1506), a masterpiece of the High Renaissance, just as it is in Caravaggio's *Madonna of the Rosary* (1601), a stirring Counter-Reformation altarpiece.

Interior staircase

Explore Ashore

Take the U-Bahn from Vorgarten-straße to Karlsplatz. From here it's a five-minute stroll to the museum, or you can change to line 2 and jump off at Museumsquartier, which is even closer. You could spend an entire day in this museum, but a couple of hours will allow you to see the highlights.

❶ Need to Know

KHM, Museum of Art History; www.khm.at; 01, Maria-Theresien-Platz; adult/child incl Neue Burg museums €15/free; ◷10am-6pm Fri-Wed, to 9pm Thu; Ⓤ Museumsquartier, Volkstheater

In the final rooms, dedicated to Spanish, French and English painting, the undoubted star is Spanish court painter Velázquez.

Kunstkammer

The Habsburgs filled their *Kunstkammer* (cabinet of art and curiosities) with an encyclopaedic collection of the rare and the precious: from narwhal-tusk cups to table holders encrusted with fossilised shark teeth. Its 20 rooms containing 2200 artworks open a fascinating window on the obsession with collecting curios in royal circles in Renaissance and baroque times.

Egyptian & Near Eastern Collection

Decipher the mysteries of Egyptian civili-sations with a chronological romp through this miniature Giza of a collection. Here

the **Offering Chapel of Ka-ni-nisut** spells out the life of the high-ranking 5th-dynasty official in reliefs and hieroglyphs.

In the Near Eastern collection, the representation of a prowling lion from Babylon's triumphal Ishtar Gate (604–562 BC) is the big attraction.

Greek & Roman Antiquities

This rich Greek and Roman repository reveals the imperial scope for collecting classical antiquities, with 2500 objects traversing three millennia from the Cypriot Bronze Age to early medieval times.

Among the Greek art is a fragment from the Parthenon's northern frieze, while the Roman stash includes the 4th-century AD *Theseus Mosaic* from Salzburg and the captivating 3rd-century AD *Lion Hunt* relief.

Vienna's Historic Centre

This walk takes you from the cathedral through the historic centre of Vienna, with highlights from many historical periods.

Start Stephansdom
Distance 3km
Duration 1½ hours

5 Hoher Markt, Vienna's oldest square, is now a busy commercial street; highlights include the **Römer Museum** (www.wienmuseum.at; Hoher Markt 3).

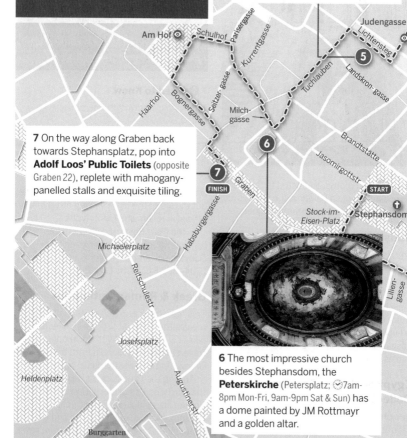

7 On the way along Graben back towards Stephansplatz, pop into **Adolf Loos' Public Toilets** (opposite Graben 22), replete with mahogany-panelled stalls and exquisite tiling.

6 The most impressive church besides Stephansdom, the **Peterskirche** (Petersplatz; ⏰7am-8pm Mon-Fri, 9am-9pm Sat & Sun) has a dome painted by JM Rottmayr and a golden altar.

N   0 _____ 200 m
     0 _____ 0.1 miles

Take a Break... Hit historic **Griechenbeisl** (www.griechenbeisl.at; 01, Fleischmarkt 11; mains €15-28; 11.30am-11.30pm) off the Fleischmarkt.

Classic Photo The seductive lines of Heiligenkreuzerhof.

Danube Canal

4 Busy **Fleischmarkt** is the heart of the Greek quarter of Vienna. Climb the stairs to Judengasse, centre of the traditional Jewish quarter.

Griechenbeisl

Fleischmarkt

Rotgasse

Laurenzerberg

Köllnerhof-gasse

Grashofgasse

3 Enter **Heiligenkreuzerhof** from the eastern side. During Christmas this lovely courtyard is filled with traditional decorations.

Rotenturmstr

Lugeck

Sonnenfels-gasse

Schönlatern-gasse

Dominikaner

Bibers

Rosenbursenstr

Stubenring (Ringstrasse)

Strobel-gasse

Essig-gasse

Bäckerstr

Jesuiten-gasse

Postgasse

Prediger-gasse

Dominikanerkirche

Wollzeile

Blutgasse

Domgasse

Schulerstr

Grünangergasse

1 Wind through the atmospheric backstreets to **Mozarthaus Vienna** (p84), where the great composer lived for three years.

2 Inside **Jesuitenkirche** (Dr-Ignaz-Seipel-Platz 1; 7am-7pm Mon-Sat, 8am-7pm Sun), frescoes create the illusion of a dome, while the **Dominikanerkirche** (Postgasse 4; 7am-7pm) is Vienna's finest early baroque church.

Kaiserburg

ARAGAMI12345/SHUTTERSTOCK ©

Exploring Nuremberg's Altstadt

Nuremberg has one of the largest and most history-packed old towns in the business and a wander around its crooked, steep lanes, covered bridges and intact city defences is one of the high points of any visit to Bavaria.

Great For...

☑ Don't Miss

Ehekarussell Brunnen (Weisser Turm U-Bahn), a grotesque sculptural work depicting six interpretations of marriage.

Kaiserburg

This enormous **castle complex** (Imperial Castle; ☎0911-244 6590; www.kaiserburg-nuernberg.de; Auf der Burg; adult/child incl Sinwell Tower €7/free, Palas & Museum €5.50/free; ☉9am-6pm Apr-Sep, 10am-4pm Oct-Mar) above the Altstadt poignantly reflects Nuremberg's medieval might. The main attraction is a tour of the newly renovated **Palas** (residential wing) to see the lavish Knights' and Imperial Hall, a Romanesque double chapel and an exhibit on the inner workings of the Holy Roman Empire. This segues to the **Kaiserburg Museum**, which focuses on the castle's military and building history.

St Sebalduskirche

Nuremberg's **oldest church** (www.sebal duskirche.de; Winklerstrasse 26; ☉9.30am-4pm Jan-Mar, to 6pm Apr-Dec) was built in

St Sebalduskirche altar

Explore Ashore

The cruise dock is 5km from the old town; it's easiest to use the company's shuttle service to reach it. Allow three to four hours at least to explore the sights here, give or take any time you wish to spend in museums.

❶ Need to Know

The Altstadt is served by the Weisser Turm and Lorenzkirche U-Bahn stations.

rusty pink-veined sandstone in the 13th century. Its exterior is replete with religious sculptures and symbols; check out the ornate carvings over the **Bridal Doorway** to the north, showing the Wise and Foolish Virgins. Inside, the bronze shrine of St Sebald (Nuremberg's own saint) is a Gothic and Renaissance masterpiece that took its maker, Peter Vischer the Elder, and his two sons more than 11 years to complete.

Stadtmuseum Fembohaus

Offering an entertaining overview of the city's history, highlights of the **Stadtmuseum Fembohaus** (📞0911-231 2595; Burgstrasse 15; adult/child €6/1.50; ⏰10am-5pm Tue-Fri, to 6pm Sat & Sun) include the restored historic rooms of this 16th-century merchant's house. Also here, **Noricama** takes you on a flashy Hollywoodesque multi-

media journey (in German and English) through Nuremberg's history.

Albrecht-Dürer-Haus

Dürer, Germany's most famous Renaissance draughtsman, lived and worked at the **Albrecht-Dürer-Haus** (📞0911-231 2568; Albrecht-Dürer-Strasse 39; adult/child €6/1.50; ⏰10am-5pm Tue, Wed & Fri, to 8pm Thu, to 6pm Sat & Sun, to 5pm Mon Jul-Sep) from 1509 until his death in 1528. After a multimedia show, there's an audio guide tour of the four-storey house, which is narrated by 'Agnes', Dürer's wife.

Germanisches Nationalmuseum

Spanning prehistory to the early 20th century, this **museum** (German National Museum; 📞0911-133 10; www.gnm.de; Kartäusergasse 1; adult/child €8/5; ⏰10am-6pm Tue & Thu-Sun, to 9pm Wed) is the German-speaking world's biggest and most important museum of Teutonic culture. It features works by German painters and sculptors, an archaeological collection, arms and armour, musical and scientific instruments, and toys.

Vienna, Austria

Baroque streetscapes and imperial palaces set the stage for Vienna's artistic and musical masterpieces alongside its coffee-house culture and vibrant epicurean and design scenes.

SIGHTS

The Hofburg & Around

Hofburg   Palace
(Imperial Palace; www.hofburg-wien.at; 01, Michaelerkuppel; adult/child €13.90/8.20; ◷9am-5.30pm; 📷1A, 2A Michaelerplatz, 🚋D, 1, 2, 46, 49, 71 Burgring, ⓊHerrengasse) Nothing symbolises Austria's resplendent cultural heritage more than its Hofburg, home base of the Habsburgs from 1273 to 1918. The oldest section is the 13th-century **Schweizerhof** (Swiss Courtyard), named after the Swiss guards who used to protect its precincts. The Renaissance **Swiss gate** dates from 1553. The courtyard adjoins a larger courtyard, **In der Burg**, with a monument to Emperor Franz II adorning its centre. The palace now houses the Austrian president's offices and a raft of museums.

Kaiserappartements   Palace
(Imperial Apartments; www.hofburg-wien.at; 01, Michaelerplatz; adult/child €13.90/8.20, incl guided tour €16.90/9.70; ◷9am-6pm Jul & Aug, to 5.30pm Sep-Jun; ⓊHerrengasse) The Kaiserappartements, once the official living quarters of Franz Josef I and Empress Elisabeth, are dazzling in their chandelier-lit opulence. The highlight is the **Sisi Museum** (📞01-533 75 70; 01, Michaelerkuppel; adult/child €13.90/8.20, incl guided tour €16.90/9.70; ◷9am-6pm Jul & Aug, to 5.30pm Sep-Jun), devoted to Austria's most beloved empress, which has a strong focus on the clothing and jewellery of Austria's monarch. Multilingual audio guides are included in the admission price. Guided tours take in the Kaiserappartements, the Sisi Museum and the **Silberkammer** (Silver Depot, Imperial Silver Collection; adult/child €13.90/8.20, incl guided tour €16.90/9.70; ◷9am-6pm Jul &

Aug, to 5.30pm Sep-Jun), whose largest silver service caters for 140 dinner guests.

Kaiserliche Schatzkammer   Museum
(Imperial Treasury; www.kaiserliche-schatz kammer.at; 01, Schweizerhof; adult/child €12/free; ◷9am-5.30pm Wed-Mon; ⓊHerrengasse) The Hofburg's Kaiserliche Schatzkammer contains secular and ecclesiastical treasures (including devotional images and altars, particularly from the baroque era) of priceless value and splendour – the sheer wealth of this collection of crown jewels is staggering. As you walk through the rooms you'll see magnificent treasures such as a golden rose, diamond-studded Turkish sabres, a 2680-carat Colombian emerald and, the highlight of the treasury, the imperial crown.

The Museum District & Neubau

The **MuseumsQuartier** (Museum Quarter, MQ; www.mqw.at; 07, Museumsplatz; ◷information & ticket centre 10am-7pm; ⓊMuseumsquartier, Volkstheater) is a remarkable ensemble of museums, cafes, restaurants and bars inside former imperial stables designed by Fischer von Erlach. This breeding ground of Viennese cultural life is the perfect place to hang out and watch or meet people on warm evenings. With over 90,000 sq metres of exhibition space, the complex is one of the world's most ambitious cultural hubs.

Leopold Museum   Museum
(www.leopoldmuseum.org; 07, Museumsplatz 1; adult/child €13/8; ◷10am-6pm Fri-Wed, to 9pm Thu; ⓊVolkstheater, Museumsquartier) Part of the MuseumsQuartier, the Leopold Museum is named after ophthalmologist Rudolf Leopold, who after buying his first Egon Schiele for a song as a young student in 1950, amassed a huge private collection of mainly 19th-century and modernist Austrian artworks. In 1994 he sold the lot – 5266 paintings – to the Austrian government for €160 million (individually, the paintings would have made him €574 million), and

ONDERTUR/SHUTTERSTOCK ©

Statue of Franz I, Hofburg

the Leopold Museum was born. **Café Leopold** (www.cafeleopold.wien; 07, ⊘9.30am-1am Mon-Fri, 9.30am-midnight Sat & Sun; 🤶) is located on the top floor.

MUMOK — Gallery

(Museum Moderner Kunst, Museum of Modern Art; www.mumok.at; 07, Museumsplatz 1; adult/child €12/free; ⊘2-7pm Mon, 10am-7pm Tue, Wed & Fri-Sun, 10am-9pm Thu; 🚌49 Volkstheater, ⓤVolkstheater, Museumsquartier) The dark basalt edifice and sharp corners of the Museum Moderner Kunst are a complete contrast to the MuseumsQuartier's historical sleeve. Inside, MUMOK contains Vienna's finest collection of 20th-century art, centred on fluxus, nouveau realism, pop art and photo-realism. The best of expressionism, cubism, minimal art and Viennese Actionism is also represented in a collection of 9000 works that are rotated and exhibited by theme – but note that sometimes all this Actionism is packed away to make room for temporary exhibitions.

Burgtheater — Theatre

(📞01-514 44 4140; www.burgtheater.at; 01, Universitätsring 2; tours adult/child €7/3.50; ⊘tours 3pm; 🚋D, 1, 2 Rathaus, ⓤRathaus) This stately Renaissance-style theatre sits with aplomb on the Ringstrasse. Designed by Gottfried Semper and Karl Hasenauer in 1888, it was restored to its pre-WWII glory in 1955. The company dates to 1741, making it Europe's second oldest. If the walls could talk, they'd tell of musical milestones like the premiere of Mozart's *The Marriage of Figaro* (1786) and Beethoven's *First Symphony* (1800). For a behind-the-scenes look at this magnificent theatre, join one of the regular guided tours.

◉ Stephansdom & the Historic Centre

Stephansdom — Cathedral

(St Stephen's Cathedral; www.stephanskirche. at; 01, Stephansplatz; tours adult/child €6/2.50; ⊘6am-10pm Mon-Sat, 7am-10pm Sun, tours 10.30am Mon-Sat; ⓤStephansplatz) Vienna's Gothic masterpiece Stephansdom – or Steffl (Little Stephan), as it's ironically

Vienna

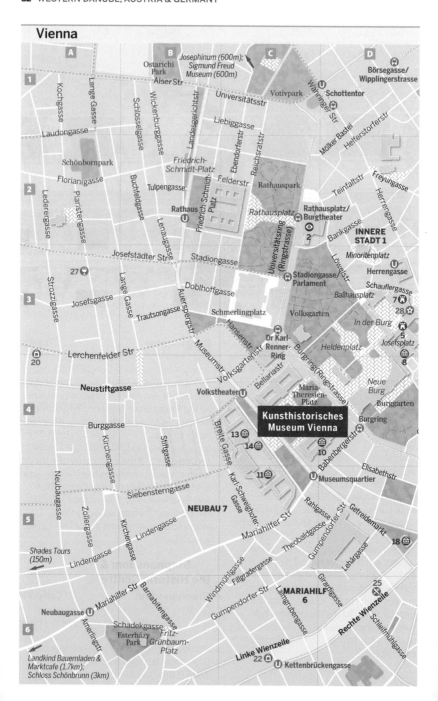

A · B · C · D

1 · 2 · 3 · 4 · 5 · 6

Ostarichi Park
Josephinum (600m);
Sigmund Freud Museum (600m)
Alser Str
Universitätsstr
Börsegasse/ Wipplingerstrasse
Votivpark
Schottentor
Kochgasse
Lange Gasse
Wickenburggasse
Landesgerichtstr
Wahringer Str
Laudongasse
Schlösselgasse
Liebiggasse
Ebendorferstr
Reichsratstr
Mölker Bastel
Helferstorferstr
Schönbornpark
Friedrich-Schmidt-Platz
Teinfaltstr
Freyungass
Florianigasse
Felderstr
Rathauspark
Herrengasse
Ledererergasse
Piaristengasse
Buchfeldgasse
Tulpengasse
Rathaus
Friedrich-Schmidt-Platz
Rathausplatz
Rathausplatz/ Burgtheater
INNERE STADT 1
Lenaugasse
Stadiongasse
Universitätsring (Ringstrasse)
Bankgasse
Minoritenplatz
Josefstädter Str
27
Doblhoffgasse
Stadiongasse Parlament
Löwelstr
Herrengasse
Schauflergasse
Strozzigasse
Lange Gasse
Josefsgasse
Trautsongasse
Schmerlingplatz
Ballhausplatz
Volksgarten
In der Burg
7
28
Auerspergstr
Hansenstr
Dr Karl-Renner-Ring
Heldenplatz
5
Josefsplatz
Lerchenfelder Str
Museumstr
Volksgartenstr
Burgring (Ringstrasse)
8
20
Neustiftgasse
Bellariastr
Neue Burg
Volkstheater
Maria-Theresien-Platz
Burggarten
Burggasse
Kunsthistorisches Museum Vienna
Burgring
Kirchengasse
Stiftgasse
Breite Gasse
13
14
Babenbergerstr
10
Neubaugasse
Zollergasse
Siebensterngasse
Karl-Schweighofer
11
Museumsquartier
Elisabethstr
NEUBAU 7
Lindengasse
Mariahilfer Str
Rahlgasse
Theobaldgasse
Gumpendorfer Str
Getreidemarkt
Shades Tours (150m)
Lindengasse
Windmühlgasse
Lehárgasse
18
Neubaugasse
Mariahilfer Str
Barnabitengasse
Fillgradergasse
Gumpendorfer Str
MARIAHILF 6
Girardigasse
25
Amerlingstr
Schadekgasse
Fritz-Grünbaum-Platz
Linke Wienzeile
Lamgrubengasse
Rechte Wienzeile
Schleifmühlgasse
Esterházy-Park
22
Kettenbrückengasse
Landkind Bauernladen & Marktcafe (1.7km); Schloss Schönbrunn (3km)

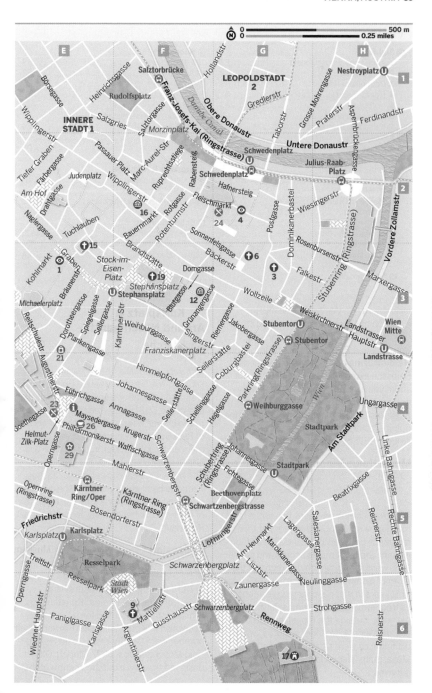

0 500 m
0 0.25 miles

E

F

G

H

Salztorbrücke

Nestroyplatz

LEOPOLDSTADT
2

Franz-Josefs-Kai (Ringstrasse)

Donau Canal

Obere Donaustr

Holandstr

Gredlerstr

Grosse Mohrengasse

Praterstr

Aspernbrückengasse

Ferdinandstr

Borsegasse

Heinrichsgasse

Rudolfsplatz

Wipplingerstr

INNERE
STADT 1

Salzgries

Saltorgasse

Morzinplatz

Taborstr

Untere Donaustr

Tiefer Graben

Passauer Platz

Marc-Aurel-Str

Schwedenplatz

Schwedenplatz

Julius-Raab-
Platz

Judenplatz

Färbergasse

Am Hof

Drahtgasse

Wipplingerstr

Ruprechtsstiege

Rabensteig

Hafnersteig

Fleischmarkt

Postgasse

Wiesingerstr

Vordere Zollamtstr

Naglergasse

Tuchlauben

Bauernmarkt

16

Rotgasse

Rotenturmstr

24

4

Sonnenfelsgasse

Dominikanerbastei

Rosenbursenstr

Stubenring (Ringstrasse)

Marxergasse

Kohlmarkt

Graben

1

15

Brandtstätte

Stock-im-
Eisen-
Platz

19

Domgasse

Bäckerstr

6

3

Falkestr

Michaelerplatz

Dorotheergasse

Spiegelgasse

Seilergasse

Stephansplatz

Stephansplatz

Blutgasse

12

Grünangergasse

Singerstr

Riemergasse

Jakobergasse

Wollzeile

Weiskirchnerstr

Stubenring (Ringstrasse)

Stubentor

Stubentor

Landstrasser
Hauptstr

Wien
Mitte

Landstrasse

Reitschulestr

Augustinerstr

Plankengasse

21

Kärntner Str

Weihburggasse

Franziskanerplatz

Seilerstätte

Coburgbastei

Parkring (Ringstrasse)

Himmelpfortgasse

Fuhrichgasse

Johannesgasse

Annagasse

Seilerstätte

Schellinggasse

Hegelgasse

Wien

Weihburggasse

Ungargasse

23

Maysedergasse

26

Krugerstr

Walfischgasse

Schwarzenbergstr

Stadtpark

Am Stadtpark

Linke Bahngasse

Goethegasse

Helmut-
Zilk-Platz

Philharmonikerstr

29

Mahlerstr

Schubertring
(Ringstrasse)

Johannesgasse

Fichtegasse

Stadtpark

Beatrixgasse

Opernring
(Ringstrasse)

Kärntner
Ring/Oper

Kärntner Ring
(Ringstrasse)

Bösendorferstr

Beethovenplatz

Schwarzenbergstrasse

Rechte Bahngasse

Reisnerstr

Friedrichstr

Karlsplatz

Karlsplatz

Dorotheergasse

Schwarzenbergstr

Lothringerstr

Lagergasse

Marokkanergasse

Salesianergasse

Neulinggasse

Strohgasse

Opernring

Treitlstr

Resselpark

Resselpark

Stadt
Wien

Mattiellistr

9

Gusshausstr

Schwarzenbergplatz

Am Heumarkt

Lisztstr

Zaunergasse

Rennweg

Reisnerstr

Wiedner Hauptstr

Paniglgasse

Karlsgasse

Argentinierstr

Schwarzenbergplatz

17

Vienna

nicknamed – is Vienna's pride and joy. A church has stood here since the 12th century, and reminders of this are the Romanesque **Riesentor** (Giant Gate) and **Heidentürme** (Towers of the Heathens). From the exterior, the first thing that will strike you is the glorious tiled roof, with its dazzling row of chevrons and Austrian eagle. Inside, the magnificent Gothic stone pulpit presides over the main nave, fashioned in 1515 by Anton Pilgrim.

Mozarthaus Vienna   Museum
(☏01-512 17 91; www.mozarthausvienna.at; 01, Domgasse 5; adult/child €11/4.50, incl Haus der Musik €18/8; ⊙10am-7pm; ⓤStephansplatz) The great composer spent two and a half happy and productive years at this residence between 1784 and 1787. Exhibits include copies of music scores and paintings, while free audio guides recreate the story of his time here. Mozart spent a total of 11 years in Vienna, changing residences frequently and sometimes setting up his home outside the Ringstrasse in the cheaper *Vorstädte* (inner suburbs) when his finances were tight. Of these, the Mozarthaus Vienna is the only one that survives.

◎ Karlsplatz & Around Naschmarkt

Karlskirche   Church
(St Charles Church; www.karlskirche.at; 04, Karlsplatz; adult/child €8/4; ⊙9am-6pm Mon-Sat, noon-7pm Sun; ⓤKarlsplatz) Built between 1716 and 1739, after a vow by Karl VI at the end of the 1713 plague, Vienna's finest baroque church rises at the southeast corner of Resselpark. It was designed and commenced by Johann Bernhard Fischer von Erlach and completed by his son Joseph. The huge elliptical copper dome reaches 72m; the highlight is the lift to the cupola (included in admission) for a close-up view of the intricate frescoes by Johann Michael Rottmayr.

Secession   Museum
(www.secession.at; 01, Friedrichstrasse 12; adult/child €9/6; ⊙10am-6pm Tue-Sun; ⓤKarlsplatz) In 1897, 19 progressive artists swam away from the mainstream Künstlerhaus artistic establishment to form the *Wiener Secession* (Vienna Secession). Among their number were Gustav Klimt, Josef Hoffman, Kolo Moser and Joseph M Olbrich. Olbrich designed the new exhibition centre of the

Secessionists, which combined sparse functionality with stylistic motifs. Its biggest draw is Klimt's exquisitely gilded *Beethoven Frieze*. Guided tours in English (€3) lasting one hour take place at 11am Saturday. An audio guide costs €3.

◎ Schloss Belvedere to the Canal

Schloss Belvedere   Palace

(www.belvedere.at; Prinz-Eugen-Strasse 27; adult/child Oberes Belvedere €16/free, Unteres Belvedere €14/free, combined ticket €22/free; ⊙9am-6pm Sat-Thu, to 9pm Fri; 🚃D, 71 Schwarzenbergplatz, Ⓤ Taubstummengasse, Südtiroler Platz) A masterpiece of total art, Schloss Belvedere is one of the world's finest baroque palaces. Designed by Johann Lukas von Hildebrandt (1668–1745), it was built for the brilliant military strategist Prince Eugene of Savoy, conqueror of the Turks in 1718. What giddy romance is evoked in its sumptuously frescoed halls, replete with artworks by Klimt, Schiele and Kokoschka; what stories are conjured in its landscaped gardens, which drop like the fall of a theatre curtain to reveal Vienna's skyline.

⊙ TOURS

Space & Place   Walking

(📞0680 125 43 54; http://spaceandplace.at; walking tours €10, Coffeehouse Conversations €11) For the inside scoop on Vienna, join Eugene on one of his fun, quirky tours. The alternative line-up keeps growing: from Vienna Ugly tours, homing in on the capital's ugly side, to Smells Like Wien Spirit, a playful exploration of the city through smell, and the sociable Coffeehouse Conversations. See the website for dates, further details and meeting points.

Shades Tours   Walking

(📞01-997 19 83; www.shades-tours.com; Impact Hub Vienna, Lindengasse 56; walking tours €18) A world apart from the bog-standard city tour, Shades reveals central Vienna from a unique perspective, with two-hour walks guided by formerly homeless residents.

🍴◎ Viennese Specialities

Vienna has a strong repertoire of traditional dishes. One or two are variations on dishes from other regions. Classics include:

Schnitzel *Wiener Schnitzel* should always be crumbed veal, but pork is gaining ground in some places.

Goulash *Rindsgulasch* (beef goulash) is everywhere in Vienna.

Tafelspitz Traditionally this boiled prime beef swims in the juices of locally produced *Suppengrün* (fresh soup vegetables), before being served with *Kren* (horseradish) sauce.

Beuschel Offal, usually sliced lung and heart, with a slightly creamy sauce.

Backhendl Fried, breaded chicken, often called *steirisches Backhendl* (Styrian fried chicken).

Zwiebelrostbraten Slices of roast beef smothered in gravy and fried onions.

Schinkenfleckerln Oven-baked ham and noodle casserole.

Bauernschmaus Platter of cold meats.

The undeniable monarchs of all desserts are *Kaiserschmarrn* (sweet pancake with raisins) and *Apfelstrudel* (apple strudel), but also look out for *Marillenknödel* (apricot dumplings) in summer.

Zwiebelrostbraten
POSINOTE/SHUTTERSTOCK ©

Offered in English and German, the tours are a real eye-opener. It also provides integration-aimed tours led by refugees.

Bitzinger Würstelstand am Albertinaplatz

See the website for dates, bookings and meeting points.

🔒 SHOPPING

Dorotheum Antiques

(www.dorotheum.com; 01, Dorotheergasse 17; ⊘10am-6pm Mon-Fri, 9am-5pm Sat; ⓊStephansplatz) The Dorotheum is among the largest auction houses in Europe, and for the casual visitor it's more like a museum, housing everything from antique toys and tableware to autographs, antique guns and, above all, lots of quality paintings. You can bid at the regular auctions held here; otherwise just drop by (it's free) and enjoy browsing.

Dirndlherz Clothing

(http://dirndlherz.at; 07, Lerchenfelder Strasse 50; ⊘11am-6pm Thu & Fri, to 4pm Sat; ⓊVolks theater) Putting her own spin on alpine fashion, Austrian designer Gabriela Urabl creates one-of-a-kind, high-fashion *Dirndls* (women's traditional dress), from sassy purple-velvet bosom-lifters to 1950s-style gingham numbers, and *Dirndls* emblazoned

with quirky motifs like pop-art and punk-like conical metal studs. T-shirts with tag-lines such as *'Mei Dirndl is in da Wäsch'* ('My Dirndl is in the wash') are also available.

🍴 EATING

Naschmarkt Market €

(06, Linke & Rechte Wienzeile; ⊘6am-7.30pm Mon-Fri, to 6pm Sat; ⓊKarlsplatz, Kettenbrück-engasse) Vienna's aromatic Naschmarkt unfurls over 500m along Linke Wienzeile between the U4 stops of Kettenbrücken-gasse and Karlsplatz. The western (Ket-tengasse) end has all sorts of meats, fruit and vegetables (including exotic varieties), spices, wines, cheeses, olives, Indian and Middle Eastern specialities and fabulous kebab and felafel stands. In all, there are 123 fixed stalls, including a slew of sit-down restaurants.

Bitzinger Würstelstand am Albertinaplatz Street Food €

(www.bitzinger-wien.at; 01, Albertinaplatz; sausages €3.50-4.70; ⊘8am-4am; 🚋D, 1, 2, 71 Kärntner Ring/Oper, ⓊKarlsplatz, Stephansplatz) Behind the Staatsoper, Vienna's best sausage stand has cult status. Bitzinger offers the contrasting spectacle of ladies and gents dressed to the nines, sipping beer, wine or Joseph Perrier Champagne (€19.90 for 0.2L) while tucking into sausages at outdoor tables or the heated counter after performances. Mustard comes in *süss* (sweet, ie mild) or *scharf* (fiercely hot).

Landkind Bauernladen
& Marktcafe   Market €€

(☏0668 801 7132; www.landkind.wien; 29 Schwendermarkt, Stand 16; meals €6-22; ⊘9am-9pm Tue-Fri, 9am-3pm Sat; 🚋52, 60,) 🌱 Part bio-organic market stall, part cafe and local community hang-out, Landkind is a local favourite for its excellent food, rough-and-ready mix of furniture, retro crockery and endless creative ways to find a table for guests, despite the tight space. Produce and menu items are seasonally sourced from small-scale sustainable farmers hand-picked by the friendly owners Nina, Beni and Stefan.

ef16   Austrian €€

(☏01-513 23 18; www.ef16.net; Fleischmarkt 16; mains €16.50-32.50; ⊘5.30-11.30pm; 🚋1, 2, 31 Schwedenplatz, Ⓤ Schwedenplatz) What a joy it is to step into this quirkily named restaurant and wine bar, where you'll dine by candlelight in a vaulted, red-walled space. In summer, the vine-rimmed *Schanigarten* (courtyard-garden) is among Vienna's prettiest. The beautifully presented food reveals profound flavours in such dishes as venison carpaccio with black nuts and cranberry mayonnaise, and guinea fowl with olive polenta.

🍷 DRINKING & NIGHTLIFE

Café Sacher   Coffee

(www.sacher.com; 01, Philharmonikerstrasse 4; ⊘8am-midnight; 🚋D, 1, 2, 71 Kärntner Ring/Oper, Ⓤ Karlsplatz) With a battalion of waiters, and air of nobility, this grand cafe is celebrated for its *Sacher Torte,* a wonderfully rich iced-chocolate cake with apricot jam once favoured by Emperor Franz Josef. It has a covered pavement terrace, but for the

The
Flohmarkt

One of the best flea markets in Europe, this Vienna **institution** (05, Linke Wienzeile; ⊘6.30am-6pm Sat; Ⓤ Kettenbrückengasse) adjoining the Naschmarkt's southwestern end brims with antiques and *Altwaren* (old wares). Stalls hawking books, clothes, records, ancient electrical goods, old postcards, ornaments, carpets, you name it, stretch for several blocks. Arrive early, as it gets increasingly crammed as the morning wears on, and be prepared to haggle.

full-blown experience, head to the opulent chandelier-lit interior.

Weinstube Josefstadt   Wine Bar

(08, Piaristengasse 27; ⊘4pm-midnight Apr-Dec; Ⓤ Rathaus) Weinstube Josefstadt is one of the loveliest *Stadtheurigen* (city wine taverns) in Vienna. A leafy green oasis spliced between towering residential blocks, its tables of friendly, well-liquored locals are squeezed in between the trees and shrubs looking onto a pretty, painted *Salettl,* or wooden summerhouse. Wine is local and cheap, food is typical, with a buffet-style meat and fritter selection.

🎭 ENTERTAINMENT

Staatsoper   Opera

(☏01-514 44 7880; www.wiener-staatsoper.at; 01, Opernring 2; tickets €13-239, standing room €3-4; Ⓤ Karlsplatz) The glorious Staatsoper is Vienna's premier opera and classical-music venue. Productions are lavish, formal affairs, where people dress up accordingly. In the interval, wander the foyer and refreshment rooms to fully appreciate the gold-and-crystal interior. Opera is not performed here in July and August (but tours still take place). Tickets can be purchased up to two months in advance.

Spanish
Riding School   Performing Arts

(Spanische Hofreitschule; ☎01-533 90 31-0; www.srs.at; 01, Michaelerplatz 1; tickets €25-217; ⊙hours vary; ⬛1A, 2A Michaelerplatz, ⒰Herrengasse) The world-famous Spanish Riding School is a Viennese institution truly reminiscent of the imperial Habsburg era. This unequalled equestrian show is performed by Lipizzaner stallions formerly kept at an imperial stud established at Lipizza (hence the name). These graceful stallions perform an equine ballet to a program of classical music while the audience watches from pillared balconies – or from a cheaper standing-room area – and the chandeliers shimmer above.

ⓘ INFORMATION

Tourist Info Wien (☎01-245 55; www.wien.info; 01, Albertinaplatz; ⊙9am-7pm; 🛜; ⬛D, 1, 2, 71 Kärntner Ring/Oper, ⒰Stephansplatz) Vienna's main tourist office, with a ticket agency, hotel booking service, free maps and every brochure under the sun.

ⓘ GETTING AROUND

Vienna's Innere Stadt centred around Stephansdom is compact and easily walkable.

U-Bahn Fast, comfortable and safe. Trains run from 5am to midnight Monday to Thursday and continuously from 5am Friday through to midnight Sunday. Tickets are sold at machines or windows at stations. Validate tickets prior to boarding.

Tram Slower but more enjoyable. Depending on the route, trams run from around 5.15am to

about 11.45pm. Buy tickets at kiosks or from the driver (more expensive). Validate tickets when boarding.

Bus Reliable, punctual, with several very useful routes for visitors. Most run from 5am to midnight; services can be sporadic or nonexistent on weekends. Buy tickets from the driver or a *Tabakladen* (tobacconist). Validate tickets on boarding.

Bike Over 120 **Citybike Wien** (Vienna City Bike; www.citybikewien.at; 1st/2nd/3rd hr free/€1/2, per hr thereafter €4) bike-share stands are located across the city. A credit card and €1 registration fee is required to hire bikes; swipe your card in the machine and follow the multilingual instructions. The bikes are intended as an alternative to public transport and can only be locked up at a bike station (unless you use your own lock).

Passau, Germany

The power of flowing water has quite literally shaped the picturesque town of Passau on the border with Austria. The Altstadt remains pretty much as it was when the powerful prince-bishops built its tight lanes, tunnels and archways with an Italianate flourish.

◎ SIGHTS
Dom St Stephan   Church

(www.bistum-passau.de; Domplatz; ⊙6.30am-7pm) There's been a church on this spot since the late 5th century, but what you see today is much younger thanks to the fire of 1662, which ravaged much of the medieval town, including the cathedral. The rebuilding contract went to a team of Italians, notably the architect Carlo Lurago and the stucco master Giovanni Battista Carlone. The result is a top-heavy baroque interior with a posse of saints and cherubs gazing down at the congregation from countless cornices and capitals.

Veste Oberhaus

Dreiflusseck   Landmark

(Three River Corner) The very nib of the Alt-stadt peninsula, the point where the rivers merge, is known as the Dreiflusseck. From the north the little Ilz sluices brackish water down from the peat-rich Bavarian Forest, meeting the cloudy brown of the Danube as it flows from the west and the pale snow-melt jade of the Inn from the south to create a murky tricolour. The effect is best observed from the ramparts of the Veste Oberhaus.

Veste Oberhaus   Fortress

(☎0851-396 800; www.oberhausmuseum.de; adult/child €5/4; ⊗9am-5pm Mon-Fri, 10am-6pm Sat & Sun mid-Mar–mid-Nov) A 13th-century defensive fortress, built by the prince-bishops, Veste Oberhaus towers over Passau with patriarchal pomp. Not surprisingly, views of the city and into Austria are superb from up here. Inside the bastion is the **Oberhausmuseum**, a regional history museum where you can uncover the mysteries of medieval cathedral building, learn what it took to become a knight and explore

Passau's period as a centre of the salt trade. Displays are labelled in English.

EATING

Heilig-Geist-Stifts-Schenke   Bavarian €€

(☎0851-26 07; www.stiftskeller-passau. de; Heilig-Geist-Gasse 4; mains €10-20; ⊗11am-midnight, closed Wed; 🎅) Not only does this historical inn have a succession of walnut-panelled ceramic-stove-heated rooms, a candlelit cellar (from 6pm) and a vine-draped garden, but the food is equally inspired. Amid the river fish, steaks and seasonal dishes there are quite gourmet affairs such as beef fillet in flambéed cognac sauce. Help it all along with one of the many Austrian and German wines in stock.

INFORMATION

Tourist Office (☎0851-955 980; www.tourism. passau.de; Rathausplatz 3; ⊗8.30am-6pm Mon-Fri, 9am-4pm Sat & Sun Easter–mid-Oct, shorter hours mid-Oct–Easter) **Passau's main tourist**

office is located in the Altstadt. There's another smaller office opposite the **Hauptbahnhof** (Bahn hofstrasse 28; ⊘9am-5pm Mon-Thu, to 4pm Fri, 10.30am-3.30pm Sat & Sun Easter-Sep, shorter hours Oct-Easter).

❶ GETTING AROUND

Central Passau is sufficiently compact to explore on foot. The CityBus links the Bahnhof with the Altstadt (€1) up to four times an hour. Longer trips within Passau cost €2; a day pass costs €4.50.

The walk up the hill to the Veste Oberhaus via Luitpoldbrücke and Ludwigsteig path, takes about 30 minutes. From April to October, a shuttle bus operates every 30 minutes from Rathausplatz (€2).

Regensburg, Germany

Regensburg dates back to Roman times and was the first capital of Bavaria. Two thousand years of history bequeathed the city some of the region's finest architectural heritage, a fact recognised by Unesco in 2006.

◉ SIGHTS

Schloss Thurn und Taxis   Castle

(www.thurnundtaxis.de; Emmeramsplatz 5; tours adult/child €13.50/11; ⊘tours hourly 10.30am-4.30pm late Mar-early Nov, to 3.30pm Sat & Sun Nov-Mar) In the 15th century, Franz von Taxis (1459–1517) assured his place in history by setting up the first European postal system, which remained a monopoly until the 19th century. In recognition of his services, the family was given the former Benedictine monastery St Emmeram, henceforth known as Schloss Thurn and Taxis. It was soon one of the most modern palaces in Europe and featured such luxuries as flushing toilets. Today it is the world's largest inhabited building.

Dom St Peter   Church

(www.bistum-regensburg.de; Domplatz; ⊘6.30am-7pm Jun-Sep, to 6pm Apr, May & Oct,

to 5pm Nov-Mar) It takes a few seconds for your eyes to adjust to the dim interior of Regensburg's soaring landmark, the Dom St Peter, one of Bavaria's grandest Gothic cathedrals with its stunning kaleidoscopic stained-glass windows and an opulent, silver-sheathed main altar. The cathedral is home of the Domspatzen, a 1000-year-old boys' choir that accompanies the 10am Sunday service (only during the school year). The Domschatzmuseum (Cathedral Treasury) brims with monstrances, tapestries and other church treasures.

❌ EATING

Historische Wurstkuchl   German €

(☏0941-466 210; www.wurstkuchl.de; Thundorferstrasse 3; 6 sausages €9.60; ⊘9am-7pm) Completely submerged several times by the Danube's fickle floods, this titchy eatery has been serving the city's traditional finger-size sausages, grilled over beech wood and dished up with its own sauerkraut and sweet grainy mustard, since 1135 and lays claim to being the world's oldest sausage kitchen.

Dicker Mann   Bavarian €€

(☏0941-573 70; www.dicker-mann.de; Krebsgasse 6; mains €9-21; ⊘9am-1am; 🖥) The 'Chubby Chappy', a stylish, tranquil and very traditional inn, is one of the oldest restaurants in town, allegedly dating back to the 14th century. All the staples of Bavarian sustenance are plated up, plus a few other dishes for good measure. On a balmy eve, be sure to bag a table in the lovely beer garden out the back.

Storstad   International €€€

(☏0941-5999 3000; www.storstad.de; Watmarkt 5; 3 courses from €40; ⊘noon-2pm, plus 6.30-9.30pm Tue-Thu, from 6pm Fri & Sat; 🖥) If you are looking for something a bit more creative on your plate than hunks of pork and dumplings, book a table at this 21st-century gourmet restaurant. The menus feature rare ingredients for Bavaria such as lamb, cod and mackerel, enjoyed paired with German

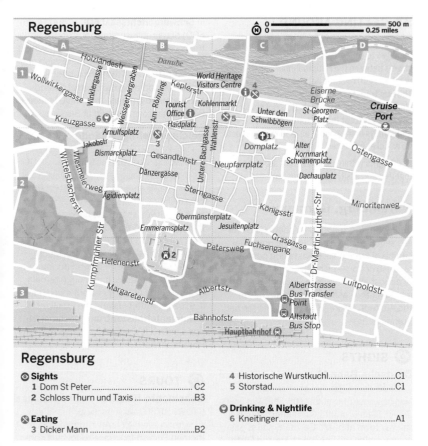

Regensburg

◎ Sights
1 Dom St Peter..C2
2 Schloss Thurn und Taxis B3

✖ Eating
3 Dicker Mann B2

4 Historische Wurstkuchl.............................C1
5 Storstad..C1

🍷 Drinking & Nightlife
6 Kneitinger...A1

and other European wine in the ultramodern, if rather overlit, dining room.

🍷 DRINKING & NIGHTLIFE

Kneitinger   Pub
(www.kneitinger.de; Arnulfsplatz 3; ⊙9am-midnight) Kneitinger is Regensburg's local beer and there's no better place to head in the city for some hearty home cooking, delicious house suds and outrageous oompah frolics than the brewery's own tavern. It's been in business since 1530.

ℹ️ INFORMATION

Tourist Office (📞0941-507 4410; https://tourismus.regensburg.de; Rathausplatz 4; ⊙9am-6pm Mon-Fri, to 4pm Sat, 9.30am-4pm Sun Apr-Oct, to 2.30pm Sun Nov-Mar; 🛜) In the historic Altes Rathaus. Sells tickets, tours, rooms and an audio guide for self-guided tours.

World Heritage Visitors Centre (📞0941-507 4410; www.regensburg-welterbe.de; Weisse-Lamm-Gasse 1; ⊙10am-7pm) **FREE** Visitors centre by the Steinerne Brücke, focusing on the city's Unesco World Heritage Sites. Interesting interactive multimedia exhibits.

GETTING AROUND

On weekdays the Altstadtbus (€1.10) somehow manages to squeeze its way through the narrow streets between the Hauptbahnhof and the Altstadt every 10 minutes between 9am and 7pm. The **bus transfer point** (Albertstrasse) is one block north of the Hauptbahnhof. Tickets for all city buses (except the Altstadtbus) cost €2.40 for journeys in the centre; an all-day ticket costs €5 at ticket machines.

All sights within the Innenstadt are close together and easily walked between.

Nuremberg, Germany

Energetic Nuremberg (Nürnberg) is Bavaria's second-largest city and the unofficial capital of Franconia. Painstaking post-WWII reconstruction – using the original stone – of almost all the city's main buildings, including the castle and old churches in the Altstadt, returned the city to its former grandeur.

 SIGHTS

Deutsche Bahn Museum   Museum
(☑0800-3268 7386; www.dbmuseum.de; Lessingstrasse 6; adult/child €6/3; ☺9am-5pm Tue-Fri, 10am-6pm Sat & Sun) Nuremberg is a railway town at heart. Germany's first passenger trains ran between here and Fürth, a fact reflected in the unmissable German Railways Museum. which explores the history of Germany's legendary rail system. The huge exhibition that continues across the road is one of Nuremberg's top sights, especially if you have a soft spot for things that run on rails.

**Memorium
Nuremberg Trials**   Memorial
(☑0911-3217 9372; www.memorium-nuremberg. de; Bärenschanzstrasse 72; adult/child incl audio guide €6/1.50; ☺9am-6pm Mon & Wed-Fri, 10am-6pm Sat & Sun Apr-Oct, slightly shorter hours Nov-Mar) Göring, Hess, Speer and 21 other Nazi leaders were tried for crimes against peace and humanity by the Allies

in **Schwurgerichtssaal 600** (Court Room 600) of this still-working courthouse. Today the room forms part of an engaging exhibit detailing the background, progression and impact of the trials using film, photographs, audiotape and even the original defendants' dock. To get here, take the U1 towards Bärenschanze and get off at Sielstrasse.

Reichsparteitagsgelände   Historic Site
(Luitpoldhain; ☑0911-231 7538; www.museen. nuernberg.de/dokuzentrum; Bayernstrasse 110; grounds free, Documentation Centre adult/child incl audio guide €6/1.50; ☺grounds 24hr, Documentation Centre 9am-6pm Mon-Fri, 10am-6pm Sat & Sun) If you've ever wondered where the infamous B&W images of ecstatic Nazi supporters hailing their Führer were taken, it was here in Nuremberg. Much of the grounds were destroyed during Allied bombing raids, but enough remain to get a sense of the megalomania behind it, especially after visiting the excellent **Dokumentationszentrum** (Documentation Centre). It's served by tram 8 from the Hauptbahnhof.

 TOURS

Geschichte für Alle   Cultural
(☑0911-307 360; www.geschichte-fuer-alle.de; adult/concession €8/7) An intriguing range of themed English-language tours by a nonprofit association. The 'Albrecht Dürer' and 'Life in Medieval Nuremberg' tours come highly recommended.

Old Town Walking Tours   Walking
(☑0170-141 1223; www.nuernberg-tours.de; tour €10; ☺1pm May-Oct) English-language Old Town walking tours are run by the tourist office – tours leave from the Hauptmarkt branch and take two hours.

Nuremberg Tours   Walking
(www.nurembergtours.com; adult/concession €22/19; ☺11.15am Mon, Wed & Sat Apr-Oct) Four-hour walking and public transport tours taking in the city centre and the Reichsparteitagsgelände. Groups meet at the entrance to the Hauptbahnhof.

NORBERT PROBST/GETTY IMAGES ©

Reichsparteitagsgelände

🅰 SHOPPING

Bier Kontor — Alcohol
(An der Mauthalle 2; ⏱11am-2pm & 2.30-7pm Mon-Sat) This small shop just off the tourist drag stocks a whopping 350 types of beer, from local Franconian suds to Hawaiian ales, fruity Belgian concoctions to British porters. And staff really know their stuff when it comes to the amber nectar.

Handwerkerhof — Market
(www.handwerkerhof.de; Am Königstor; ⏱9am-6.30pm Mon-Fri, 10am-4pm Sat Apr-Dec, shorter hours Jan-Mar) A recreation of an old-world Nuremberg crafts quarter, the Handwerkerhof is a walled tourist market by the Königstor. If you're in the market for souvenirs you may find some decent merchandise here, such as gingerbread wooden toys and traditional ceramics, and there is plenty of bratwurst to go round, too.

🅧 EATING

Nuremberg has all kinds of cuisines, but it's the cosy Franconian taverns serving dark *Landbier* (regional beer) and the city's famous bratwurst that will leave a lasting culinary memory.

Café am Trödelmarkt — Cafe €
(Trödelmarkt 42; dishes €4-10; ⏱9am-6pm Mon-Sat, 10am-6pm Sun) A gorgeous place on a sunny day, this multilevel waterfront cafe overlooks the covered Henkersteg bridge. It's especially popular for its continental breakfasts, and has fantastic cakes, as well as good blackboard lunchtime specials between 11am and 2pm.

Bratwursthäusle — Franconian €€
(http://die-nuernberger-bratwurst.de; Rathausplatz 1; meals €7.50-11.50; ⏱11am-10pm) Seared over a flaming beech-wood grill, the little links sold at this rustic inn next to the

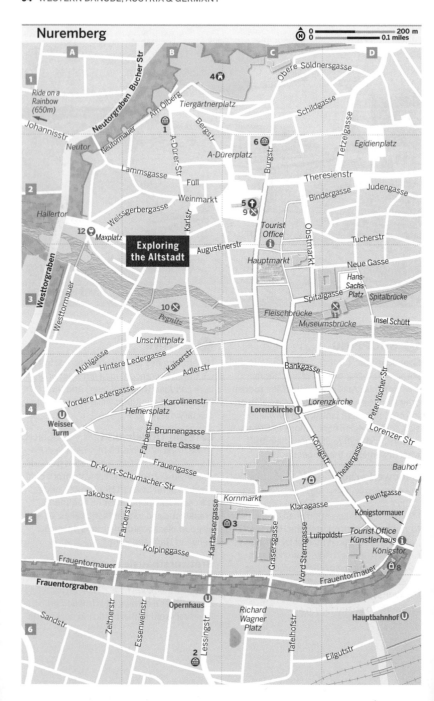

Nuremberg

⊙ N 0 ————— 200 m
0 ————— 0.1 miles

Ride on a
Rainbow
(650m)

Johannisstr

Neutorgraben Bucher Str

Neutor

Neutormauer

Lammsgasse

Hallertor

Westtorgraben

Weissgerbergasse

Westtormauer

Am Ölberg

A-Dürer-Str

Füll

Karlstr

Weinmarkt

Maxplatz

**Exploring
the Altstadt**

Tiergärtnerplatz

Bergstr

A-Dürerplatz

Augustinerstr

Hauptmarkt

Pegnitz

Unschlittplatz

Mühlgasse

Hintere Ledergasse

Kaiserstr

Adlerstr

Vordere Ledergasse

Hefnersplatz

Karolinenstr

Farberstr

Brunnengasse

Breite Gasse

Frauengasse

Dr-Kurt-Schumacher-Str

Jakobstr

Farberstr

Kolpinggasse

Kartäusergasse

Kornmarkt

Gräsersgasse

Frauentormauer

Frauentorgraben

Sandstr

Zeltnerstr

Essenweinstr

Lessingstr

Opernhaus

Richard
Wagner
Platz

Tafelhofstr

Ellgutstr

Obere Söldnersgasse

Schildgasse

Tetzelgasse

Egidienplatz

Theresienstr

Bindergasse

Judengasse

Burgstr

Tourist
Office

Obstmarkt

Tucherstr

Neue Gasse

Hans-
Sachs-
Platz

Spitalgasse

Spitalbrücke

Fleischbrücke

Museumsbrücke

Insel Schütt

Bankgasse

Lorenzkirche

Lorenzkirche

Königstr

Theatergasse

Peter-Vischer-Str

Lorenzer Str

Bauhof

Peuntgasse

Klaragasse

Königstormauer

Luitpoldstr

Vord-Sterngasse

Tourist Office
Künstlerhaus

Königstor

Frauentormauer

Königstor

Hauptbahnhof

**Weisser
Turm**

1

2

3

4

5

6

A

B

C

D

4

1

6

5
9

12

10

3

7

8

2

11

Nuremberg

Sebalduskirche arguably set the standard across the land. You can dine in the timbered restaurant or on the terrace with views of the Hauptmarkt. Service can be flustered at busy times and it's cash only when the bill comes.

Heilig-Geist-Spital   Bavarian €€
(📞0911-221 761; www.heilig-geist-spital.de; Spitalgasse 16; mains €7-18; ⊘11.30am-11pm) Lots of dark carved wood, a herd of hunting trophies and romantic candlelight make this former hospital, suspended over the Pegnitz, one of the most atmospheric dining rooms in town. Sample the delicious, seasonally changing menu inside or out in the pretty courtyard. A real treat if you are looking for somewhere traditional to dine.

🍷 DRINKING & NIGHTLIFE
Kettensteg   Beer Garden
(Maxplatz 35; ⊘11am-11pm) At the end of the chain bridge and in the shadow of the Halletor you'll find this classic Bavarian beer garden complete with its gravel floor, folding slatted chairs, fairy lights, tree shade and river views. Zirndorfer, Lederer and Tucher beers are on tap and some of the food comes on heart-shaped plates.

ℹ️ INFORMATION

Tourist office branches at Hauptmarkt and in the Künstlerhaus sell the Nuremberg Card (€23) with two days of free museum entry and public transport. Staff also offer maps, info and advice.

Tourist Office Hauptmarkt (📞0911-233 60; www.tourismus.nuernberg.de; Hauptmarkt 18; ⊘9am-6pm Mon-Sat, 10am-4pm Sun) **Haupt-**markt branch of the tourist office. Has extended hours during Christkindlesmarkt which takes place on its doorstep.

Tourist Office Künstlerhaus (📞0911-233 60; www.tourismus.nuernberg.de; Königstrasse 93; ⊘9am-7pm Mon-Sat, 10am-4pm Sun) **Publishes** the excellent *See & Enjoy* booklet, a comprehensive guide to the city.

ℹ️ GETTING AROUND

The best transport around the Altstadt is at the end of your legs. Timed tickets on the VGN bus, tram and U-Bahn/S-Bahn networks cost from €1.30. A day pass costs €8.10. Passes bought on Saturday are valid all weekend.

Nuremberg has ample bike lanes along busy roads and the Altstadt is pretty bike friendly. For bike hire, try the excellent **Ride on a Rainbow** (📞0911-397 337; www.ride-on-a-rainbow.de; Adam-Kraft-Strasse 55; per day from €9).

EASTERN DANUBE, HUNGARY & SERBIA

Eastern Danube, Hungary & Serbia

The two great cities of this stretch of the Danube are the capitals of Hungary and Serbia respectively. Budapest has something for everyone – from dramatic history and flamboyant architecture to healing thermal waters. Outspoken, adventurous, proud and audacious: Belgrade ('White City') is by no means a 'pretty' capital, but its gritty exuberance makes it one of Europe's most happening cities. While it hurtles towards a brighter future, its chaotic past unfolds before your eyes: socialist blocks are squeezed between art-nouveau masterpieces, and remnants of the Habsburg legacy contrast with Ottoman relics.

With One Day in Budapest

Spend your morning in Budapest on Castle Hill, taking in the views from the **Royal Palace** (p101) and establishing the lay of the land. There are museums aplenty up here, but don't be greedy: you only have time for one. We recommend either the **Hungarian National Gallery** (p100) for fine Hungarian art or the **Castle Museum** (p101) for a seamless introduction to the city's long and tortuous past. In the afternoon head to the nearby **Gellért Baths** (p103) for a relaxing soak.

Best Places for...

Wine Doblo, Budapest (p110)

Pastries Pekara Trpković, Belgrade (p111)

History Belgrade Fortress, Belgrade (p111)

Art Hungarian National Gallery, Budapest (p100)

Markets Nagycsarnok, Budapest (p106)

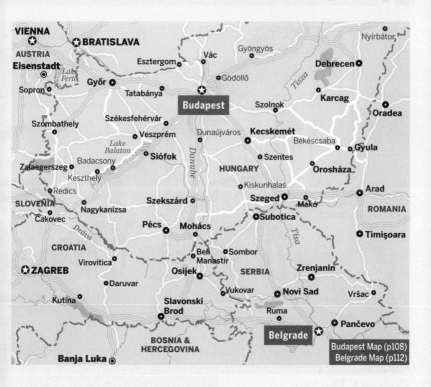

VIENNA
BRATISLAVA
AUSTRIA   Nyírbátor
Eisenstadt   Esztergom   Vác   Gyöngyös
          Lake   Debrecen
          Fertő   Győr   Gödöllő
Sopron   Tatabánya   Tisza
                                                          Karcag
Szombathely   Székesfehérvár   Budapest   Szolnok   Oradea
          Veszprém   Dunaújváros   Kecskemét
          Lake   Békéscsaba   Gyula
          Balaton   Siófok   Szentes
Zalaegerszeg Badacsony   Danube   HUNGARY   Orosháza
   Keszthely
     Redics   Kiskunhalas   Arad
SLOVENIA   Szekszárd   Szeged   Makó
   Cakovec   Nagykanizsa   ROMANIA
                 Pécs   Mohács   Subotica
          Dráva   Tisza   Timişoara
CROATIA   Beli Sombor
   ZAGREB   Virovitica   Manastir   Zrenjanin
                 Osijek   SERBIA
          Daruvar
   Kutina   Slavonski   Vukovar   Novi Sad   Vršac
                 Brod   Ruma
                                   Belgrade   Pančevo
          BOSNIA &   Budapest Map (p108)
          HERCEGOVINA   Belgrade Map (p112)
   Banja Luka

Getting from the Ports

Budapest Ships dock along a long stretch of the Danube, mostly on the east bank to the south of the centre. Depending on your berth, you may be within easy walking distance or better off getting a bus.

Belgrade Cruise ships dock on the Sava River, just north of Brankov Most (bridge). There's a tram stop here (Tram 2), which makes accessing the rest of the city easy.

Fast Facts

Currencies Forint (Ft) in Budapest; Serbian dinar (RSD) in Belgrade

Languages Hungarian in Budapest; Serbian in Belgrade

Free Wi-fi There are free wi-fi hotspots through the centre of the cities, and many restaurants and bars have networks.

Money ATMs and banks are plentiful throughout both city centres.

Tourist Information Budapest Info has a centre on the Pest side of the river; there's an information centre in the Belgrade City Library.

Castle Museum

Royal Palace, Budapest

The enormous Royal Palace has been razed and rebuilt six times over the past seven centuries. Today the palace contains two important museums, the national library and an abundance of statues and monuments. It is the focal point of Buda's Castle Hill and the city's most visited sight.

Great For...

 Don't Miss

Late-Gothic altarpieces, Gothic statues and heads, and the Renaissance door frame.

Hungarian National Gallery

The **Hungarian National Gallery** (Magyar Nemzeti Galéria; ☏1-201 9082; www.mng.hu; I Szent György tér 2, Bldgs A-D; adult/concession 1800/900Ft, audio guide 800Ft; ⊙10am-6pm Tue-Sun; ☐16, 16A, 116) is an overwhelming collection spread across four wings of the palace that traces Hungarian art from the 11th century to the present day. The largest collections include medieval and Renaissance stonework, Gothic wooden sculptures and panel paintings, and late-Gothic winged altars. There's also an important collection of Hungarian paintings and sculpture from the 19th and 20th centuries.

The gallery is currently in a state of flux, with the late-Renaissance and baroque art collection in the Museum of Fine Arts ahead of the National Gallery's relocation to a purpose-built building in City Park.

Hungarian National Gallery

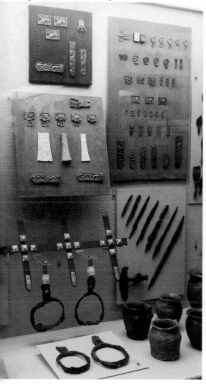

IAKOV FILIMONOV/SHUTTERSTOCK ®

Royal Palace **🅖**

⚓

Explore Ashore

Cruise ships mostly dock on the east side of the river a little south of the centre. Depending on where your ship ties up, the castle should be clearly visible on the other side of the river. It's a pleasant 15-minute walk to the top, but there's also a funicular and buses.

🛈 Need to Know

Royal Palace, Királyi Palota; I Szent György tér; 🚌16, 16A, 116

Castle Museum

Castle Museum (Vármúzeum; 📞1-487 8800; www.btm.hu; I Szent György tér 2, Bldg E; adult/concession 2400/1200Ft; ⊗10am-6pm Tue-Sun Mar-Oct, to 4pm Tue-Sun Nov-Feb; 🚌16, 16A, 116, 🚋19, 41) explores the city's 2000-year history over four floors. Restored palace rooms dating from the 15th century can be entered from the two-level basement, where there are three vaulted halls.

On the ground floor, exhibits showcase Budapest during the Middle Ages, with important Gothic statues of courtiers, squires and saints. There are also artefacts recently recovered from a well dating from Turkish times, most notably a 14th-century tapestry of the Hungarian coat of arms with the fleur-de-lis of the House of Anjou. On the 1st floor, the wonderful multimedia 'Light & Shadow: 1000 Years of a Capital'

exhibit traces the history of Budapest from the arrival of the Magyars and the Turkish occupation to modern times, looking at housing, ethnic diversity and other topics.

On the 2nd floor the exhibits reach way back – from prehistoric times to the end of the Avar period in the 8th century. The excellent audio guide is 1200Ft.

Buda Castle Labyrinth

This 1200m-long **cave system** (Budavári Labirintus; 📞1-212 0207; http://labirintus.eu; I Úri utca 9 & I Lovas út 4/a; adult/under 12yr/senior & student 2500/600/2000Ft; ⊗10am-7pm; 🚌16, 16A, 116), located some 16m (and 45 steps) under the Castle District, contains a motley collection of displays in its joined-up labyrinths. Expect the history of Dracula (supposedly imprisoned here), dry-ice mist and a ghostly masked ball. It's all good fun and it's always 20°C down here. There are two entrances.

Széchenyi Baths

Thermal Baths & Spas, Budapest

Budapest sits on a crazy quilt of almost 125 thermal springs, and 'taking the waters' is very much a part of everyday life here. Some baths date from Turkish times, others are art nouveau marvels and still others are chic modern spas boasting all the mod cons.

Great For...

☑ **Don't Miss**

The sight of locals playing chess on floating boards (regardless of the weather) at Széchenyi Baths.

History of a Spa City

The remains of two sets of baths at Aquincum indicate the Romans took advantage of Budapest's thermal waters almost two millennia ago. But it wasn't until the Turkish occupation of the 16th and 17th centuries that bathing became an integral part of Budapest life. In the late 18th century, Habsburg Empress Maria Theresia ordered that Budapest's waters be analysed at the Treasury's expense. By the 1930s Budapest had become a fashionable spa resort.

Healing Waters

The mineral-rich waters are said to relieve a number of complaints, from arthritis and muscle pain to poor blood circulation and post-traumatic stress. They're also a miracle cure for that most unpleasant of afflictions, the dreaded hangover.

Gellért Baths

MARTCHAN/SHUTTERSTOCK ©

Explore Ashore

The Gellért and Rudas baths are both centrally located on the west bank of the Danube. Depending on where your ship docks, they may be within very easy walking distance. Allow a couple of hours to soak up all the options.

❶ Need to Know

Budapest Spas and Hot Springs (www.spasbudapest.com) has excellent up-to-date information.

Gellért Baths (Gellért Gyógyfürdő; ☑06 30 849 9514, 1-466 6166; www.gellertbath.hu; XI Kelenhegyi út 4, Danubius Hotel Gellért; incl locker/cabin Mon-Fri 5600/6000Ft, Sat & Sun 5800/6200Ft; ◷6am-8pm; 🚊7, 86, Ⓜ M4 Szent Gellért tér, 🚋18, 19, 47, 49) Soaking in these art nouveau baths, open to men and women at all times, has been likened to taking a bath in a cathedral.

Széchenyi Baths (Széchenyi Gyógyfürdő; ☑1-363 3210, 06 30 462 8236; www.szechenyi bath.hu; XIV Állatkerti körút 9-11; tickets incl locker/cabin Mon-Fri 5200/5700Ft, Sat & Sun 5400/5900Ft; ◷6am-10pm; Ⓜ M1 Széchenyi fürdő) The gigantic 'wedding-cake' building in City Park houses these baths, which are unusual for three reasons: their immensity; the bright, clean atmosphere; and the high temperature of the water (up to 40°C).

Veli Bej Baths (Veli Bej Fürdője; ☑1-438 8587; www.irgalmasrend.hu/site/velibej/sprachen/en; II Árpád fejedelem útja 7; 6am-noon 2240Ft, 3-7pm 2800Ft, after 7pm 2240Ft; ◷6am-noon & 3-9pm; 🚊9, 109, 🚋4, 6, 17, 19) One of the oldest (1575) and most beautiful Ottoman-era baths in Budapest, with five thermal pools of varying temperatures.

Choosing a Bath

The choice of bathhouses is legion, and which you choose is a matter of personal taste.

Rudas Baths (Rudas Gyógyfürdő; ☑1-356 1322; http://en.rudasfurdo.hu; I Döbrentei tér 9; incl cabin Mon-Fri/Sat & Sun 3500/4000Ft, morning/night ticket 2800/5100Ft; ◷men 6am-8pm Mon & Wed-Fri, women 6am-8pm Tue, mixed 10pm-4am Fri, 6am-8pm & 10pm-4am Sat, 6am-8pm Sun; 🚊7, 86, 🚋18, 19) These renovated baths (1566) are the most Turkish in Budapest, with an octagonal pool, domed cupola and eight massive pillars. They're mostly men-only during the week, but turn into a zoo on mixed weekend nights.

Zindan Gate

PHOTO OZ/SHUTTERSTOCK ©

Belgrade Fortress

Some 115 battles have been fought over imposing, impressive Belgrade Fortress (aka Kalemegdan) and the citadel was destroyed more than 40 times throughout the centuries. The fort's bloody history is discernible despite today's jolly cafes and funfairs.

Great for

☑ **Don't Miss**

The intriguing interior of Ružica Church.

Military Museum

In the Upper Town area of the fortress, this **museum** (www.muzej.mod.gov.rs; adult/child 200/100RSD; ⊙10am-5pm Tue-Sun) presents the complete military history of the former Yugoslavia. Gripping displays include captured Kosovo Liberation Army weapons, bombs and missiles (courtesy of NATO), rare guns and bits of the American stealth fighter shot down in 1999. You'll find the museum through the Stambol Gate, built by the Turks in the mid-1700s and used for public executions.

Roman Well

The daring can peek down this mysterious 60m-deep hole (more cistern than well). Of dubious origin and shrouded in horrifying legends, the pit is so eerie that it apparently creeped out Alfred Hitchcock!

Ružica Church

KEITH LEVIT/DESIGN PICS/GETTY IMAGES ©

Explore Ashore

Happily, Belgrade Fortress is right by where the cruise ships dock, so it's easily accessed by a 15-minute walk. There's a lot to explore in this area, so allow at least a couple of hours.

❶ Need to Know

Beogradska tvrđava; www.beogradskatvrd java.co.rs; ⊗24hr; FREE

Bicenko. The church was originally an arsenal, then a military chapel before its restoration in 1925.

Big Gunpowder Magazine

The huge, **Gunpowder Magazine** (200RSD; ⊗11am-7pm) was set up by the Austrians in 1718 as a safe place to hide artillery; today it houses a collection of stone monuments, including Roman sarcophagi, tombstones and altars. Tickets must be purchased in advance from the souvenir shop within the Inner Stambol Gate.

Nebojša Tower

A former dungeon, the tower (1460) – the largest and best preserved in the fortress – now serves as a museum, with some excellent exhibits on the Ottoman era, the First Serbian Uprising and Balkan freedom fighter Rigas Feraios, a Greek revolutionary who was jailed and murdered here.

Lower Town

The Lower Town slopes down towards the mouth of the Sava and the Danube. Enter through the 15th-century **Despot's Gate**, consisting of inner and outer ramparts. The tall **Castellan's Tower** beside it houses the Observatory of Belgrade's Astronomical Society. Next is the massive 15th-century **Zindan Gate**, with two rounded towers and a bridge.

Ružica Church

The ivy-swathed Ružica Church looks innocuous from the outside; inside, you'll find chandeliers made by WWI Serbian soldiers from spent bullet casings, swords, rifles and cannon parts, as well as numerous frescoes, including those by famous Russian academy artist Andrei

Budapest, Hungary

Budapest has something for everyone – from dramatic history and flamboyant architecture to healing thermal waters and a nightlife that is unrivalled in Eastern and Central Europe.

SIGHTS

Great Synagogue Synagogue

(Nagy Zsinagóga; ☎1-413 5584, 1-413 1515; www.greatsynagogue.hu/gallery_syn.html; VII Dohány utca 2; adult/concession/family incl museum 4000/3000/9000Ft; ⊙10am-7.30pm Sun-Thu, to 3.30pm Fri May-Sep, 10am-5.30pm Sun-Thu, to 3.30pm Fri Mar, Apr & Oct, 10am-3.30pm Sun-Thu, to 1.30pm Fri Nov-Feb; Ⓜ M2 Astoria, 🚊47, 49) Budapest's stunning Great Synagogue is the world's largest Jewish house of worship outside New York City. Built in 1859, the synagogue has both Romantic and Moorish architectural elements. Inside, the **Hungarian Jewish Museum & Archives** (Magyar Zsidó Múzeum és Levéltár; ☎1-413 5500; www.milev.hu) contains objects relating to both religious and everyday life. On the synagogue's north side, the **Holocaust Tree of Life Memorial** presides over the mass graves of those murdered by the Nazis.

House of Terror Museum

(Terror Háza; ☎1-374 2600; www.terrorhaza.hu; VI Andrássy út 60; adult/concession 3000/1500Ft, audio guide 1500Ft; ⊙10am-6pm Tue-Sun; Ⓜ M1 Vörösmarty utca, 🚊4, 6) The headquarters of the dreaded ÁVH secret police houses the disturbing House of Terror, focusing on the crimes and atrocities of Hungary's fascist and Stalinist regimes in a permanent exhibition called Double Occupation. But the years after WWII leading up to the 1956 Uprising get the lion's share of the exhibition space (almost three-dozen spaces on three levels). The reconstructed prison cells in the basement and the Perpetrators' Gallery on the staircase, featuring photographs of the turncoats, spies and torturers, are chilling.

Basilica of St Stephen Cathedral

(Szent István Bazilika; ☎1-338 2151, 06 30 703 6599; www.basilica.hu; V Szent István tér; requested donation 200Ft; ⊙9am-7pm Mon-Sat, 7.45am-7pm Sun; Ⓜ M3 Arany János utca) FREE Budapest's neoclassical cathedral is the most sacred Catholic church in all of Hungary and contains its most revered relic: the mummified right hand of the church's patron, King St Stephen. It was built over half a century to 1905. Much of the interruption during construction had to do with a fiasco in 1868 when the dome collapsed during a storm, and the structure had to be demolished and then rebuilt from the ground up. The view from the **dome** (Panoráma kilátó; adult/child 600/400Ft; ⊙10am-6pm Jun-Sep, to 5.30pm Apr, May & Oct, to 4.30pm Nov-Mar) is phenomenal.

Hungarian State Opera House Notable Building

(Magyar Állami Operaház; ☎06 30 279 5677, 1-332 8197; www.operavisit.hu; VI Andrássy út 22; adult/concession 2490/2200Ft; ⊙tours in English 2pm, 3pm & 4pm; Ⓜ M1 Opera) The neo-Renaissance Hungarian State Opera House was designed by Miklós Ybl in 1884 and is among the most beautiful buildings in Budapest. Its facade is decorated with statues of muses and opera greats such as Puccini, Mozart, Liszt and Verdi, while its interior dazzles with marble columns, gilded vaulted ceilings, chandeliers and near-perfect acoustics. You can join one of the three 45-minute daily tours. Tickets are available from a desk in the lobby.

SHOPPING

Nagycsarnok Market

(Great Market Hall; ☎1-366 3300; www.piaconline.hu; IX Vámház körút 1-3; ⊙6am-5pm Mon, to 6pm Tue-Fri, to 3pm Sat; Ⓜ M4 Fővám tér, 🚊47, 49) This is Budapest's biggest market (1897), though it has become a tourist magnet since its renovation for the millecentenary celebrations in 1996. Still, plenty of locals come here for fruit, vegetables, deli items, fish and meat. Head up to the 1st floor for Hungarian folk costumes, dolls,

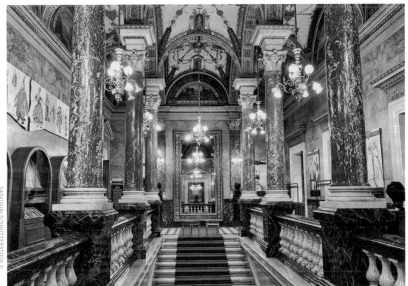

Hungarian State Opera House

painted eggs, embroidered tablecloths, carved hunting knives and other souvenirs.

Bestsellers — Books

(✆1-312 1295; www.bestsellers.hu; Ⓥ Október 6 utca 11; ⊙9am-6.30pm Mon-Fri, 11am-6pm Sat, noon-6pm Sun; 🚊15, 115, ⓂM1/2/3 Deák Ferenc tér) Still top of the pops for English-language bookshops in Budapest, with fiction, travel guides and lots of Hungarica, as well as a large selection of newspapers and magazines overseen by master bookseller Tony Láng. Helpful staff are at hand to advise and recommend.

EATING

Budavári Rétesvár — Hungarian €

(Strudel Castle; ✆06 70 408 8696; www. budavariretesvar.hu; Ⓘ Balta köz 4; strudel 350Ft; ⊙8am-8pm; 🚊16, 16A, 116) Strudel in all its permutations – from poppyseed with sour cherry to dill with cheese and cabbage – is available at this hole-in-the-wall dispensary in a narrow alley of the Castle District.

Kispiac — Hungarian €€

(✆1-269 4231, 06 30 430 0142; www.kispiac.eu; Ⓥ Hold utca 13; mains 2450-4450Ft; ⊙noon-10pm Mon-Sat; ⓂM3 Arany János utca) This small retro-style restaurant – an absolute favourite of ours – serves seriously Hungarian things like stuffed *csülök* (pig's trotter – and way better than it sounds; 2950Ft), roast *malac* (piglet; 3250Ft) and the ever-popular wild boar spare ribs (3950Ft) as well as an infinite variety of *savanyúság* (pickled vegetables). Perfectly selected wine list and a warm welcome.

Borkonyha — Hungarian €€€

(Wine Kitchen; ✆1-266 0835; www.borkonyha. hu; Ⓥ Sas utca 3; mains 3450-7950Ft; ⊙noon-4pm & 6pm-midnight Mon-Sat; 🚊15, 115, ⓂM1 Bajcsy-Zsilinszky út) Chef Ákos Sárközi's approach to Hungarian cuisine at this Michelin-starred restaurant is contemporary, and the menu changes every week or two. Go for the signature foie gras appetiser with apple and celeriac and a glass of sweet Tokaji Aszú wine. If *mangalica* (a special type of Hungarian pork) is on the menu, try it with a glass of dry *furmint*.

Budapest

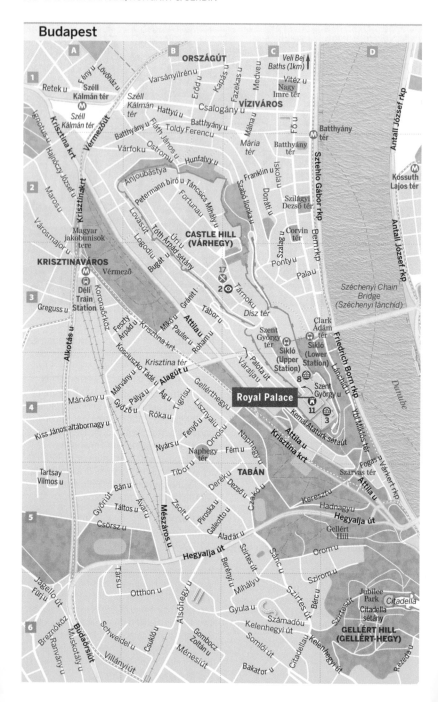

ORSZÁGÚT

Veli Bej
Baths (1km)

Retek u
Fény u
Lövőház u
Varsányi Irén u
Erőd u
Kapás u
Fazekas u
Medve u
Vitéz u
Nagy
Imre tér

Széll
Kálmán tér

Széll
Kálmán tér

Széll
Kálmán
tér
Hattyú u
Csalogány u

VÍZIVÁROS

Batthyány u
Fiáth János u
Toldy Ferenc u
Málna u

Batthyány
tér

Krisztina krt
Ignotus u
Hajnóczy József u
Vérmező út
Batthyány u
Ostrom u
Várfoku
Hunfalvy u
Mária
tér
Batthyány
tér

Várfoku

Anjoubástya
Franklin u
Iskola u
Szabó Ilonka u

Marosu
Petermann bíró u
Táncsics Mihály u
Fortuna u
Donáti u

Szilágyi
Dezső tér

Városmajor u
Magyar
jakobinusok
tere
Lovas út
Tóth Árpád sétány
Úri u
Bugát u
CASTLE HILL
(VÁRHEGY)
Hess András tér
Corvin
tér
Bem rkp

KRISZTINAVÁROS

Vérmező
Logodi u

17
2

Pontyu
Palau

Széchenyi Chain
Bridge
(Széchenyi lánchíd)

Déli
Train
Station
Greguss u
Koronaőr köz
Feszty
Árpád u
Krisztina krt
Miklós u
Pauler u
Attila u
Tábor u
Gránit l.
Roham u
Disz tér

Clark
Ádám
tér

Alkotás u
Kosciuszko Tádé u
Krisztina tér
Szent
György
tér
Siklo
(Upper
Station)
Siklo
(Lower
Station)

Márvány u
Tádé u
Márvány u
Pálya u
Alagút u
Ág u
Gellérthegy u
Palota út
Váralja u
8
Szent
György u

Győző u
Róka u
Tigris u
Lisznyai u
Royal Palace
11
3

Kiss János altábornagy u
Nyárs u
Fenyő u
Orvos u
Naphegy u
Kemal Atatürk sétaút
Attila u
Krisztina krt

Naphegy
tér
Fém u

Tartsay
Vilmos u
Tibor u
TABÁN
Szarvas tér

Mészáros u
Győri út
Táltos u
Avar u
Bán u
Zsolt u
Deták u
Piroska u
Dezső u
Czakó u
Galeotti u
Keresztu
Hadnagy u
Hegyalja út

Csörsz u
Aladár u
Gellért
Hill

Hegyalja út
Szirtes út
Sánc u
Orom u
Szirom u

Jagelló út
Fürj u
Otthon u
Alsóhegy u
Mihály u
Bérc u
Szirtes út
Jubilee
Park
Citadella

Breznó köz
Muskotály u
Budaörsi út
Schweidel u
Csukló u
Gyula u
Kelenhegyi út
Számadó u
Citadella
sétány
GELLÉRT HILL
(GELLÉRT-HEGY)

Ranváry u
Villányi út
Gombocz
Zoltán u
Ménesi út
Somlói út
Bakator u

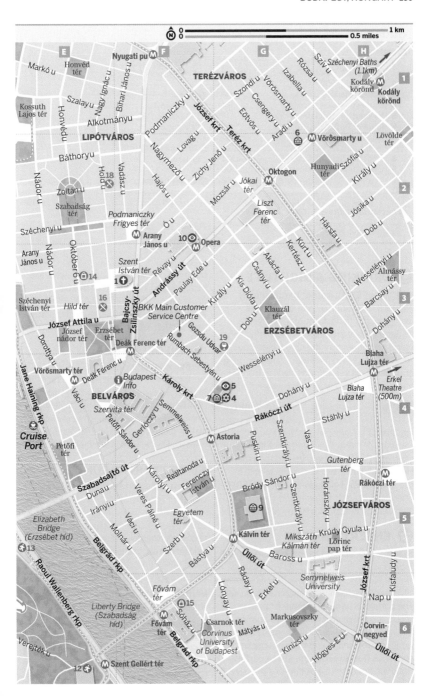

Budapest

🍷 DRINKING & NIGHTLIFE

In recent years, Budapest has justifiably gained a reputation as one of Europe's leading nightlife destinations. Alongside its age-old cafe culture, it offers a magical blend of unique drinking holes, fantastic wine, home-grown firewaters and emerging craft beers, all served with a warm Hungarian welcome and a wonderful sense of fun.

Doblo   Wine Bar
(☏06 20 398 8863; www.budapestwine.com; VII Dob utca 20; ⊘2pm-2am Sun-Wed, to 4am Thu-Sat; Ⓜ M1/2/3 Deák Ferenc tér) Brick-lined and candlelit, Doblo is where you go to taste Hungarian wines, with scores available by the 1.5cL (15mL) glass for 900Ft to 2150Ft. There's food such as meat and cheese platters and live music nightly at 9pm.

🎭 ENTERTAINMENT

Hungarian State Opera House Opera
(Magyar Állami Operaház; ☏1-814 7100, box office 1-332 7914; www.opera.hu; VI Andrássy út 22; ⊘box office 10am-5pm Mon-Fri; Ⓜ M1 Opera) The gorgeous neo-Renaissance opera house is worth a visit as much to admire the incredibly rich decoration inside as to view a performance and hear the perfect acoustics. Tours (p106) are still departing while the opera house undergoes massive renovations (due to be completed in 2020),

but most of the operas and musicals are being staged in the **Erkel Theatre** (Erkel Színház; VIII II János Pál pápa tér 30; ⊘box office 10am-8pm; ☐7, Ⓜ M2 Keleti pályaudvar), Budapest's 'other' opera house.

ℹ️ INFORMATION

The **Budapest Info** (☏1-576 1401; www.budapestinfo.hu; V Sütő utca 2; ⊘8am-8pm; Ⓜ M1/2/3 Deák Ferenc tér, ☐47, 49) office near Deák Ferenc tér is about the best single source of information about Budapest; stocks information about attractions and has purchasable maps; can be crowded in summer.

ℹ️ GETTING AROUND

Budapest's transport system, run by **BKK** (www.bkk.hu; VII Rumbach Sebestyén utca 19-21.; ⊘9am-5pm Mon, Tue & Thu, 9am-7pm Wed, 9am-3pm Fri; Ⓜ M1/2/3 Deák Ferenc tér), is one of the most comprehensive in Europe. Travel passes valid for one day to one month are valid on all trams, buses, trolleybuses, HÉV suburban trains (within the city limits) and metro lines.

Metro The quickest but least scenic way to get around. Runs 4.30am to about 11.50pm.

Bus Extensive network of regular buses runs from around 4.30am to between 9pm and 11.50pm; from 11.50pm to 4.30am a network of 40 night buses (three digits beginning with '9' – 901 to 999) kicks in.

Tram More pleasant for sightseeing than buses. Tram 6 on the Big Ring Rd runs overnight.

Trolleybus Mostly useful for getting to and around City Park in Pest.

Belgrade, Serbia

Outspoken, adventurous, proud and audacious: Belgrade ('White City') is by no means a 'pretty' capital, but its gritty exuberance makes it one of Europe's most happening cities.

SIGHTS

Museum of Yugoslavia Museum

(www.muzej-jugoslavije.org; Botićeva 6; 400RSD, incl entry to Marshal Tito's Mausoleum, 4-6pm 1st Thu of month free; ⊙10am-6pm Tue-Sun) This must-visit museum houses an invaluable collection of more than 200,000 artefacts representing the fascinating, tumultuous history of Yugoslavia. Photographs, artworks, historical documents, films, weapons, priceless treasure: it's all here. It can be a lot to take in; English-speaking guides are available if booked in advance via email, or you can join a free tour on weekends (11am in English, Serbian at noon). **Marshal Tito's Mausoleum** (Kuća Cveća) is also on the museum grounds; admission is included in the ticket price.

Nikola Tesla Museum Museum

(www.nikolateslamuseum.org; Krunska 51; admission incl guided tour in English 500RSD; ⊙10am-8pm Tue-Sun) Meet the man on the 100RSD note at one of Belgrade's best museums, where you can release your inner nerd with some wondrously sci-fi-ish interactive elements. Tesla's ashes are kept here in a glowing, golden orb: debate has been raging for years between the museum (and its secular supporters) and the church as to whether the remains should be moved to Sveti Sava Temple.

🄯 ACTIVITIES

Belgrade Alternative Guide Walking

(☑063 743 3055; www.belgradealtguide.com; tours per person 1700-9800RSD) Run by passionate locals, these tours explore Savamala rooftop hang-outs, central art galleries, street art, the history of Zemun, farmers markets, secret eateries and surrounding villages. Tours generally run between three and four hours.

iBikeBelgrade Cycling

(☑066 900 8386; www.ibikebelgrade.com; Braće Krsmanović 5; 1 hr/day €2/8; ⊙Apr-Oct) Wheel around town on tailored cycle tours that take in everywhere from Ada Ciganlija to Zemun. Daily tours (three hours, €24 per person) are available.

🄰 SHOPPING

Parfimerija Sava Perfume

(Sava Perfumery; www.facebook.com/parfemisava; Kralja Petra 75; ⊙10am-1pm & 4-7pm Mon-Fri, to 2pm Sat; 📶) With its old-fashioned interior, gorgeous vintage bottles and delectable scents wafting throughout, this traditional perfumery is a doorway into the Belgrade of yore. Established in 1954 by the father of current owner, Nenad, this is the last of its kind in Belgrade, where scents are mixed by hand in a mysterious room behind a heavy curtain and labelled by typewriter.

Makadam Arts & Crafts

(www.makadam.rs; Kosančićev venac 20; ⊙noon-8pm Tue-Sun; 📶) Make your way to Makadam across the original Turkish cobblestones of Kosančićev venac, a lovely slice of old Belgrade. The concept store only sells handmade items from across Serbia. Shoppers will find an impressive selection of carefully chosen items by local craftspeople and designers, with the accent on the use of natural and traditional materials.

EATING

Pekara Trpković Bakery €

(www.facebook.com/pekaratrpkovic; Nemanjina 32; burek per 100g 32-55RSD; ⊙6am-8.30pm Mon-Sat, to 4pm Sun) The fact that this family business has existed for over a century in Belgrade's competitive bakery market is quite an achievement. The Serbian tradition of making pastries has reached its peak in this case. Trpković delicacies

Belgrade

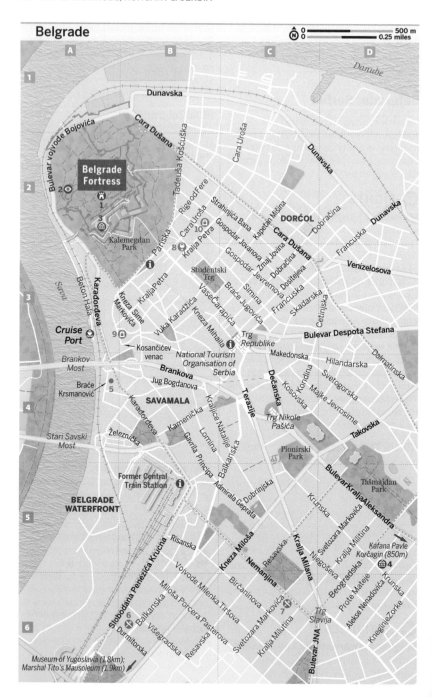

N · 0 —————— 500 m
0 —————— 0.25 miles

Danube

Dunavska

Cara Dušana

Bulevar vojvode Bojovića

Belgrade Fortress

Tadeuša Košćuška

Rige od Fere

Cara Uroša

Dunavska

Dunavska

Strahinjića Bana

Kapetan Mišina

DORĆOL

Dobračina

Francuska

Venizelosova

Kalemegdan Park

Pančiská

Cara Uroša

Gospodar Jovanova

Kralja Petra

Zmaj Jovina

Cara Dušana

Dobračina

Dositejeva

Francuska

Kneza Sime Marković

Kralja Petra

Studentski Trg

Vase Čarapića

Braće Jugovića

Simina

Skadarska

Cetinjska

Gospodar Jevremova

Vuka Karadžića

Kneza Mihaila

Trg Republike

Makedonska

Bulevar Despota Stefana

Dalmatinska

Hilandarska

Svetogorska

Cruise Port

Suru

Beton Hala

Karađorđeva

Kosančićev venac

National Tourism Organisation of Serbia

Kondina

Kosovska

Majke Jevrosime

Brankov Most

Braće Krsmanović

Brankova

Jug Bogdanova

SAVAMALA

Dečanska

Takovska

Stari Savski Most

Karađorđeva

Železnička

Kamenička

Kraljice Natalije

Lomina

Gavrila Principa

Balkanska

Terazije

Trg Nikole Pašića

Pionirski Park

Tašmajdan Park

Former Central Train Station

Admirala Geprata

BELGRADE WATERFRONT

Slobodana Penezića Krcuna

Risanska

Kneza Miloša

Nemanjina

Resavska

Kralja Milana

Krunska

Svetozara Markovića

Njegoševa

Kralja Militina

Bulevar Kralja Aleksandra

Kafana Pavle Korčagin (850m)

Beogradska

Prote Mateje

Krunska

Museum of Yugoslavia (1.8km); Marshal Tito's Mausoleum (1.9km)

Durmitorska

Balkanska

Višegradska

Miloša Porcera Pasterova

Vojvode Milenka Tiršova

Birčaninova

Resavska

Svetozara Markovića

Kralja Militina

Trg Slavija

Bulevar JNA

Alekse Nenadovića

Kneginje Zorke

Belgrade

and sandwiches are extremely popular and there are often queues, especially for breakfast and lunch breaks.

Iris New Balkan Cuisine Serbian €€€
(☑064 129 6377; www.newbalkancuisine.com/iris; Sarajevska 54; tasting menus veg/nonveg 3000-3700RSD, with wine 5600/6300RSD; ⊗12.30-10pm Wed-Sat; ☐☑) ✔ Belgrade's best foodie bang for the buck is this newcomer clandestinely occupying a 1st-floor apartment south of the old train station. Courses from the tasting menu are based around a single ingredient – whatever head chef Vanja Puškar has procured from organic farmers that week – and taken to new heights without leaving behind their Serbian origins.

🍷 DRINKING & NIGHTLIFE

Bar Central Cocktail Bar
(www.facebook.com/BarCentral011; Kralja Petra 59; ⊗9am-midnight Sun-Thu, to 1am Fri & Sat; ☐) This is the HQ of Serbia's Association of Bartenders, a fact made evident after one sip of any of the sublime cocktails (515RSD to 1165RSD) on offer. With an interior as polished as a bottle flip-pour, this ain't the place for tacky tikis and those little umbrellas – this is serious mixology territory.

Kafana Pavle Korčagin Taverna
(☑011 240 1980; www.kafanapavlekorcagin.rs; Ćirila i Metodija 2a; ⊗7.30am-2am Mon-Fri, 10am-2am Sat, 11am-midnight Sun) Raise a glass at this frantic, festive *kafana* (tavern). Lined with communist memorabilia and packed

to the rafters with revellers and grinning accordionists, this table-thumping throwback fills up nightly; reserve a table via the website in advance.

ℹ️ INFORMATION

Tourist Organisation of Belgrade hosts tourist information centres at **Knez Mihailova** (Turistički informativni centri; ☑011 263 5622; www.tob.rs; Knez Mihailova 56, Belgrade City Library; ⊗9am-8pm) and the now decommissioned **Central Train Station** (☑011 361 2732; ⊗9am-2pm Mon-Sat).

The National Tourism Organisation of Serbia operates the information centre at **Trg Republike** (☑011 328 2712; www.serbia.travel; Trg Republike 5; ⊗10am-9pm Mon-Fri, to 6pm Sun) and **Mt Avala** (☑011 390 8517; Mt Avala Tower; ⊗9am-8pm Mar-Sep, to 5pm Oct-Feb). More info points are planned.

ℹ️ GETTING AROUND

GSP Belgrade (www.gsp.rs) runs the city's trams and trolleybuses, which ply limited routes, but buses chug all over town. Rechargeable **BusPlus** (www2.busplus.rs) smart cards can be bought (250RSD) and topped up (89RSD per ticket) at kiosks and other outlets (Maxi supermarkets etc) across the city; tickets are 150RSD if you buy from the driver. Fares are good for 90 minutes. Unlimited paper BusPlus passes relevant to tourists are available for one, three and five days for 250RSD, 700RSD and 1000RSD, respectively.

SEINE,
FRANCE

Seine, France

Paris has a timeless familiarity, with instantly recognisable architectural icons, memorable cuisine and chic boutiques. Dining is a quintessential part of the Parisian experience, and its art repository is one of the best, showcasing priceless treasures in palatial museums. With its soaring Gothic cathedral, beautifully restored medieval quarter, excellent museums and vibrant cultural life, Rouen is one of Normandy's most engaging and historically rich destinations. At the mouth of the Seine, Le Havre is a love letter to modernism, evoking France's postwar energy and optimism.

With One Day in Paris

Start at the **Eiffel Tower** (p118), then head by metro to Charles de Gaulle–Étoile (a 2km walk). Admire the **Arc de Triomphe** (p128), then promenade down the glamorous Champs-Élysées. Make your way to the labyrinthine **Louvre** (p120). Next, cross to Île de la Cité and inspect the exterior of fire-damaged **Notre Dame** (p124). Then cross back and explore the bars and restaurants of the **Marais district** (p124).

Best Places for...

Art Musée du Louvre, Paris (p121)

Pastries Jacques Genin, Paris (p135)

Sweets Le Bonbon au Palais, Paris (p134)

Cocktails Bar Hemingway, Paris (p136)

Market Marché aux Puces de St-Ouen, Paris (p137)

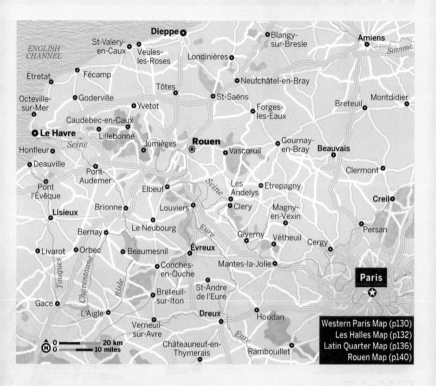

Western Paris Map (p130)
Les Halles Map (p132)
Latin Quarter Map (p136)
Rouen Map (p140)

Getting from the Ports

Paris The two cruise ship docks in Paris are located a couple of kilometres southwest of the centre on the Seine. Quai de Grenelle is the closer, with Bir Hakeim metro stop a five-minute walk away. Quai André Citroën is a little further downstream, and served by Javel-André Citroën metro stop and Javel RER.

Rouen It's only 2km from the dock to the city centre. Taxis are readily available to take you on the 10-minute ride into town. Otherwise it's a 25-minute walk.

Le Havre The cruise terminal is 2.5km from the city centre. Many cruise companies offer a shuttle service into town.

Fast Facts

Currency Euro (€)

Language French

Free Wi-fi Free wi-fi for customers in many cafes and bars. Numerous free wi-fi zones in public areas.

Money ATMs are common throughout the cities.

Tourist Information The main branch in Paris is at the Hôtel de Ville; in Rouen, you'll find a centre opposite the cathedral, and there's an office on the western edge of the Le Havre centre.

MARINADA/SHUTTERSTOCK ©

Eiffel Tower

No one could imagine Paris today without it. But Gustave Eiffel only constructed this elegant, 324m-tall signature spire as a temporary exhibit for the 1889 World's Fair. Climb it to admire Paris laid out at your feet.

Great For...

☑ **Don't Miss**

A glass of bubbly in the top-floor Champagne Bar (open noon to 5.15pm and 6.15pm to 10.45pm).

It took 300 workers, 2.5 million rivets and two years of nonstop labour to assemble. Upon completion the tower became the tallest human-made structure in the world (324m or 1063ft) – a record held until the completion of the Chrysler Building in New York in 1930. A symbol of the modern age, it faced massive opposition from Paris' artistic and literary elite, and the 'metal asparagus', as some Parisians snidely called it, was originally slated to be torn down in 1909. It was spared only because it proved an ideal platform for the transmitting antennas needed for the newfangled science of radiotelegraphy.

1st Floor

Of the tower's three floors, the 1st floor (57m) has the most space but the least impressive views. The glass-enclosed **Pavillon Ferrié** – open since summer 2014 – houses

Observation deck

DROP OF LIGHT/SHUTTERSTOCK ©

Explore Ashore

The Eiffel Tower is one of the closest sights to the cruise ship docks. From Quai de Grenelle, it's walkable in under 10 minutes. From André Citroën, stroll for 20 or grab the RER train from nearby Javel station to Champ de Mars. For a trip to the top, allow two to 2½ hours depending on queue lengths.

❶ Need to Know

Map p130; www.toureiffel.paris; Champ de Mars, 5 av Anatole France, 7e; adult/child lift to top €25/12.50, lift to 2nd fl €16/8, stairs to 2nd fl €10/5; ☻lifts & stairs 9am-12.45am mid-Jun–Aug, lifts 9.30am-11.45pm, stairs 9.30am-6.30pm Sep–mid-Jun; Ⓜ Bir Hakeim or RER Champ de Mars–Tour Eiffel

an immersion film along with a small cafe and souvenir shop, while the outer walkway features a discovery circuit to help visitors learn more about the tower's ingenious design. Check out the sections of glass flooring that proffer a dizzying view of the ant-like people walking on the ground far below.

2nd Floor

Views from the 2nd floor (115m) are the best – impressively high, but still close enough to see the details of the city below. Telescopes and panoramic maps placed around the tower pinpoint locations in Paris and beyond. Story windows give an overview of the lifts' mechanics, and the vision well allows you to gaze through glass panels to the ground.

Top Floor

Views from the wind-buffeted top floor (276m) stretch up to 60km on a clear day,

though at this height the panoramas are more sweeping than detailed. Afterwards peep into Gustave Eiffel's restored top-level office where lifelike wax models of Eiffel and his daughter Claire greet Thomas Edison. To access the top floor, take a separate lift on the 2nd floor (closed during heavy winds).

Nightly Sparkles

Every hour on the hour, the entire tower sparkles for five minutes with 20,000 6-watt lights. They were first installed for Paris' millennium celebration in 2000 – it took 25 mountain climbers five months to install the current bulbs and 40km of electrical cords. For the best view of the light show, head across the Seine to the Jardins du Trocadéro.

KIEV.VICTOR/SHUTTERSTOCK ©

Musée du Louvre

Few art galleries are as prized or daunting as the Musée du Louvre, Paris' pièce de résistance. One of the world's largest and most diverse museums, it showcases an unbelievable 35,000-odd works of art. It would take nine months to glance at every piece.

Great For...

☑ Don't Miss

Da Vinci's bewitching *Mona Lisa;* the Mesopotamian and Egyptian collections.

The Louvre rambles over four floors and through three wings: the **Sully Wing** creates the four sides of the Cour Carrée (literally 'Square Courtyard') at the eastern end of the complex; the **Denon Wing** stretches 800m along the Seine to the south; and the northern **Richelieu Wing** skirts rue de Rivoli. The 'Grand Louvre' project, inaugurated by the late President François Mitterrand in 1989, doubled the museum's exhibition space. New and renovated galleries include the state-of-the-art **Islamic art galleries** (lower ground floor, Denon) in the stunningly restored Cour Visconti.

Priceless Antiquities

Both **Mesopotamia** (ground floor, Richelieu) and **Egypt** (ground and 1st floors, Sully) are well represented in the Louvre; seek out the *Code of Hammurabi* (Room 227, ground floor, Richelieu) and *The Seated*

Sphinx, Egypt Collection

⚓ Explore Ashore

You'll need to change lines a couple of times to reach the Palais Royal Musée du Louvre metro station from the cruise ship docks. Allow at least half an hour to get there. Seeing everything in the Louvre would take you 75 days(!), but if you select your highlights carefully, three to four hours will give you a good taste.

❶ Need to Know

Map p130; ☎01 40 20 53 17; www.louvre.fr; rue de Rivoli & quai des Tuileries, 1er; adult/child €15/free, 6-9.45pm 1st Sat of month free; ⊗9am-6pm Mon, Thu, Sat & Sun, to 9.45pm Wed, Fri & 1st Sat of month; Ⓜ Palais Royal–Musée du Louvre

Scribe (Room 635, 1st floor, Sully). Room 307 (ground floor, Sully) holds impressive friezes and an enormous **two-headed-bull column** from the Darius Palace in ancient Persia, while an enormous seated **statue of Pharaoh Ramesses II** highlights the temple room (Room 324, Sully).

The lower ground floor culminates with the famous armless duo, the **Venus de Milo** (Room 346, ground floor, Sully) and the **Winged Victory of Samothrace** (Room 703, 1st floor, Denon).

French & Italian Masterpieces

The 1st floor of the Denon Wing, where the *Mona Lisa* is found, is easily the most popular. Rooms 700 through 702 are hung with monumental **French paintings**: look for the *Consecration of the Emperor Napoléon I* (David), *The Raft of the Medusa* (Géricault) and *Grande Odalisque* (Ingres).

Rooms 710, 711, 712 and 716 are also must-visits, filled with classic works by **Renaissance masters** (Raphael, Titian, Uccello, Botticini). Contemplate Botticelli's graceful frescoes (Room 1) and the superbly detailed *Wedding Feast at Cana* (Room 711). On the ground floor are Italian sculptures, including Michelangelo's *The Dying Slave* and Canova's *Psyche and Cupid* (Room 403).

Mona Lisa

Easily the Louvre's most admired work is Leonardo da Vinci's *La Joconde* (in French; *La Gioconda* in Italian), the lady with the enigmatic smile known as *Mona Lisa* (Room 711, 1st floor, Denon). Infrared technology has confirmed her identity as Lisa Gherardini (c 1479–1542). Scientists also discovered that her dress was covered in a gauze veil worn by pregnant women or new mothers.

The Louvre

A HALF-DAY TOUR

Successfully visiting the Louvre is a fine art. Its complex labyrinth of galleries and staircases spiralling across three wings and four floors renders discovery a snakes-and-ladders experience. Initiate yourself with this three-hour itinerary – a playful mix of *Mona Lisa*–obvious and up-to-the-minute unexpected.

Arriving in the newly renovated **❶ Cour Napoléon** beneath IM Pei's glass pyramid, pick up colour-coded floor plans at an information stand, then ride the escalator up to the Sully Wing and swap passport or credit card for a multimedia guide (there are limited descriptions in the galleries) at the wing entrance.

The Louvre is as much about spectacular architecture as masterful art. To appreciate this, zip up and down Sully's Escalier Henri II to admire **❷ Venus de Milo**, then up parallel Escalier Henri IV to the palatial displays in **❸ Cour Khorsabad**. Cross Room 236 to find the escalator up to the 1st floor and the opulent **❹ Napoléon III apartments**. Next traverse 25 consecutive galleries (thank you, floor plan!) to flip conventional contemplation on its head with Cy Twombly's **❺ The Ceiling**, and the hypnotic **❻ Winged Victory of Samothrace**, which brazenly insists on being admired from all angles. End with the impossibly famous **❼ Raft of the Medusa**, **❽ Mona Lisa** and **❾ Virgin & Child**.

Napoléon III Apartments
1st Floor, Richelieu
Napoléon III's gorgeous gilt apartments were built from 1854 to 1861, featuring an over-the-top decor of gold leaf, stucco and crystal chandeliers that reaches a dizzying climax in the Grand Salon and State Dining Room.

Jardin du Carrousel

Galerie du Carrousel Entrances

Porte des Lions

TOP TIPS

➡ Don't even consider entering the Louvre's maze of galleries without a floor plan, free from the information desk in the Hall Napoléon.

➡ The Denon Wing is always packed; visit on late nights (Wednesday or Friday) or trade Denon in for the notably quieter Richelieu Wing.

➡ Tickets to the Louvre are valid for the whole day, meaning that you can nip out for lunch.

LOUVRE AUDITORIUM

Classical-music concerts are staged several times a week at the Louvre Auditorium (off the main entrance hall). Don't miss the Thursday lunchtime concerts featuring emerging composers and musicians. The season runs from September to April or May, depending on the concert series.

Mona Lisa
Room 711, 1st Floor, Denon
No smile is as enigmatic or bewitching as hers. Da Vinci's diminutive *La Joconde* hangs opposite the largest painting in the Louvre – sumptuous, fellow Italian Renaissance artwork *The Wedding at Cana*.

The Raft of the Medusa
Room 700, 1st Floor, Denon
Decipher the politics behind French romanticism in Théodore Géricault's *Raft of the Medusa*.

Cour Khorsabad
Ground Floor, Richelieu
Time travel with a pair of winged human-headed bulls to view some of the world's oldest Mesopotamian art. **DETOUR»** Night-lit statues in Cour Puget.

PRYZMAT / SHUTTERSTOCK ©

The Ceiling
Room 663, 1st Floor, Sully
Admire the blue shock of Cy Twombly's 400-sqmetre contemporary ceiling fresco – the Louvre's latest, daring commission. **DETOUR»** *The Braque Ceiling*, Room 662.

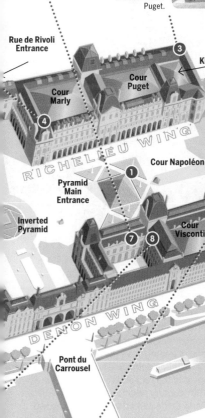

Rue de Rivoli Entrance

SULLY WING

Cour Khorsabad

❸

Cour Puget

Cour Marly

❹

Cour Carrée

RICHELIEU WING

❺

Cour Napoléon

❶

Pyramid Main Entrance

❷

Inverted Pyramid

❻

Cour Visconti

❼ ❽

❾

DENON WING

Pont des Arts

Pont du Carrousel

Venus de Milo
Room 346, Ground Floor, Sully
No one knows who sculpted this seductively realistic goddess from Greek antiquity. Naked to the hips, she is a Hellenistic masterpiece.

Winged Victory of Samothrace
Room 703, 1st Floor, Sully
Draw breath at the aggressive dynamism of this headless, handless Hellenistic goddess. **DETOUR»** The razzle-dazzle of the Apollo Gallery's crown jewels.

Virgin & Child
Grande Galerie, 1st Floor, Denon
In the spirit of artistic devotion save the Louvre's most famous gallery for last: a feast of Virgin-and-child paintings by Da Vinci, Raphael, Domenico Ghirlandaio, Giovanni Bellini and Francesco Botticini.

TUTTI/FRUTTI / SHUTTERSTOCK ©

Front facade and towers of Notre Dame, largely undamaged in the fire of 2019

Cathédrale Notre Dame de Paris

A vision of stained-glass rose windows, flying buttresses and frightening gargoyles, Paris' glorious cathedral is the city's geographic and spiritual heart – so much so that distances from Paris to every part of metropolitan France are measured from its location.

Great For...

Notre Dame Closed

The cathedral suffered a devastating fire in 2019. Visitors will most likely not be able to enter Notre Dame for many years.

A blaze broke out under the cathedral's roof on the evening of 15 April 2019. Though firefighters were able to control the fire and ultimately save the church, it suffered devastating damage. The fire destroyed most of the roof and toppled its spire, a 19th-century addition. However, the oldest parts of the cathedral – notably the two bell towers, the rose windows and the west facade – were all saved. At the time of the fire, Notre Dame was undergoing a planned restoration, and this spared several statues and other artefacts, which had been taken off-site to be restored.

Despite the damage, the awesome exterior of the cathedral, and its surrounding squares, are well worth a visit – for the sublime Gothic architecture and the church's historical and cultural significance.

Rose window

ARTEM NEDOLUZHKO/SHUTTERSTOCK ©

⚓

Explore Ashore

The quickest way of getting here from the cruise ship docks is via the RER to Saint-Michel–Notre-Dame. From Grenelle, walk to the Champ de Mars stop near the Eiffel Tower; from André Citroën, use Javel. Allow 25 minutes.

❶ Need to Know

Map p132; www.notredamedeparis.fr; 6 Parvis Notre Dame – place Jean-Paul-II, 4e; ⊘closed indefinitely; Ⓜ Cité

Rebuilding Notre Dame

After the fire, French President Emmanuel Macron said he'd like the cathedral to be rebuilt by 2024, in time for the Olympic Games, but others estimate that a full restoration could take decades. There is debate over the form that the restoration should take: should it be restored to its original era, to the 19th-century update or something more modern still?

Though it will be a long while before visits to the interior can resume, the cathedral's significance has not dimmed. The gothic structure stands strong and continues to inspire awe and devotion more than 800 years after it was first built.

Architecture

Built on a site occupied by earlier churches and, a millennium prior, a Gallo-Roman temple, the construction of Notre Dame was begun in 1163 and largely completed by the early 14th century. The cathedral was badly damaged during the Revolution, prompting architect Eugène Emmanuel Viollet-le-Duc to oversee extensive renovations between 1845 and 1864.

Notre Dame is known for its sublime balance, though if you look closely you'll see all sorts of minor asymmetrical elements introduced to avoid monotony, in accordance with standard Gothic practice. These include the slightly different shapes of each of the three main portals, whose statues were once brightly coloured to make them more effective as a *Biblia pauperum* – a 'Bible of the poor' to help the illiterate faithful understand Old Testament stories, the Passion of the Christ and the lives of the saints.

Rose Windows

A cathedral highlight, the three rose windows are Notre Dame's most spectacular feature. All three windows appear to have survived the 2019 fire, with no catastrophic damage.

Walking Tour: Arty Montmartre

This walk takes you through the heart of hilltop Montmartre where artists lived, worked and partied hard in the 19th century. With its ivy-clad buildings and steep narrow lanes, this is cinematic Paris at its best.

Start M Abbesses
Distance 1km
Duration One hour

4 Le Passe-Muraille on place Marcel Aymé portrays Dutilleul, hero of Aymé's short story *The Walker Through Walls*.

Cimetière
St-Vincent

R St-Vincent

R de l'Abreuvoir

Sq Suzanne
Buisson

R Girardon

Av Junot

4
Pl Marcel
Aymé

3 Windmill **Moulin Blute Fin**, on rue Lepic, was immortalised by Renoir in his 1876 *Bal du Moulin de la Galette*.

3

R Lepic

R Norvins

R d'Orchampt

R Gabrielle

Pl Émile
Goudeau

R Berthe

R Durantin

R des
Trois Frères

R des Abbesses

Passage des Abbesses

Sq J
Rictus

2

1 Admire Hector Guimard's iconic art nouveau metro entrance (1900) on **place des Abbesses**.

R de la Vieuville

START M Abbesses

5 Uphill is Montmartre's oldest building, the 17th-century manor house that's now **Musée de Montmartre** (www.museedemontmartre.fr; 12 rue Cortot).

6 The 12th-century **Église St-Pierre de Montmartre** (www.saintpierredemontmartre.net; 2 rue du Mont Cenis; ☺9am-7.30pm Sat-Thu, to 6pm Fri) witnessed the founding of the Jesuits, who met in the crypt.

Take a Break... Hardware Société (https://hardwaresociete.com; 10 Rue Lamarck; ☺9am-4pm Mon-Fri, to 4:30pm Sat & Sun) is great for coffee, breakfast or lunch.

R Cortot 5

R des Saules

R Norvins

R du Mont Cenis

Pl du Tertre 7 FINISH 6

Basilique du Sacré Cœur

R Lamarck

Classic Photo A selfie in front of the city of romance's most seductive wall, Le Mur des je t'aime.

7 Lap up the local life on **place du Tertre**, packed with buskers, portrait artists and cafe terraces.

2 Learn 'I love you!' in many languages with the artwork **Le Mur des je t'aime** (www.lesjetaime.com) in Sq Jehan Rictus.

Pl St-Pierre

Ⓝ 0 — 100 m / 0 — 0.05 miles

Paris

Paris' monument-lined boulevards, museums, classical bistros and boutiques are enhanced by a new wave of multimedia galleries, creative wine bars, design shops and tech start-ups.

◎ SIGHTS

◎ Eiffel Tower & Western Paris

Musée Marmottan Monet   Gallery

(Map p130; ☎01 44 96 50 33; www.marmottan. fr; 2 rue Louis Boilly, 16e; adult/child €12/8.50; ⊙10am-6pm Tue, Wed & Fri-Sun, to 9pm Thu; MLa Muette) This museum showcases the world's largest collection of works by impressionist painter Claude Monet (1840–1926) – about 100 – as well as paintings by Gauguin, Sisley, Pissarro, Renoir, Degas, Manet and Berthe Morisot. It also contains an important collection of French, English, Italian and Flemish illuminations from the 13th to 16th centuries.

◎ Champs-Élysées & Grands Boulevards

Arc de Triomphe   Landmark

(Map p130; www.paris-arc-de-triomphe.fr; place Charles de Gaulle, 8e; viewing platform adult/child €12/free; ⊙10am-11pm Apr-Sep, to 10.30pm Oct-Mar; MCharles de Gaulle–Étoile) If anything rivals the Eiffel Tower (p118) as the symbol of Paris, it's this magnificent 1836 monument to Napoléon's victory at Austerlitz (1805), which he commissioned the following year. The intricately sculpted triumphal arch stands sentinel in the centre of the Étoile (Star) roundabout. From the viewing platform on top of the arch (50m up via 284 steps and well worth the climb), you can see the dozen avenues.

◎ Louvre & Les Halles

Centre Pompidou   Museum

(Map p132; ☎01 44 78 12 33; www.centrepom pidou.fr; place Georges Pompidou, 4e; museum, exhibitions & panorama adult/child €14/free, panorama only ticket €5/free; ⊙11am-9pm Wed-Mon, temporary exhibits to 11pm Thu; MRambu teau) Renowned for its radical architectural statement, the 1977-opened Centre Pompidou brings together galleries and cutting-edge exhibitions, hands-on workshops, dance performances, cinemas and other entertainment venues, with street performers and fanciful fountains outside. The **Musée National d'Art Moderne**, France's national collection of art dating from 1905 onwards, is the main draw; a fraction of its 100,000-plus pieces – including Fauvist, cubist, surrealist, pop art and contemporary works – is on display. Don't miss the spectacular Parisian panorama from the rooftop.

◎ Montmartre & Northern Paris

Basilique du Sacré-Cœur   Basilica

(Map p132; ☎01 53 41 89 00; www.sacre -coeur-montmartre.com; Parvis du Sacré-Cœur, 18e; basilica free, dome adult/child €6/4, cash only; ⊙basilica 6am-10.30pm, dome 8.30am-8pm May-Sep, 9am-5pm Oct-Apr; MAnvers or Abbesses) Begun in 1875 in the wake of the Franco-Prussian War and the chaos of the Paris Commune, Sacré-Cœur is a symbol of the former struggle between the conservative Catholic old guard and the secular, republican radicals. It was finally consecrated in 1919, standing in contrast to the bohemian lifestyle that surrounded it. The view over Paris from its parvis is breathtaking. Avoid walking up the steep hill by using a regular metro ticket aboard the **funicular** (www.ratp.fr; place St-Pierre, 18e; ⊙6am-12.45am; MAnvers or Abbesses) to the **upper station** (www.ratp.fr; rue du Cardinal Dubois, 18e; ⊙6am-12.45am; MAbbesses).

◎ Le Marais & Around

Cimetière du Père Lachaise   Cemetery

(Map p132; ☎01 55 25 82 10; www.pere-lachaise. com; 16 rue du Repos & 8 bd de Ménilmontant, 20e; ⊙8am-6pm Mon-Fri, from 8.30am Sat, from 9am Sun mid-Mar–Oct, shorter hours Nov–mid-Mar; MPère Lachaise or Gambetta) Opened in 1804, Père Lachaise is today the world's most visited cemetery. Its 70,000 ornate tombs of the rich and famous form a verdant, 44-hectare sculpture garden. The most visited are those of 1960s rock star

Arc de Triomphe

Jim Morrison (division 6) and Oscar Wilde (division 89). Pick up cemetery maps at the **conservation office** (Bureaux de la Conservation; ☎01 55 25 82 10; 16 rue du Repos, 20e; ⏰8.30am-12.30pm & 2-5pm Mon-Fri; ⓂPhilippe Auguste, Père Lachaise) near the main bd de Ménilmontant entrance. Other notables buried here include composer Chopin, playwright Molière, poet Apollinaire, and writers Balzac, Proust, Stein and Colette.

Musée National Picasso   Museum
(Map p132; ☎01 85 56 00 36; www.museepicasso paris.fr; 5 rue de Thorigny, 3e; adult/child €12.50/ free; ⏰10.30am-6pm Tue-Fri, from 9.30am Sat & Sun; ⓂChemin Vert or St-Paul) One of Paris' most treasured art collections is showcased inside the mid-17th-century Hôtel Salé, an exquisite private mansion owned by the city since 1964. The Musée National Picasso is a staggering art museum devoted to Spanish artist Pablo Picasso (1881–1973), who spent much of his life living and working in Paris. The collection includes more than 5000 drawings, engravings, paintings, ceramic works and sculptures by the *grand maître* (great master), although they're not all displayed at the same time.

◎ **Latin Quarter**

Panthéon   Mausoleum
(Map p136; ☎01 44 32 18 00; www.paris-pan theon.fr; place du Panthéon, 5e; adult/child €9/ free; ⏰10am-6.30pm Apr-Sep, to 6pm Oct-Mar; ⓂMaubert-Mutualité or RER Luxembourg) The Panthéon's stately neoclassical dome is an icon of the Parisian skyline. Its vast interior is an architectural masterpiece: originally an abbey church dedicated to Ste Geneviève and now a mausoleum, it has served since 1791 as the resting place of some of France's greatest thinkers, including Voltaire, Rousseau, Braille and Hugo. A copy of Foucault's pendulum, first hung from the dome in 1851 to demonstrate the rotation of the earth, takes pride of place.

◎ **St-Germain & Les Invalides**

Musée d'Orsay   Museum
(Map p130; ☎01 40 49 48 14; www.musee-orsay. fr; 1 rue de la Légion d'Honneur, 7e; adult/child €14/free; ⏰9.30am-6pm Tue, Wed & Fri-Sun,

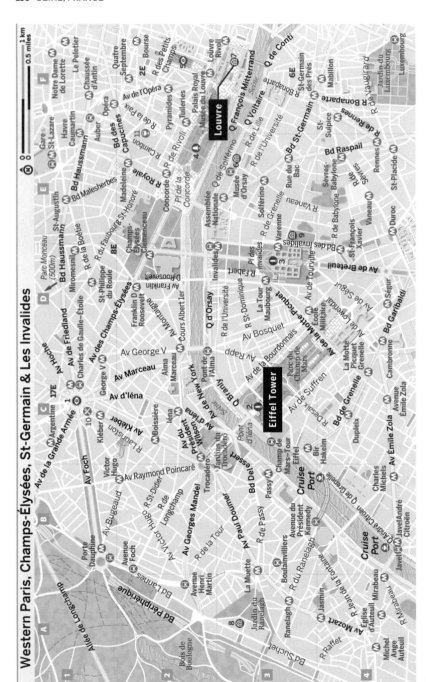

Western Paris, Champs-Élysées, St-Germain & Les Invalides

Western Paris, Champs-Élysées, St-Germain & Les Invalides

to 9.45pm Thu; M Assemblée Nationale or RER Musée d'Orsay) The home of France's national collection from the impressionist, post-impressionist and art nouveau movements spanning from 1848 to 1914 is the glorious former Gare d'Orsay train station – itself an art nouveau showpiece – where a roll call of masters and their world-famous works are on display.

Top of every visitor's must-see list is the painting collection, centred on the world's largest collection of impressionist and post-impressionist art. Allow ample time to swoon over masterpieces by Manet, Monet, Cézanne, Renoir, Degas, Pissarro and Van Gogh.

Musée Rodin   Museum, Garden

(Map p130; 📞01 44 18 61 10; www.musee-rodin. fr; 79 rue de Varenne, 7e; adult/child €10/free, garden only €4/free; ⊙10am-5.45pm Tue-Sun; M Varenne or Invalides) Sculptor, painter, sketcher, engraver and collector Auguste Rodin donated his entire collection to the French state in 1908 on the proviso that it dedicate his former workshop and showroom, the beautiful 1730 Hôtel Biron, to displaying his works. They're now installed not only in the mansion itself, but also in its rose-filled garden – one of the most peaceful places in central Paris and a wonderful spot to contemplate his famous work *The Thinker*. Prepurchase tickets online to avoid queuing.

Hôtel des Invalides   Monument, Museum

(Map p130; www.musee-armee.fr; 129 rue de Grenelle, 7e; adult/child €12/free; ⊙10am-6pm Apr-Oct, to 5pm Nov-Mar; M Varenne or La Tour Maubourg) Flanked by the 500m-long Esplanade des Invalides lawns, Hôtel des

Invalides was built in the 1670s by Louis XIV to house 4000 *invalides* (disabled war veterans). On 14 July 1789, a mob broke into the building and seized 32,000 rifles before heading on to the prison at Bastille and the start of the French Revolution.

Admission includes entry to all Hôtel des Invalides sights (temporary exhibitions cost extra). Hours for individual sites can vary – check the website for updates.

🎫 TOURS & COURSES

Parisien d'un Jour – Paris Greeters   Walking

(www.greeters.paris; by donation) See Paris through local eyes with these two- to three-hour city tours. Volunteers – mainly knowledgeable Parisians passionate about their city – lead groups (maximum six people) to their favourite spots. Minimum two weeks' notice is needed.

La Cuisine Paris   Cooking

(Map p132; 📞01 40 51 78 18; www.lacuisineparis. com; 80 quai de l'Hôtel de Ville, 4e; 2hr cooking class/walking tour & class from €69/165; M Pont Marie, Hôtel de Ville) Classes in English range from how to make bread and croissants to macarons as well as market classes and gourmet 'foodie walks'.

Meeting the French   Cultural, Tours

(📞01 42 51 19 80; www.meetingthefrench.com; tours & courses from €12) Cosmetics workshops, backstage cabaret tours, fashion-designer showroom visits, French table decoration, art embroidery classes, market tours, baking with a Parisian baker – the repertoire of cultural and gourmet tours and behind-the-scenes experiences offered

Les Halles, Marais & Montmartre

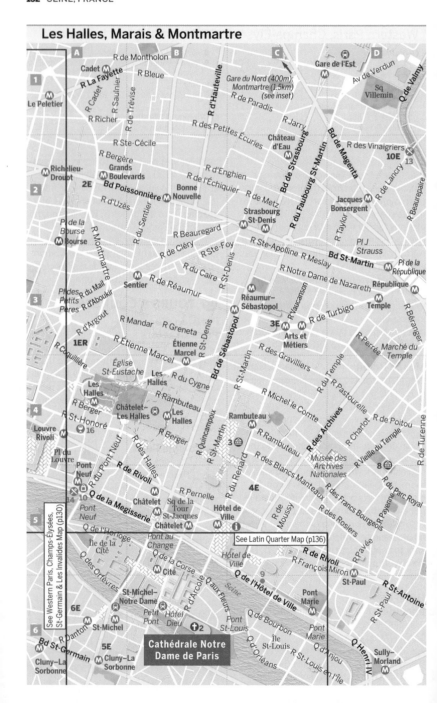

R de Montholon

Cadet Ⓜ

R La Fayette

R Cadet

R Bleue

R Saulnier

R de Trévise

Ⓜ Le Peletier

R Richer

R d'Hauteville

R de Paradis

Gare du Nord (400m);
Montmartre (1.5km)
(see inset)

Gare de l'Est Ⓜ

Av de Verdun

Sq Villemin

Q de Valmy

R Ste-Cécile

R des Petites Ecuries

R Jarry

R Bergère

Château
d'Eau

R des Vinaigriers

10E 13

Ⓜ Richelieu-
Drouot

Grands
Ⓜ Boulevards

R d'Enghien

R de l'Échiquier

Bd de Strasbourg

R du Faubourg St-Martin

Bd de Magenta

R de Lancry

2E

Bd Poissonnière

Bonne
Nouvelle

R de Metz

Jacques
Bonsergent Ⓜ

R Taylor

R Beaurepaire

R d'Uzès

Strasbourg
St-Denis Ⓜ

R Ste-Apolline R Meslay

Pl J
Strauss

Pl de la
Bourse

R Beauregard

R Notre Dame de Nazareth

Pl de la
République

Ⓜ Bourse

R de Cléry

R Ste-Foy

Bd St-Martin

R Montmartre

R du Sentier

R St-Denis

République Ⓜ

R Béranger

R du Mail

R du Caire

Temple Ⓜ

Pl des
Petits
Pères

Sentier Ⓜ

R de Réaumur

Réaumur–
Sébastopol Ⓜ

R Vaucanson

R de Turbigo

R d'Aboukir

R Mandar

R Greneta

3E Ⓜ

R Perrée

Marché du
Temple

R d'Argout

1ER

R Étienne Marcel

Étienne
Marcel Ⓜ

R St-Denis

Bd de Sébastopol

Arts et
Métiers

R du Temple

R Coquillière

Église
St-Eustache

Les
Halles

R du Cygne

R des Gravilliers

R Charlot

R de Poitou

R de Turenne

Les
Halles

R du Temple

R Pastourelle

Châtelet–
Les Halles Ⓜ

Les
Halles Ⓜ

R Rambuteau

R Michel le Comte

R Vieille du Temple

8E 🏛

Ⓜ Louvre
Rivoli

R Berger

R St-Honoré

R Berger

Rambuteau Ⓜ

R Rambuteau

R St-Martin

3 🏛

R des Archives

R du Parc Royal

Pl du
Louvre

R Quincampoix

R des Blancs Manteaux

Musée des
Archives
Nationales

R Payenne

Pont
Neuf Ⓜ

R de Rivoli

R du Pont Neuf

R des Halles

R du Renard

4E

R des Francs Bourgeois

R Pavée

14 ⓧ 10

Q de la Megisserie

R Pernelle

R des Rosiers

Châtelet

Sq de la
Tour
St-Jacques

Hôtel de
Ville 🅘

R de
Moussy

Pont
Neuf

Q de l'Horloge

Châtelet Ⓜ

See Western Paris, Champs-Élysées,
St-Germain & Les Invalides Map (p130)

See Latin Quarter Map (p136)

Île de la
Cité

Pont au
Change

Q de la Corse

Hôtel de
Ville

R de Rivoli

R François Miron

St-Paul Ⓜ

R St-Antoine

Q des Orfèvres

Ⓜ Cité

Q de l'Hôtel de Ville

9

Pont
Marie

R St-Paul

R St-Antoine

St-Michel–
Notre Dame Ⓜ

R d'Arcole

Q aux Fleurs

Seine

Q de Bourbon

Pont
Marie Ⓜ

Sully–
Morland Ⓜ

6E

Petit
Pont

Hôtel
Dieu

🕇**2**

Pont
St-Louis

Île
St-Louis

Q d'Anjou

Q Henri IV

Ⓜ St-Michel

**Cathédrale Notre
Dame de Paris**

Q d'Orléans

R St-Louis en l'Île

Bd St-Germain

5E

Cluny–La
Sorbonne

Cluny–La
Sorbonne

R Danton

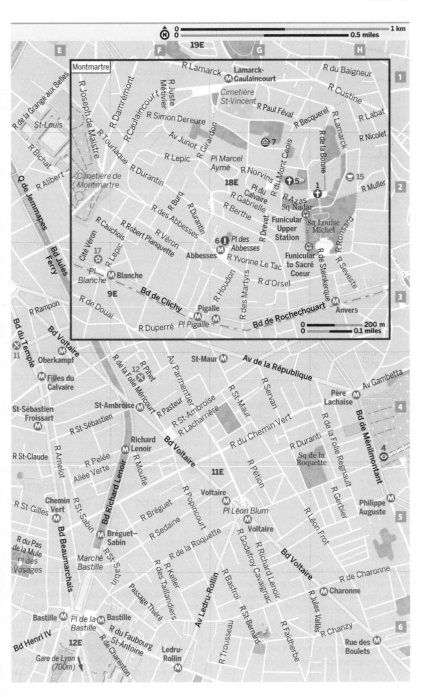

0 1 km
0 0.5 miles

19E

Montmartre

R Lamarck

Lamarck-Caulaincourt

R du Baigneur

E

F

G

H

1

R de la Grange aux Belles

R Joseph de Maistre

R Damrémont

R Caulaincourt

R Juste Métivier

R Lamarck

R Simon Dereure

Cimetière St-Vincent

R Custine

R Paul Féval

R Becquerel

R Labat

R Nicolet

St-Louis

R Bichat

R Tourlaque

Av Junot

Girardon

R de la Bonne

R Lamarck

Q de Jemmapes

R Alibert

Cimetière de Montmartre

R Durantin

R Lepic

Pl Marcel Aymé

7

R du Mont Cenis

R Muller

15

1

2

R Norvins

Pl du Calvaire

5

R Azas

R des Abbesses

R Gabrielle

Sq Nadar

18E

R Durantin

R Berthe

Funicular Upper Station

Sq Louise Michel

R Robert Planquette

R Cauchois

Cité Véron

R Lepic

R Véron

6

Pl des Abbesses

Abbesses

R Drevet

R Yvonne Le Tac

Funicular to Sacré Coeur

R de Steinkerque

R Ronsard

R Seveste

17

Pl Blanche

Blanche

R Houdon

R d'Orsel

R des Martyrs

9E

Bd de Clichy

Pigalle

Anvers

R Rampon

R de Douai

R Duperré

Pl Pigalle

Bd de Rochechouart

0 200 m
0 0.1 miles

3

Bd Jules Ferry

Bd du Temple

11

St-Maur

Av de la République

Oberkampf

R de la Folie Méricourt

R Pihet

12

Av Parmentier

R Pasteur

R St-Maur

R Servan

Père Lachaise

Av Gambetta

Filles du Calvaire

St-Ambroise

St-Sébastien Froissart

R St-Sébastien

R St-Ambroise

R Lacharrière

R du Chemin Vert

R Duranti

R de la Folie Regnault

Bd de Ménilmontant

4

R St-Claude

R Amelot

R Pelée

Allée Verte

Richard Lenoir

R Moufle

Bd Voltaire

11E

R Pétion

Sq de la Roquette

R Gerbier

4

Chemin Vert

R St-Gilles

R St-Sabin

Bd Richard Lenoir

Voltaire

Pl Léon Blum

Voltaire

R Léon Frot

Philippe Auguste

5

R du Pas de la Mule

Pl des Vosages

Bd Beaumarchais

Bréguet–Sabin

Marché Bastille

R Bréguet

R Sedaine

R de la Roquette

R St-Sabin

Passage Thiéré

R Popincourt

R Keller

R des Taillandiers

R Richard Lenoir

R Godefroy Cavaignac

Bd Voltaire

R de Charonne

Charonne

6

Bastille

Bd Henri IV

12E

Pl de la Bastille

Bastille

R du Faubourg St-Antoine

R de Charenton

Ledru-Rollin

Av Ledru-Rollin

R Bastfroi

R Trousseau

R St-Bernard

R Faidherbe

R Jules Vallès

R Chanzy

Rue des Boulets

Gare de Lyon (700m)

Les Halles, Marais & Montmartre

by Meeting the French is truly outstanding. All courses and tours are in English.

⊕ SHOPPING

Bouquinistes   Books

(Map p132; quai Voltaire, 7e, to quai de la Tournelle, 5e, & Pont Marie, 4e, to quai du Louvre, 1er; ⊙11.30am-dusk) With some 3km of forest-green boxes lining the Seine – containing over 300,000 secondhand (and often out-of-print) books, rare magazines, postcards and old advertising posters – Paris' *bouquinistes* are integral to the cityscape. Many open only from spring to autumn (and many shut in August), but year-round you'll still find some to browse.

Le Bonbon au Palais   Food

(Map p136; ☎01 78 56 15 72; www.lebonbonau palais.com; 19 rue Monge, 5e; ⊙10.30am-7.30pm Tue-Sat; Ⓜ Cardinal Lemoine) Kids and kids-at-heart will adore this sugar-fuelled *tour de France*. The school-geography-themed boutique stocks rainbows of artisanal sweets from around the country. Old-fashioned glass jars brim with treats like *calissons* (diamond-shaped, icing-sugar-topped ground fruit and almonds from Aix-en-Provence), *rigolettes* (fruit-filled pillows from Nantes), *berlingots* (striped, triangular boiled sweets from Carpentras and elsewhere) and *papalines* (herbal liqueur-filled pink-chocolate balls from Avignon).

Le Bon Marché   Department Store

(Map p136; ☎01 44 39 80 00; www.24sevres. com; 24 rue de Sèvres, 7e; ⊙10am-8pm Mon-Wed, Fri & Sat, 10am-8.45pm Thu, 11am-7.45pm Sun; Ⓜ Sèvres-Babylone) Built by Gustave Eiffel as Paris' first department store in 1852, this is the epitome of style, with a superb concentration of men's and women's fashions, homewares, stationery, books and toys. Break for a coffee, afternoon tea or a light lunch at the Rose Bakery tearoom on the 2nd floor.

The icing on the cake is its glorious **food hall** (www.lagrandeepicerie.com; 38 rue de Sèvres, 7e; ⊙8.30am-9pm Mon-Sat, 10am-8pm Sun).

⊗ EATING

⊗ Eiffel Tower & Western Paris

Bustronome   Gastronomy $$$

(Map p130; ☎09 54 44 45 55; www.bustronome. com; 2 av Kléber, 16e; 4-course lunch €65, 6-course dinner €100; ⊙by reservation 12.15pm, 12.45pm, 7.45pm & 8.45pm; ⊘⍗; Ⓜ Kléber, Charles de Gaulle–Étoile) A true moveable feast, Bustronome is a voyage into French gastronomy aboard a glass-roofed bus, with Paris' famous monuments – the Arc de Triomphe, Grand Palais, Palais Garnier, Notre Dame and Eiffel Tower – gliding by as you dine on seasonal creations prepared in the purpose-built vehicle's lower-deck galley. Children's menus for lunch/dinner cost

€40/50; vegetarian, vegan and gluten-free menus are available.

Louvre & Les Halles
Maison Maison Mediterranean $$
(Map p132; ☑09 67 82 07 32; www.restaurant -maisonmaison.com; 63 Parc Rives de Seine, 1er; 2-/3-course lunch menu €20/25, small plates €7-16; ⊘kitchen 7-10pm Mon, noon-3pm & 7-10pm Tue-Sun, bar to 2am; MPont Neuf) Halfway down the stairs by Pont Neuf is this wonderfully secret space beneath the *bouquinistes* (used-book sellers), where you can watch the *bateaux-mouches* (river-cruise boats) float by as you dine on creations such as beetroot and pink-grapefruit-cured bonito or gnocchi with white asparagus and broccoli pesto. In nice weather, cocktails at the glorious riverside terrace are not to be missed.

 Montmartre & Northern Paris
Le Verre Volé Bistro $
(Map p132; ☑01 48 03 17 34; www.leverrevole.fr; 67 rue de Lancry, 10e; mains €11-22, sandwiches €7.90; ⊘bistro 12.30-2.30pm & 7.30-11.30pm, wine bar 10am-2am; 🡒; MJacques Bonsergent) The tiny 'Stolen Glass' – a wine shop with a few tables – is one of Paris' most popular wine bar–restaurants, with outstanding natural and unfiltered wines and expert advice. Unpretentious, hearty *plats du jour* are excellent. Reserve in advance for meals, or stop by to pick up a gourmet sandwich (such as mustard-smoked burrata with garlic-pork sausage) and a bottle.

Le Marais & Around
Jacques Genin Pastries $
(Map p132; ☑01 45 77 29 01; www.jacquesgenin. fr; 133 rue de Turenne, 3e; pastries €9; ⊘11am-7pm Tue-Fri & Sun, to 7.30pm Sat; MOberkampf or Filles du Calvaire) Wildly creative *chocolatier* Jacques Genin is famed for his flavoured caramels, *pâtes de fruits* (fruit jellies) and exquisitely embossed *bonbons de chocolat* (chocolate sweets). But what completely steals the show at his elegant chocolate showroom is the *salon de dégustation* (aka tearoom), where you can order a pot of outrageously thick hot chocolate and

legendary Genin *millefeuille*, assembled to order.

La Cave de l'Insolite Bistro $$
(Map p132; ☑01 53 36 08 33; www.lacavedelin solite.fr; 30 rue de la Folie Méricourt, 11e; 2-/3-course midweek lunch menus €18/20, mains €20-36; ⊘12.15-2.30pm & 7.30-10.30pm Tue-Sat; 🡒; MSt-Ambroise, Parmentier) Brothers Axel and Arnaud, who have worked at some of Paris' top addresses, run this rustic-chic wine bar with barrels, timber tables and a wood-burning stove. Duck pâté with cider jelly, haddock rillettes with lime and endive confit, and beef with mushroom and sweetbread sauce are among the seasonal dishes; its 100-plus hand-harvested wines come from small-scale French vineyards.

Latin Quarter
Café de la Nouvelle Mairie Cafe $
(Map p136; ☑01 44 07 04 41; 19 rue des Fossés St-Jacques, 5e; mains €11-17; ⊘8am-12.30am Mon-Fri, kitchen noon-2.30pm & 8-10.30pm Mon-Thu, 8-10pm Fri; MCardinal Lemoine) Shhhh... just around the corner from the Panthéon (p129) but hidden away on a small, fountained square, this hybrid cafe-restaurant and wine bar is a tip-top neighbourhood secret, serving natural wines and delicious seasonal bistro fare from oysters and ribs (*à la française*) to grilled lamb sausage over lentils. It takes reservations for dinner but not lunch – arrive early.

Restaurant AT Gastronomy $$$
(Map p136; ☑01 56 81 94 08; www.atsushitanaka. com; 4 rue du Cardinal Lemoine, 5e; 6-course lunch menu €55, 12-course dinner tasting menu €95, with paired wines €170; ⊘12.15-2pm & 8-9.30pm Mon-Sat; MCardinal Lemoine) Trained by some of the biggest names in gastronomy (Pierre Gagnaire included), chef Atsushi Tanaka showcases abstract artlike masterpieces incorporating rare ingredients (charred bamboo, kohlrabi turnip cabbage, juniper berry powder, wild purple fennel, Nepalese Timut pepper) in a blank-canvas-style dining space on stunning outsized plates. Reservations essential.

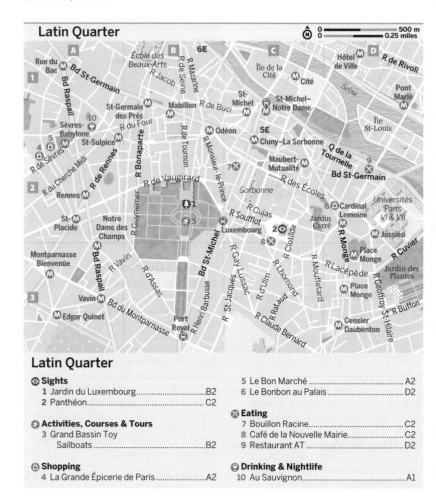

Latin Quarter

Sights
1 Jardin du Luxembourg B2
2 Panthéon C2

Activities, Courses & Tours
3 Grand Bassin Toy
   Sailboats B2

Shopping
4 La Grande Épicerie de Paris A2

5 Le Bon Marché A2
6 Le Bonbon au Palais D2

Eating
7 Bouillon Racine C2
8 Café de la Nouvelle Mairie.........................C2
9 Restaurant AT D2

Drinking & Nightlife
10 Au Sauvignon A1

St-Germain & Les Invalides

Bouillon Racine Brasserie $$

(Map p136; ☎01 44 32 15 60; www.bouillonracine.
fr; 3 rue Racine, 6e; 2-course weekday lunch
menu €17.50, 3-course menu €35, mains €17-
24.50; ⊙noon-11pm; ♿; ⓂCluny–La Sorbonne)
Inconspicuously situated in a quiet street,
this heritage-listed art nouveau 'soup
kitchen', with mirrored walls, floral motifs
and ceramic tiling, was built in 1906 to feed
market workers. Despite the magnificent
interior, the food – inspired by age-old
recipes – is no afterthought and superbly
executed (stuffed, spit-roasted suckling
pig, pork shank in Rodenbach red beer,
scallops and shrimps with lobster coulis).

DRINKING & NIGHTLIFE

Bar Hemingway Cocktail Bar

(Map p130; www.ritzparis.com; Hôtel Ritz Paris,
15 place Vendôme, 1er; ⊙6pm-2am; ☎; ⓂOpéra)
Black-and-white photos and memorabilia
(hunting trophies, old typewriters and
framed handwritten letters by the great
writer) fill this snug bar inside the Ritz.
Head bartender Colin Peter Field mixes

monumental cocktails, including three different Bloody Marys made with juice from freshly squeezed seasonal tomatoes. Legend has it that Hemingway himself, wielding a machine gun, helped liberate the bar during WWII.

Le Garde Robe   Wine Bar

(Map p132; ✆01 49 26 90 60; 41 rue de l'Arbre Sec, 1er; ⊙noon-1am Mon-Sat; Ⓜ︎Louvre Rivoli) Le Garde Robe is possibly the world's only bar to serve alcohol alongside a detox menu. While you probably shouldn't come here for the full-on cleansing experience, you can definitely expect excellent, affordable natural wines, a casual atmosphere and a good selection of food, ranging from cheese and charcuterie plates to adventurous options (tuna gravlax with black quinoa and guacamole).

Au Sauvignon   Wine Bar

(Map p136; ✆01 45 48 49 02; www.ausauvignon. com; 80 rue des Sts-Pères, 7e; ⊙8am-11pm Mon-Sat, 9am-10pm Sun; Ⓜ︎Sèvres-Babylone) Grab a table in the evening light at this wonderfully authentic wine bar or head to the quintessential bistro interior, with original zinc bar, tightly packed tables and hand-painted ceiling celebrating French viticultural tradition. A plate of casse-croûtes au pain Poilâne (toast with ham, pâté, terrine, smoked salmon and foie gras) is the perfect accompaniment.

ENTERTAINMENT

Moulin Rouge   Cabaret

(Map p132; ✆01 53 09 82 82; www.moulinrouge. fr; 82 bd de Clichy, 18e; show only from €87, lunch & show from €165, dinner & show from €190; ⊙show only 2.45pm, 9pm & 11pm, lunch & show 1.45pm, dinner & show 7pm; Ⓜ︎Blanche) Immortalised in Toulouse-Lautrec's posters and later in Baz Luhrmann's film, Paris' legendary cabaret twinkles beneath a 1925 replica of its original red windmill. Yes, it's packed with bus-tour crowds, but from the opening bars of music to the last high can-can kick, it's a whirl of fantastical costumes, sets, choreography and Champagne. Book

Flea Market Treasure Trove

Spanning 9 hectares, the **Marché aux Puces de St-Ouen** (www.marcheauxpuces-saintouen.com; rue des Rosiers, St-Ouen; ⊙Sat-Mon; Ⓜ︎Porte de Clignancourt) is a vast flea market, founded in 1870 and said to be Europe's largest. Over 2000 stalls are grouped into 15 *marchés* (markets) selling everything from 17th-century furniture to 21st-century clothing. Each market has different opening hours – check the website for details. There are miles upon miles of 'freelance' stalls; come prepared to spend some time.

Marché aux Puces de St-Ouen

in advance and dress smartly (no trainers or sneakers).

INFORMATION

Paris Convention & Visitors Bureau (Paris Office de Tourisme; Map p132; ✆01 49 52 42 63; www.parisinfo.com; 29 rue de Rivoli, 4e; ⊙9am-7pm May-Oct, 10am-7pm Nov-Apr; ☎; Ⓜ︎Hôtel de Ville) Paris' main tourist office is at the Hôtel de Ville. It sells tickets for tours and several attractions, plus museum and transport passes.

ⓘ GETTING AROUND

BICYCLE & WALKING

Paris is increasingly bike-friendly, with more cycling lanes and efforts from the city of Paris to reduce the number of cars on the roads. The **Vélib'** (✆01 76 49 12 34; www.velib-metropole.fr; day/week subscription €5/15, standard bike

Parisian Parks

For apartment-dwelling Parisians, the city's parks are a communal backyard where they can stroll in style or bust out cheese and wine.

The **Jardin du Luxembourg** (Map p136; www.senat.fr/visite/jardin; 6e; ⊘hours vary; MMabillon, St-Sulpice, Rennes, Notre Dame des Champs or RER Luxembourg) is an oasis of formal terraces, chestnut groves and lush lawns. Napoléon dedicated the 23 gracefully laid-out hectares to the children of Paris, and many Parisians spent their childhood prodding 1920s wooden **sailboats** (sailboat rental per 30min €4; ⊘11am-6pm Apr-Oct) with long sticks on the octagonal Grand Bassin.

The formal 28-hectare **Jardin des Tuileries** (Map p130; rue de Rivoli, 1er; ⊘7am-9pm Apr-late Sep, 7.30am-7.30pm late Sep-Mar; MTuileries or Concorde) was laid out in its present form in 1664 by André Le Nôtre, architect of the gardens at Versailles. It's filled with fountains, ponds and sculptures, and is now part of the Banks of the Seine Unesco World Heritage Site.

The **Jardin du Palais Royal** (Map p130; www.domaine-palais-royal.fr; 2 place Colette, 1er; ⊘8am-10.30pm Apr-Sep, to 8.30pm Oct-Mar; MPalais Royal–Musée du Louvre) is perfect for a picnic, or shopping in the trio of beautiful arcades that frame it. However, it's the southern end, polka-dotted with sculptor Daniel Buren's 260 black-and-white striped columns, that has become the garden's signature feature.

Elegant **Parc Monceau** (www.paris.fr/ equipements/parc-monceau-1804; 35 bd de Courcelles, 8e; ⊘7am-10pm May-Aug, to 9pm Sep, to 8pm Oct-Apr; MMonceau) has an Egyptian-style pyramid, a bridge modelled after Venice's Rialto, a Renaissance arch and a Corinthian colonnade. There are play areas, a carousel and scheduled puppet shows.

hire up to 30/60min free/€1, electric bike €1/2) bike-share scheme changed operators in 2018; check the website for the latest information. When the handover is complete, it will put tens of thousands of bikes (30% of them electric) at 1400 stations throughout Paris.

Paris is a beautiful city to stroll, and walking is the best way to soak up the ambience. Sights gathered along and around the Seine are easy and picturesque to walk between if you have the time.

PUBLIC TRANSPORT

Paris' underground network consists of two separate but linked systems: the metro and the Réseau Express Régional (RER) suburban train line. The metro has 14 numbered lines; the RER has five main lines (but you'll probably only need to use A, B and C). When buying tickets, consider how many zones your journey will cover.

For information on the metro, RER and bus systems, visit www.ratp.fr. Metro maps are available for free at ticket windows, or download them for free from the website.

The Mobilis and Paris Visite passes are valid on the metro, the RER, SNCF's suburban lines, buses, night buses, trams and the Montmartre funicular railway.

Mobilis Allows unlimited travel for one day and costs €7.50 (for two zones) to €17.80 (five zones).

Paris Visite Unlimited travel and other discounts. The 'Paris Centre' pass (zones 1 to 3) costs €12/26.65 for one/three days.

Rouen

With its soaring Gothic cathedral, beautifully restored medieval quarter, imposing ancient churches, excellent museums and vibrant cultural life, Rouen is one of Normandy's most engaging and historically rich destinations.

 SIGHTS

Cathédrale Notre Dame   Cathedral
(www.cathedrale-rouen.net; place de la Cathédrale; ⊘2-7pm Mon, 9am-7pm Tue-Sat, 8am-6pm Sun Apr-Oct, shorter hours Nov-Mar) Rouen's stunning Gothic cathedral, built

between the late 12th and 16th centuries, was famously the subject of a series of canvases painted by Monet at various times of the day and year. The 75m-tall **Tour de Beurre** (Butter Tower) was financed by locals in return for being allowed to eat butter during Lent – or so the story goes. A free sound-and-light spectacular is projected on the façade every night from June (at 11pm) to late September (at 9.30pm).

Abbatiale St-Ouen   Church
(place du Général de Gaulle; ⊘10am-noon & 2-6pm Tue-Thu, Sat & Sun) This largely empty 14th-century abbey is a gloriously sublime and quite stunning example of the Rayonnant Gothic style, with a colossal interior dappled with the light from the gorgeous stained glass; it's quite a mind-blowing spectacle. The entrance is through the lovely garden on the south side, facing rue des Faulx.

Musée des Beaux-Arts   Gallery
(☎02 35 71 28 40; www.mbarouen.fr; esplanade Marcel Duchamp; ⊘10am-6pm Wed-Mon) FREE Housed in a very grand structure flung up

in 1870, Rouen's simply outstanding fine-arts museum features canvases by Rubens, Modigliani, Pissarro, Renoir, Sisley (lots) and, of course, several works by Monet, as well as a fine collection of Flemish oils. There's also one jaw-dropping painting by Caravaggio as well as a very serene cafe. Drop your bag in the lockers provided and follow the route through the galleries, arranged chronologically.

Historial Jeanne d'Arc   Museum
(☎02 35 52 48 00; www.historial-jeannedarc.fr; 7 rue St-Romain; adult/child €10.50/7.50; ⊘10am-6pm Tue-Sun) For an introduction to the great 15th-century heroine and the events that earned her fame – and shortly thereafter condemnation – don't miss this excellent site. It's less of a museum, and more of an immersive, theatre-like experience, where you walk through medieval corridors and watch (and hear via headphones, in seven languages) the dramatic retelling of Joan's visions, her victories, the trial that sealed her fate, and the mythologising that followed in the years after her death.

Cathédrale Notre Dame interior, Rouen

KIEV VICTOR/SHUTTERSTOCK ©

Rouen

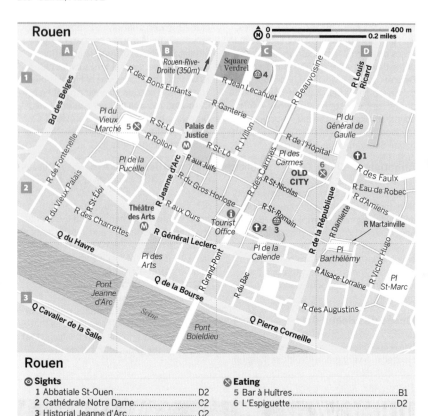

Rouen

⊚ **Sights**

✕ **Eating**

✕ EATING

Bar à Huîtres   Seafood $

(place du Vieux Marché; mains €10-16, oysters per half-dozen/dozen from €10/17; ⊙10am-2pm Tue-Sat) Grab a seat at the horseshoe-shaped bar at this casual but polished eatery located inside Rouen's covered market for uber-fresh seafood. Specials change daily based on what's fresh, from giant shrimp to dorado and fillet of sole, but each is cooked up to perfection. Don't neglect the restaurant's namesake – the satisfying *huîtres* (oysters) with several different varieties on offer.

L'Espiguette   Bistro $

(☑02 35 71 66 27; 25 place St-Amand; weekday lunch menus €13, mains €17-24; ⊙noon-10pm Tue-Sat) This charmingly decorated eatery serves excellent bistro classics – think *osso bucco* (veal casserole), fillet of sole, beef tartare – with the day's offerings up on a chalkboard. It's quite popular with locals, so reserve ahead, even at lunchtime (the lunch *menu* is a great deal). Grab a seat at one of the outdoor tables on a warm day.

ⓘ INFORMATION

Tourist Office (☎02 32 08 32 40; www.rouen
tourisme.com; 25 place de la Cathédrale; ⊗9am-
7pm Mon-Sat, 9.30am-12.30pm & 2-6pm Sun
May-Sep, 9.30am-12.30pm & 1.30-6pm Mon-Sat
Oct-Apr) Housed in a terrific 1500s Renaissance
building facing the cathedral. Rouen's only
exchange bureau is tucked away at the back.

ⓘ GETTING AROUND

Central Rouen and all the sights around the
old city on the Right Bank are small enough to
navigate on foot.

Le Havre

A Unesco World Heritage Site since 2005,
Le Havre is a love letter to modernism,
evoking, more than any other French city,
France's postwar energy and optimism. The
centre was completely rebuilt by the Belgian architect Auguste Perret, whose airy
modernist vision remains, miraculously,
largely intact.

◉ SIGHTS

Église St-Joseph   Church
(bd François 1er; ⊗10am-6pm) Perret's masterful, 107m-high Église St-Joseph, visible
from all over town, was built using bare
concrete from 1951 to 1959. Some 13,000
panels of coloured glass make the soaring,
sombre interior particularly striking when
it's sunny. Stained-glass artist Marguerite
Huré created a cohesive masterpiece in her
collaboration with Perret, and her use of
shading and colour was thoughtfully conceived, evoking different moods depending
on where the sun is in the sky – and the
ensuing colours created by the illumination.

Musée Malraux   Gallery
(MuMa; ☎02 35 19 62 62; www.muma-lehavre.fr/
en; 2 bd Clemenceau; adult/under 26yr €7/free;
⊗11am-6pm Tue-Fri, to 7pm Sat & Sun) Near

the waterfront, this luminous and tranquil
space houses a fabulous collection of vivid
impressionist works – the finest in France
outside Paris – by masters such as Monet
(who grew up in Le Havre), Pissarro, Renoir
and Sisley. You'll also find works by the Fauvist painter Raoul Dufy, born in Le Havre,
and paintings by Eugène Boudin, a mentor
of Monet and another Le Havre native.

✖ EATING

La Taverne Paillette   Brasserie $$
(☎02 35 41 31 50; www.taverne-paillette.com; 22
rue Georges Braque; lunch menus €15.50-31.20,
mains €16-26; ⊗noon-midnight daily) Solid
brasserie food is served up at this Le Havre
institution whose origins, in a former in-
carnation, go back to the late 16th century.
Think bowls overflowing with mussels, generous salads, gargantuan seafood platters
and, in the Alsatian tradition, eight types
of *choucroute* (sauerkraut). Diners leave
contentedly well-fed and many are here for
its famous beer too.

ⓘ INFORMATION

Tourist Office (☎02 32 74 04 04; www.lehavre
tourisme.com; 186 bd Clemenceau; ⊗2-6pm
Mon, 10am-12.30pm & 2-6pm Tue-Sat Nov-Mar,
9.30am-1pm & 2-7pm Apr-Nov) Has a map in
English for a two-hour walking tour of Le Havre's
architectural highlights and details on cultural
events. Situated at the western edge of the city
centre, one block south of the La Plage tram
terminus.

ⓘ GETTING AROUND

Two modern tram lines run by LiA (www.trans
ports-lia.fr) link the **train station** (Gare du Havre;
www.voyages-sncf.com; cours de la République)
with the city centre and the beach. A single ride
costs €1.70; travelling all day is €3.80.

Downtown Le Havre is compact and easily
walkable.

ELBE,
CZECH REPUBLIC
& GERMANY

Elbe, Czech Republic & Germany

Covering the Czech Republic and a thick slice of eastern Germany, Elbe cruises are under-the-radar options. Prague, not on the Elbe but usually included on river cruises, is the equal of Paris in terms of beauty. Its maze of cobbled lanes and hidden courtyards is a paradise for the aimless wanderer. The classic view of Dresden from the Elbe's northern bank takes in spires, towers and domes belonging to palaces, churches and stately buildings: hard to believe that the city was all but wiped off the map by Allied bombings in 1945. Wittenberg is first and foremost about Martin Luther, the monk who triggered the German Reformation in 1517.

With One Day in Prague

With a day in Prague, wander through the courtyards of Prague Castle (p146), visit **St Vitus Cathedral** (p156) and the the **Old Royal Palace** (p148); try and time things to catch the changing of the guard at noon. Descend from the castle to the **Old Town Square** (p156); after watching the Astronomical Clock do its thing, climb to the top of the **Old Town Hall Tower** (p156) for a great view of the square. As day fades, stroll across **Charles Bridge** (p156) in the evening light.

Best Places for...

History Prague Castle (p146)

Palace Zwinger, Dresden (p162)

Wine Vinograf, Prague (p161)

Beer Hall Lokál, Prague (p160)

Reconstruction Frauenkirche, Dresden (p152)

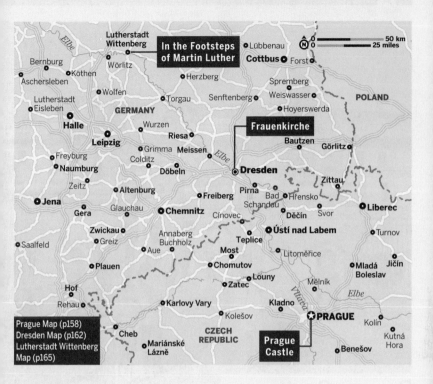

In the Footsteps of Martin Luther

Frauenkirche

Prague Castle

Prague Map (p158)
Dresden Map (p162)
Lutherstadt Wittenberg
Map (p165)

Getting from the Ports

Prague River cruises do not normally enter Prague; you will likely be transported here by bus from Mělník, 50km north.

Dresden You are even closer, docking right up against the historic centre.

Wittenberg Boats dock on the river just five minutes' walk from the old town.

Fast Facts

Currencies Euro (€) in Germany; Koruna česká (Kč, or Czech crown) in Prague

Languages German in Wittenberg and Dresden; Czech in Prague

Free Wi-fi Widely available in bars and cafes.

Money ATMs are common in all three towns.

Tourist Information The office in Wittenberg is conveniently close to Schlosskirche. In Dresden, there's an office near Frauenkirche. In Prague, you'll find one in the Old Town Hall.

Gate of Titans

STOCKPHOTOASTUR/SHUTTERSTOCK ©

Prague Castle

Looming above the Vltava River, Prague Castle dominates the city like a fairy-tale fortress. Within lies a fascinating collection of historic buildings, museums and galleries housing artistic and cultural treasures.

Great For...

☑ Don't Miss

Story of Prague Castle, Lobkowicz Palace, Royal Garden, Basilica of St George and the Old Royal Palace.

There are three main kinds of ticket (A, B, C; each valid for two days), which allow entry to different combinations of sights. Most short-term visitors will be satisfied with the reduced-price option B, which includes the major highlights. Bring photo ID and prepare to queue to get in at busy times.

First Courtyard

The First Courtyard lies within the castle's main gate on Hradčany Square (Hradčanské náměstí), flanked by huge, baroque statues of battling **Titans** (1767–70) that dwarf the castle guards standing beneath them. The **changing of the guard** takes place every hour on the hour, but the longest and most impressive display is at noon, when banners are exchanged while a brass band plays a fanfare from the windows of

Entrance to Palace ballroom

VIACHESLAV KOTOV/SHUTTERSTOCK ©

Explore Ashore

You will likely be bussed into Prague at the end of the Elbe cruise, so you will probably make your way here from your accommodation. You'll need at least three hours to see everything here.

❶ Need to Know

Pražský hrad; ☑224 372 423; www.hrad.cz; Hradčanské náměstí 1; adult/concession from 250/125Kč; ☺grounds 6am-10pm, gardens 10am-6pm Apr-Oct, historic buildings 9am-5pm Apr-Oct, to 4pm Nov-Mar; Ⓜ Malostranská, ☒22, 23

the Plečnik Hall, which overlooks the First Courtyard.

St Vitus Treasury

On the right of the Second Courtyard, the Chapel of the Holy Cross (1763) houses the **St Vitus Treasury** (Svatovítský poklad; ☑224 373 442; www.hrad.cz; nádvoří II, Pražský hrad; adult/child 300/150Kč, admission incl with Prague Castle Tour C ticket; ☺10am-6pm Apr-Oct, to 5pm Nov-Mar), a spectacular collection of ecclesiastical bling that was founded by Charles IV in the 14th century. Gold and silver reliquaries crusted in diamonds, emeralds and rubies contain saintly relics ranging from fragments of the True Cross to the withered hand of a Holy Innocent. The oldest items include a reliquary arm of St Vitus dating from the early 10th century, while the most impressive treasures

include a gold coronation cross of Charles IV (1370) and a diamond-studded baroque monstrance from 1708.

Royal Garden

A gate on the northern side of the Second Courtyard leads to **Powder Bridge** (Prašný most; 1540), which spans the Stag Moat and leads to the **Royal Garden** (Královská zahrada; ☺10am-6pm Apr-Oct; ☒22, 23) **FREE**, which started life as a Renaissance garden built by Ferdinand I in 1534. It is graced by several gorgeous Renaissance structures.

The most beautiful of the garden's buildings is the 1569 **Ball-Game House** (Míčovna), a masterpiece of Renaissance sgraffito where the Habsburgs once played a primitive version of badminton. To the east is the **Summer Palace** (Letohrádek), or Belvedere (1538–60), the most authentic Italian Renaissance building outside Italy; to the west is the 1695 former **Riding**

School (Jízdárna; ⊙10am-6pm). All three are used as venues for temporary exhibitions.

Picture Gallery

The Swedish army that looted the famous bronzes in the **Wallenstein Garden** (Valdštejnská zahrada; www.senat.cz; Letenská 10; ⊙7.30am-6pm Mon-Fri, 10am-6pm Sat & Sun Mar-Oct, to 7pm daily Jun-Sep; Ⓜ Malostranská, 🚊12, 15, 20, 22) FREE in 1648 also nicked Rudolf II's art treasures. This **gallery** (adult/child 100/50Kč, admission incl with Prague Castle Tour C ticket; ⊙9am-5pm Apr-Oct, to 4pm Nov-Mar; 🚊22) in the castle's beautiful Renaissance stables houses an exhibition of 16th- to 18th-century European art, based on the Habsburg collection that was begun in 1650 to replace the lost paintings; it includes works by Cranach, Holbein, Rubens, Tintoretto and Titian.

Old Royal Palace

The **Old Royal Palace** (Starý královský palác; Prague Castle; ⊙9am-5pm, to 4pm Nov-Mar; 🚊22, 23) at the courtyard's eastern end is one of the oldest parts of the castle, dating from 1135. It was originally used only by Czech princesses, but from the 13th to the 16th centuries it was the king's own palace.

The **Vladislav Hall** (Vladislavský sál) is famous for its beautiful, late-Gothic vaulted ceiling (1493–1502) designed by Benedikt Rejt. Though more than 500 years old, the flowing, interwoven lines of the vaults have almost an art-nouveau feel, in contrast to the rectilinear form of the Renaissance windows. The vast hall was used for banquets, councils and coronations, and for indoor jousting tournaments – hence the **Riders' Staircase** (Jezdecké schody), through an arch on the northern side, designed to admit

Basilica of St George

a knight on horseback. All the presidents of the republic have been sworn in here.

A door in the hall's southwestern corner leads to the former offices of the **Bohemian Chancellery** (České kanceláře). On 23 May 1618, in the second room, Protestant nobles rebelling against the Bohemian Estates and the Habsburg emperor threw two of his councillors and their secretary out of the window. They survived, as their fall was broken by the dung-filled moat, but this **Second Defenestration of Prague** sparked off the Thirty Years' War.

> ★ **Top Tip**
> The castle grounds are open all day from 6am to 11pm. Although the historic buildings are closed, an early-morning or late-evening stroll through the castle courtyards minus the daytime crowds is wonderfully atmospheric.

S4SVISUALS/SHUTTERSTOCK ©

At the eastern end of the Vladislav Hall a door to the right leads to a terrace with great views of the city. To the right of the Riders' Staircase you'll spot an unusual Renaissance doorway framed by twisted columns, which leads to the **Diet** (Sněmovna), or Assembly Hall, which displays another beautifully vaulted ceiling.

Basilica of St George

St George Sq (Jiřské náměstí), the plaza to the east of St Vitus Cathedral, lies at the heart of the castle complex.

The striking, brick-red, early-baroque facade that dominates the square conceals the Czech Republic's best-preserved Romanesque **basilica** (Jiřské náměstí; admission incl with Prague Castle tour A & B tickets), established in the 10th century by Vratislav I (the father of St Wenceslas). What you see today is mostly the result of restorations made between 1887 and 1908.

The austerity of the Romanesque nave is relieved by a baroque double staircase leading to the apse, where fragments of 12th-century frescoes survive. In front of the stairs lie the tombs of Prince Boleslav II (d 997; on the left) and Prince Vratislav I (d 921), the church's founder. The arch beneath the stairs allows a glimpse of the 12th-century crypt; Přemysl kings are buried here and in the nave.

On the right side of the crypt is a gruesome statue of a decomposing corpse, complete with a snake coiled in its abdominal cavity. Dating from the 16th century, it is an allegory of Vanity, although it is known as Brigita after a Prague legend. An Italian sculptor murdered his girlfriend, a local girl named Brigita, but when her buried body was discovered he was driven by remorse to create this sculpture of her decaying corpse.

> ✕ **Take a Break**
> Enjoy lunch with a river view on the terraces at **Villa Richter** (www.villarichter.cz; Staré zamecké schody 6; ⊙11am-11pm Mar-Oct; mains 150-300Kč, 3-course dinner 945Kč), below the castle's east gate.

Prague River Walk

The Vltava River runs through the heart of Prague and served as muse for composer Bedřich Smetana in writing his moving *Vltava (Moldau)* symphony. But you don't need to be a musician to enjoy the river's breathtaking bridges and backdrops on this extended walk along the waterway.

Start Convent of St Agnes
Distance 8km
Duration Three hours

2 Amble around **Letná Gardens** (p161) and take in the view of the old town and Malá Strana below.

Royal Garden (Královská zahrada)

Brusnice

Old Castle Steps (Staré Zámecké schody)

Malostranská Ⓜ

Valdštejnská

MALÁ STRANA

❸

Thunovská

Nerudova

Wallenstein Garden (Valdštejnská zahrada)

Vojan Gardens (Vojanovy sady)

Malá Strana Square (Malostranské náměstí)

Josefská

Tržiště

Mostecká

Karmelitská

Na Kampě

Čertovka

Classic Photo Photogenic Prague Castle from any angle.

3 Enjoy views over the Vltava and the red roofs of Malá Strana from the ramparts of **Prague Castle** (p146) or from the beautifully manicured royal gardens.

6 The whimsical yet elegant **Dancing House** (http://tadu.cz; Rašínovo nábřeží 80), by architects Vlado Milunić and Frank Gehry, surprisingly fits in with its ageing neighbours.

Matoušova

SMÍCHOV

Ⓝ 0 ———————— 500 m
0 ———————— 0.25 miles

1 The **Convent of St Agnes** (U Milosrdných 17; ⏰10am-6pm Tue-Sun) is the oldest Gothic building in Bohemia – building began in 1231 – and is supposedly haunted.

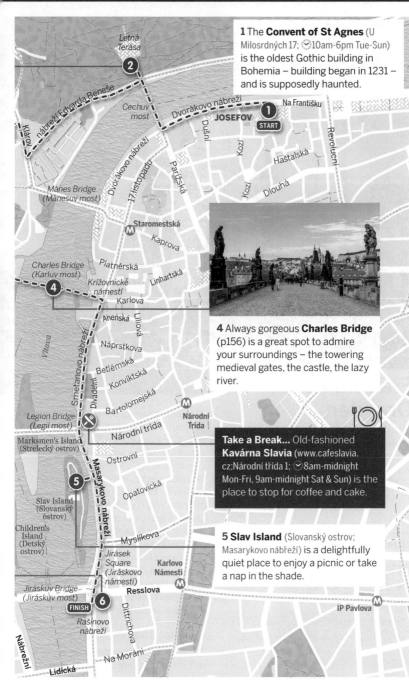

4 Always gorgeous **Charles Bridge** (p156) is a great spot to admire your surroundings – the towering medieval gates, the castle, the lazy river.

Take a Break... Old-fashioned **Kavárna Slavia** (www.cafeslavia.cz;Národní třída 1; ⏰8am-midnight Mon-Fri, 9am-midnight Sat & Sun) is the place to stop for coffee and cake.

5 **Slav Island** (Slovanský ostrov; Masarykovo nábřeží) is a delightfully quiet place to enjoy a picnic or take a nap in the shade.

3 DUNCAN ANDISON/SHUTTERSTOCK © 4 SVETLANASF/SHUTTERSTOCK © 6 VLADIMIR SAZONOV/SHUTTERSTOCK ©

Frauenkirche, Dresden

Dresden's top sight, the unmissable Frauenkirche, has become a symbol of East Germany's post-communist renewal. Destroyed by Allied bombs in 1945, it was a heap of baroque rubble until rebuilding work began in 1994.

Great For...

☑ **Don't Miss**

The altar, reassembled from nearly 2000 fragments, is especially striking.

Standing in perfect baroque wedding-cake symmetry on the pretty Neumarkt, the domed Frauenkirche – Dresden's most beloved symbol – returned to Dresden's cityscape in 2005 following a decade of building work. The original graced its skyline for two centuries before collapsing after the WWII bombing raid that turned Dresden into an inferno and destroyed most of the city centre. It had been left as a war memorial – the East German authorities weren't keen on rebuilding churches – but once the DDR's regime was swept away in 1989, plans for the church's comeback, which had been drawn up in 1985, were quickly accelerated.

Original Building

The former Frauenkirche dated to the first half of the 18th century, but a church has

MARCUS_HOFMANN/SHUTTERSTOCK ©

Frauenkirche interior

⚓ Explore Ashore

Cruise ships mostly dock in a brilliant location just a couple of minutes' walk from the Frauenkirche, which looms over this section of the Elbe. Leave an hour at least to cover it, with guided tours and audio tours also ranging between 30 minutes to one hour.

❶ Need to Know

☏ 0351-6560 6100; www.frauenkirche-dres-den.de; Neumarkt; audio guide €2.50, cupola adult/student €8/5; ⊙ 10am-noon & 1-6pm Mon-Fri, weekend hours vary

stood on this spot since the 11th century. The design you see today replaced a smaller building and was completed for the first time in 1743. Its most striking feature is the 96m-high sandstone dome, weighing 12,000 tonnes. It was a remarkable feat of engineering for the time, comparable to the dome of St Paul's in London. The rounded structure is a prominent feature on the Dresden skyline.

Destruction

Dresden city centre was infamously destroyed in a massive air raid launched by British and American planes on 13 February, 1945. Over 1200 bombers hurled some 3900 tonnes of explosives on the city. The resulting firestorm killed around 25,000 people and left Dresden a smouldering shell. The Frauenkirche stood throughout the two-day raid, finally collapsing on 15 February.

Resurrection

The reconstruction work cost €180 million and was financed largely by donations raised by the Society to Promote the Reconstruction of the Church of Our Lady and Dresdner Bank. In a symbolic act of reconciliation, the cross and orb that tops the Frauenkirche were created by a British goldsmith whose father was involved in the February 1945 air raid.

A spitting image of the original, it may not bear the gravitas of age but that only slightly detracts from its festive beauty inside and out. The cupola can be climbed, and the galleried interior is a wonderful place for concerts, meditations and services. Check the website for the current schedule or stop by the Frauenkirche Visitors Centre.

Lutherhaus interior

In the Footsteps of Martin Luther, Wittenberg

Lutherstadt Wittenberg bears the name of Martin Luther (1483–1546), the man whose Ninety-Five Theses criticising certain practices of the Catholic church launched the Protestant Reformation over 500 years ago. Various Reformation-related sites dot the town.

Great For...

☑ Don't Miss

The excellent displays at the Lutherhaus.

Lutherhaus

Even those with no previous interest in the Reformation will likely be fascinated by the state-of-the-art exhibits in the **Lutherhaus** (☎03491-420 3118; www.martinluther. de; Collegienstrasse 54; adult/concession €8/6; ⊙9am-6pm), the former monastery turned Luther family home, operated as a museum since 1883. Through an engaging mix of accessible narrative, artefacts, famous oil paintings and interactive multimedia stations, you'll learn about the man, his times and his impact on world history. Highlights include Cranach's *Ten Commandments* in the refectory and an original room furnished by Luther in 1535.

Lutherhaus exterior

TAKASHI IMAGES/SHUTTERSTOCK ©

Explore Ashore

River cruises dock by the bridge, from where it's a five-minute walk north to the compact old town. You can easily spend hours wandering the sights here, so set aside at least two hours.

❶ Need to Know

The Luther sights are all very close to each other in this small town.

Schlosskirche

Did he or didn't he nail those *Ninety-Five Theses* to the door of the **Schlosskirche** (Castle Church; ☏03491-402 585; www.schloss-kirche-wittenberg.de; Schlossplatz; ⊗10am-6pm Mon-Sat, from 11.30am Sun)? We'll never know for sure, since the original portal was destroyed by fire in 1760 and replaced in 1858 with a massive bronze version inscribed with Martin Luther's theses in Latin. Luther himself is buried inside the church below the pulpit, opposite his friend and fellow reformer Philipp Melanchthon.

Stadtkirche Wittenberg

The **Stadt- und Pfarrkirche St Marien** (☏03491-628 30; www.stadtkirchengemeinde-wittenberg.de; Jüdenstrasse 35; ⊗10am-6pm Mon-Sat, from 11.30am Sun) was where Luther's ecumenical revolution began, with the world's first Protestant worship services in 1521. It was also here that Luther preached his famous Lectern sermons in 1522, and where he married ex-nun Katharina von Bora three years later. Ongoing renovations continue.

Luthereiche

This **oak tree** (Luther Oak; cnr Lutherstrasse & Am Bahnhof) marks the spot where, on 10 December 1520, Luther burned the papal bull (a treatise issued by Pope Leo X ordering his excommunication) and a number of other books on church law; the tree itself was only planted around 1830.

Prague, Czech Republic

Prague is the equal of Paris in terms of beauty, with history stretching back a millennium. The maze of cobbled lanes and hidden courtyards is a paradise for the aimless wanderer, always beckoning you to explore a little further.

◎ SIGHTS

Charles Bridge   Bridge

(Karlův most; ☺24hr; 🚊2, 17, 18 to Karlovy lázně, 12, 15, 20, 22 to Malostranské náměstí) Strolling across Charles Bridge is everybody's favourite Prague activity. However, by 9am it's a 500m-long fairground, with an army of tourists squeezing through a gauntlet of hawkers and buskers beneath the impassive gaze of the baroque statues that line the parapets. If you want to experience the bridge at its most atmospheric, try to visit it at dawn.

St Vitus Cathedral   Church

(Katedrála sv Víta; ✆257 531 622; www.katedral asvatehovita.cz; Prague Castle; ☺9am-5pm, from noon Sun, to 4pm Nov-Mar; 🚊22, 23) Built over a time span of almost 600 years, St Vitus is one of the most richly endowed cathedrals in central Europe. It is pivotal to the religious and cultural life of the Czech Republic, housing treasures that range from the 14th-century mosaic of the Last Judgement and the tombs of St Wenceslas and Charles IV, to the baroque silver tomb of St John of Nepomuk, the ornate Chapel of St Wenceslas and art nouveau stained glass by Alfons Mucha.

St Nicholas Church   Church

(Kostel sv Mikuláše; ✆257 534 215; www. stnicholas.cz; Malostranské náměstí 38; adult/ child 70/50Kč; ☺9am-5pm Mar-Oct, to 4pm rest of year; 🚊12, 15, 20, 22) Malá Strana is dominated by the huge green cupola of St Nicholas Church, one of Central Europe's finest baroque buildings. (Don't confuse it with the other Church of St Nicholas on Old Town Square.) On the ceiling, Johann Kracker's 1770 *Apotheosis of St Nicholas* is

Europe's largest fresco (clever trompe l'oeil techniques have made the painting merge almost seamlessly with the architecture).

Wenceslas Square   Square

(Václavské náměstí; Ⓜ Můstek, Muzeum) More a broad boulevard than a typical city square, Wenceslas Square has witnessed a great deal of Czech history – a giant Mass was held here during the revolutionary upheavals of 1848; in 1918 the creation of the new Czechoslovak Republic was celebrated here; and it was here in 1989 where many anticommunist protests took place. Originally a medieval horse market, the square was named after Bohemia's patron saint during the nationalist revival of the mid-19th century.

National Museum   Museum

(Národní muzeum; ✆224 497 111; www.nm.cz; Václavské náměstí 68; adult/child 250/170Kč; ☺10am-6pm; Ⓜ Muzeum) Looming above Wenceslas Square is the neo-Renaissance bulk of the National Museum, designed in the 1880s by Josef Schulz as an architectural symbol of the Czech National Revival. Its magnificent interior is a shrine to the cultural, intellectual and scientific history of the Czech Republic. The museum's main building reopened in 2018 after several years of renovation work.

Old Town Square   Square

(Ⓜ Staroměstská) FREE One of Europe's biggest and most beautiful urban spaces, Old Town Square (Staroměstské náměstí, or Staromák for short) has been Prague's principal public square since the 10th century, and was its main marketplace until the beginning of the 20th century.

Old Town Hall   Historic Building

(Staroměstská radnice; ✆236 002 629; www. staromestskaradnicepraha.cz; Staroměstské náměstí 1; adult/child 250/150Kč; ☺11am-6pm Mon, 9am-6pm Tue-Sun; Ⓜ Staroměstská) Prague's Old Town Hall, founded in 1338, is a hotchpotch of medieval buildings built piecemeal over the centuries, presided over by a tall Gothic tower with a splendid Astronomical Clock. As well as housing the Old

St Vitus Cathedral

Town's main tourist information office, the town hall has several historic attractions, and hosts art exhibitions on the ground and 2nd floors.

Prague Jewish Museum   Museum
(Židovské muzeum Praha; ☑222 749 211; www. jewishmuseum.cz; Reservation Centre, Maiselova 15; combined-entry ticket adult/child 350/250Kč; ☺9am-6pm Sun-Fri, to 4.30pm Nov-Mar; Ⓜ Staroměstská) This museum consists of six Jewish monuments clustered together in Josefov: the Maisel Synagogue; the Pinkas Synagogue; the Spanish Synagogue; the Klaus Synagogue; the Ceremonial Hall; and the Old Jewish Cemetery. There is also the Old-New Synagogue, which is still used for religious services, and requires a separate ticket or additional fee.

⊙ TOURS
AlenaGuide   Tours
(☑724 129 201; www.alenagu ide.com; tours from 2300Kč) Alena Vopalkova is a graduate of La Salle University in Philadelphia, USA, who has returned to Prague to lead private, customised tours of her home city. Subjects range from general sightseeing to more specialised tours covering the Jewish Museum, food or shopping, and from three-hour walking tours to day trips exploring off-the-beaten-track spots such as the scenic Český raj (Bohemian Paradise).

Taste of Prague   Food & Drink
(☑775 577 275; www.tasteofprague.com; per person 2700Kč) Locals Jan and Zuzi are passionate about Prague's restaurant scene. They lead four-hour foodie tours of the city, tasting trad and modern Czech dishes and drinks in a variety of venues, with intriguing asides on Czech history and culture along the way. Private one- or two-day tasting tours of Moravian vineyards can also be arranged.

World War II in Prague   Tours
(☑605 918 596; www.ww2inprague.com; per person 600Kč; ☺10am & 2pm) Highly recommended tour for anyone interested in military history, with a chance to visit the underground HQ of the Prague resistance, and compare archive photos of WWII

Central Prague

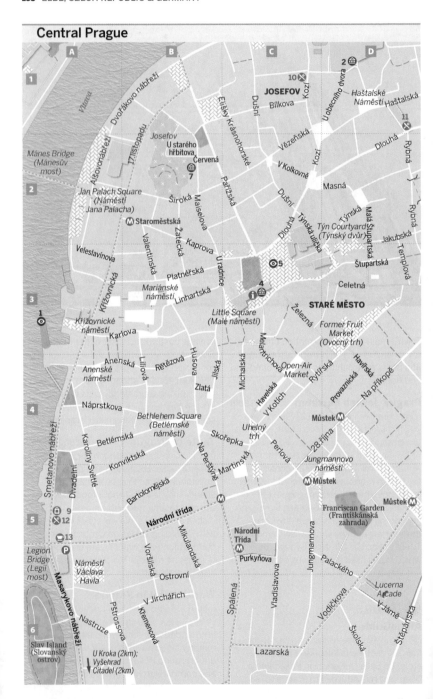

Vltava

Máltava

A **B** **C** **D**

1

Dvořákovo nábřeží

10 ✗
2 🏛
JOSEFOV

Elišky Krásnohorské

Kozí

Bílkova

U obecního dvora

Haštalské
Náměstí Haštalská

11 ✗

Dušní

Vězeňská

Josefov
U starého
hřbitova
Červená

Kozí

Dlouhá

Rybná

Máltava

Alšovo nábřeží

17.listopadu

2

Máltava

Máttava

Máttava

Máttava

Máttava

Máttava

Pařížská

V Kolkovně

Masná

Máltava

Máltava

Jan Palach Square
(Náměstí
Jana Palacha)

Maiselova

Dušní

Týnská

Malá Štupartská

Rybná

Ⓜ Staroměstská

Široká

Dlouhá

Týnská ulička

Tým Courtyard
(Týnský dvůr)

Jakubská

Templová

Žatecká

Kaprova

U radnice

5

Štupartská

Veleslavínova

Valentinská

Křižovnická

Platnéřská

Celetná

3

Mariánské
náměstí

Linhartská

4 🏛
ⓘ

STARÉ MĚSTO

1

Křížovnické
náměstí

Karlova

Little Square
(Malé náměstí)

Železná

Former Fruit
Market
(Ovocný trh)

Anenská

Liliová

Řetězová

Husova

Jilská

Michalská

Melantrichova

Open-Air
Market

Rytířská

Havířská

Na příkopě

Anenské
náměstí

Zlatá

Havelská

Provaznická

Náprstkova

V Kotcích

Můstek Ⓜ

4

Bethlehem Square
(Betlémské
náměstí)

Skořepka

Uhelný
trh

Perlová

28. října

Jungmannovo
náměstí

Můstek Ⓜ

Karolíny Světlé

Betlémská

Konviktská

Na Perštýně

Martinská

Smetanovo nábřeží

Divadelní

Bartolomějská

Národní třída Ⓜ

Můstek Ⓜ

Franciscan Garden
(Františkánská
zahrada)

5

🔒 9
✗ 12

📷 13

**Národní
Třída**
Ⓜ
Purkyňova

Mikulandská

Jungmannova

Palackého

Lucerna
Arcade

Legion
Bridge
(Legii
most)

Ⓟ

Náměstí
Václava
Havla

Voršilská

Ostrovní

Spálená

Vladislavova

Vodičkova

V Jámě

Štěpánská

V Jirchářích

Masarykovo nábřeží

Nastruze

Pštrossova

Křemencová

Školská

6

Slav Island
(Slovanský
ostrov)

U Kroka (2km);
↓ Vyšehrad
Citadel (2km)

Lazarská

Máltava

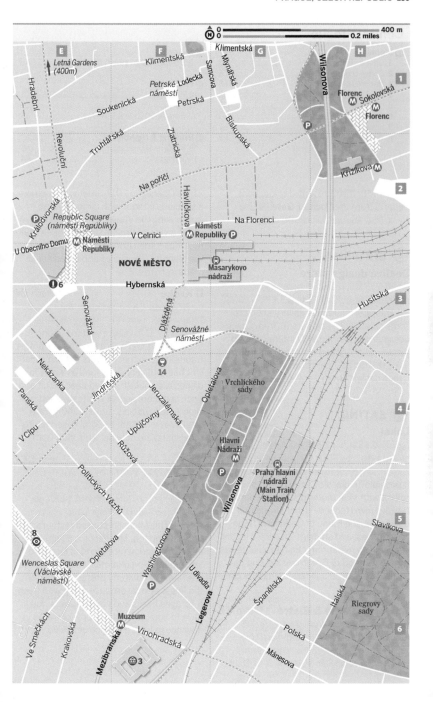

Central Prague

Prague with their present-day locations. Departs from the **Powder Gate** (Prašná brána; Na příkopě; Ⓜ Náměstí Republiky).

🔒 SHOPPING

Deelive design store   Design

(☏222 263 526; www.deelive.cz; Smetanovo nábřeží 334/4; ◷10am-8pm; 🚊3, 6, 9, 17, 18, 22, 23) This airy, minimalist gallery-shop presents carefully selected items from Czech designers, predominantly interior design pieces, jewellery and clothing. Feel free to ask the shop assistants questions about Czech design; they're enthusiasts!

⊗ EATING

Lokál   Czech €

(☏734 283 874; www.lokal-dlouha.ambi.cz; Dlouhá 33; mains 155-265Kč; ◷11am-1am, to midnight Sun; 🛜; 🚊6, 8, 15, 26) Who'd have thought it possible? A classic Czech beer hall (albeit with slick modern styling); excellent *tankové pivo* (tanked Pilsner Urquell); a daily-changing menu of traditional Bohemian dishes; and smiling, efficient, friendly service! Top restaurant chain Ambiente has turned its hand to Czech cuisine, and the result has been so successful that the place is always busy.

SmetanaQ Café & Bistro   Bistro €€

(☏722 409 757; http://smetanaq.cz/#cafe-bistro; Smetanovo nábřeží 334/4; breakfast 105-279Kč, salads 149-239Kč; ◷8am-9pm Mon-Sat, 9am-8pm Sun; 🛜; 🚊3, 6, 9, 13, 17, 18,

22, 23) Opened in 2017, SmetanaQ features a spacious interior with large windows overlooking the Vltava River and, in winter, offers a view of Prague Castle. Coffee (49Kč to 70Kč) comes from a local roaster, and the plentiful cakes, pies and bread are all made in-house.

U Kroka   Czech €€

(☏775 905 022; www.ukroka.cz; Vratislavova 12, Vyšehrad; mains 170-295Kč; ◷11am-11pm; 🛜; 🚊2, 3, 7, 17, 21) Cap a visit to historic Vyšehrad Citadel with a hearty meal at this traditional pub that delivers not just excellent beer but very good food as well. Classic dishes like goulash, boiled beef, rabbit and duck confit are served in a festive setting. Daily lunch specials (around 140Kč) are available from 11am to 3pm. Reservations (advisable) are only possible after 3pm.

Field   Czech €€€

(☏222 316 999; www.fieldrestaurant.cz; U Milosrdných 12; mains 590-620Kč, 6-course tasting menu 2800Kč; ◷11am-2.30pm & 6-10.30pm Mon-Fri, noon-3pm & 6-10pm Sat & Sun; 🛜; 🚊17) ✐ This Michelin-starred restaurant is unfussy and fun. The decor is an amusing art-meets-agriculture blend of farmyard implements and minimalist chic, while the chef creates painterly presentations from the finest of local produce along with freshly foraged herbs and edible flowers. You'll have to book at least a couple of weeks in advance to have a chance of a table.

🍸 DRINKING & NIGHTLIFE

Vinograf   Wine Bar

(📞214 214 681; www.vinograf.cz; Senovážné náměstí 23; ⏰11.30am-midnight, from 5pm Sat & Sun; 📶; 🚊3, 5, 6, 9, 14, 24) With knowledgeable staff, a relaxed atmosphere and an off-the-beaten-track feel, this appealingly modern wine bar is a great place to discover Moravian wines. There's good finger food, mostly cheese and charcuterie, to accompany your wine, with food and wine menus (in Czech and English) on big blackboards behind the bar. Very busy at weekends, when it's worth booking a table.

There's another branch in **Malá Strana** (📞604 705 730; www.vinograf.cz; Míšeňská 8; ⏰4pm-midnight Mon-Sat, 2-10pm Sun; 📶; 🚊12, 15, 20, 22).

Letná Beer Garden   Beer Garden

(📞233 378 200; www.letenskyzamecek.cz; Letenské sady 341; ⏰11am-11pm May-Sep; 🚊1, 8, 12, 25, 26) No accounting of watering holes in the neighbourhood would be complete without a nod towards the city's best beer garden, with an amazing panorama, situated at the eastern end of the **Letná Gardens** (⏰24hr; 🚻). Buy a takeaway beer from a small kiosk and grab a picnic table. Kiosks also sell small food items like chips and sandwiches.

ℹ️ INFORMATION

Prague City Tourism – Old Town Hall (Prague Welcome; 📞221 714 714; www.prague.eu; Staroměstské náměstí 1, Old Town Hall; ⏰9am-7pm, to 6pm Jan & Feb; Ⓜ️Staroměstská) The busiest of the Prague City Tourism branches occupies the ground floor of the Old Town Hall.

ℹ️ GETTING AROUND

Central Prague is easily managed on foot (though be sure to wear comfortable shoes). For longer trips, the city has a reliable public transport system of metros, trams and buses.

Where Beer is God

The best beer in the world just got better. Since the invention of Pilsner Urquell in 1842, the Czechs have been famous for producing some of the world's finest brews. But the internationally famous brand names – Urquell, Staropramen and Budvar – have been equalled, and even surpassed, by a bunch of regional Czech beers and microbreweries that are catering to a renewed interest in traditional brewing. Never before have Czech pubs offered such a wide range of brews – names you'll now have to get your head around include Kout na Šumavě, Primátor, Únětice and Matuška.

Staropramen beer
MATEUSZ_SZYMANSKI/SHUTTERSTOCK ©

The system is integrated, meaning that the same tickets are valid on all types of transport, and for transfers between them.

Walking Central Prague is compact, and individual neighbourhoods are easily explored on foot.

Tram Extensive network; best way to get around shorter distances between neighbourhoods.

Metro Fast and frequent, good for visiting outlying areas or covering longer distances.

Bus Not much use in the city centre, except when travelling to/from the airport; operates in areas not covered by tram or metro.

Taxi Relatively cheap but prone to rip-off drivers.

Dresden, Germany

There are few city silhouettes more striking than Dresden's. The classic view from the Elbe's northern bank takes in spires, towers and domes belonging to palaces, churches and stately buildings, and indeed it's hard to believe that the city was all but wiped off the map by Allied bombings in 1945.

◎ SIGHTS

Key sights cluster in the compact Altstadt on the Elbe's south bank. From here, Augustusbrücke leads across the river to the Neustadt.

Zwinger   Palace

(🕿 0351-4914 2000; www.der-dresdner-zwinger. de; Theaterplatz 1; ticket for all museums adult/ concession €12/9, courtyard free; ⏰6am-10pm Apr-Oct, to 8pm Nov-Mar) A collaboration between the architect Matthäus Pöppelmann and the sculptor Balthasar Permoser, the Zwinger was built between 1710 and 1728 on the orders of Augustus the Strong who, having returned from seeing Louis XIV's palace at Versailles, wanted something similar for himself. Primarily a party palace for royals, the Zwinger has ornate portals that lead into the vast fountain-studded courtyard, which is framed by buildings lavishly adorned with evocative sculpture. Today it houses three superb museums within its baroque walls.

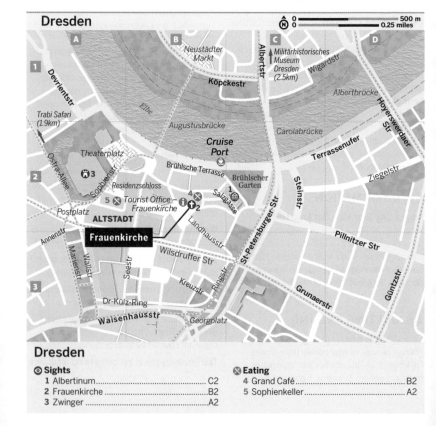

Dresden

Albertinum — Gallery

(Galerie Neue Meister; ☑0351-4914 2000; www.
skd.museum; enter from Brühlsche Terrasse
or Georg-Treu-Platz 2; adult/concession/child
under 17yr €10/7.50/free; ⊙10am-6pm Tue-Sun)
The Renaissance-era former arsenal is
the stunning home of the **Galerie Neue
Meister** (New Masters Gallery), which
displays an array of paintings by some
of the great names in art from the 18th
century onwards. Caspar David Friedrich's
and Claude Monet's landscapes compete
with the abstract visions of Marc Chagall
and Gerhard Richter, all in gorgeous rooms
orbiting a light-filled courtyard. There's also
a superb sculpture collection spread over
the lower floors.

Militärhistorisches
Museum Dresden — Museum

(☑0351-823 2803; www.mhmbw.de; Olbricht-
platz 2; adult/concession €5/3; ⊙10am-6pm
Thu-Sun & Tue, to 9pm Mon; 🚋7 or 8 to Stauffen-
bergallee) Even devout pacifists will be awed
by this engaging museum, housed in a
19th-century arsenal bisected by a bold
glass-and-steel wedge designed by Daniel
Libeskind. Exhibits have been updated for
the 21st century, so don't expect a roll call
of military victories or a parade of weapons.
Instead, you'll find a progressive – and
often artistic – look at the roots and ramifi-
cations of war and aggression.

TOURS

Trabi Safari — Driving

(☑0351-8990 0110; www.trabi-safari.de; Bremer
Strasse 35; adult/child under 17yr €49/free) Get
behind the wheel of the ultimate GDR-
mobile for this 1½-hour guided drive around
the city, taking in sights from all eras. The
price depends on the number of people in
the car; four people to a car is the best value.

EATING

Grand Café — Saxon €€

(☑0351-496 2444; www.coselpalais-dresden.
de; An der Frauenkirche 12; mains €15-20;
⊙11am-11pm) The imaginative mains (try

Dresden
& WWII

Between 13 and 15 February 1945,
British and American planes unleashed
3900 tonnes of explosives on Dresden
in four huge air raids. Bombs and incen-
diary shells whipped up a mammoth
firestorm, and ashes rained down on villages 35km away. When the blazes had
died down and the dust settled, tens of
thousands of Dresdners had lost their
lives and 20 sq km of this once-elegant
baroque city lay in smouldering ruins.

Historians still argue over whether
this constituted a war crime committed
by the Allies on an innocent civilian
population. Some claim that with the
Red Army at the gates of Berlin, the
war was effectively won, and the Allies
gained little military advantage from the
destruction of Dresden. Others have
said that, as the last urban centre in the
east of the country left intact, Dresden
could have provided shelter for German
troops returning from the east and was
a viable target.

Dresden, 1946
SPUTNIK/ALAMY STOCK PHOTO ©

roasted pike-perch on crispy Dijon mustard
rösti with lemon and vegetables) and
sumptuous cakes are good, but they act
more as appetisers for the gold-trimmed
baroque Coselpalais, which houses the cafe
and makes for a stylish (if slightly formal)
refuelling stop.

Sophienkeller — Saxon €€

(☑0351-497 260; www.sophienkeller-dresden.
de; Taschenberg 3; mains €12-20; ⊙11am-1am)

The 1730s theme, complete with waitresses trussed up in period garb, may be a bit overcooked, but the local specialities certainly aren't. It's mostly rib-sticking fare, such as the boneless half-duck with red cabbage or the spit-roasted suckling pig. Wash it down with a mug of dark Bohemian Krušovice, and enjoy the ambience of vaulted ceilings in the Taschenbergpalais building.

ℹ INFORMATION

Tourist Office – Frauenkirche (☎0351-501 501; www.dresden.de; QF Passage, Neumarkt 2; ⊙10am-7pm Mon-Fri, to 6pm Sat, to 3pm Sun) Go to the basement of the shopping mall to find the city's most central tourist office, with helpful English-speaking staff.

ℹ GETTING AROUND

Buses and trams are run by **Dresdner Verkehrsbetriebe** (DVB; ☎0351-857 1011; www.dvb.de/en). Fares within town cost €2.30, and a day pass €6, valid until 4am the following morning. Buy tickets from vending machines at stops or aboard trams, and remember to validate them in the machines provided.

Lutherstadt Wittenberg, Germany

As its full name suggests, Wittenberg is first and foremost about Martin Luther, the monk who triggered the German Reformation by publishing his *Ninety-Five Theses* against church corruption in 1517, as the story goes, by provocatively nailing it to the door of the Schlosskirche in this very town.

◎ SIGHTS

Melanchthon Haus Museum
(☎03491-420 3110; www.martinluther.de; Collegienstrasse 60; adult/concession €5/2.50; ⊙10am-6pm) This museum, expanded in 2013, occupies the former quarters of Philipp Melanchthon, an expert in ancient languages who helped Luther translate the Bible into German from Greek and Hebrew, becoming the preacher's friend and most eloquent advocate. The historic wing

Melanchthon Haus

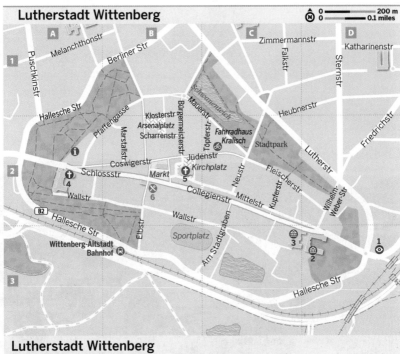

Lutherstadt Wittenberg

authentically recreates the atmosphere in which Melanchthon lived. The modern annex houses an exhibition on his life, work and influence.

⊗ EATING

Brauhaus Wittenberg   German €€

(☏03491-433 130; www.brauhaus-wittenberg. de; Markt 6, Im Beyerhof; mains €8-18; ⊙11am-11pm) Wittenberg's brewhouse, with its cobbled courtyard, indoor brewery and shiny copper vats, thrums with the noise of people having a good time. The menu is hearty, but also features smaller dishes for waist-watchers. Oh, and there's beer also. Lots of fun.

ⓘ INFORMATION

Lutherstadt Wittenberg Tourist Office

(☏03491-498 610; www.lutherstadt-wittenberg. de/en/service/tourist-information; Schlossplatz 2; ⊙9am-6pm Mon-Fri, 10am-4pm Sat & Sun)

ⓘ GETTING AROUND

The town is easily explored on foot or by bike.

For bike rental, try **Fahrradhaus Kralisch** (☏03941-403 703; www.fahrradhaus-kralisch.de; Jüdenstrasse 11; bikes per 24hr €9; ⊙9am-6pm Mon-Fri, to noon Sat).

MOSELLE, GERMANY

Moselle, Germany

Having traversed France and Luxembourg, the Moselle heads through Germany to meet its destiny with the Rhine at Koblenz. It's a very pretty stretch of river flanked by vineyards, and makes for great leisurely cruising and exploration. With an astounding nine Unesco World Heritage Sites, gorgeous Trier shelters Germany's finest ensemble of Roman monuments, and is enlivened by a characterful medieval centre and large student population. Bernkastel-Kues are lovely twin settlements in the heart of wine country, while Cochem's castle and pretty buildings make it a visual highlight of the Moselle.

With One Day in Trier

With a day in Trier, focus on the **Roman sites** (p170). The amphitheatre, Porta Nigra, Kaiserthermen and the Konstantin Basilika are the must-see sites. In the afternoon, visit the adjacent **cathedral** and **Liebfrauenbasilika** (p174) for a contrast, then check out the beautiful buildings around the nearby **Hauptmarkt** (p174).

Best Places for...

Food Weinwirtschaft Friedrich-Wilhelm, Trier (p175)

Museum Rheinisches Landesmuseum, Trier (p174)

Wine Tasting Mosel Vinothek, Bernkastel-Kues (p172)

Wine Shopping VinoForum, Cochem (p179)

Potatoes Kartoffel Kiste, Trier (p175)

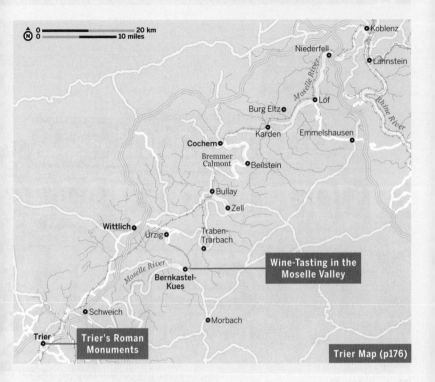

Getting from the Ports

Trier Cruise ships dock at the Zurlauben area, north of the centre, about a 1.5km walk to the heart of the old town. Buses run from the nearby bridge.

Bernkastel-Kues Ships dock on the eastern bank close to the heart of Bernkastel. Kues is a short walk across the bridge.

Cochem Cruises dock right by the spectacular old town.

Fast Facts

Currency Euro (€)

Language German

Free Wi-fi Most bars and cafes offer free networks.

Money ATMs are common in each of the towns.

Tourist Information The Trier tourist office is at the Porta Nigra. The office in Bernkastel-Kues is on the Bernkastel side of the river. Cochem's office is on Endertplatz.

Porta Nigra

Trier's Roman Monuments

A Unesco-protected site, Germany's oldest city is home to its finest ensemble of Roman monuments, among them a mighty gate, amphitheatre, thermal baths, imperial throne room, and the country's oldest bishop's church, which retains Roman sections.

Great For...

☑ **Don't Miss**

The Konstantin Basilika's new organ has 6500 pipes and generates a sevenfold echo.

Porta Nigra

Blackened by time (the name is Latin for 'black gate'), this brooding 2nd-century **Roman city gate** (adult/child €4/2.50; ⊘9am-6pm Apr-Sep, to 5pm Mar & Oct, to 4pm Nov-Feb) is a marvel of engineering held together by gravity and iron clamps.

In the 11th century it was turned into a church to honour Simeon, a Greek hermit who spent six years walled up in the east tower. After his death in 1134, he was buried inside the gate and later became a saint.

Konstantin Basilika

Constructed around AD 310 as Constantine's throne room, the brick-built **basilica** (Constantine's Throne Room; ☏0651-9949 1200; www.konstantin-basilika.de; Konstantinplatz 10; ⊘10am-6pm Mon-Sat, 1-6pm Sun Apr-Oct, 10am-noon & 2-4pm Tue-Sat, 1-3pm Sun Nov-Mar) FREE

Konstantin Basilika

Explore Ashore

It's about a 1.5km walk from the dock north of the centre to the heart of the old town. Alternatively, catch a bus (87 works) from near the bridge just south of the dock. You can spend half a day easily taking in all the monuments.

❶ Need to Know
The three-day TrierCard (€9.90) gives 10% to 25% off museum and monument admissions, and unlimited use of public transport.

is now an austere Protestant church. With built-to-impress dimensions (67m long, 27m wide and 33m high), it's the largest single-room Roman structure in existence.

Amphitheatre

The **amphitheatre** (Olewiger Strasse; adult/child €4/2.50; ⏱9am-6pm Apr-Sep, to 5pm Mar & Oct, to 4pm Nov-Feb) could accommodate 20,000 spectators for gladiator tournaments and animal fights. Beneath the arena are dungeons, where prisoners waited next to starving beasts for the final showdown.

Kaiserthermen

Consider the layout of this vast Roman **thermal bathing complex** (Imperial Baths; Weberbachstrasse 41; adult/child €4/2.50; ⏱9am-6pm Apr-Sep, to 5pm Mar & Oct, to 4pm Nov-Feb), with its striped brick-and-stone

arches, from the corner lookout tower, then descend into an underground labyrinth of cavernous hot- and cold-water baths, boiler rooms and heating channels.

Römerbrücke

Spanning the Mosel, Germany's oldest **bridge** (Roman Bridge; Karl Marx Strasse) uses 2nd-century stone pilings (AD 144–52), built from black basalt from the Eifel mountains, which have been holding it up since legionnaires crossed on chariots.

Thermen am Viehmarkt

Found by accident in 1987 during the construction of a parking garage – buried beneath WWII air-raid shelters, the remains of a 17th-century Capuchin monastery, one-time vineyards and cemeteries – these **thermal baths** (Forum Baths; Viehmarktplatz; adult/child €4/2.50; ⏱9am-5pm Tue-Sun) are sheltered by a dramatic glass cube.

Vineyard on the Moselle

JÖRG GREUEL/GETTY IMAGES ©

Wine Tasting in the Moselle Valley

Disciples of the grape will love the Moselle, where you can sample arguably the country's best whites as you cruise the river. Bernkastel-Kues has some of the best wine experiences, with Cochem a close second.

Great For...

☑ **Don't Miss**

Try some of the less well-known grape types such as Elbling, Dornfelder and Kerner.

Mosel-Weinmuseum

Part of the St-Nikolaus-Hospital (p177) complex, the small **Mosel-Weinmuseum** (Moselle Wine Museum; ☎06531-4141; www.moselweinmuseum.de; Cusanusstrasse 2, Kues; adult/child €5/2.50; ⊙10am-6pm mid-Apr–Oct, 2-5pm Nov–mid-Apr) has interactive screens (best appreciated by German speakers) and features such as an Aromabar (you have to guess what you're smelling). The main event, though, is the cellar of the adjacent **Mosel Vinothek** (☎06531-4141; www.moselvinothek.de; Cusanusstrasse 2; wine tasting per person summer/winter €18/12; ⊙10am-6pm Apr-Oct, 11am-5pm Feb, Mar, Nov & Dec), where you can indulge in an 'all you can drink' wine tasting (€18) with about 150 vintages to choose from. In winter the selection is more limited, but tastings cost just €12.

Weinstube Spitzhäuschen

FOTO-SELECT/SHUTTERSTOCK ©

Explore Ashore

Most of these attractions are close to the bridge in Bernkastel-Kues, a short walk from where the boats tie up. To spread out your wine consumption, allow half a day for these sights.

❶ Need to Know

A wine route map is available from all of the region's tourist offices.

Weingut Dr Pauly-Bergweiler

Tastings of renowned wines produced by **Dr Pauly-Bergweiler** (📞06531-3002; www. pauly-bergweiler.com; Gestade 15; wine tastings €11.50; ⊙wine tastings by reservation 1-6pm Mon-Fri, from 2pm Sat) can take place in an atmospheric vaulted cellar, chapel and baroque hall. It's popular with groups, so book ahead.

Weinstube Spitzhäuschen

Wine bars don't come cuter than this crooked half-timbered **building** (📞06531-7476; www.spitzhaeuschen.de; Karlstrasse 13, Bernkastel; ⊙4-10pm Mon-Fri, from 3pm Sat & Sun Easter-Oct, 3-10pm Sat Nov-Dec, other times by appointment). The Moselle's oldest (dating from 1416), it resembles a giant bird's house: its narrow base is topped by a much larger, precariously leaning upper floor that allowed carriages to pass through the narrow alley to the marketplace. Taste over 50 of the Schmitz family's local wines; small snacks are also available.

VinoForum

Barrels are suspended from the ceiling at this ultra-contemporary Vinothek (p179). Taste and buy exceptional wines made from grapes grown on the hillside behind and in the surrounding area, and look out for events, such as brunches, dinners and jazz concerts on the elevated terrace overlooking the Moselle. It's in the hamlet of Ernst, 4km east of Cochem.

Trier

With an astounding nine Unesco World Heritage Sites, Germany's oldest city shelters the country's finest ensemble of Roman monuments, among them a mighty gate, amphitheatre, elaborate thermal baths, imperial throne room, and the country's oldest bishop's church, which retains Roman sections.

◉ SIGHTS

Liebfrauenbasilika   Church

(Church of Our Lady; www.trierer-dom.de; Lieb-frauenstrasse; ◷10am-6pm Mon-Fri, to 4.30pm Sat, 12.30-6pm Sun Apr-Oct, 11am-5pm Mon-Fri, to 4.30pm Sat, 12.30-5pm Sun Nov-Mar) Germany's oldest Gothic church was built in the 13th century. It has a cruciform structure supported by a dozen pillars symbolising the 12 Apostles (look for the black stone from where all 12 articles of the Apostle's Creed painted on the columns are visible) and some colourful postwar stained glass.

Trierer Dom   Cathedral

(☏0651-979 0790; www.trierer-dom.de; Liebfrau-enstrasse 12; ◷6.30am-6pm Apr-Oct, to 5.30pm Nov-Mar) Looming above the Roman palace of Helena (Emperor Constantine's mother), this cathedral is Germany's oldest bishop's church and still retains Roman sections. Today's edifice is a study in nearly 1700 years of church architecture with Romanesque, Gothic and baroque elements. Intriguingly, its floorplan is of a 12-petalled flower, symbolising the Virgin Mary.

To see some dazzling ecclesiastical equipment and peer into early Christian history, head upstairs to the **Domschatz** (Cathedral Treasury; ☏0651-710 5378; www. trierer-dom.de/bauwerk/domschatz; adult/ child €1.50/0.50; ◷10am-5pm Mon-Sat, from 12.30pm Sun Apr-Oct & Dec, 11am-4pm Tue-Sat, from 12.30pm Sun Nov & Jan-Mar) or around the corner to the **Museum am Dom Trier** (☏0651-710 5255; www.bistum-trier.de/ museum; Bischof-Stein-Platz 1; adult/child €3.50/2; ◷9am-5pm Tue-Sat, from 1pm Sun).

Rheinisches Landesmuseum   Museum

(Roman Archaeological Museum; www.landes museum-trier.de; Weimarer Allee 1; adult/child incl audio guide €8/4; ◷10am-5pm Tue-Sun) A scale model of 4th-century Trier and rooms filled with tombstones, mosaics, rare gold coins (including the 1993-discovered Trier Gold Hoard, the largest preserved Roman gold hoard in the world, with over 2600 gold coins) and some fantastic glass are highlights of this museum, which affords an extraordinary look at local Roman life.

Hauptmarkt   Square

Anchored by a 1595 fountain dedicated to St Peter and the Four Virtues, Trier's central market square is surrounded by medieval and Renaissance architectural treasures such as the **Rotes Haus** (Red House; Diet-richstrasse 53; ◷interior closed to the public), and the **Steipe**, which now houses the **Spielzeugmuseum** (Toy Museum; ☏0651-758 50; www.spielzeugmuseum-trier.de; adult/child €5/2.50; ◷11am-5pm Tue-Sun; ⊞), as well as the Gothic **St-Gangolf-Kirche** (◷7am-6pm).

Small market stalls (flowers, sausages etc) set up most days, except Sunday.

Museum Karl-Marx-Haus   Museum

(www.fes.de/museum-karl-marx-haus; Brück-enstrasse 10; adult/child €5/3.50; ◷9am-6pm Apr-Oct, 1-5pm Mon, 10am-5pm Tue-Sun Nov-Mar) Revamped in 2018 on the 200th anniversary of Marx' birth, the early-18th-century baroque townhouse in which the author of *The Communist Manifesto* and *Das Kapital* was born in 1818 now houses exhibits covering his life, work, allies and enemies, social democracy, his decades of exile in London, where he died in 1883, and his intellectual and political legacy.

⊕ TOURS & ACTIVITIES

City Walking Tour   Walking

(adult/child €7.90/4.50; ◷1pm May-Oct) Guided 75-minute walking tours in English begin at the tourist office.

Weinkulturpfad · Hiking

(Wine Culture Path) Panoramic views unfold from **Petrisberg**, the vine-covered hill just east of the Roman amphitheatre. Halfway up, the Weinkulturpfad leads through the grapes to Olewig (1.6km). Next to the Petrisberg/Aussicht stop for buses 4 and 85, a **multilingual panel** (Sickingenstrasse) traces local history from the first known human habitation (30,000 years ago) through the last ice age to the Romans.

Radstation · Cycling

(Fahrradservicestation; ☏0651-148 856; www.bues-trier.de; Bahnhofsplatz; adult/child/electric bike per day from €12/6/30; ☺9am-6pm May-Sep, 10am-6pm Mon-Fri, to 2pm Sat Oct-Apr) Bikes in tip-top condition can be rented at the Hauptbahnhof's Radstation, next to track 11. Staff are enthusiastic about cycling and can provide tips on routes.

EATING

Kartoffel Kiste · German €

(www.kistetrier.de; Fahrstrasse 13-14; mains €7-17; ☺11.30am-10pm; 🅿🧒) Fronted by a bronze fountain, local favourite Kartoffel Kiste specialises, as its name suggests, in baked, breaded, gratinéed, soupified and sauce-doused potatoes. If you're after something heartier (albeit pricier), it also does great schnitzel and steaks. There are 220 seats inside and, in warmer weather, another 120 on the terrace.

Weinwirtschaft Friedrich-Wilhelm · German €€

(☏0651-994 7480; www.weinwirtschaft-fw.de; Weberbach 75; mains €12.50-27.50; ☺11.30am-2.30pm & 5.30-10pm Mon-Fri, 11.30am-10pm Sat & Sun) A historical former wine warehouse with exposed brick and joists now houses this superb restaurant. Creative dishes incorporate local wines, such as trout poached in sparkling white wine with mustard sauce and white asparagus, or local sausage with Riesling sauerkraut and fried potatoes. Vines trail over the trellis-covered garden; the attached wine shop is a great place to stock up.

Alt Zalawen · German €€

(☏0651-286 45; www.altzalawen.de; Zurlaubener Ufer 79; mains €6-18; ☺kitchen 11am-10pm, closed Sun Nov-Mar; 🐀) The pick of the cluster of bar-restaurants right on the riverfront, with terraces extending to the path running along the grassy bank, timber-panelled Alt Zalawen is a picturesque spot for traditional German specialities (schnitzels, sausages, *Spätzle*) and local Trierer Viez cider. If you're here in December, it's fêted for its roast goose.

Weinhaus Becker · International €€€

(☏0651-938 080; www.beckers-trier.de; Olewiger Strasse 206; 1-/3-course lunch menu €18/28, 3-/4-course dinner menu €45/58, mains €21-34; ☺noon-2pm & 6-10pm Tue-Sun) Within the Becker's hotel complex, 3km southeast of the centre, this supremely elegant wine-house serves sublime internationally influenced dishes like cod with pumpkin, banana and macadamia nuts, or quail with parsnip foam and roasted mushrooms, accompanied by (very) local wines made from grapes grown on the hillside opposite. Also here is the ultragourmet, twin-Michelin-starred **Becker's Restaurant** (☏0651-938 080; 5-/8-course dinner menu €125/158; ☺7-9pm Tue-Sat).

ℹ INFORMATION

Tourist Office (☏0651-978 080; www.trier-info.de; An der Porta Nigra; ☺9am-6pm Mon-Sat, 10am-5pm Sun Mar-Dec, 10am-5pm Mon-Sat Jan & Feb)

ℹ GETTING AROUND

The city centre is easily explored on foot. Buses (www.vrt-info.de) cost €2; a public transport day pass costs €5.90. The Olewig wine district is served by buses 6, 16 and 81. There are bus stops on Bahnhofsplatz.

Bikes can be rented at the Hauptbahnhof's Radstation, next to track 11, and from the tourist office, as well as many hotels.

Trier

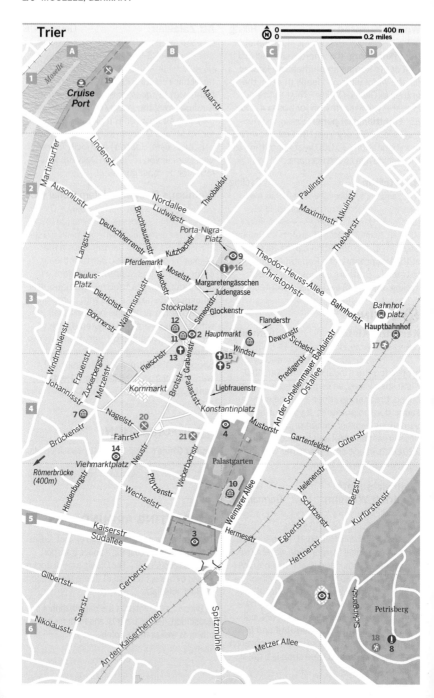

0 ——— 400 m
0 ——— 0.2 miles

A · B · C · D

Moselle

Cruise Port 19

Martinsurferr
Ausoniustr
Lindenstr
Langstr
Deutschherrenstr
Nordallee
Maarstr
Theobaldstr
Ludwigstr
Bruchhausenstr
Paulinstr
Maximinstr
Alkuinstr
Thebäerstr
Porta-Nigra-Platz 9
16
Kutzbachstr
Pferdemarkt
Paulus-Platz
Dietrichstr
Böhmerstr
Walramsneustr
Jakobstr
Moselstr
Simeonstr
Theodor-Heuss-Allee
Christophstr
Bahnhofstr
Margaretengässchen
Judengasse
Stockplatz
Glockenstr
Flanderstr
12
11 2 **Hauptmarkt** 6
Deworastr
Sichelstr
Predigerstr
An der Schellenmauer
Baldiunstr
Ostallee
13
15
5
Windstr
Liebfrauenstr
Kornmarkt
Brotstr
Grabenstr
Palaststr
Fleischstr
Frauenstr
Zuckerbergstr
Metzelstr
Windmühlenstr
Johannisstr
7
Nagelstr
20
Konstantinplatz
Mustorstr
4
Gartenfeldstr
Güterstr
Brückenstr
Fahrstr
14
21
Neustr
Weberbachstr
Palastgarten
10
Helenenstr
Schützenstr
Egbertstr
Bergstr
Kurfürstenstr
Viehmarktplatz
Römerbrücke (400m)
Pfützenstr
Wechselstr
Weimarer Allee
Hinderburgstr
Kaiserstr
Südallee
3
Hermesstr
Hettnerstr
Gilbertstr
Gerberstr
Saarstr
Nikolausstr
An den Kaiserthermen
Spitzmühle
Metzer Allee
Sickingenstr
1
Petrisberg
18
8

Bahnhof-platz
Hauptbahnhof
17

Trier

Bernkastel-Kues

These charming twin towns are the hub of the *Mittelmosel* (Middle Moselle) region. Bernkastel, on the right (eastern) bank, is a symphony in half-timber, stone and slate, and teems with wine taverns. Kues, the birthplace of theologian Nicolaus Cusanus (1401–64), is less quaint but is home to some key historical sights and has a lovely riverfront promenade.

SIGHTS

Burg Landshut
Ruins

(☏06531-972 770; www.burglandshut.de; Bernkastel; ☺noon-9pm Thu-Tue) A rewarding way to get your heart pumping is heading from the Marktplatz up to this ruined 13th-century castle, framed by vineyards and forests on a bluff above Bernkastel. It's a very steep 750m from town; allow 30 minutes. You'll be rewarded with glorious valley views. The spectacularly renovated restaurant was unveiled in 2018; during restoration, a 4th-century Roman tower's foundations were also discovered. An hourly shuttle bus from the riverfront costs €5 uphill, €3.50 downhill, or €7 return.

Marktplatz
Square

Bernkastel's pretty Marktplatz, a block inland from the bridge, is enclosed by a romantic ensemble of half-timbered houses with beautifully decorated gables. Look for the iron handcuffs, to which criminals were attached, on the facade of the 1608-built Rathaus.

St-Nikolaus-Hospital
Historic Building

(www.cusanus.de; Cusanusstrasse 2, Kues; guided tour €7; ☺9am-6pm Sun-Fri, to 3pm Sat, guided tour 10.30am Tue & 3pm Fri Apr-Oct) **FREE** Most of Kues' sights, including the Mosel-Weinmuseum (p172) and Mosel Vinothek (p172), are conveniently grouped near the bridge in the late-Gothic St-Nikolaus-Hospital, an old-age home founded by Cusanus in 1458 for 33 men (one for every year of Jesus' life). You're free to explore the cloister and Gothic *Kapelle* (chapel) at leisure, but the treasure-filled library can only be seen on a guided tour.

⊙ TOURS

MTB Trailscout
Cycling

(☏017 620 730 681; www.mtbtour-mosel.de; tours from €25; ☺Easter-Oct) Guided mountain-bike tours offer a local perspective of the valley (English tours are possible by arrangement). Two- to three-hour beginner tours cover 25km; experienced (and fit!) mountain bikers can take a challenging six-hour, 50km tour. Departure points vary. Rates don't include bikes or compulsory helmets; rent both from Fun Bike Team, or **Fahrräder Wildmann** (☏06532-954 367; www.fahrraeder-wildmann.de; Uferallee 55, Zeltingen-Rachtig; standard/electric bike hire per

Reichsburg, Cochem

day €10/22, bike transport from €80; ☺9am-noon & 4-6pm Wed-Mon Apr-Oct, shorter hours Nov-Mar).

🔒 SHOPPING

Bonbon Willi Food

(www.bonbon-willi.de; Burgstrasse 8, Bernkastel; ☺11am-5.30pm Mon-Sat) Watch sweets being boiled and crafted using century-old techniques and tools at this traditional shop. Some of the more unusual flavours include Riesling and *Federweiser* (red wine); it also makes liquorice, marzipan and chocolates.

🍴 EATING

Restaurant Burg Landshut German €€

(☎06531-972 770; www.burglandshut.de; Burg Landshut, Bernkastel; mains €14-25; ☺noon-2pm & 6-9pm Thu-Tue Easter-Nov) Opened in 2018 in the ruined castle Burg Landshut, this state-of-the-art restaurant is worth the steep climb (or shuttle-bus ride) for modern German cuisine such as sauerkraut and blood-sausage soup, and pike-perch with bacon and cabbage mash, topped off by desserts like Black Forest mousse with berry coulis and Riesling sorbet with poached local peaches. Panoramic views unfold over town.

Rotisserie Royale European €€

(☎06531-6572; www.rotisserie-royale.de; Burgstrasse 19, Bernkastel; mains €14.50-24.50, 5-course dinner menu €46.50; ☺noon-2pm & 5-9pm Thu-Tue) Seriously good cooking inside this half-timbered house spans starters like pan-fried foie gras on a potato-and-apple rösti or sautéed calf's liver with black truffle foam, followed by mains such as catfish-stuffed cabbage with white asparagus mousse, and desserts like chocolate ganache on eggnog foam with walnut sorbet to finish.

ℹ️ INFORMATION

Tourist Office (☎06531-500 190; www.bern kastel.de; Gestade 6, Bernkastel; audio guides 3hr/1 day €6/8; ☺9am-5pm Mon-Fri, from 10am Sat, to 1pm Sun May-Oct, 9.30am-4pm Mon-Fri

Nov-Apr) Has an ATM and rents out audio guides to explore the two towns.

GETTING AROUND

In Bernkastel, **Fun Bike Team** (📞06531-940 24; www.funbiketeam.de; Schanzstrasse 22, Bernkastel; standard/electric bike per day €12/25; 🕐9am-1pm & 2-6.30pm Mon-Fri, 9am-2pm Sat Apr-Oct, shorter hours Nov-Mar) rents bikes.

The town is quite compact across both sides of the river, and can easily be seen on foot.

Cochem

Cochem, with its bank of pastel-coloured, terrace-fronted restaurants lining the waterfront, tangle of narrow alleyways and dramatic castle precipitously perched on a rock, is one of the Moselle's most visited towns.

SIGHTS

Reichsburg   Castle

(📞02671-255; www.reichsburg-cochem.de; Schlossstrasse 36; tours adult/child €6/3; 🕐tours 9am-5pm mid-Mar–Oct, shorter hours Nov–mid-Mar) Like many others in the area, Cochem's original 11th-century castle fell victim to French troops in 1689, then stood ruined for centuries until wealthy Berliner Louis Ravene snapped it up for a pittance in 1868 and had it restored to its current – if not always architecturally faithful – glory. The 40-minute tours (some in English; leaflet/audio guide otherwise available) take in the decorative rooms that reflect 1000 years' worth of tastes and styles.

Bundesbank Bunker   Historic Site

(📞02671-915 3540; www.bundesbank-bunker.de; Am Wald 35; adult/child €10/5, shuttle bus one-way/return €2.50/4; 🕐tours hourly 11am-3pm May-Oct, 2hr 11am-4pm Nov-Apr) Camouflaged as residential buildings and built to survive a nuclear war, this extraordinary Cold War secret bunker owned by the German Federal Bank was stocked with 15 billion Deutsche Marks to roll out in the event of war. One-hour guided tours descend 100 steps into the bunker, where the year-round temperature is 12°C (bring a jacket). From May to October, shuttle buses run from the tourist office; otherwise it's a steep 1km walk or drive from the centre.

SHOPPING

VinoForum   Wine

(📞02671-917 1777; www.vinoforum-ernst.de; Moselstrasse 12-13, Ernst; 🕐10am-6pm Apr-Oct, 1-5pm Nov-Mar) Barrels are suspended from the ceiling at this ultra-contemporary *Vinothek*. Taste and buy exceptional wines made from grapes grown on the hillside behind and in the surrounding area, and look out for events, such as brunches, dinners and jazz concerts on the elevated terrace overlooking the Moselle. It's in the hamlet of Ernst, 4km east of Cochem.

EATING

Alt Thorschenke   German €€

(📞02671-7059; www.thorschenke.de; Brücken-strasse 3; mains €10.50-19; 🕐11am-9pm; 🛜) Wedged into the old medieval walls, away from the busy riverfront restaurants, Alt Thorschenke is a diamond find for regional specialities, such as herring with apple and onions, pork neck with mustard-cream sauce, and several different types of schnitzel – accompanied by wines from local producers.

INFORMATION

Tourist Office (📞02671-600 40; www.ferien land-cochem.de; Endertplatz 1; 🕐9am-5pm Mon-Sat, 10am-3pm Sun mid-Jun–Sep, shorter hours Oct–mid-Jun)

Getting Around

Cochem is best navigated on foot, with the sights easily reachable via walking along and across the river, via the picturesque waterfront.

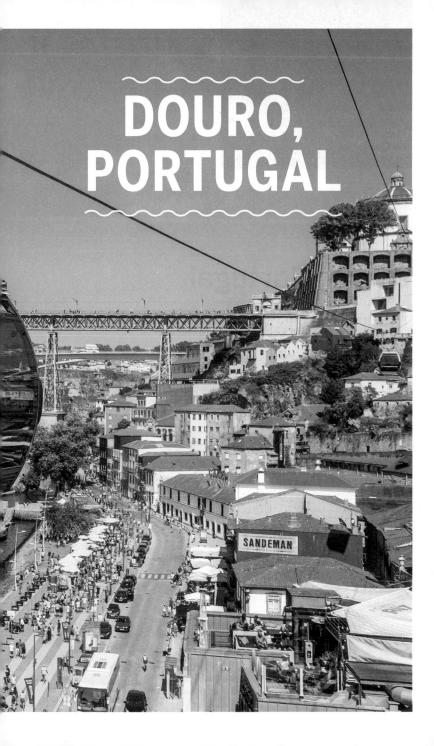

DOURO, PORTUGAL

Douro, Portugal

The Douro region, home to port wine, is simply one of the most glorious spots on earth. The Douro Valley showcases steep terrace vineyards carved into mountains, granite bluffs, whitewashed quintas (estates) and 18th-century wine cellars that draw visitors from around the world. Humble-yet-opulent Porto entices with its higgledy-piggledy medieval centre, divine food and wine, and charismatic locals. Its charms are as subtle as the nuances of an aged tawny port, best savoured slowly.

With One Day in Porto

Begin with knockout views of the historic centre from the **Sé** (p184), the city's fortress-like Romanesque cathedral. From here, dive into Ribeira's knot of alleys, passing sorbet-hued townhouses, which topple haphazardly down the hillside, then nip into the **Igreja da Misericórdia** (p188) for a glimpse at the church's extraordinary tiles. After lunch, walk across the top level of the bridge to reach **Jardim do Morro** (p187) for precipitous views of Ribeira. Swing down to Vila Nova da Gaia's **waterfront** (p186) in the cable car, then hit one of the **port wine lodges** (p186) for a cellar tour and tasting.

Best Places for...

Port Graham's, Porto (p186)

Wine Prova, Porto (p196)

Food DOP, Porto (p195)

Baroque Igreja de São Francisco, Porto (p184)

Gallery Museu Nacional Soares dos Reis, Porto (p190)

Previous page: View of Ponte de Dom Luís I from the Teleférico de Gaia cable car (p187)
Benny Marty/shutterstock ©

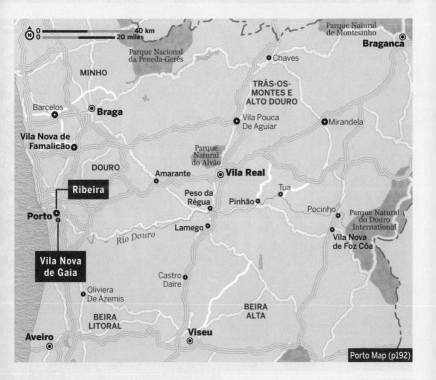

Porto Map (p192)

Getting from the Ports

Porto Most cruises are berthed at Cais de Gaia, in front of the port lodges on the south side of the river in the centre. Some moor at Freixo, around 3km east of the centre.

Peso da Régua The quaint old town is one block uphill from the scenic riverfront. Wineries are best visited by an arranged tour.

Pinhão Cruises dock at the small waterfront on the north bank. Most companies arrange for winery visits from the ship, and the town centre is only a short stroll away.

Fast Facts

Currency Euro (€)

Language Portuguese

Free Wi-fi Many cafes, bars and restaurants in Porto offer free wi-fi, and there's a free public network in the centre of town. Upriver, it's a lot scarcer.

Money ATMs are widespread. Not all small, family-run shops, restaurants and guesthouses accept credit cards.

Tourist Information Porto's main tourist office is in the city centre. In Peso da Régua, it faces the river west of the Museo do Douro. The tiny *turismo* in Pinhão is almost never open.

Igreja de São Francisco

ROB VAN ESCH/SHUTTERSTOCK ©

Ribeira

Ribeira is Porto's biggest heart-stealer, with its Unesco World Heritage maze of medieval alleys zigzagging down to the Rio Douro. Exploring this postcard-perfect neighbourhood is a must for every visitor.

Great For...

☑ Don't Miss

Ponte de Dom Luís I – admire, photograph and walk across Porto's main bridge.

Churches & Palaces

Sitting on Praça Infante Dom Henrique, **Igreja de São Francisco** (Jardim do Infante Dom Henrique; adult/child €6/5; ⊘9am-8pm Jul-Sep, to 7pm Mar-Jun & Oct, to 5.30pm Nov-Feb) looks from the outside to be an austerely Gothic church, but inside it hides one of Portugal's most dazzling displays of baroque finery. Hardly a centimetre escapes unsmothered, as otherworldly cherubs and sober monks are drowned by nearly 100kg of gold leaf.

Porto's **Sé** (Terreiro da Sé; cloisters adult/student €3/2; ⊘9am-7pm Mon-Sat, 9.30am-12.30pm & 2.30-7pm Sun Apr-Oct, 9am-6pm Mon-Sat, 9am-12.30pm & 2.30-6pm Sun Nov-Mar) is a hulking, hilltop fortress of a cathedral, founded in the 12th century though largely

Palácio da Bolsa

⚓ Explore Ashore

Many travellers base themselves near here before beginning the cruise. The principal berth is just across the bridge at Cais de Gaia. Leave a few hours to enjoy the winding streets.

❶ Need to Know

The local metro stop is São Bento (yellow metro line D).

rebuilt a century later and extensively altered during the 18th century. You can still make out the church's Romanesque origins in the barrel-vaulted nave. Inside, a rose window and a 14th-century Gothic cloister remain from its early days.

The splendid neoclassical **Palácio da Bolsa** (Stock Exchange; www.palaciodabolsa. com; Rua Ferreira Borges; tours adult/child €10/6.50; ◷9am-6.30pm Apr-Oct, 9am-12.30pm & 2-5.30pm Nov-Mar) honours Porto's past and present money merchants. Just beyond the entrance is the glass-domed Pátio das Nações (Hall of Nations), where the exchange once operated. But this pales in comparison with rooms deeper inside; to visit these, join one of the half-hour guided tours (every 30 minutes).

Ponte de Dom Luís I

Completed in 1886 by a student of Gustave Eiffel, this **bridge's** top deck is now reserved for pedestrians, as well as one of the city's metro lines; the lower deck bears regular traffic, as well as narrow walkways for those on foot. The views of the river and old town are simply stunning, as are the daredevils who leap from the lower level. Prior to the bridge's construction, the area's foot traffic navigated a bridge made from old port boats lashed together.

Cais da Ribeira

This riverfront **promenade** is postcard Porto, taking in the whole spectacular sweep of the city, from Ribeira's pastel houses stacked like Lego bricks to the barcos rabelos (flat-bottomed boats) once used to transport port from the Douro. Early-evening buskers serenade crowds and chefs fire up grills in the hole-in-the-wall fish restaurants and tascas (taverns) in the old arcades.

Graham's

M.SCERERA/ALAMY STOCK PHOTO ©

Vila Nova de Gaia

Vila Nova de Gaia (simply 'Gaia' to locals) takes you back to the 17th-century beginnings of port-wine production, when British merchants transformed wine into the post-dinner tipple of choice. Sampling port-wine is one of the main reasons to head to Porto, and Gaia is the place to do it.

Great For...

☑ Don't Miss

A tasting session at Graham's, Porto's finest port-wine lodge.

Wine Lodges

Start at riverside **Espaço Porto Cruz** (www.myportocruz.com; Largo Miguel Bombarda 23; ⏱11am-7pm Tue-Sun), a swanky emporium in a restored 18th-century building that celebrates all things port. In addition to tastings (€7.50 for three ports), there are exhibition halls, a rooftop terrace and a restaurant. Established way back in 1820, British-founded big-name **Graham's** (☏223 776 490, 223 776 492; www.grahams-port.com; Rua do Agro 141; tours incl tasting from €15; ⏱9.30am-6.30pm Apr-Oct, to 6pm Nov-Mar) features a small museum and is a popular choice for tours (30 minutes), which dip into atmospheric barrel-lined cellars and conclude with a tasting of three to eight port wines. British-run **Taylor's** (☏223 772 973; www.taylor.pt; Rua do Choupelo 250; tours

Taylor's

HERACLES KRITIKOS/SHUTTERSTOCK ©

Afurada   *Vila Nova de Gaia*   Ⓜ Jardim do Morro

⚓ Explore Ashore

The principal dock for river cruises is just below here at Cais de Gaia. Allow at least half a day to catch the cable car and see the monastery as well as savour port tastings.

❶ Need to Know

Metro line D runs through the Jardim do Morro stop.

incl tasting adult/child €15/6; ⊙10am-6pm) boasts lovely, oh-so-English grounds with tremendous views of Porto. Its one-hour tours include a tasting of three top-of-the-range port wines, and the cellars are simply staggering, piled to the rafters with huge barrels. **Croft** (☑220 109 825; www.croftport. com; Rua Barão de Forrester 412; tours incl tasting €14; ⊙10am-7.30pm) and **Cálem** (☑916 113 451; www.calem.pt; Avenida Diogo Leite 344; tours incl tasting €12; ⊙10am-7pm May-Oct, to 6pm Nov-Apr) are also recommended.

Cable Car & Jardim do Morro

Don't miss a five-minute ride on the **Teleférico de Gaia** (www.gaiacablecar.com; Calçada da Serra 143; one way/return €6/9; ⊙10am-8pm May-Sep, to 6pm Oct-Mar), an aerial gondola that provides fine views over

the Douro and Porto. It runs between the southern end of the Ponte de Dom Luís I and the riverside. At the bridge end of the *teleférico* is the hilltop **Jardim do Morro** (Avenida da República). Shaded by palms, these gardens are all about the view. From here, Porto is reduced to postcard format, with the pastel-hued houses of Ribeira on the opposite side of the snaking river below.

Mosteiro da Serra de Pilar

Watching over Gaia is this 17th-century hilltop **monastery** (Rampa do Infante Santo; adult/child €4/2; ⊙10am-6.30pm Tue-Sun Apr-Oct, to 5.30pm Nov-Mar), with its striking circular cloister, church with gilded altar, and stellar river views. Requisitioned by the future Duke of Wellington during the Peninsular War (1807–14), it still belongs to the Portuguese military and can only be visited on 40-minute guided tours.

Porto City Centre

This walking tour winds its way through the city centre, skirting the edge of Ribeira before running along the river. The route takes in some of the city's architectural highlights and two of the best waterfront dining areas.

Start Torre dos Clérigos
Distance 2km
Duration Two to three hours

1 Begin with unrivalled views from the 76m-high baroque tower of the **Torre dos Clérigos** (Rua de São Filipe de Nery; €5; ⏲9am-7pm).

R Cândido dos Reis

Pç de Lisboa

Jardim da Cordoaria

START ❶

3 Near the end of Rua das Flores stands Nicolau Nasoni's baroque masterpiece, the **Igreja da Misericórdia**. (www.mmipo.pt; Rua das Flores 5; ⏲10am-6.30pm Apr-Sep, to 5.30pm Oct-Mar)

❸

R Ferreira Borges

R Sousa Viterbo

R Infante Dom Henrique

❹

❺

4 Check out the main courtyard of neoclassical **Palácio da Bolsa** (p185) – once Porto's stock exchange.

5 Just next door is the **Igreja de São Francisco** (p184), its severe Gothic facade hiding a jaw-dropping golden interior.

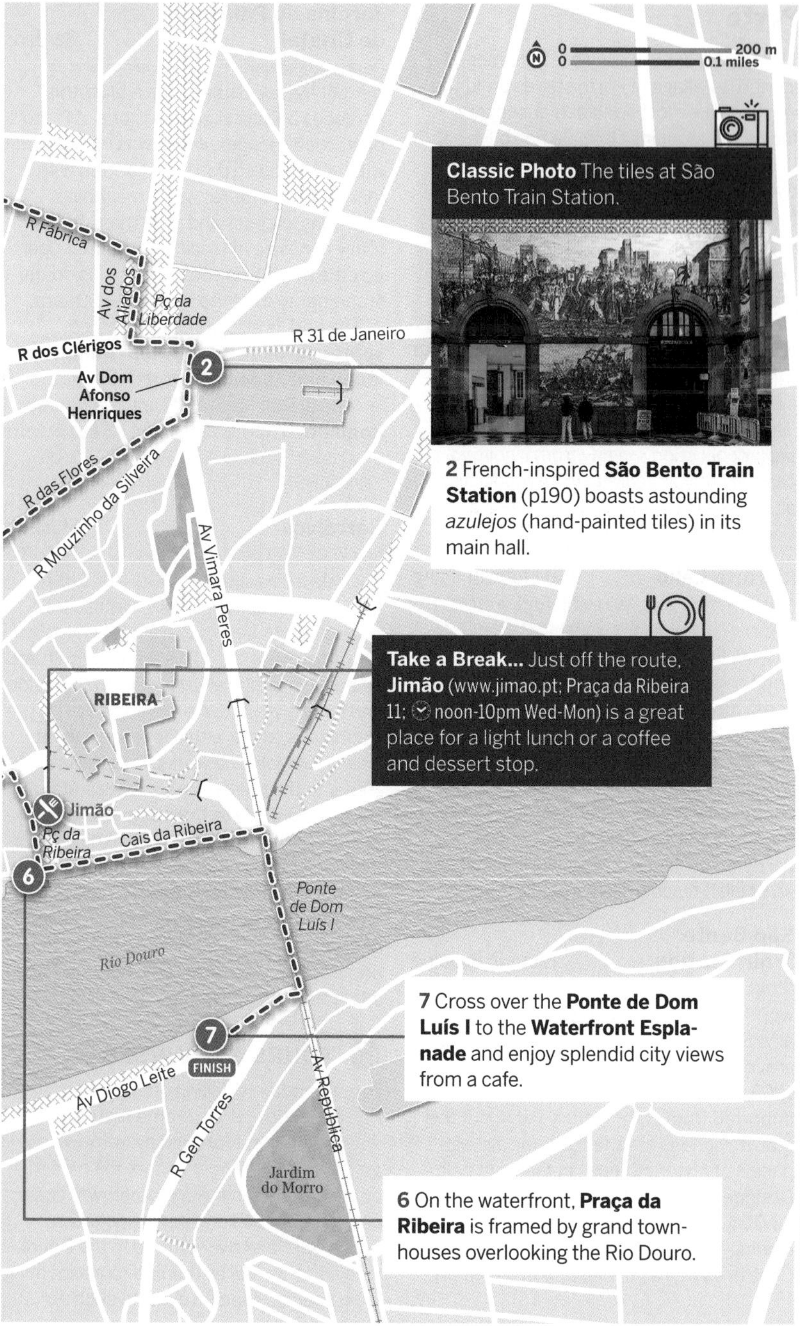

0   200 m
0   0.1 miles

R Fábrica

Av dos Aliados

Pç da Liberdade

R dos Clérigos

R 31 de Janeiro

Av Dom Afonso Henriques

R das Flores

R Mouzinho da Silveira

Av Vimara Peres

RIBEIRA

Jimão

Pç da Ribeira

Cais da Ribeira

Rio Douro

Ponte de Dom Luís I

Av Diogo Leite

R Gen Torres

Av República

Jardim do Morro

FINISH

Classic Photo The tiles at São Bento Train Station.

2 French-inspired **São Bento Train Station** (p190) boasts astounding *azulejos* (hand-painted tiles) in its main hall.

Take a Break... Just off the route, **Jimão** (www.jimao.pt; Praça da Ribeira 11; ◷ noon-10pm Wed-Mon) is a great place for a light lunch or a coffee and dessert stop.

7 Cross over the **Ponte de Dom Luís I** to the **Waterfront Esplanade** and enjoy splendid city views from a cafe.

6 On the waterfront, **Praça da Ribeira** is framed by grand townhouses overlooking the Rio Douro.

Porto

The setting could hardly be more magnificent. The village of Porto stands amid the west coast's most spectacular scenery, facing the stunning Golfe de Porto – a Unesco World Heritage Site, cradled between flame-red cliffs – and with a thickly forested valley to its rear.

◎ SIGHTS

Museu Nacional
Soares dos Reis   Museum
(www.museusoaresdosreis.pt; Rua Dom Manuel II 44; adult/child €5/free; ◷10am-6pm Tue-Sun) Porto's best art museum presents a stellar collection ranging from Neolithic carvings to Portugal's take on modernism, all housed in the formidable Palácio das Carrancas.

Livraria Lello   Historic Building
(www.livralialello.pt; Rua das Carmelitas 144; €5; ◷10am-7.30pm Mon-Fri, to 7pm Sat, 11am-7pm Sun; ⚐) Even if you're not after books, don't miss this exquisite 1906 neo-Gothic confection, with its lavishly carved plaster resembling wood and a stained-glass skylight. Feels magical? Its intricately wrought, curiously twisting staircase was supposedly the inspiration for the one in the Harry Potter books, which JK Rowling partly wrote in Porto while working here as an English teacher from 1991 to 1993.

São Bento
Train Station   Historic Building
(Praça Almeida Garrett; ◷5am-1am) One of the world's most beautiful train stations, beaux arts São Bento wings you back to a more graceful age of rail travel. Completed in 1903, its mansard roof seems to have been imported from 19th-century Paris, but the real attractions are the dramatic *azulejo* panels of historic scenes in the front hall. Designed by Jorge Colaço in 1930, some 20,000 tiles depict historic battles (including Henry the Navigator's conquest of Ceuta), as well as the history of transport.

Jardins do Palácio
de Cristal   Gardens
(Rua Dom Manuel II; ◷8am-9pm Apr-Sep, to 7pm Oct-Mar; ⚐) Sitting atop a bluff, this gorgeous botanical garden is one of Porto's best-loved escapes, with lawns interwoven with sun-dappled paths and dotted with fountains, sculptures, giant magnolias, camellias, cypress and olive trees. It's actually a mosaic of small gardens that open up little by little as you wander – as do the stunning views of the city and Rio Douro.

The park is also home to a domed **sports pavilion**, the high-tech **Biblioteca Municipal Almeida Garrett** (◷2-6pm Mon, 10am-6pm Tue-Sat; ☎) and the **Museu Romântico** (Quinta da Macieirinha; Rua de Entre Quintas 220; adult/child weekdays €2.20/free, Sat & Sun free; ◷10am-5.30pm Tue-Sun).

Serralves   Museum
(www.serralves.pt; Rua Dom João de Castro 210; adult/child museums & park €10/free, park only €5/free, 10am-1pm 1st Sun of the month free; ◷10am-7pm Mon-Fri, to 8pm Sat & Sun May-Sep, reduced hours Oct-Apr) This fabulous cultural institution combines a museum, a mansion and extensive gardens. Cutting-edge exhibitions, along with a fine permanent collection featuring works from the late 1960s to the present, are showcased in the **Museu de Arte Contemporânea**, an arrestingly minimalist, whitewashed space designed by the eminent Porto-based architect Álvaro Siza Vieira. The delightful, pink **Casa de Serralves** is a prime example of art deco, bearing the imprint of French architect Charles Siclis. One ticket gets you into both museums.

◉ TOURS & COURSES

Forget randomly ticking off the sights – Porto is endowed with some first-rate special-interest tours, led by in-the-know guides proud to show visitors the hidden corners of their beloved hometown. There are in-depth food and port-wine tours, pub crawls, and river cruises to the Douro vineyards, as well as themed tours zooming in on specific aspects of Porto such as

KIEV.VICTOR/SHUTTERSTOCK ©

Livraria Lello

azulejos, traditional trades and crafts, and Jewish heritage. Advance booking is usually required.

Taste Porto   Food & Drink

(☑920 503 302; www.tasteporto.com; Downtown Food Tour adult/child €65/42, Vintage Food Tour €70/42; ☺Downtown Food Tour 10.45am & 4pm Tue-Sat, Vintage Food Tour 10am & 4.15pm Mon-Sat, Photo Food Experience 9.45am daily) Loosen a belt notch for Taste Porto's superb downtown food tours, where you'll sample everything from Porto's best slow-roast-pork sandwich to éclairs, fine wines, cheese and coffee. Friendly, knowledgeable guide André and his team lead these indulgent and insightful 3½-hour walking tours, which take in viewpoints and historic back lanes en route to restaurants, grocery stores and cafes.

Other Side   Tours

(☑916 500 170; www.theotherside.pt; Rua Souto 67; ☺9am-8pm) Well-informed, congenial guides reveal their city on half-day walking tours of hidden Porto (€19), a walking and food tour (€49), and wine tours (€55). They also venture further afield with full-

day trips to the Douro's vineyards (€95), and to Guimarães and Braga (€85).

Worst Tours   Walking

(www.theworsttours.weebly.com; Praça do Marquês de Pombal) **FREE** A trio of out-of-work architects got together to offer free and fun offbeat tours of Porto on foot, each with a different theme. While the tours are technically free, tips are naturally very welcome; pay as much as you wish. Tours meet at Praça do Marquês de Pombal and last around two to three hours. Book ahead online.

Be My Guest   Walking

(☑938 417 850; www.bemyguestinporto.com; 3hr tours €20) To get better acquainted with Porto, sign up for one of Be My Guest's terrific themed walking tours of the city, skipping from an insider's peek at *azulejos* to belle époque architecture and urban art. Run by two incredibly passionate guides – Nuno and Fred – it also arranges four-hour cookery workshops (€35) and wine-tasting tours (€25). Meeting points vary. Check in advance.

Porto

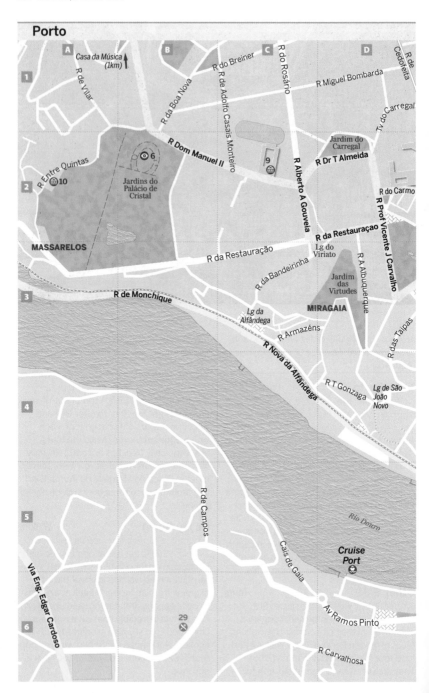

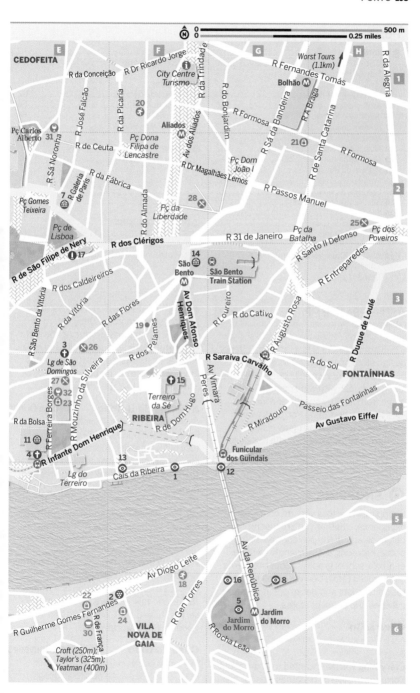

CEDOFEITA E

R da Conceição

R Dr Ricardo Jorge F

City Centre Turismo

R da Trindade

Worst Tours (1.1km)

R Fernandes Tomás G

Bolhão Ⓜ H

R da Picaria

R José Falcão

R da Alegria

1

20 ⓘ

R A Braga

R do Bonjardim

R Formosa

R Sá da Bandeira

R de Santa Catarina

Pç Carlos Alberto

31 ⓘ

R Sá Noronha

R de Ceuta

Aliados Ⓜ

Av dos Aliados

Pç Dona Filipa de Lencastre

R Dr Magalhães Lemos

Pç Dom João I

21

R Formosa

R da Fábrica

7 ⓘ

R Galeria de Paris

R do Almada

28 ✕

R Passos Manuel

2

Pç Gomes Teixeira

Pç de Lisboa

Pç da Liberdade

R 31 de Janeiro

Pç da Batalha

25 ✕

Pç dos Poveiros

R de São Filipe de Nery

17 ⓘ

R dos Clérigos

14 ⓘ **São Bento** Ⓜ

São Bento Train Station

R Santo Il Defonso

R Entreparedes

R Duque de Loulé

3

R São Bento da Vitória

R dos Caldeireiros

R da Vitória

R das Flores

Av Dom Afonso Henriques

R Loureiro

R do Cativo

R Augusto Rosa

R do Sol

FONTAÍNHAS

19 ●

R dos Pelames

3 ⓘ 26 ✕

Lg de São Domingos

R dos Sapateiros

27 ✕

32

23

R da Bolsa

11 ⓘ

4 ⓘ

R Mouzinho da Silveira

15 ⓘ

Terreiro da Sé

RIBEIRA

R de Dom Hugo

Av Vimara Peres

R Saraiva Carvalho

R Miradouro

Passeio das Fontainhas

Av Gustavo Eiffel

4

R Ferreira Borges

R Infante Dom Henrique

13

Cais da Ribeira

1

12

Funicular dos Guindais

Lg do Terreiro

5

Av da República

Av Diogo Leite

18 ⓘ

22

2

24

30

R Guilherme Gomes Fernandes

R de França

VILA NOVA DE GAIA

R Gen Torres

16

5

Jardim do Morro

8

Jardim do Morro Ⓜ

R Rocha Leão

Croft (250m); Taylor's (325m); Yeatman (400m)

6

0   500 m
0   0.25 miles
Ⓝ

Porto

Workshops Pop Up Cooking

(☎966 974 119; www.workshops-popup.com; Rua do Almada 275; 3hr class incl lunch or dinner €35) This cool indie arts, crafts and interior design store hosts regular three-hour, hands-on cookery workshops, followed by lunch or dinner with wine pairing. Themes range from healthy snacks and Indian food to Cook and Taste Portugal, where you'll learn to cook Portuguese classics like *bacalhau à lagareiro* (codfish cooked in extra virgin olive oil) and *pastéis de nata* (Portuguese-style custard tarts).

🔒 SHOPPING

Shopping in Porto is very much a local experience, whether you are tasting port before selecting the perfect take-home bottle, nattering to the friendly *senhora* at an old-school grocery about the merits of *tremoços* (lupin beans), or talking to resident artists and designers at pop-ups, galleries and concept stores.

Oliva & Co Food

(www.facebook.com/pg/OlivaeCo; Rua Ferreira Borges 60; ⊙10am-7pm Sun-Fri, to 8pm Sat) Everything you ever wanted to know about Portuguese olive oil becomes clear at this

experiential store, which maps out the country's six Protected Designation of Origin (PDO) regions producing the extra-virgin stuff. Besides superb oils and olives, you'll find biscuits, chocolate and soaps made with olive oil. Try before you buy or join one of the in-depth tastings.

A Pérola do Bolhão Food & Drinks

(Rua Formosa 279; ⊙9.30am-7.30pm Mon-Fri, 9am-1pm Sat) Founded in 1917, this delightfully old-school deli sports Porto's most striking art nouveau facade and is stacked to the rafters with smoked sausages and pungent mountain cheeses, olives, dried fruits and nuts, wine and port. The beautiful *azulejos* depict flowers and two goddess-like women bearing *café* (coffee) and *chá* (tea) plants.

Porto Wine House Food & Drinks

(www.portowinehouse.com; Rua Cândido dos Reis 4-10; ⊙9am-8pm) Stock up on fine whites, rubies and tawnies here, as well as *conservas* (tinned fish), preserves and other goodies. Ships worldwide.

Casa do Galo Gifts & Souvenirs

(www.acasadogalo.com; Av Diogo Leite 50; ⊙10.30am-8.30pm) An ode to all things

Portuguese, this shop is well stocked with gifts from the kitsch to the classy. You'll find *galo de Barcelos* cockerels, as well as ceramics, textiles (lace and *lenços dos namorado,* or sweetheart handkerchiefs), cork products and edibles such as honey, preserves, tinned fish in retro wrappings and, naturally, port wine.

 EATING

Porto's food scene has gone through the roof in recent years. Hot at the moment are *petiscos* (small Portuguese plates, ideal for sharing), lazy weekend brunches, creative vegetarian buffet-style restaurants with bags of charm and imaginative riffs on hand-me-down recipes, and old-school taverns championing slow food. And don't forget the temptation of local cafes and patisseries around nearly every corner.

Cafe Santiago   Portuguese €

(🖉222 055 797; www.caferestaurantesantiago.com.pt; Rua Passos Manuel 226; mains €8-12; ⊘noon-11pm Mon-Sat) This is hands down one of the best places to try Porto's classic gut-busting treat, the *francesinha* – a thick, open-faced sandwich piled with cheese, sausage, egg and/or assorted meats, plus a tasty, rich beer sauce. This classic will set you back €9.75, which might seem pricey for a sandwich, but trust us: it's a meal in itself.

Cantina 32   Portuguese €€

(🖉222 039 069; www.cantina32.com; Rua das Flores 32; petiscos €3.50-20; ⊘12.30-3pm & 6.30-10.30pm Mon-Sat; 🐾) Industrial-chic meets boho at this delightfully laid-back haunt, with its walls of polished concrete, mismatched crockery, verdant plants, and vintage knick-knacks ranging from a bicycle to an old typewriter. The menu is just as informal – *petiscos* such as *pica-pau* steak (bite-sized pieces of steak in a garlic-white-wine sauce), quail egg croquettes, and cheesecake served in a flower pot reveal a pinch of creativity.

Flor dos Congregados   Portuguese €€

(🖉222 002 822; www.flordoscongregados.pt; Travessa dos Congregados 11; mains €8-16; ⊘7-10pm Mon-Wed, noon-3pm & 7-11pm Thu-Sat) Tucked away down a narrow alley, this softly lit, family-run restaurant brims with stone-walled, wood-beamed, art-slung nooks. The frequently changing blackboard menu goes with the seasons.

DOP   Gastronomy €€€

(🖉222 014 313; www.doprestaurante.pt; Palácio das Artes, Largo de São Domingos 18; mains €25-28, tasting menus €80-90; ⊘7.30-11pm Mon, 12.30-3pm & 7.30-11pm Tue-Sat; 🐾) Housed in a grand edifice, DOP is one of Porto's most stylish addresses, with its high ceilings and slick, monochrome interior. Much-feted chef Rui Paula puts a creative, seasonal twist on outstanding ingredients, with dish after delicate, flavour-packed dish skipping from octopus carpaccio to cod with lobster rice.

Pedro Lemos   Gastronomy €€€

(🖉220 115 986; www.pedrolemos.net; Rua do Padre Luís Cabral 974; tasting menus €110-130; ⊘12.30-3pm & 7.30-11pm Tue-Sat) One of Porto's two Michelin-starred restaurants, Pedro Lemos is sheer delight. With a love of seasonally sourced produce and robust flavours, the eponymous chef creates culinary fireworks using first-class ingredients from land and sea – be it ultrafresh Atlantic bivalves or Alentejano black pork cooked to smoky deliciousness with wild mushrooms. Choose between the subtly lit, cosy-chic dining room or the roof terrace.

Yeatman   Gastronomy €€€

(🖉220 133 100; www.the-yeatman-hotel.com; Yeatman Hotel, Rua do Choupelo 88; tasting menus €140-170, wine pairing €60-70; ⊘7.30-11pm) With its polished service, elegant setting and dazzling views over the river and city, the two-Michelin-starred restaurant at the five-star Yeatman Hotel is sheer class. Chef Ricardo Costa puts his imaginative spin on seasonal ingredients from lobster to pheasant – all skilfully cooked, served with

Port Wine

You can't say you've been to Porto until you've tasted the Douro's oak-barrel-aged nectar and learned to tell a mellow, nutty tawny from a complex, sophisticated vintage. Ever since the 17th century, the swanky lodges spilling down Vila Nova de Gaia's hillside have been the nerve centre of port production – as they still are today.

Grapes are harvested in autumn and immediately crushed (sometimes still by foot) and allowed to ferment until alcohol levels reach 7%. At this point, one part brandy is added to every five parts wine. Fermentation stops immediately, leaving the unfermented sugars that make port sweet. The quality of the grapes, together with the ways the wine is aged and stored, determines the kind of port you get. The most common include the following:

Ruby Made from average-quality grapes, and aged at least two years in vats; rich, red colours and sweet, fruity flavours.

Tawny Made from average-quality grapes, and aged for two to seven years in wooden casks; mahogany colours, drier than ruby, with nuttier flavours.

Aged tawny Selected from higher-quality grapes, then aged in wooden casks for 10, 20, 30 or 40 years (reflected in the price, respectively). Subtler and silkier than regular tawny; drinks more like brandy or cognac than wine.

Vintage Made from the finest grapes from a single year, aged in barrels for two years, then aged in bottles for at least 10 years; dark ruby colours, fruity yet extremely subtle and complex.

Late-bottled vintage (LBV) Made from very select grapes of a single year, aged for around five years in wooden casks, then bottled; similar to vintage, but ready for immediate drinking once bottled, and usually smoother and lighter bodied.

flair and expertly matched with wines from the 1000-bottle cellar that is among the country's best.

Vinum   Portuguese €€€
(✆220 930 417; www.vinumatgrahams.com; Graham's Port Lodge, Rua do Agro 141; mains €24-29, menus €50-100; ⏰12.30-11pm) Vinum manages the delicate act of combining 19th-century port-lodge charm with contemporary edge. Peer through to the barrel-lined cellar from the pine-beamed restaurant, or out across the Douro and Porto's rooftops from the conservatory and terrace. Portuguese menu stunners include green ceviche fresh from Matasinhos fish market and dry-aged Trás-os-Montes beef, complemented by a stellar selection of wines and ports.

🅾 DRINKING & NIGHTLIFE

While Porto isn't going to steal the clubbing crown any time soon, *tripeiros* (Porto residents) love to get their groove on, especially in the Galerias, with its speakeasy-style bars and the party spilling out onto the streets. With just enough urban edge to keep the scene fresh-faced, a night out here can easily jump from indie clubs to refined rooftop bars.

7G Roaster   Coffee
(www.facebook.com/7groaster; Rua de França 26; ⏰10am-6pm Mon-Thu, to 7pm Fri-Sun) The baristas really know their stuff at this speciality coffee roasters. In the cool, monochrome, wood-floored space, you can sip a perfectly made espresso or go for brunch (€12), which includes everything from sheep's cheese to homemade granola, pastries and fresh-pressed juice. Sit on the terrace to gaze up at the vertical garden.

Prova   Wine Bar
(www.prova.com.pt; Rua Ferreira Borges 86; ⏰5pm-1am Wed-Sun; 📶) Diogo, the passionate owner, explains the finer nuances of Portuguese wine at this chic, stone-walled bar, where relaxed jazz plays. Stop by for a two-glass tasting (€5), or sample wines

Aduela

by the glass – including beefy Douros, full-bodied Dãos and crisp Alentejo whites. These marry well with sharing plates of local hams and cheeses (€14). Diogo's port tonics are legendary.

Aduela   Bar
(Rua das Oliveiras 36; ⊙3pm-2am Mon, 10am-2am Tue-Thu, to 4am Fri & Sat, 3pm-midnight Sun) Retro and hip but not self-consciously so, chilled Aduela bathes in the nostalgic orange glow of its glass lights, which illuminate the green walls and mishmash of vintage furnishings. Once a sewing machine warehouse, today it's where friends gather to converse over wine and appetising *petiscos* (€3 to €8).

ENTERTAINMENT

Casa da Música   Concert Venue
(House of Music; ☑220 120 220; www.casadamusica.com; Avenida da Boavista 604; ⊙box office 9.30am-7pm Mon-Sat, to 6pm Sun) Grand and minimalist, sophisticated yet populist, Porto's cultural behemoth boasts

a shoebox-style concert hall at its heart, meticulously engineered to accommodate everything from jazz duets to Beethoven's Ninth, and from blues to fado and electronica. The hall hold concerts most nights of the year, with occasional summer concerts staged outdoors in the adjoining plaza.

ⓘ INFORMATION

The main city **turismo** (☑300 501 920; www.visitporto.travel; Rua Clube dos Fenianos 25; ⊙9am-8pm May-Jul & Sep-Oct, to 9pm Aug, to 7pm Nov-Apr) has a detailed city map, a transport map and the *Agenda do Porto* cultural calendar, among other printed materials.

ⓘ GETTING AROUND

Metro Porto's compact, six-line metro network runs from 6am to 1am daily. It's handy for zipping between neighbourhoods and getting to/from the airport and beaches north of the city. A map is available at http://en.metrodoporto.pt.

Tram Porto's vintage trams are transport at its atmospheric best. There are three lines:

The Alto Douro

Heading upriver from Peso da Régua, terraced vineyards blanket every hillside, with whitewashed *quintas* (estates) perched high above the Douro. This dramatic landscape is the jaw-dropping by-product of over 2000 years of winemaking. While villages are small and architectural monuments few and far between, it's worth the trip simply for the panoramic ride itself. Its allure has clearly not gone unnoticed. In 2001 Unesco designated the entire Alto Douro wine-growing region a World Heritage Site.

Further east towards Spain, the soil is drier, with the sculpted landscape giving way to more rugged terrain. But despite the aridity – and the blisteringly hot summers – the land around Vila Nova de Foz Côa produces fine grapes, olives and nuts.

Most recently, the construction of the Foz-Tua dam – completed in 2017 just metres from the Alto Douro – has sparked controversy among Portuguese environmental groups and the region's wine producers.

Vineyards along the Douro
MAURICIO ABREU/GETTY IMAGES ©

1 running along the river from the historic centre to Foz, 18 between Massarelos and Carmo, and 22 doing a loop through the centre from Carmo to Batalha/Guindais.

Bus Central hubs of Porto's extensive bus system include the Jardim da Cordoaria, Praça da Liberdade and São Bento station.

Taxi To cross town expect to pay between €5 and €8. There's a 20% surcharge at night. There are taxi ranks throughout the centre.

Peso da Régua

Gateway to the Alto Douro, the sun-bleached town of Peso da Régua abuts the Rio Douro at the western edge of the demarcated port-wine region. Most tourists stick to the scenic riverfront, but the quaint old town one block uphill is an almost exclusively local scene, and well worth a wander.

SIGHTS

Museu do Douro   Museum
(www.museudodouro.pt; Rua Marquês de Pombal; adult/concession €6/3; ☺10am-6pm Mar-Oct, to 5.30pm Nov-Feb) Bringing the Douro Valley's wine producing history vividly to life, this wonderful museum has a wealth of arte-facts and engaging displays, from a vast wall-size map of the river, annotated kilo-metre by kilometre, to old leather-bound texts, vintage port-wine posters and the remains of an old flat-bottomed port haul-er. You'll find it all in a gorgeous converted riverside warehouse, with a restaurant and bar on-site. The gift shop, stocked with wine, handmade soaps, ceramics and jewellery, is also brilliant.

⊗ EATING

Taberna do Jéréré   Portuguese €€
(☎254 323 299; Rua Marquês de Pombal 38; mains €8-18; ☺noon-3pm & 7.30-10.30pm Mon-Sat) Excellent Portuguese dishes, including the house speciality *bacalhau á Jéréré* (dried salt-cod with shrimp, mushroom and spinach), are served in a tastefully rustic dining room with a beamed ceiling and granite floors. Great-value lunch specials.

Castas e Pratos   Portuguese €€€
(☎254 323 290; www.castasepratos.com; Avenida José Vasques Osório; mains €20-35; ☺10.30am-11pm) The coolest dining room in town is set in a restored wood-and-stone railyard warehouse with exposed original

timbers. You can order grilled *alheira* sausage or octopus salad from the tapas bar downstairs, or opt for green asparagus risotto or roasted kid goat and potatoes with turnip sprouts in the mezzanine.

 INFORMATION

Loja Interativa de Turismo (254 318 152; www.cm-pesoregua.pt; Avenida do Douro; 9.30am-12.30pm & 2-6pm) Régua's high-tech tourist office, facing the Douro 1km west of the station, supplies information about the town and the region, including local accommodation and vineyards.

 GETTING AROUND

Cruise ships dock centrally in Régua, and it's easy to make your way around on foot from here.

Pinhão

Encircled by terraced hillsides that produce some of the world's best port – and some stellar table wines, too – pretty little Pinhão sits on a particularly lovely bend of the Rio Douro, about 25km upriver from Peso da Régua. Wineries and their competing signs dominate the scene. Even the delightful train station has *azulejos* depicting the grape harvest. The town itself, cute though it is, holds little of interest, but you are right in the heart of wine country here.

 ACTIVITIES

Quinta do Bomfim   Wine
(254 730 370; www.symington.com/visit-us; tours incl tasting from €17; 10.30am-7pm daily Mar-Oct, 9.30am-6.30pm Tue-Sun Nov-Feb) Conveniently located in downtown Pinhão, Symington's swank *quinta* showcases a small museum inside a restored historic winery. Multilingual guided tours (advance reservation required) offer views of the vineyards' ancient dry stone terraces and visit the 19th-century lodge where young wine is still aged in old wooden vats. Tours

end in the gorgeous tasting room with its terrace overlooking the Douro.

Quinta das Carvalhas   Wine
(254 738 050; www.realcompanhiavelha.pt/ pages/quintas/4; self-guided walk €10, bus/ jeep tour €12.50/35, vintage tour incl premium wine tasting €90; 10am-7.30pm Apr-Oct, to 6pm Nov-Mar) Just across the bridge from Pinhão, this *quinta* on the Douro's south bank welcomes visitors to its spiffy modern tasting room and wine shop and offers a variety of vineyard tours climbing to a ridgeline with gorgeous views. Choose from a self-guided walk, an open-top bus tour, a 4WD tour or a personalised vintage tour guided by the in-house agronomist.

 EATING

Veladouro   Portuguese €€€
(254 738 166; Rua da Praia 3; mains €15-25; 10am-midnight) Wood-grilled meats and fish are the speciality at this schist-walled restaurant by the riverfront. On sunny days, the vine-shaded front terrace is the place to be, with views of local fishermen under their umbrellas on the adjacent dock.

Cozinha da Clara   Portuguese €€€
(254 732 254; www.quintadelarosa.com/ content/cozinha-da-clara; M590, Pinhão; tapas €2.50-15, mains €20-26, 3-course menu incl wine €50; lunch 1-3pm, tapas 3-6pm, dinner 7-9.30pm) Whether you come for drinks, tapas and sunset over the river, or for one of the splendid three-course 'dinner parties' hosted by chef Pedro Cardoso, Quinta de la Rosa's recently launched restaurant is a delightful place to dine. Snag a table on the outdoor terrace if you can – views of the vineyards and the Douro flowing far below are breathtaking.

 GETTING AROUND

Cruises pull up right in the heart of little Pinhão, so it's easy to get around on foot.

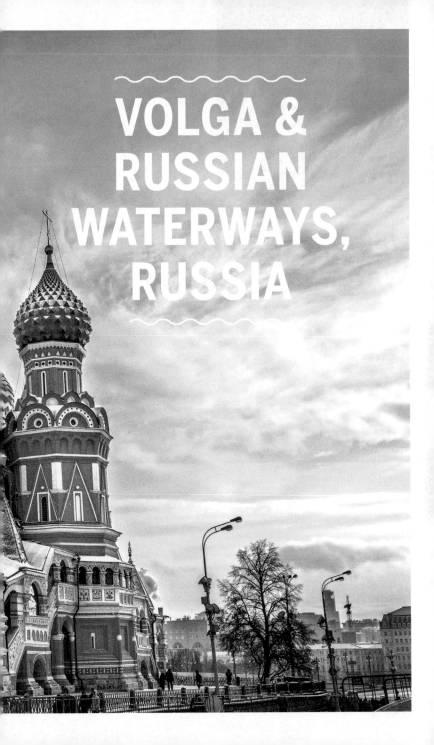

VOLGA &
RUSSIAN
WATERWAYS,
RUSSIA

Volga & Russian Waterways, Russia

A variety of cruises are available on Russian waterways, the most popular of which travel between Moscow and St Petersburg, navigating various canal systems and rivers, including the Volga, Europe's longest river. On the Moskva River, Moscow thrills visitors during any season with its artistry, history and majesty – and it all starts right in the centre at the Kremlin and Red Square. In St Petersburg, situated on the Neva, you cannot tire of exploring its amazing art collections, nor be bored by its grand facades and canalside palaces.

With One Day in Moscow

Arrive at the Kremlin ticket office at 9.30am sharp to reserve your time to enter the **Armoury** (p204). Dedicate your morning to inspecting the ancient icons, gold and gems in the **Kremlin** (p204). Afterwards, stroll through Alexander Garden and catch the changing of the guard at the **Tomb of the Unknown Soldier** (p218). Then jump right into the queue on Red Square for **Lenin's Mausoleum** (p209) before it closes at 1pm. Stroll through Kitay Gorod, discovering the countless 17th-century churches and check out Park Zaryadye. For the evening, book tickets in advance for a show at the **Bolshoi Theatre** (p223).

Best Places for...

Art State Hermitage Museum, St Petersburg (p210)

Local Food Banshiki, St Petersburg (p228)

High-end Dining Cafe Pushkin, Moscow (p222)

Market Danilovsky Market, Moscow (p222)

Contemporary Art Garage Museum, Moscow (p218)

Previous page: St Basil's Cathedral (p209), Moscow

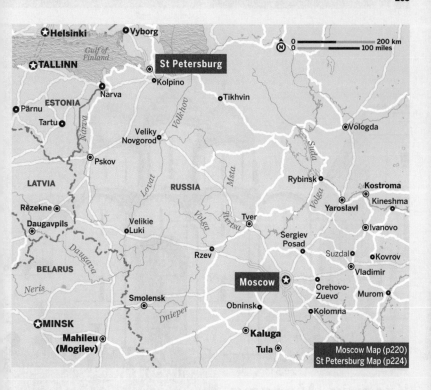

Getting from the Ports

Moscow Renovations at the Northern Cruise Terminal in Moscow should be completed by the time you read this. The terminal is 16km north of the city centre, about a 10-minute walk from Rechnoy vokzal metro stop, which is itself a half-hour ride from the centre.

St Petersburg The river terminal is in the southeast of the city, around 10 minutes' walk from Proletarskaya metro station (Line 3, green line). It's five stops to Gostiny Dvor in the historic heart.

Fast Facts

Currency Rouble (R)

Language Russian

Free Wi-fi Available in many bars, restaurants and cafes, as well as on the metro and at hotspots around the cities.

Money ATMs are common throughout Moscow and St Petersburg. Look for signs that say 'bankomat' (БАНКОМАТ).

Tourist Information In 2012, a network of tourist information centres were introduced in Moscow's city centre, including one in Revolution Sq. St Petersburg's main office is in the historic heart of the city.

Assumption Cathedral

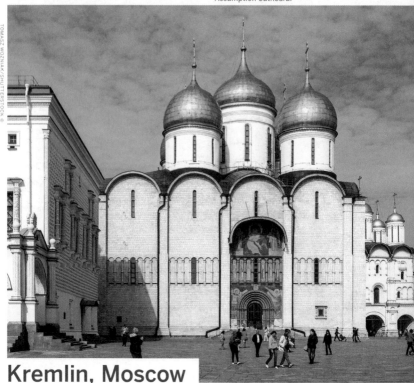

Kremlin, Moscow

The apex of Russian political power, the Kremlin is the kernel of not just Moscow, but the whole country. From here, autocratic tsars, communist dictators and modern-day presidents have governed Russia.

Great For...

☑ **Don't Miss**

The exquisite decorative detail of the Archangel Cathedral.

Assumption Cathedral

With five golden helmet domes and four semicircular gables, **Assumption Cathedral** (Успенский собор) was the focal church of prerevolutionary Russia and is the burial place of most of the heads of the Russian Orthodox Church from the 1320s to 1700. A striking 1660s fresco of the Virgin Mary faces Sobornaya pl, above the door once used for royal processions. If you have limited time, come straight here. The visitors' entrance is at the western end.

Armoury

The **Armoury** (Оружейная палата; adult/child R1000/free; ⊙tours 10am, noon, 2.30pm & 4.30pm Fri-Wed; Ⓜ Aleksandrovsky Sad) dates to 1511, when it was founded under Vasily III to manufacture and store weapons, imperi-

Archangel Cathedral

VALERY EGOROV/SHUTTERSTOCK ©

Assumption Cathedral **Kremlin** Ivan the Great Bell Tower
Alexandrovsky Sad
Armoury
Archangel Cathedral
Kremlevskaya nab Moscow River

Explore Ashore

From the northern cruise terminal, it's a 10-minute walk to Rechnoy vokzal metro stop. From here, take line 2 to Teatralnaya (25 minutes), from where it's another 10-minute walk to the Kremlin. You'll need two to three hours to see the separate museums and cathedrals.

ℹ Need to Know

Кремль; ☏ 495-695 4146; www.kreml.ru; R700; ⏱ 9.30am-6pm 15 May-30 Sep, ticket office 9am-5pm Fri-Wed, 10am-5pm 1 Oct-14 May, ticket office 9.30am-4.30pm Fri-Wed; Ⓜ Aleksandrovsky Sad

al arms and regalia for the royal court. Later it also produced jewellery, icon frames and embroidery. To this day, the Armoury contains plenty of treasures for ogling, and remains a highlight of any visit to the Kremlin. If possible, buy your time-specific ticket to the Armoury when you buy your ticket to the Kremlin.

Archangel Cathedral

The **Archangel Cathedral** (Архангельский собор), at the southeastern corner of Sobornaya pl, was for centuries the coronation, wedding and burial church of tsars. It was built by Ivan Kalita in 1333 to commemorate the end of the great famine, and dedicated to Archangel Michael, guardian of the Moscow princes. By the turn of the 16th century it had fallen into disrepair and

was rebuilt between 1505 and 1508 by the Italian architect Alevisio Novi. Like the Assumption Cathedral, it has five domes and is essentially Byzantine-Russian in style. However, the exterior has many Venetian Renaissance features, notably the distinctive scallop-shell gables and porticoes.

Ivan the Great Bell Tower

With its two golden domes rising above the eastern side of Sobornaya pl, **Ivan the Great Bell Tower** (Колокольня Ивана Великого; R250; ⏱ 10am-5pm Apr-Oct) is the Kremlin's tallest structure – a landmark visible from 30km away. Before the 20th century it was forbidden to build anything higher in Moscow. Purchase a ticket to the architectural exhibit inside for a specifically timed admission to climb the 137 steps to the top for sweeping views.

The Kremlin

A DAY AT THE KREMLIN

Only at the Kremlin can you see 800 years of Russian history and artistry in one day. Enter the ancient fortress through the Trinity Gate Tower and walk past the impressive Arsenal, ringed with cannons. Past the Patriarch's Palace, you'll find yourself surrounded by white-washed walls and golden domes. Your first stop is ❶ **Assumption Cathedral** with the solemn fresco over the doorway. As the most important church in prerevolutionary Russia, this 15th-century beauty was the burial site of the patriarchs. The ❷ **Ivan the Great Bell Tower** now contains a nifty multimedia exhibit on the architectural history of the Kremlin. The view from the top is worth the price of admission. The tower is flanked by the massive ❸ **Tsar Cannon & Bell**.

In the southeast corner, ❹ **Archangel Cathedral** has an elaborate interior, where three centuries of tsars are laid to rest. Your final stop on Sobornaya pl is ❺ **Annunciation Cathedral**, rich with frescoes and iconography.

Walk along the Great Kremlin Palace and enter the ❻ **Armoury** at the time designated on your ticket. After gawking at the goods, exit the Kremlin through Borovitsky Gate and stroll through the Alexander Garden to the ❼ **Tomb of the Unknown Soldier**.

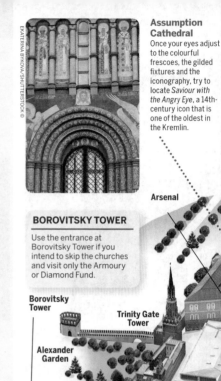

Assumption Cathedral
Once your eyes adjust to the colourful frescoes, the gilded fixtures and the iconography, try to locate *Saviour with the Angry Eye*, a 14th-century icon that is one of the oldest in the Kremlin.

Arsenal

BOROVITSKY TOWER

Use the entrance at Borovitsky Tower if you intend to skip the churches and visit only the Armoury or Diamond Fund.

Borovitsky Tower

Trinity Gate Tower

Alexander Garden

⑥

Great Kremlin Palace

TOP TIPS

➡ **Online Purchase** Full-price tickets to the Kremlin churches and the Armoury can be purchased in advance on the Kremlin website.

➡ **Lunch** There are no eating options. Plan to eat before you arrive or stash a snack.

Armoury
Take advantage of the free audio guide to direct you to the most intriguing treasures of the Armoury, which is chock-full of precious metalworks and jewellery, armour and weapons, gowns and crowns, carriages and sledges.

Tomb of the Unknown Soldier

Visit the Tomb of the Unknown Soldier honouring the heroes of the Great Patriotic War. Come at the top of the hour to see the solemn synchronicity of the changing of the guard.

ANDREW KOTURANOV/SHUTTERSTOCK ©

Patriarch's Palace

Ivan the Great Bell Tower

Check out the artistic electronic renderings of the Kremlin's history, then climb 137 steps to the belfry's upper gallery, where you will be rewarded with super, sweeping vistas of Sobornaya pl and beyond.

Moscow River

Sobornaya pl

Tsar Cannon & Bell

Peer down the barrel of the monstrous Tsar Cannon and pose for a picture beside the oversized Tsar Bell, both of which are too big to serve their intended purpose.

Archangel Cathedral

See the final resting place of princes and emperors who ruled Russia for more than 300 years, including the visionary Ivan the Great, the tortured Ivan the Terrible and the tragic Tsarevitch Dmitry.

Annunciation Cathedral

Admire the artistic mastery of Russia's greatest icon painters who are responsible for many of the icons in the deesis and festival rows of the iconostasis.

EKATERINA BYKOVA/SHUTTERSTOCK ©

Red Square and St Basil's Cathedral

TANATAT PONGPHIBOOL, THAILAND/GETTY IMAGES ©

Red Square & St Basil's Cathedral, Moscow

Immediately outside the Kremlin's northeastern wall is the celebrated Red Square, the 400m-by-150m cobble-stoned heart of Moscow. Commanding the square from the southern end is St Basil's Cathedral.

Great For...

☑ **Don't Miss**

The view of Red Square and St Basil's at night.

Red Square

The panorama of the square never fails to set the heart aflutter, especially at night. The word *krasnaya* in the name means 'red' now, but in old Russian it meant 'beautiful' and Krasnaya pl lives up to this epithet. Furthermore, it evokes an incredible sense of import to stroll across the place where so much of Russian history has unfolded.

Next to the cathedral, an elevated platform, known as the Place of Skulls, was used for reading out decrees and proclamations in the old ages and became the setting for Pussy Riot's anti-Putin video clip in 2011.

⚓ Explore Ashore

From the northern cruise terminal, it's a 10-minute walk to Rechnoy vokzal metro stop. From here, take line 2 to Teatralnaya (25 minutes), from where it's a five-minute walk to Red Square. You can cover the square in an hour.

❶ Need to Know

Красная площадь; Krasnaya pl; Ⓜ Ploshchad Revolyutsii

St Basil's Cathedral

At the southern end of Red Square stands the icon of Russia: **St Basil's Cathedral** (Покровский собор, Храм Василия Блаженного; ☑ 495-698 3304; www.shm.ru; adult/concession R1000/150; ⊙ 11am-5pm Nov-Apr, to 6pm May-Oct, from 10am Jun-Aug). This crazy confusion of colours, patterns and shapes is the culmination of a style that is unique to Russian architecture. In 1552, Ivan the Terrible captured the Tatar stronghold of Kazan on the Feast of Intercession. He commissioned this landmark church, officially the Intercession Cathedral, to commemorate the victory. Created from 1555 to 1561, this masterpiece would become the ultimate symbol of Russia.

Lenin's Mausoleum

Although Vladimir Ilych requested that he be buried beside his mum in St Petersburg, he still lies in state in this **mausoleum** (Мавзолей Ленина; www.lenin.ru; Krasnaya pl; ⊙ 10am-1pm Tue-Thu & Sat) FREE at the foot of the Kremlin wall, receiving visitors who come to pay their respects. Line up at the western corner of the square (near the entrance to Alexander Garden) to see the embalmed leader, who has been here since 1924. Note that photography is not allowed and stern guards ensure that all visitors remain respectful and silent.

Winter Palace (p212)

State Hermitage Museum, St Petersburg

The Hermitage fully lives up to its sterling reputation. You can be absorbed by its treasures for days and still come out wanting more.

Great For...

[icons: painting, notebook/pen, camera]

[map showing: Great (Old) Hermitage, Hermitage Theatre, Small Hermitage, **Hermitage**, New Hermitage, Winter Palace, General Staff Building, Admiralteyskaya, Nevsky pr]

ℹ️ Need to Know

Государственный Эрмитаж; www.hermitage museum.org; Dvortsovaya pl 2; combined ticket R700; ⏰10.30am-6pm Tue, Thu, Sat & Sun, to 9pm Wed & Fri; Ⓜ Admiralteyskaya

☑ **Don't Miss**
Rembrandt (Room 254)
Great Church (Room 271)
Treasure Gallery
Peacock Clock (Room 204)

The Collection

The Hermitage first opened to the public in 1852. Today, for the price of admission, anybody can parade down the grand staircases and across parquet floors, gawping at crystal chandeliers, gilded furniture and an amazing art collection that once was for the Tsar's court's eyes only.

The main complex consists of five connected buildings – the **Winter Palace** (Зимний дворец), the **Small Hermitage** (Малый Эрмитаж), the **Great (Old) Hermitage** (Большой (Старый) Эрмитаж), also known as the Large Hermitage, the **New Hermitage** (Новый Эрмитаж) and the **Hermitage Theatre** (https://hermitagetheater. com; Dvortsovaya nab 32; online tickets from R8300) – and is devoted to items from prehistoric times up until the mid-19th century.

Impressionist, post-impressionist and modern works are found in the new galleries of the **General Staff Building** (Здание Главного штаба; Dvortsovaya pl 6-8; R300, incl main Hermitage museum & other buildings R700; ⊙10.30am-6pm Tue, Thu, Sat & Sun, to 9pm Wed & Fri) across Palace Sq.

The Western European Collection, in particular, does not miss much: Spanish, Flemish, Dutch, French, English and German art are all covered from the 15th to the 18th centuries, while the Italian collection goes back all the way to the 13th century, including the Florentine and Venetian Renaissance, with priceless works by Leonardo da Vinci, Raphael, Michelangelo and Titian. A highlight is the enormous collection of Dutch and Flemish paintings, in particular the spectacular assortment of

Hermitage gallery

Rembrandt, most notably his masterpiece *Return of the Prodigal Son*.

Treasure Gallery

For lovers of things that glitter and the applied arts, the Hermitage's **Treasure Gallery** (tour of Diamond or Gold Rooms R350) should not be missed. These two special collections, guarded behind vault doors, are open only by guided tour, for which you should either call ahead to reserve a place or buy a ticket at the entrance. The Golden Rooms collection focuses on a hoard of fabulous Scythian and Greek gold and silver from the Caucasus, Crimea and Ukraine, dating from the 7th to 2nd centuries BC; the Diamond Rooms section has fabulous jewellery from Western Europe and pieces from as far apart as China, India and Iran.

Peacock Clock

The centrepiece of the Pavilion Hall (Room 204) is the incredible Peacock Clock, created by James Cox and gifted to Catherine the Great in 1781 by Grigory Potemkin. A revolving dial in one of the toadstools tells the time: as it strikes the hour the automaton peacock spreads its wings and the toadstools, owl and cock come to life in once-weekly performances at 7pm on Wednesday.

POPOVA VALERIYA/SHUTTERSTOCK ©

⚓ Explore Ashore

The river terminal is around a 10-minute walk from Proletarskaya metro station, from where it's a 20-minute ride to Gostiny Dvor. From here, a 20-minute stroll down the main boulevard, Nevsky Prospekt, will get you to the Hermitage, or you could jump on one of the many buses running along this street. To see everything here you need around 60 days (!), but if you plan your highlights carefully in advance, half a day will allow you to see them.

★ Top Tips

● Avoid possibly long entrance queues by buying your ticket online. The printed-out voucher or PDF on a wi-fi–enabled device is valid for 180 days.

● Alternatively, pay at the computerised ticket machines in the main entrance courtyard and be sure to wait for your tickets to be printed at the end of the transaction (they come after the payment receipt).

● If you leave jackets and bags in the cloakroom, be aware that you can't go back for anything without leaving the museum.

● Handbags, small shoulder bags and plastic bags are allowed in the Hermitage, but backpacks aren't.

The Hermitage

A HALF-DAY TOUR

Successfully navigating the State Hermitage Museum, with its four vast interconnecting buildings and around 360 rooms, is an art form in itself. Our half-day tour of the highlights can be done in four hours, or easily extended to a full day.

Once past ticket control start by ascending the grand **❶ Jordan Staircase** to Neva Enfilade and Great Enfilade for the impressive staterooms, including the former throne room St George's Hall and the 1812 War Gallery (Room 197), and the Romanovs' private apartments. Admire the newly restored **❷ Great Church**, then circle back through the throne room and walk down the Dutch art and Medieval art galleries (261 and 259) to the **❸ Pavilion Hall** with its view onto the Hanging Garden and the gilded Peacock Clock, always a crowd pleaser.

Make your way along the series of smaller galleries in the Large Hermitage hung with Italian Renaissance art, including masterpieces by **❹ Da Vinci** and **❺ Caravaggio**. The Loggia of Raphael (Room 227) is also impressive. Linger a while in the galleries containing Spanish art before taking in the Dutch collection, the highlight of which is the hoard of **❻ Rembrandt** canvases in Room 254.

Descend the Council Staircase (Room 206), noting the giant malachite vase, to the ground floor where the fantastic Egyptian collection awaits in Room 100 as well as the galleries of Greek and Roman Antiquities. If you have extra time, it's well worth booking tours to see the special exhibition in the **❼ Gold Rooms** of the Treasure Gallery.

TOP TIPS

➜ Reserve tickets online to skip the long lines.

➜ You can also get tickets at the self-service kiosks in the courtyard.

➜ Wear comfortable shoes.

➜ Bear in mind the only cloakroom is before ticket control, so you can't go back and pick up a sweater.

GERMAN S/SHUTTERSTOCK ©

Jordan Staircase
Originally designed by Rastrelli, in the 18th century this incredible white marble construction was known as the Ambassadorial Staircase because it was the way into the palace for official receptions.

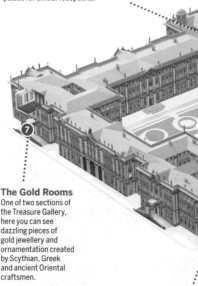

The Gold Rooms
One of two sections of the Treasure Gallery, here you can see dazzling pieces of gold jewellery and ornamentation created by Scythian, Greek and ancient Oriental craftsmen.

IMAGE SOURCE/GETTY IMAGES ©

Great Church
This stunningly ornate church was the Romanovs' private place of worship and the venue for the marriage of the last tsar, Nicholas II, to Alexandra Feodorovna in 1895.

Rembrandt
A moving portrait of contrition and forgiveness, *Return of the Prodigal Son* (Room 254) depicts the biblical scene of a wayward son returning to his father.

Da Vinci
Along with the *Benois Madonna*, also here, *Madonna and Child (Madonna Litta;* Room 214) is one of just a handful of paintings known to be the work of Leonardo da Vinci.

St George's Hall

Hermitage Theatre

Pavilion Hall
Apart from the Peacock Clock, the Pavilion Hall also contains beautifully detailed mosaic tables made by Italian and Russian craftsmen in the mid-19th century.

Caravaggio
The Lute Player (Room 232) is the Hermitage's only Caravaggio, and a work that the master of light and shade described as the best piece he'd ever painted.

St Petersburg's Historic Heart

This stroll explores the venerable centre of St Petersburg, taking in some of its main monuments as you criss-cross its waterways.

Start Dvortsovaya pl
Distance 2km
Duration Three hours

2 Cross the river over **Pevchesky Most** and head north to the residence of Russia's most celebrated poet at the **Pushkin Flat-Museum** (www.museumpushkin.ru; ⊘10.30am-6pm Wed-Mon).

1 At the corner of Nevsky pr, the **Alexander Column** is perfectly framed under the triumphal arch with the **Winter Palace** (p212) behind.

Dvortsovy most

Winter Palace

Pushkin Flat-Museum

nab reki Moyki

START

Alexander Garden

Bolshaya Konyushennaya ul

Malaya Konyushennaya ul

Admiralteyskaya Ⓜ

Gorokhovaya ul

Malaya Morskaya ul

Kazansky most

Kazan Cathedral

6 At the junction of Nevsky pr and nab kanala Griboyedova, admire the Style Moderne **Singer Building**, in contrast to the **Kazan Cathedral** (⊘8.30am-7.30pm) opposite.

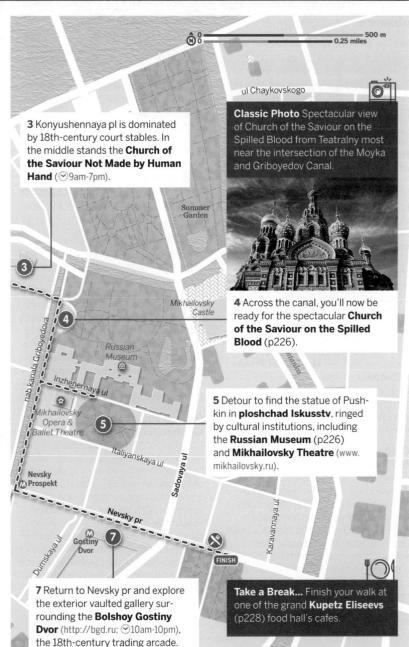

N 0 —— 500 m
0 —— 0.25 miles

ul Chaykovskogo

3 Konyushennaya pl is dominated by 18th-century court stables. In the middle stands the **Church of the Saviour Not Made by Human Hand** (🕙9am-7pm).

Classic Photo Spectacular view of Church of the Saviour on the Spilled Blood from Teatralny most near the intersection of the Moyka and Griboyedov Canal.

Summer Garden

Mikhailovsky Castle

4 Across the canal, you'll now be ready for the spectacular **Church of the Saviour on the Spilled Blood** (p226).

Russian Museum

nab kanala Griboyedova

Inzhenernaya ul

Mikhailovsky Opera & Ballet Theatre

5 Detour to find the statue of Pushkin in **ploshchad Iskusstv**, ringed by cultural institutions, including the **Russian Museum** (p226) and **Mikhailovsky Theatre** (www.mikhailovsky.ru).

Italiyanskaya ul

Sadovaya ul

Nevsky Prospekt

Nevsky pr

Karavannaya ul

Dumskaya ul

Gostiny Dvor

FINISH

7 Return to Nevsky pr and explore the exterior vaulted gallery surrounding the **Bolshoy Gostiny Dvor** (http://bgd.ru; 🕙10am-10pm), the 18th-century trading arcade.

Take a Break... Finish your walk at one of the grand **Kupetz Eliseevs** (p228) food hall's cafes.

2 LISA-LISA/SHUTTERSTOCK © 4 ROMAN EVGENEV/SHUTTERSTOCK © 6 DINA PHOTO STORES/SHUTTERSTOCK ©

Moscow

Moscow lives and breathes Russian history, from the ancient Kremlin on the city's founding site to the ubiquitous legacy of the Soviet period. During any season, at any hour of the day, Moscow thrills visitors with its artistry, history and majesty.

◉ SIGHTS

Pushkin Museum
of Fine Arts   Museum

(Музей изобразительных искусств им Пушкина; ☏495-697 9578; www.arts-museum.ru; ul Volkhonka 12; single/combined galleries R400/600; ⊙11am-7pm Tue, Wed, Sat & Sun, to 9pm Thu & Fri; ⓂKropotkinskaya) This is Moscow's premier foreign-art museum, split over three branches and showing off a broad selection of European works, including masterpieces from ancient civilisations, the Italian Renaissance and the Dutch Golden Age. To see the incredible collection of impressionist and post-impressionist paintings, visit the **19th & 20th Century Art Gallery** (adult/student R300/150; ⊙11am-7pm Tue-Sun, to 9pm Thu). The **Museum of Private Collections** (Музей личных коллекций; www.artprivatecollections.ru; ul; entry prices vary; ⊙noon-8pm Wed-Sun, to 9pm Thu) shows off complete collections donated by private individuals.

Cathedral of Christ
the Saviour   Church

(Храм Христа Спасителя; www.xxc.ru; ul Volkhonka 15; ⊙1-5pm Mon, from 10am Tue-Sun; ⓂKropotkinskaya) ᴴᴿᴱᴱ This opulent and grandiose cathedral was completed in 1997 – just in time to celebrate Moscow's 850th birthday. The cathedral's sheer size and splendour guarantee its role as a love-it-or-hate-it landmark. Considering Stalin's plan for this site (a Palace of Soviets topped with a 100m statue of Lenin), Muscovites should at least be grateful they can admire the shiny domes of a church instead of the shiny dome of Ilyich's head.

State Tretyakov
Gallery Main Branch   Gallery

(Государственная Третьяковская Галерея; www.tretyakovgallery.ru; Lavrushinsky per 10; adult/concession R700/150; ⊙10am-6pm Tue, Wed & Sun, to 9pm Thu-Sat, last tickets 1hr before closing; ⓂTretyakovskaya) The exotic boyar (high-ranking noble) castle on a little lane in Zamoskvorechie contains the main branch of the State Tretyakov Gallery, housing the world's best collection of Russian icons and an outstanding collection of other prerevolutionary Russian art. Show up early to beat the queues. The neighbouring **Engineer's Building** is reserved for special exhibits.

Gorky Park   Park

(Парк Горького; ⊙24hr; ⓯; ⓂOktyabrskaya) ᴴᴿᴱᴱ Moscow's main city escape isn't your conventional expanse of nature preserved inside an urban jungle. It's not a fun fair either, though it used to be one. Its official name says it all – Maxim Gorky's Central Park of Culture and Leisure. That's exactly what it provides: culture and leisure in all shapes and forms. Designed in the 1920s by avant-garde architect Konstantin Melnikov as a piece of communist utopia, these days it showcases the enlightened transformation Moscow has recently undergone.

Garage Museum of
Contemporary Art   Museum

(☏495-645 0520; www.garagemca.org; ul Krymsky val 9/32; adult/student R300/150; ⊙11am-10pm; ⓂOktyabrskaya) The brainchild of Moscow art fairy Darya Zhukova, Garage is one of the capital's hottest modern-art venues. In 2015, the museum moved to spectacular new digs in Gorky Park – a derelict Soviet-era building, renovated by the visionary Dutch architect Rem Koolhaas. It hosts exhibitions, lectures, films and interactive educational programs, featuring Russian and international artists. A good cafe and a bookstore are also on the premises.

Tomb of the
Unknown Soldier   Memorial

(Могила неизвестного солдата) The Tomb of the Unknown Soldier contains the remains

Exterior detail, Cathedral of Christ the Saviour

of one soldier who died in December 1941 at Km41 of Leningradskoe sh – the nearest the Nazis came to Moscow. This is a kind of national pilgrimage spot, where newly-weds bring flowers and have their pictures taken. The inscription reads: 'Your name is unknown, your deeds immortal.' Every hour on the hour, the guards perform a perfectly synchronised ceremony to change the guards on duty.

😊 ACTIVITIES

Sanduny Baths   Bathhouse
(📞495-782 1808; www.sanduny.ru; ul Neglinnaya 14; R1800-2800; ⏰8am-10pm Wed-Mon, 2nd male top class 10am-midnight Tue-Fri, 8am-10pm Sat & Sun; Ⓜ Kuznetsky Most) Sanduny is the oldest and most luxurious *banya* (hot bath) in the city. The Gothic Room is a work of art with its rich woodcarving, while the main shower room has an aristocratic Roman feel to it. There are several classes, as on trains; regulars say that the second male top class is actually better than the premium class.

Capital Shipping Co   Boating
(ССК, Столичная Судоходная Компания; 📞495-225 6070; www.cck-ship.ru; adult/child 1hr cruise R900/700, 2-day pass R2400/2000) Originally, these ferries were simply a form of transportation, but visitors realised that riding the entire route was a great way to see the city, and CCK eventually developed fixed routes with higher prices. Nowadays, ferries ply the Moscow River from May to September; board at one of six docks for a cruise ranging from one to two hours.

🔒 SHOPPING

GUM   Mall
(ГУМ; www.gum.ru; Krasnaya pl 3; ⏰10am-10pm; Ⓜ Ploshchad Revolyutsii) Behind its elaborate 240m-long facade on the northeastern side of Red Square, GUM is a bright, bustling shopping mall with hundreds of fancy stores and restaurants. With a skylight roof and three-level arcades, the spectacular interior was a revolutionary design when it was built in the 1890s, replacing the Upper Trading Rows that previously occupied this site.

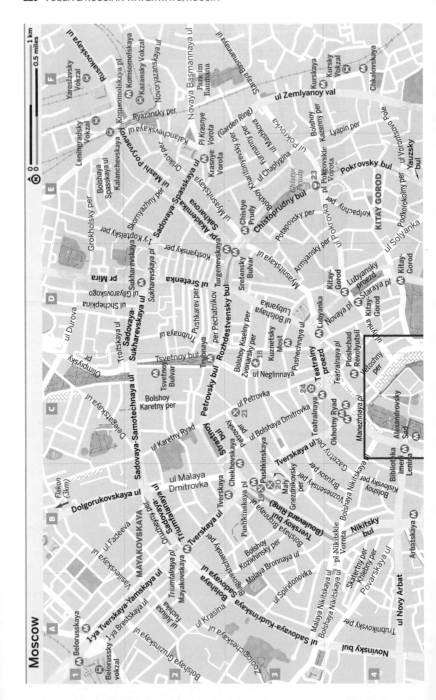

Moscow

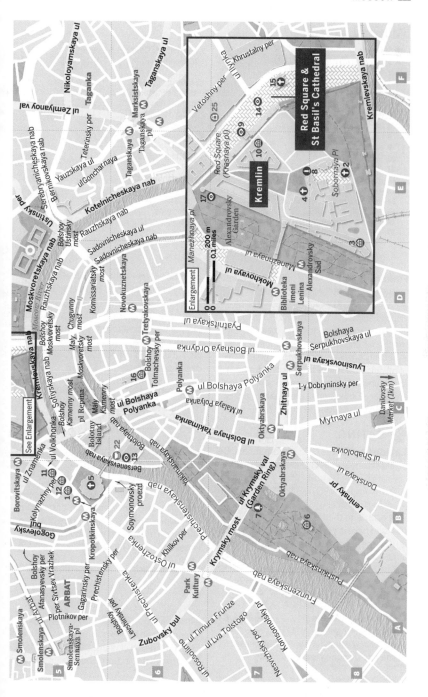

Enlargement

0   200 m
0   0.1 miles

Manezhnaya pl

Kremlin

**Red Square &
St Basil's Cathedral**

Red Square
(Krasnaya pl)

Alexandrovsky
Garden

Mokhovaya ul

Manezhnaya ul

Biblioteka
imeni
Lenina

Alexandrovsky
Sad

Sobornaya Pl

ul Ilyinka

Vetoshny per

Khrustalny per

Kremlevskaya nab

See Enlargement

Nikoloyamskaya ul

ul Zemlyanoy val

Taganka

Taganskaya ul

Nikoloyamskaya nab

Serebryanicheskaya nab

Bernikovskaya nab

Yauzskaya ul

ul Goncharnaya

Marksistskaya

Taganskaya
pl

Taganskaya

Ustinsky per

Kotelnicheskaya nab

Rauzhskaya ul

Sadovnicheskaya ul

Sadovnicheskaya nab

Teterinsky per

Bolshoy
Ustinsky
most

Kotelnicheskaya nab

Moskvoretskaya nab

Moscow River

Bolshoy
Moskvoretsky
most

Maly.
Chugunny
most

Komissariatsky
most

Novokuznetskaya

Pyatnitskaya ul

Bolshoy
Moskvoretsky
most

Sofiyskaya nab

Bolshoy
Kamenny most

Maly.
Kamenny
most

pl Repina

Bolotny
Island

Bolotnaya nab

Bersenevskaya nab

Vodootvodny

ul Bolshaya Ordynka

ul Bolshaya Polyanka

ul Malaya Polyanka

Polyanka

Tretyakovskaya

Tolmachevsky per

Bolshaya
Serpukhovskaya ul

Serpukhovskaya

1-y Dobryninsky per

Mytnaya ul

Lyusinovskaya ul

Zhitnaya ul

Oktyabrskaya

Oktyabrskaya

Danilovsky Market (1km)

ul Shabolovka

Donskaya ul

Leninsky pr

Komsomolsky pr

Nesvizhsky per

ul Timura Frunze

ul Lva Tolstogo

ul Rossolimo

ul Prechistenka

Park
Kultury

Khilkov per

ul Ostozhenka

Prechistensky per

Soymonovsky
proezd

Krymsky most

Krymsky val
(Garden Ring)

Frunzenskaya nab

Pushkinskaya nab

Pushkinskaya nab

Yakimanskaya nab

ul Bolshaya Yakimanka

ul Bolshaya
Polyanka

ul Volkhonka

Znamenka

Borovitskaya

Kolymazhny per

Gogolevsky bul

Plotnikov per

Smolenskaya-
Sennaya pl

Smolenskaya

ul Arbat

ARBAT

Bolshoy
Afanasyevsky per

per Sivtsev Vrazhek

Gagarinsky per

Bolshoy
Lestinsky per

Zubovsky bul

Moscow

Flakon   Shopping Centre

(www.flacon.ru; ul Bolshaya Novodmitrovskaya 36;
Ⓜ Dmitrovskaya) Flakon is arguably the most
visually attractive of all the redeveloped
industrial areas around town, looking a bit
like the far end of London's Portobello Rd,
especially on weekends. Once a glassware
plant, it is now home to dozens of funky
shops and other businesses. Shopping for
designer clothes and unusual souvenirs is
the main reason for coming here.

EATING

Lavka-Lavka   International €€

(Лавка-Лавка; ☑495-621 2036; www.restoran.
lavkalavka.com; ul Petrovka 21 str 2; mains R500-
1100; ⊙noon-midnight Tue-Thu & Sun, to 1am Fri
& Sat, 6pm-midnight Mon; 🛜🛗; Ⓜ Teatralnaya)
🖋 Welcome to the Russian Portlandia – all
the food here is organic and hails from little
farms where you can rest assured all the
lambs and chickens lived a very happy life
before being served to you on a plate. This
is a great place to sample local food cooked
in a funky improvised style.

Danilovsky Market   Market €€

(www.danrinok.ru; Mytnaya ul 74; mains R400-
600; ⊙8am-8pm; Ⓜ Tulskaya) A showcase
of the city's ongoing gentrification, this

giant Soviet-era farmers market is now
largely about deli food cooked and served
in myriad little eateries, including such
gems as a Dagestani dumpling shop and a
Vietnamese *pho* kitchen. The market itself
looks very orderly, if a tiny bit artificial,
with uniformed vendors and thoughtfully
designed premises.

Khachapuri   Georgian €€

(Хачапури; ☑8-985-764 3118; www.hacha.
ru; Bolshoy Gnezdnikovsky per 10; khachapuri
R220-420, mains R460-720; ⊙10am-11pm, to
1am Fri & Sat; ❄🛜; Ⓜ Pushkinskaya) Unassum-
ing, affordable and appetising, this urban
cafe exemplifies what people love about
Georgian culture: the warm hospitality
and the freshly baked *khachapuri* (cheese
bread). Aside from eight types of delicious
khachapuri, there's also an array of soups,
shashlyk (meat kebabs), *khinkali* (dumplings) and other Georgian favourites.

Cafe Pushkin   Russian €€€

(Кафе Пушкинь; ☑495-739 0033; www.
cafe-pushkin.ru; Tverskoy bul 26a; business lunch
R660-990, mains R1000-3400; ⊙24hr; ❄🛜;
Ⓜ Pushkinskaya) The tsarina of *haute-russe*
dining, offering an exquisite blend of Russian and French cuisines. Service and food
are done to perfection. The lovely 19th-

century building has a different atmosphere on each floor, including a richly decorated library and a pleasant rooftop cafe.

DRINKING & NIGHTLIFE

Ukuleleshnaya   Bar
(Укулелешная; ☏495-642 5726; www.uku-uku.
ru; ul Pokrovka 17 str 1; ☺noon-midnight Sun-
Thu, noon-4am Fri & Sat; Ⓜ Chistye Prudy) In
its new location, this is now more of a bar
than a musical instrument shop, although
ukuleles still adorn the walls, prompting an
occasional jam session. Craft beer prevails
on the drinks list, but Ukuleleshnaya also
serves experimental cocktails of its own invention. Live concerts happen regularly and
resident Pomeranian spitz Berseny (cute
dog) presides over the resulting madness.

Bar Strelka   Cafe, Club
(www.barstrelka.com; Bersenevskaya nab 14/5,
bldg 5a; ☺9am-midnight Mon-Thu, to 3am Fri,
noon-3am Sat, noon-midnight Sun; ☏; Ⓜ Kropot-
kinskaya) Located just below the Patriarshy
most, the bar-restaurant at the **Strelka
Institute** (www.strelkainstitute.ru) is the ideal
starting point for an evening in the **Red October** (Завод Красный Октябрь) complex. The
rooftop terrace has unbeatable Moscow
River views, but the interior is equally cool
in a shabby-chic sort of way. The bar menu
is excellent and there is usually somebody
tinkling the ivories.

✪ ENTERTAINMENT

Bolshoi Theatre   Ballet, Opera
(Большой театр; ☏495-455 5555; www.bolshoi.
ru; Teatralnaya pl 1; tickets R5500-12,000;
☺closed late Jul–mid-Sep; Ⓜ Teatralnaya)
An evening at the Bolshoi is still one of
Moscow's most romantic and entertaining options for a night on the town. The
glittering six-tier auditorium has an electric
atmosphere, evoking over 240 years of
premier music and dance. Both the ballet
and opera companies perform a range of
Russian and foreign works here.

ⓘ INFORMATION

Discover Moscow (https://um.mos.ru/en/
discover-moscow) A comprehensive site organised by the City of Moscow.

Tourist Hotline (☏8-800-220 0001, 8-800-
220 0002, 495-663 1393)

ⓘ GETTING AROUND

Most visitors won't need anything but Moscow's
super-efficient metro system, which allows
you to get to pretty much anywhere in the city
without thinking about complicated bus or tram
routes. Connecting to the metro, an overground
railway ring line (Moscow Central Ring) circles
the city, which may be useful for some sights on
the outskirts.

Moscow has a unified ticketing system. All
tickets are essentially smart cards that you
must tap on the reader at the turnstiles before
entering a metro station or on the bus. Most
convenient for short-term visitors is the red
Ediny (Единый) ticket, which is good for all kinds
of transport and available at metro stations.
Depending on your time and logistics, you can
choose between buying a ticket good for a single
trip for R55, two trips for R110, 20 trips for R720,
40 trips for R1440 or 60 trips for R1700.

St Petersburg

The sheer grandeur and history of Russia's
imperial capital never fail to amaze, but this
is also a city with a revolutionary spirit. It
remains a city of majestic architecture, high
artistic culture and historical significance,
augmented with a brilliant restaurant, bar
and cafe scene and exciting creative design
clusters.

SIGHTS

Palace Square   Square
(Дворцовая площадь; Dvortsovaya pl; Ⓜ Admiralteyskaya) This vast expanse is simply one
of the most striking squares in the world,
still redolent of imperial grandeur almost
a century after the end of the Romanov

St Petersburg

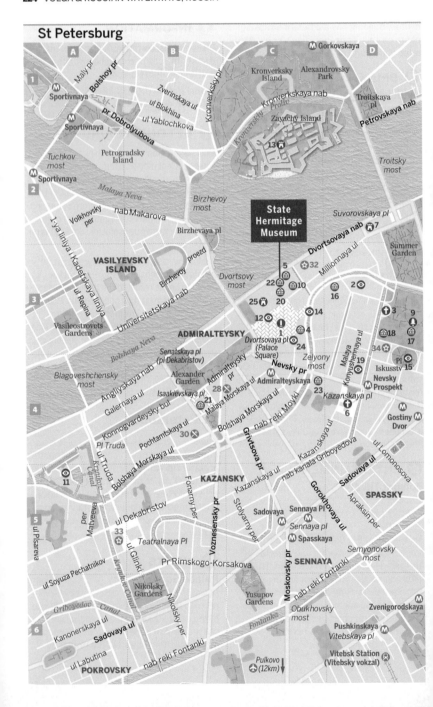

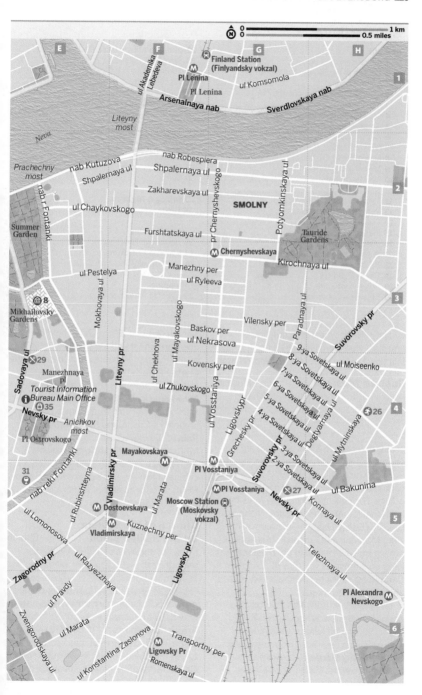

N

0
0

1 km
0.5 miles

E **F** **G** **H**

Finland Station
(Finlyandsky vokzal)

Pl Lenina

Pl Lenina

ul Komsomola

ul Akademika Lebedeva

Arsenalnaya nab

Sverdlovskaya nab

1

Liteyny most

Neva

Prachechny most

nab Kutuzova

nab Robespiera

Shpalernaya ul

Shpalernaya ul

Zakharevskaya ul

pr Chernyshevskogo

SMOLNY

Potyomkinskaya ul

2

nab r Fontanki

ul Chaykovskogo

Summer Garden

Furshtatskaya ul

Tauride Gardens

Chernyshevskaya

Kirochnaya ul

ul Pestelya

Manezhny per

ul Ryleeva

Mokhovaya ul

Paradnaya ul

Suvorovsky pr

3

8

Mikhailovsky Gardens

Vilensky per

Baskov per

ul Nekrasova

ul Mayakovskogo

Liteyny pr

ul Chekhova

9-ya Sovetskaya ul

ul Moiseenko

8-ya Sovetskaya ul

7-ya Sovetskaya ul

Sadovaya ul

29

Manezhnaya pl

Tourist Information
Bureau Main Office

35

Nevsky pr

Anichkov most

Pl Ostrovskogo

Kovensky per

ul Zhukovskogo

ul Vosstaniya

Ligovsky pr

Grechesky pr

6-ya Sovetskaya ul

5-ya Sovetskaya ul

4-ya Sovetskaya ul

Suvorovsky pr

Degtyarnaya ul

ul Mytninskaya

26

4

31

nab reki Fontanki

ul Rubinshteyna

Vladimirsky pr

Mayakovskaya

Pl Vosstaniya

3-ya Sovetskaya ul

2-ya Sovetskaya ul

27

ul Bakunina

Konnaya ul

5

ul Lomonosova

ul Marata

Dostoevskaya

Moscow Station
(Moskovsky vokzal)

Pl Vosstaniya

Nevsky pr

Telezhnaya ul

Zagorodny pr

ul Razyezzhaya

Kuznechny per

Vladimirskaya

Ligovsky pr

ul Pravdy

Zvenigorodskaya ul

ul Marata

ul Konstantina Zaslonova

Ligovsky Pr

Transportny per

Romenskaya ul

Pl Alexandra Nevskogo

6

St Petersburg

dynasty. For the most amazing first impression, walk from Nevsky pr, up Bolshaya Morskaya ul and under the **triumphal arch**.

Russian Museum   Museum

(Русский музей; ☑812-595 4248; www.rus museum.ru; Inzhenernaya ul 4; adult/student R500/250; ☉10am-8pm Mon, 10am-6pm Wed & Fri-Sun, 1-9pm Thu; Ⓜ Nevsky Prospekt) Focusing solely on Russian art, from ancient church icons to 20th-century paintings, the Russian Museum's collection is magnificent and can easily be viewed in half a day or less. The collection includes works by Karl Bryullov, Alexander Ivanov, Nicholas Ghe, Ilya Repin, Natalya Goncharova, Kazimir Malevich and Kuzma Petrov-Vodkin, among many others, and the masterpieces keep on coming as you tour the beautiful Carlo Rossi–designed Mikhailovsky Palace and its attached wings.

Entry is either from Arts Sq or via the connected **Benois Wing** (adult/student R450/200) on nab kanala Griboyedova. There's also an entrance from the lovely **Mikhailovsky Garden** (Михайловский сад; https://igardens.ru; ☉10am-10pm May-Sep, to 8pm Oct-Mar, closed Apr) **FREE** behind the palace. Permanent and temporary exhibitions by the Russian Museum are also held at the **Marble Palace** (Мраморный дворец; www. rusmuseum.ru; adult/student R300/170), the **Mikhailovsky Castle** (Михайловский замок; adult/student R250/130), also known as the Engineer's Castle, and the **Stroganov Palace** (Строгановский дворец; adult/student R250/130). Combined tickets, available at each palace, cover entrance either to your choice of two the same day (adult/student R600/270) or to all four within a three-day period (R850/400).

Church of the Saviour on the Spilled Blood   Church

(Храм Спаса на Крови; ☑812-315 1636; http:// eng.cathedral.ru/spasa_na_krovi; Konyushennaya pl; adult/student R350/200; ☉10.30am-6pm Thu-Tue; Ⓜ Nevsky Prospekt) This five-domed dazzler is St Petersburg's most elaborate church, with a classic Russian Orthodox exterior and an interior decorated with some 7000 sq metres of mosaics. Officially called the Church of the Resurrection of Christ, its far more striking colloquial name references the assassination attempt on Tsar Alexander II here in 1881.

St Isaac's Cathedral   Museum
(Исаакиевский собор; ☎812-315 9732; www. cathedral.ru; Isaakievskaya pl; cathedral adult/ student R250/150, colonnade R150; ⊙cathedral 10.30am-10.30pm Thu-Tue May-Sep, to 6pm Oct-Apr, colonnade 10.30am-10.30pm May-Oct, to 6pm Nov-Apr; ⓜAdmiralteyskaya) The golden dome of St Isaac's Cathedral dominates the St Petersburg skyline. Its obscenely lavish interior is open as a museum, although services are held in the cathedral throughout the year. Many people bypass the museum to climb the 262 steps to the *kolonnada* (colonnade) around the drum of the dome, providing superb city views.

Peter & Paul Fortress   Fortress
(Петропавловская крепость; www.spbmuseum. ru; grounds free, SS Peter & Paul Cathedral adult/ child R450/250, combined ticket for 5 exhibitions R600/350; ⊙grounds 9.30am-8pm, cathedral & bastion 10am-7pm Mon, Thu & Fri, 10am-5.45pm Sat, 11am-7pm Sun; ⓜGorkovskaya) Housing a cathedral where the Romanovs are buried, a former prison and various exhibitions, this large defensive fortress on Zayachy Island is the kernel from which St Petersburg grew into the city it is today. History buffs will love it and everyone will swoon at the panoramic views from atop the fortress walls, at the foot of which lies a sandy riverside beach, a prime spot for sunbathing.

New Holland   Island
(Новая Голландия; www.newhollandsp.ru; nab Admiralteyskogo kanala; ⊙9am-10pm Mon-Thu, to 11pm Fri-Sun; ⓜSadovaya) This triangular island was closed for the most part of the last three centuries, and has opened to the public in dazzling fashion. There's plenty going on here, with hundreds of events happening throughout the year. There are summertime concerts, art exhibitions, yoga classes and film screenings, plus restaurants, cafes and shops. You can also come to enjoy a bit of quiet on the grass – or on one of the pontoons floating in the pond.

🏛 Worth a Trip: Peterhof

One of the greatest attractions outside of St Petersburg is the jaw-dropping collection of gilded fountains, statue-lined lanes and picturesque canals that make up the **Lower Park** (Нижний парк; www. peterhofmuseum.ru; adult/student May-Oct R750/400, Nov-Apr free; ⊙9am-7pm) of Peterhof. Even if you'd rather not brave the crowds to visit the ornate **Grand Palace** (Большой дворец; www.peterhofmuseum. ru; ul Razvodnaya; adult/student R700/400, audio guide R600; ⊙10.30am-6pm Tue-Sun, closed last Tue of month), it's still well worth a visit here to see the over-the-top Grand Cascade and other water features, including trick fountains that douse unsuspecting visitors.

It's easy and cheap to reach Peterhof by bus or *marshrutka* (minibus). From May to September, there are also expensive but highly enjoyable hydrofoils from the centre of St Petersburg.

Lower Park, Peterhof
DEN781/SHUTTERSTOCK ©

➋ ACTIVITIES
If your time is short, or you wish to avoid the long queues at the palaces, book yourself into a gu ided tour of Peterhof, Tsarskoe Selo or Pavlovsk with a travel agency, and make sure that they book your entry ticket for you. **Peter's Walking Tours** (☎812-943 1229; http://peterswalk.com; from R1320) in St Petersburg can do this for you.

Mariinsky Theatre ballet performance at the Bolshoi Theatre (p223), Moscow

SERGEY PETROV/SHUTTERSTOCK ©

DenRus
Tours

(www.denrus.ru) This long-established shore-excursion operator offers a number of different tours angled specifically towards cruise passengers. Tours can often be adapted to visitor needs and guides are well trained, experienced and speak good English.

Red October
Tours

(☏812-363 0368; www.redoctober.ru) Operating since 2000, this experienced tour agency specialises in one- to three-day shore excursions for cruise ship passengers, including tailor-made programs for private groups.

Mytninskiye Bani
Bathhouse

(Мытнинские бани; www.mybanya.spb.ru; ul Mytninskaya 17-19; per hr R200-350, lux banya per hr R1000-2000; ⊙8am-10pm Fri-Tue; M Ploshchad Vosstaniya) Unique in the city, Mytninskiye Bani is heated by a wood furnace, just like the log-cabin bathhouses still found in the Russian countryside. It's actually the oldest communal *banya* in the city; in addition to a *parilka* (steam room) and plunge pool, the private 'lux' *banya*

includes a swanky lounge area with leather furniture and a pool table.

SHOPPING

Kupetz Eliseevs
Food & Drinks

(☏812-456 6666; www.kupetzeliseevs.ru; Nevsky pr 56; ⊙10am-11pm; ☎; M Gostiny Dvor) This Style Moderne stunner is St Petersburg's most elegant grocery store, selling plenty of branded goods from tea blends to caviar and handmade chocolates as well as delicious freshly baked breads, pastries and cakes. Kids will love watching the animatronic figures in the window display and there are pleasant cafes on the ground floor and in the former wine cellar.

⊗ EATING

Banshiki
Russian €€

(Банщики; ☏8-921-941 1744; www.banshiki.spb.ru; Degtyarnaya ul 1; mains R500-1100; ⊙11am-11pm; ☎; M Ploshchad Vosstaniya) Attached to a renovated *banya* complex, this is currently the place to sample nostalgic Russian fare at affordable prices. Everything is made in-house, from its refreshing *kvas* (fermented rye bread water) to dried meats and eight types of smoked fish. Don't overlook cherry *vareniki* (dumplings) with sour cream, oxtail ragout or the rich borsch (betroot soup).

Gräs x Madbaren   Fusion €€

(☑812-928 1818; http://grasmadbaren.com; Inzhenernaya ul 7; mains R420-550, tasting menu R2500; ☺9am-11pm Sun-Thu, to 1am Fri & Sat; ☎; ⓜGostiny Dvor) Anton Abrezov is the talented exec chef behind this Scandi-cool meets Russian locavore restaurant where you can sample dishes such as a delicious corned-beef salad with black garlic and pickled vegetables or an upmarket twist on ramen noodles with succulent roast pork.

Teplo   Modern European €€

(☑812-407 2702; www.v-teple.ru; Bolshaya Morskaya ul 45; mains R360-940; ☺9am-midnight Mon-Fri, from 11am Sat & Sun; ❄☎✎♦; ⓜAdmiralteyskaya) This much-feted, eclectic and original restaurant has got it all just right. The venue itself is a lot of fun to nose around, with multiple small rooms, nooks and crannies. Service is friendly and fast (when it's not too busy) and the peppy, inventive Italian-leaning menu has something for everyone. Reservations are usually required, so call ahead.

Cococo   Russian €€€

(☑812-418 2060; www.kokoko.spb.ru; Voznesensky pr 6; mains R650-1300; ☺7-11am & 2pm-1am; ☎; ⓜAdmiralteyskaya) Cococo has charmed locals with its inventive approach to contemporary Russian cuisine. Your food is likely to arrive disguised as, say, a small bird's egg, a can of peas or a broken flowerpot – all rather gimmicky, theatrical and fun. The best way to sample what it does is with its tasting menu (R2900). Bookings are advised.

 DRINKING & NIGHTLIFE

Top Hops   Craft Beer

(☑8-966-757 0116; www.tophops.ru; nab reki Fontanki 55; ☺4pm-1am Mon-Thu, 2pm-2am Fri-Sun; ☎; ⓜGostiny Dvor) One of the nicer craft-beer bars in town, this riverside space with friendly staff serves up a regularly changing menu of 20 beers on tap and scores more in bottles. The tasty Mexican snacks and food (go for nachos and chilli) go down exceptionally well while you sample your way through its range.

 ENTERTAINMENT

Mariinsky Theatre   Ballet, Opera

(Мариинский театр; ☑812-326 4141; www.mariinsky.ru; Teatralnaya pl 1; tickets R1200-6500; ⓜSadovaya) St Petersburg's most spectacular venue for ballet and opera, the Mariinsky Theatre is an attraction in its own right. Tickets can be bought online or in person; book in advance during the summer months. The magnificent interior is the epitome of imperial grandeur, and any evening here will be an impressive experience.

 INFORMATION

Tourist Information Bureau (☑812-242 3909, 812-303 0555; http://eng.ispb.info; Sadovaya ul 14/52; ☺10am-7pm Mon-Sat; ⓜGostiny Dvor) Maps, tours, information and advice for travellers.

 GETTING AROUND

Metro Fastest way to cover long distances. Has around 70 stations and runs from approximately 5.45am to 12.45am.

Bus, Trolleybus & Marshrutka Buses are best for shorter distances in areas without good metro coverage; they can be slow going, but the views are good. Trolleybuses are slower still, but are cheap and plentiful. *Marshrutky* are the private sector's contribution – fast fixed-route minibuses that you can get on or off anywhere along their routes.

Tram With an ongoing upgrade, trams are becoming more useful, particularly in areas such as Kolomna and Vasilyevsky Island where there is little else available.

DNIEPER, UKRAINE

In This Chapter

Dnieper, Ukraine

In the beginning there was Kyiv. Long before Ukraine and Russia existed, the city's inhabitants were already striding up and down the green hills, idling away hot afternoons on the Dnipro (Dnieper) River and promenading along Khreshchatyk – then a stream, now the main avenue. From here, East Slavic civilisation spread all the way to Alaska. Odesa is a city straight from literature – an energetic, decadent boom town. Its famous Potemkin Steps sweep down to the Black Sea and Ukraine's biggest commercial port. Behind them, a cosmopolitan cast of characters makes merry among neoclassical pastel buildings lining a geometric grid of leafy streets.

With One Day in Kyiv

Stroll down the main boulevard, vul Khreshchatyk, to **Maidan Nezalezhnosti** (p238). Head on to **St Sophia's Cathedral** (p238) and **St Michael's Monastery** (p239), then head to the Kyevo-Pecherska Lavra. Return to the city centre on Kyiv's astonishingly deep metro and wander around **Shevchenka Park**, sampling *blyny* (pancakes) from a stand.

Best Places for...

Summer Nightlife Arkadia Beach, Odesa (p237)

Chilling Out Skvorechnik, Kyiv (p239)

Street Snacks Kyivska Perepichka, Kyiv (p241)

Souvenir Shopping Andriyivsky Uzviz, Kyiv (p239)

Foodie Experience City Food Market, Odesa (p245)

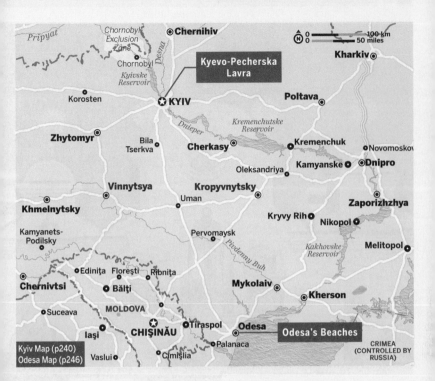

Kyiv Map (p240)
Odesa Map (p246)

Getting from the Ports

Kyiv The river port in Kyiv is about 1km north of downtown in the locale of Podil. It's very handy for Poshtova Ploshcha metro station.

Odesa Cruise ships dock at a central pier. From here, the Potemkin Steps rise into the centre of town; grab the funicular railway if you don't fancy the climb.

Fast Facts

Currency Hryvnia (uah)

Language Ukrainian

Free Wi-fi Virtually all cafes, restaurants and hotels have wi-fi, and speeds are generally very good.

Money Both ATMs and exchange booths signposted 'обмін валют' (obmin valyut) are ubiquitous.

Tourist Information In Kyiv, the city runs about a dozen information booths. See www.visitkyiv.travel.

Dormition Cathedral

Kyevo-Pecherska Lavra, Kyiv

Set on 28 hectares of grassy hills above the Dnipro River in Pechersk, tourists and Orthodox pilgrims flock to the Lavra. (Lavra is a senior monastery, while pecherska means 'of the caves'.) The monastery is a feast for the eyes, inside and out.

Great For...

☑ **Don't Miss**

The spooky mummified monks in the catacombs.

History

The Greek St Antony founded this *lavra* in 1051, after Orthodoxy was adopted as Kyivan Rus' official religion. He and his follower Feodosy dug a series of catacombs where they and other reclusive monks worshipped, studied and lived. When they died, their bodies were naturally preserved by the caves' cool temperature and dry atmosphere. The mummies survive today, confirmation for believers that these were true holy men.

Above ground, the Dormition Cathedral was built from 1073 to 1089 as Kyiv's second great Byzantine-inspired church, and the monastery became Kyivan Rus' intellectual centre, producing chronicles and icons, and training builders and artists.

Wrecked by the Tatars in 1240, the Lavra went through a series of revivals and

Cathedral altar

Explore Ashore

From Poshtova Ploshcha station, take bus 62 to Yevropeiska Sq. Change to bus 24 and get off at the Spasa na Berestovi stop, from where the monastery is a five-minute walk. Allow 30 minutes from the port to the monastery, and two to three hours to appreciate the site thoroughly.

❶ Need to Know

Києво-Печерська лавра, Caves Monastery; ☎044-406 6375; http://kplavra.kiev.ua; vul Lavrska 9; upper/lower Lavra 25uah/free; ⊘9am-7pm Apr-Sep, 9am-6pm Oct-Mar, caves 8.30am-4.30pm; Ⓜ Arsenalna

disastrous fires before being mostly rebuilt, with its prevailing baroque influences, in the 18th century. It was made a museum in 1926 but was partly returned to the Ukrainian Orthodox Church in 1988.

Historical Treasures Museum

This **museum** (Музей історичних коштовностей України; adult/student 50/30uah; ⊘10am-5.45pm, closed Mon & last Fri of month) in the Upper Lavra has an astounding collection of precious stones and metal found or made in Ukraine, including a fabulous hoard of gold jewellery worked for the Scythians by Greek Black Sea colonists. Many treasures come from a handful of circa 4th-century BC burial mounds in the Dnipropetrovsk, Zaporizhzhya and Kherson regions.

Museum of Microminiature

Beneath the Great Bell Tower, this **museum** (Музей мікромініатюр; www.microart.kiev.ua; Kyevo-Pecherska Lavra; adult/student 50/25uah; ⊘9am-1pm & 2-7pm Wed-Mon) provides something even for atheists. Russian artist Nikolai Siadristy's tiny creations include the world's smallest book, a balalaika with strings one-fortieth the width of a human hair and a flea fitted with golden horseshoes.

Lower Lavra

Things may change due to an ongoing inter-church crisis in Ukraine, but at the time of writing the lower *lavra* and cave complex was controlled by the Moscow patriarchate. It runs a separate tourism bureau, where you can book a cave excursion for a donation. From the upper *lavra*, exit through the back entrance and you're at the bureau.

Lanzheron Beach

A. LESIK/SHUTTERSTOCK ©

Odesa's Beaches

With Crimea off limits, Odesa these days is packed with Ukrainian holiday makers. A string of sandy beaches hosts a vibrant summer social and party scene.

Great For...

☑ **Don't Miss**

The lively party scene at Arkadia Beach.

Route of Health

The dystopian Soviet name has stuck to this 5.5km **stretch** (Траса здоров'я) of sandy, rocky and concrete beaches that forms the city's recreational belt. Packed like a sardine can and filled with noise and barbecue smells, the beaches are anything but idyllic, yet this is a great place for mingling with Ukrainian holidaymakers in their element. Starting at Lanzheron Beach, which boasts a wooden boardwalk, the route ends at Arkadia, the newly renovated nightlife hotspot, filled with clubs and fancy resorts.

Lanzheron Beach

Perhaps to copy Brighton Beach, New York – where half of Odesa seems to have emigrated – the authorities built a boardwalk at the **beach** (Пляж Ланжерон)

that's closest to the city centre and is the first stop on the Route of Health. It looks modern and attractive, but is small and hence often crowded. It's reachable by foot via Shevchenko Park in the city centre.

Arkadia Beach

Reconstructed to resemble the glitzy resorts across the sea in Turkey, Odesa's **main fun zone** (Пляж Аркадія) shines like a mini Las Vegas and remains crowded with revellers till the wee hours. A wide promenade lined with cafes and bars leads towards the seafront, which is jam-packed with beach clubs that double as nightlife venues after dark. Arkadia can be reached by walking, cycling or riding a park train along the Route of Health from Lanzheron Beach.

Explore Ashore

Travelling from Odesa centre to Arkadia, take tram 5 from the tram stop near the train station, in front of the McDonald's on vul Panteleymonivska, to the end of the line (45 minutes) via the lovely tree-lined bul Frantsuzsky, where Odesa's aristocracy lived in tsarist times.

From Lanzheron Beach to Arkadia Beach along the Route of Health is 5km on foot or bicycle.

❶ Need to Know

Public transport to Arkadia gets extremely crowded in summer, so consider taking a taxi (around 70uah).

Kyiv

In the beginning there was Kyiv. Long before Ukraine and Russia existed, the city's inhabitants were already striding up and down the green hills, idling hot afternoons away on the Dnipro River and promenading along Khreshchatyk.

◉ SIGHTS

St Sophia's Cathedral   Church
(pl Sofiyska; grounds/cathedral/bell tower 20/80/40uah; ⊙cathedral & museums 10am-6pm, grounds & bell tower 9am-7pm; ⓂZoloti Vorota) The interior is the most astounding aspect of Kyiv's oldest standing church. Many of the mosaics and frescoes are original, dating back to 1017–31, when the cathedral was built to celebrate Prince Yaroslav's victory in protecting Kyiv from the Pechenegs (tribal raiders). While equally attractive, the building's gold domes and 76m-tall wedding-cake bell tower are 18th-century baroque additions. It's well worth climbing the bell tower for a bird's-eye view of the cathedral and 360-degree panoramas of Kyiv.

Maidan Nezalezhnosti   Square
(майдан Незалежності, Independence Sq; ⓂMaidan Nezalezhnosti) Be it celebration or revolution, whenever Ukrainians want to get together – and they often do – 'Maidan' is the nation's meeting point. The square saw pro-independence protests in the 1990s and the Orange Revolution in 2004. But all of that was eclipsed by the Euromaidan Revolution in 2013–14, when it was transformed into an urban guerrilla camp besieged by government forces. In peaceful times, Maidan is more about festiveness than feistiness, with weekend concerts and a popular nightly fountain show.

All streets in the centre seem to spill into maidan Nezalezhnosti, and with them spills a cross-section of Kyiv life: vendors selling food and souvenirs; teenagers carousing under the watchful gaze of winged-angel statues; skate rats and snake charmers; lovers and bums.

Yet the echo of revolution is omnipresent. Makeshift memorials on vul Instytutska

St Sophia's Cathedral

RUSLAN KALNITSKYY/SHUTTERSTOCK ©

serve as a sombre reminder of those slain in Euromaidan. Images of burning tyres and army tents from that fateful winter will forever linger in the Ukrainian conscience.

Skvorechnik
Cultural Centre

(Скворечник; Birdhouse; www.facebook.com/skvorechnikcafe; Trukhaniv Island; Ⓜ Poshtova Pl) ✒ It's hard to characterise this beachfront hippie haven on Trukhaniv Island. It derives its name from the smattering of raised wooden chill-out huts that dot the grounds. While you can rent these out, Skvorechnik is about much more than birdhouses. It's like a mini, alcohol-free Burning Man festival – a zone of singalongs, yoga, zen meditation, massage, dreamcatcher-making classes – well, you get the idea. Of course there's also a beach and a busy vegetarian cafe keeping people fed and fuelled.

St Michael's Golden-Domed Monastery
Monastery

(Михайлівський Золотоверхий монастир; www.archangel.kiev.ua; vul Tryokhsvyatytelska 6; ⊘ territory 8am-7pm; Ⓜ Poshtova Pl) Looking from St Sophia's past the Bohdan Khmelnytsky statue, it's impossible to ignore the gold-domed blue church at the other end of proyizd Volodymyrsky. This is St Michael's, named after Kyiv's patron saint. As the impossibly shiny cupolas imply, this is a fresh (2001) copy of the original (1108), which was torn down by the Soviets in 1937. The church's fascinating history is explained in great detail (in Ukrainian and English placards) in a **museum** (14uah; ⊘ 10am-7pm Tue-Sun; Ⓜ Poshtova Pl) in the monastery's bell tower.

Andriyivsky Uzviz
Street

(Андріївський узвіз, Andrew's Descent; Ⓜ Kontraktova Pl) According to legend, a man walked up the hill here, erected a cross and prophesied, 'A great city will stand on this spot.' That man was the Apostle Andrew, hence the name of Kyiv's quaintest thoroughfare, a steep cobbled street that winds its way up from Kontraktova pl to vul Volodymyrska, with a vaguely Montparnasse feel. Along the length of 'the *uzviz*' you'll

Kyiv Souvenirs

You'll find more than a dozen shops selling reasonably priced national costumes, textiles and other souvenirs in the **maidan Nezalezhnosti underpass**. Quality tends to be better at speciality shops, however. Andriyivsky uzviz is the top spot for touristy stuff like *matryoshka* (Russian nesting dolls), fur hats, kitschy art, Dynamo Kyiv kit and Soviet posters and coins. Definitely bring home a bottle of *horilka* (vodka), available at any foodstore.

Matryoshka
TROOBADOOR/SHUTTERSTOCK ©

find cafes, art galleries and vendors selling all manner of souvenirs and kitsch.

The street's highlight, near the top of the hill, is the stunning gold and blue **St Andrew's Church**, a five-domed, cross-shaped baroque masterpiece that celebrates the apostle legend.

National Museum of Ukrainian History
Museum

(Національний музей історії України; ☑ 044-278 4864; www.nmiu.com.ua; vul Volodymyrska 2; adult/student 50/30uah, tour 240uah; ⊘ 10am-6pm Mon-Fri, 11am-7.30pm Sat & Sun; Ⓜ Kontraktova Pl) Located more or less at the spot where history began for Kyiv, this huge museum has been fully modernised in recent years and represents a fantastic stroll through all stages of Ukraine's past, from the Stone Age to the ongoing war with Russia in the east. Displays are in chronological order, and while not all are in English, each

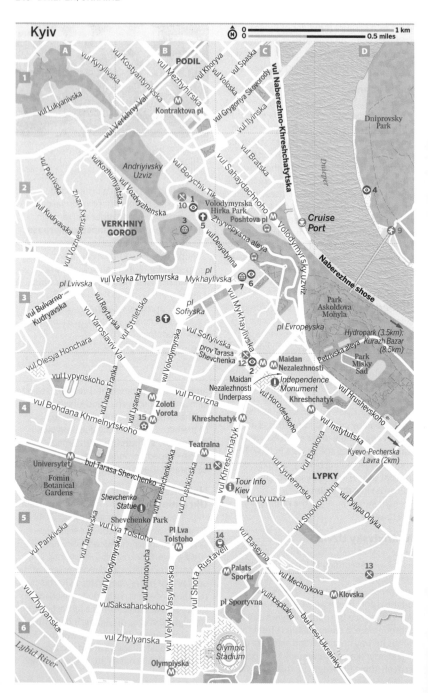

Kyiv

N

0 ——— 1 km
0 ——— 0.5 miles

PODIL

vul Kostyantynivska
vul Kyrylivska
vul Mezhyhirska
vul Khoryva
vul Spaska
vul Voloska

vul Verkhniy Val

Kontraktova pl

vul Grygoriya Skovorody
vul Ilyinska

vul Naberezhno-Khreshchatytska

Dniprovsky
Park

Dnieper

vul Lukyanivska

vul Petrivska

zakut Kyrylivska

vul Kudryavska

Andriyivsky
Uzviz
vul Kozhumyatska
vul Vozdvyzhenska

vul Borychiv Tik

vul Sahaydachnoho

vul Bratska

Cruise
Port

4

9

**VERKHNIY
GOROD**

10
1
3
5

Volodymyrska
Hirka Park
Poshtova pl
Zhyvopysna aleya

Volodymyrsky uzviz

Naberezhne shose

vul Voznesensky uzviz

vul Desyatynna

pl Lvivska
vul Velyka Zhytomyrska

pl
Mykhaylivska

7 6

Park
Askoldova
Mohyla

vul Bulvarno-
Kudryavska
vul Reytarska
vul Strieletska
vul Yaroslaviv Val

pl
Sofiyska

vul Mykhaylivska

pl Evropeyska

Hydropark (3.5km);
Kurazh Bazar
(8.5km)

8

vul Sofiyivska

prov Tarasa
Shevchenka

Petrivska aleya

Park
Misky
Sad

vul Olesya Honchara
vul Lypynskoho

vul Ivana Franka

vul Volodymrska

12
2

Maidan
Nezalezhnosti

Maidan
Nezalezhnosti
Underpass

Independence
Monument

Khreshchatyk

vul Hrushevskoho

vul Bohdana Khmelnytskoho

vul Lysenka

**Zoloti
Vorota**
15

vul Prorizna

Khreshchatyk

vul Horodetskoho

vul Instytutska

vul Bankova

Kyevo-Pecherska
Lavra (2km)

Teatralna

11

vul Khreshchatyk

vul Lyuteranska

LYPKY

vul Shovkovychna

vul Pylypa Orlyka

Universytet

bul Tarasa Shevchenko

Fomin
Botanical
Gardens

Shevchenko
Statue

Shevchenko Park

vul Tarasivska

vul Volodymyrska

vul Pushkinska

Tour Info
Kiev

Kruty uzviz

vul Pankivska

vul Lva Tolstoho

vul Antonovycha

vul Velyka Vasylkivska

14

Pl Lva
Tolstoho

vul Shota Rustaveli

vul Basevna

Palats
Sportu

pl Sportyvna

vul Mechnykova

bul Lesi Ukrainky

13

Klovska

vul Zhylyanska

vulSaksahanskoho

vul Zhylyanska

vul Hospitalna

Lybid River

Olympiyska

Olympic
Stadium

Kyiv

room has an English placard describing the period of history covered within.

🏃 ACTIVITIES

Trukhaniv Island   Beach
(M Poshtova Pl) The island opposite Podil on the Dnipro is accessible via the **Parkovy footbridge** – an experience in its own right, full of life and colour. In the summer brave souls bungee off the bridge for 200uah (we do not vouch for the safety of this!). Trukhaniv is criss-crossed by forested roads and paths – a great place for cycling.

Hydropark   Beach
(M Hydropark) The main recreational zone on the Dnipro islands, Hydropark deafens people arriving by metro with pop music blasted from dozens of bars near the entrance. Venture deeper into the park, however, and you'll find Kyivans in their element. There's an old-school outdoor gym, sports zones, shashlyk (meat kebab) stands and all manner of beach, be it gay or straight, clothed or nude.

🛍 SHOPPING

Kurazh Bazar   Market
(Кураж Базар; Art-Zavod Platforma, vul Bilo-morska 1A; 70uah; M Lisova) Kurazh Bazar is a fantastic monthly weekend flea market

on Kyiv's left (east) bank. You'll find some 400 vendors selling all manner of new and used clothes, antiques and bric-a-brac, in addition to plenty of street food, street performers, kids' activities and live music on a large central stage. The venue, **Art-Zavod Platforma** (http://artzavodplatforma.com/en), is an attraction in its own right.

🍴 EATING

Kyiv has arrived as a foodie destination, with a seemingly unlimited supply of high-quality restaurants. Nor are they expensive, as even the best restaurants cost about one-third of what you would expect to pay in Western Europe. For penny pinchers there are some great local eating options, often taking the form of *stolovye* (cafeterias) offering a smorgasbord of national cuisine.

Kyivska Perepichka   Pies €
(Київська перепічка; vul Bohdana Khmelnytskoho 3; perepichka 15uah; ◷8.30am-9pm Mon-Sat, 10am-9pm Sun; M Teatralna) A perpetually long queue moves with lightning speed towards a window where two women hand out pieces of fried dough enclosing a mouth-watering sausage. The place became a local institution long before the first 'hot dog' hit town. An essential Kyiv experience.

From left: Soviet era medals on sale at a market; *Khachapuri* (Georgian cheese bread), Taras Shevchenko National Opera Theatre

Ostannya Barikada   Ukrainian €€

(Last Barricade; ☎068 907 1991; maidan Nezalezhnosti 1; mains 130-200uah; ⊗11am-midnight; ❄🛜; Ⓜ Maidan Nezalezhnosti) Hidden in a 'secret bunker' under maidan Nezalezhnosti, this is both a nationalist shrine and one of Kyiv's best restaurants. Everything – from the cheeses and *horilka* (vodka) to the craft beer and steaks – is 100% homegrown. Ukraine's three modern revolutions are eulogised everywhere. Getting in is a quest, but as poet Taras Shevchenko said, 'Fight and you'll win.'

Start by pushing 'ОБ' on the Globus mall (west wing) elevator. Once you're in, you get a free tour of the place.

Kanapa   Ukrainian €€€

(Канапа; ☎044-425 4548; https://borysov. ua/uk/kanapa; Andriyivsky uzviz 19A; mains 250-400uah; ⊗10am-midnight; 🛜; Ⓜ Kontraktova Pl) 🍴 Sneak away from the busy *uzviz* into this beautiful old wooden house with sliding-glass doors overlooking a lush ravine out back. Kanapa serves modern cuisine largely made from its own farm's produce. Traditional it is not: green *borsch* is made of nettles and chicken Kiev is not chicken but pheasant. Ukrainian mussels, caviar and pâté are other specialities.

A good place for an affordable and highly original breakfast (10am to noon). Newly opened sister cafe **Kanapka** across the street focuses on lighter meals and wine.

Shoti   Georgian €€€

(Кафе Шоти; ☎044-339 9399; vul Mechnykova 9; mains 160-480uah; ⊗noon-11pm; ❄🛜; Ⓜ Klovska) This is modern Georgian cuisine at its finest. Try the fork-whipped egg-and-butter *khachapuri* (cheese bread) and a shoulder of lamb or charcoal-grilled catfish, all served with fresh, complimentary *shoti* flatbread. Huge racks of the finest Georgian wines, professionally decanted, tempt oenophiles. Sit outside on the broad veranda, or settle into the restaurant proper with its meticulously scuffed wood floor.

🍸 DRINKING & NIGHTLIFE

Alchemist Bar   Cocktail Bar

(vul Shota Rustaveli 12; ⊗noon-3am, to 5am Fri & Sat; 🛜; Ⓜ Palats Sportu) Kyiv's best bar

RUSLAN LYTVYN/SHUTTERSTOCK ©

is set in an intimate basement space on vibrant vul Shota Rustaveli. No pretensions, no strict *feiskontrol* (face control), just an eclectic mix of fun-loving patrons chasing good music, good drinks and good conversation. Most nights see truly excellent bands play, after which DJs take over and many people start dancing near the bar.

🎭 ENTERTAINMENT

Taras Shevchenko National Opera Theatre
Opera

(📞044-235 2606; www.opera.com.ua; vul Volodymyrska 50; tickets 20-500uah; ☺box office 11am-5.30pm, shows 7pm, closed mid-Jun–Aug; Ⓜ Zoloti Vorota) Performances at this lavish theatre (opened 1901) are grandiose affairs, but tickets are cheap. True disciples of Ukrainian culture should not miss a performance of *Zaporozhets za Dunaem* (Zaporizhzhyans Beyond the Danube), a sort of operatic, purely Ukrainian version of *Fiddler on the Roof*.

ℹ️ INFORMATION

The city runs about a dozen information booths, including near **Bessarabska Rynok** (cnr vul Khreshchatyk & vul Baseyna; ☺9am-7pm, to 5.30pm Fri). They are of moderate usefulness, but are usually staffed by an English speaker who can answer simple questions and distribute free maps and brochures. For more details, see www.visitkyiv.travel.

ℹ️ GETTING AROUND

Although often crowded, Kyiv's metro is clean, efficient, reliable and easy to use. It is also the world's deepest, requiring escalator rides of seven to eight minutes! Trains run frequently between around 6am and midnight on all three lines. Blue *zhetony* (plastic tokens) costing 8uah (good for one ride) are sold by cashiers. It gets cheaper if you buy a plastic card that can be topped up at any station. The price of one trip goes down to 6.50uah if you buy 50 trips.

Buses, trolleybuses, trams and many quicker *marshrutky* (minibuses) serve most routes. Tickets for buses, trams and trolleybuses cost

4uah and are sold at street kiosks or directly from the driver/conductor. *Marshrutky* rides usually cost 6uah.

Taxi prices in Kyiv are cheap by world standards. Expect to pay 50uah for short (less than 3km) trips within central Kyiv. Almost everyone is using taxi apps, like Uber or its local version, Uklon, these days.

Odesa

Odesa is a city straight from literature – an energetic, decadent boom town. Neoclassical pastel buildings line a geometric grid of leafy streets, leading to Odesa's famous Potemkin Steps, which sweep down to the Black Sea and Ukraine's biggest commercial port.

◎ SIGHTS

Potemkin Steps   Landmark
(Потьомкінські сходи) Fresh from a controversial renovation, which changed its original outlook, the Potemkin Steps lead down from bul Prymorsky to the sea port. Pause at the top to admire the sweeping views of the harbour. You can avoid climbing back up by taking a **funicular railway** (bul Primorsky; 3uah; ⊙8am-11pm) that runs parallel. Or, having walked halfway up, you can sneak into a passage that now connects the steps with the reconstructed **Istanbul Park**.

Prymorsky Boulevard   Street
(Приморський бульвар) Odesa's elegant facade, this tree-lined, clifftop promenade was designed to enchant the passengers of arriving boats with the neoclassical opulence of its architecture and civility, unexpected in these parts at the time of construction in the early 19th century. Imperial architects also transformed the cliff face into terraced gardens descending to the port, divided by the Potemkin Steps – the **Istanbul Park** lies east of the steps and the **Greek Park** west of them.

Vul Derybasivska   Street
(Дерибасівська вулиця) Odesa's main commercial street, pedestrian vul Derybasivska is jam-packed with restaurants, bars and, in the summer high season, tourists. At its quieter eastern end you'll discover the **statue of José de Ribas**, the Spanish-Neapolitan general who built Odesa's harbour and who also has a central street named after him. At the western end of the thoroughfare is the pleasant and beautifully renovated **City Garden**, surrounded by several restaurants.

History of Odesa
Jews Museum   Museum
(Музей історії євреїв Одеси; ☑048-728 9743; www.migdal.org.ua/migdal/museum/; vul Nizhynska 66; recommended donation 100uah, tour 200uah; ⊙1-7pm Mon-Thu, 10am-4pm Sun) Less than 2% of people call themselves Jewish in today's Odesa – against 44% in the early 1920s – but the resilient and humorous Jewish spirit still permeates every aspect of local life. Hidden inside a typical run-down courtyard with clothes drying on a rope and a rusty carcass of a prehistoric car, this modest but lovingly curated exhibition consists of items donated by Odessite families, many of whom have long emigrated to America or Israel.

🅐 SHOPPING

Privoz Market   Market
(Ринок Привіз; vul Pryvozna) Odesa is home to two of southern Ukraine's largest and most famous markets. This centrally located market is possibly the largest farmers market in the country and a must-visit for *rynok* (market) lovers. On hot days you may want to breathe through your mouth in the overheated halls. Whatever you buy, always bargain – you'll upset them if you don't.

✖ EATING

Odesa's restaurant scene easily rivals Kyiv's thanks to a new phenomenon that time has come to call – loud and clear – Odesa cuisine. It's a magic stew of Russian, Ukrainian, Jewish and Moldovan cuisines cooked up in Soviet communal kitchens

Mamalyga (a version of polenta with brynza goat's cheese or fried lard)

and fishermen's huts. Its main virtue is that it takes full advantage of the region's abundance in vegetables, fruit and seafood.

Dva Karla   Moldovan €

(Bodega 2K; ☑096 524 1601; www.facebook. com/bodega2k; vul Hretska 22; mains 70-120uah; ⏰10am-11pm) This envoy from nearby Moldova occupies a super-quaint courtyard covered with a vine canopy in summer and pleasant cellar premises in winter. Come here to try *mamalyga* (a version of polenta with *brynza* goat's cheese or fried lard), paprika stuffed with rice and chopped meat, as well as juicy *mitityay* (kebabs).

Touting itself as a bodega, 2K also treats visitors to excellent Moldovan and (more experimental) Ukrainian wine. It's also a great breakfast option.

Tyulka   Ukrainian €

(Тюлька; ☑048-233 3231; www.tulka.od.ua; vul Koblevska 46; snacks 60-70uah; ⏰10am-11pm) A clever take on Soviet nostalgia (no Lenins or red banners in sight), this cafe recreates the ambience of a 1970s working-class eatery, complete with authentic tablecloths,

beer mugs and salads served in tall glasses. Food is an assortment of classic Odesa snacks, from the namesake *tyulka* (small fish, served fried or salted) to *cheburek* (meat pastry).

City Food Market   Food Hall €€

(Міський продовольчий ринок; ☑048-702 1913; www.facebook.com/odessa.cityfood. market; Rishelyevska 9A; mains 100-200uah; ⏰11am-2am; 📶📖) Once an itinerant tribe, congregating here and there for irregular jamborees, Odesa foodies now have a rather palatial indoors base. The two-storey building is divided between shops, each with its own kitchen dedicated to a particular product – from the Vietnamese *pho* soup and Greek pita gyros, to grilled ribs and oysters.

Bernardazzi   European €€€

(Бернардацці; ☑067 000 2511; www.bernar dazzi.com; Odessa Philharmonic Hall, vul Bunina 15; mains 200-420uah; ⏰noon-midnight, to 2am Fri & Sat; ❄) Few Ukrainian restaurants have truly authentic settings, but the art nouveau dining room of this Italianesque

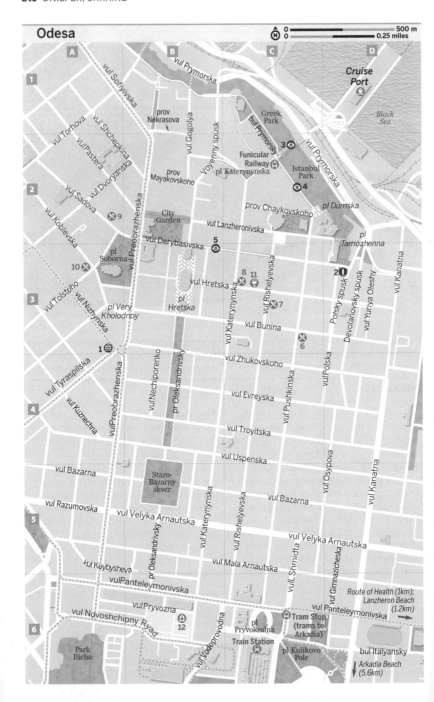

Odesa

0 — 500 m
0 — 0.25 miles

Cruise Port

Black Sea

vul Sofiyivska

vul Prymorska

prov Nekrasova

Greek Park

bul Prymorsky

vul Prymorska

vul Torhova

vul Shchepkina

vulPastera

vul Dvoryanska

vul Gogolya

Voyenny spusk

Funicular Railway

3

Istanbul Park

prov Mayakovskoho

pl Katerynynska

4

vul Sadova

prov Chaykovskoho

pl Dumska

vul Koblevska

9

City Garden

vul Lanzheronivska

pl Tamozhenna

vul Derybasivska

5

vul Preobrazhenska

pl Soborna

vul Hretska

8 11

vul Rishelyevska

2

vul Kanatna

10

pl Very Kholodnoy

pl Hretska

vul Katerynynska

7

Polsky spusk

Devolanovsky spusk

vul Yuriya Oleshy

vul Tolstoho

vul Nizhynska

vul Bunina

6

1

vul Zhukovskoho

vul Polska

vul Nechiporenko

pr Oleksandrivsky

vul Pushkinska

vul Tyraspilska

vul Evreyska

vul Kuznechna

vul Troyitska

vul Uspenska

vul Bazarna

Staro-Bazarny skver

vul Osypova

vul Kanatna

vul Razumovska

vul Velyka Arnautska

vul Katerynynska

vul Rishelyevska

vul Bazarna

vul Velyka Arnautska

pr Oleksandrivsky

vul Kuybysheva

vul Mala Arnautska

vul L Shmidta

vul Gimnazicheska

vulPanteleymonivska

Route of Health (1km); Lanzheron Beach (1.2km)

vulPryvozna

vul Panteleymonivska

vul Novoshchipny R vad

12

vul Vodoprovodna

pl Pryvozalna

Tram Stop (trams to Arkadia)

Park Ilicha

Train Station

pl Kulikovo Pole

bul Italyansky

Arkadia Beach (5.6km)

Odesa

palazzo (once a stock exchange, now the Philharmonic Hall) is the real deal. In addition to well-crafted southern and Eastern European fare, there's an award-winning wine list, occasional live music and a secluded courtyard for summertime chilling.

Kotelok Mussels Bar   Seafood €€€

(☑048-736 6030; http://kotelok-musselsbar. com; vul Sadova 17; mains 180-400uah; ☺9am-11pm, to midnight Fri & Sat) This may not be obvious, but mussels are as much a part of Odesa food culture as aubergine 'caviar' (cold vegetable stew). Furnished like a bar, with a row of seats facing an open kitchen, Kotelok is all about Black Sea mussels served with a variety of dips, including the quintessentially local mixture of paprika and *brynza*.

⊙ DRINKING & NIGHTLIFE

Shkaf   Bar

(Шкаф; ☑048-232 5017; www.shkaff.od.ua; vul Hretska 32; ☺6pm-5am) It feels like entering a *shkaf* (wardrobe) from the outside, but what you find inside is a heaving basement bar–club, a surefire antidote to Odesa's trendy beach-club scene and pick-up bars. The inconspicuous, unmarked entrance is always surrounded by smoking/chilling-out patrons, so you won't miss it.

ⓘ INFORMATION

Tourist Information Centre (☑380 94 712 2018; www.move.in.ua/en/odessa; vul Derybasivska 22; ☺8am-8pm daily)

ⓘ GETTING AROUND

From the cruise ship berth, climbing the Potemkin Steps takes you straight into town. Trolleybuses trundle up and down the main avenues for easy access to central sights.

Useful tram routes for visitors are Route 5, which connects a number of major sights ending with Arkadia, and Route 18, which travels along the beaches.

Useful trolleybus route numbers include 5 (connecting the old town centre with Arkadia), 9 (passing through the old centre and vul Derybasivska), 7 (passing the cathedral, vul Rishelievskaya and the train station) and 10 (connecting the Potemkin Steps with vul Rishelievskaya).

A typical taxi with Uber costs 30uah to 40uah in the centre, 70uah to 80uah from the centre to Arkadia.

RHÔNE,
FRANCE

Rhône, France

Commanding a strategic spot at the confluence of the Rhône and Saône Rivers, grand old Lyon is France's gastronomic capital. Downstream, the Rhône forges past Vienne's Roman ruins and the centuries-old Côtes du Rhône vineyards, opening to sunny vistas of fruit orchards, lavender fields and the distant Alps as it continues south. During the 14th century, the Provençal town of Avignon was the centre of the Roman Catholic world. Its impressive legacy of ecclesiastical architecture most notably includes the soaring, World Heritage–listed Palais des Papes.

With One Day in Lyon

Start by exploring the long peninsula between the rivers known as **Presqu'île** (p256), which is near the dock. From here, cross the Saône to the west and stroll around the medieval quarter of **Vieux Lyon** (p254), which has plenty of attractions and sights, including museums and religious buildings. But most importantly, make sure you have lunch in a traditional **bouchon** (p252) – the quintessential Lyon experience.

Best Places for...

Bistro Le Musée, Lyon (p256)

History Palais des Papes, Avignon (p260)

Gallery Musée des Beaux-Arts, Lyon (p256)

Modern Architecture Musée des Confluences, Lyon (p256)

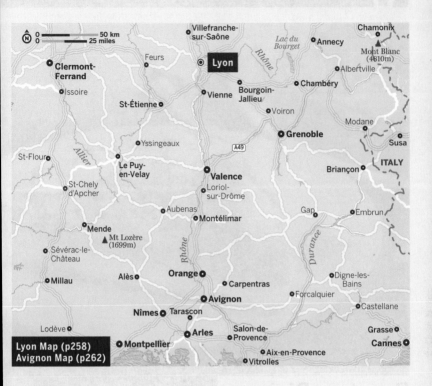

Getting from the Ports

Lyon Ships dock at the Quai Claude Bernard, at a central point on the Rhône just north of the confluence with the Saône. From here, it's a short walk into town.

Vienne Ships dock very centrally and it's less than five minutes to the town centre.

Avignon The port is on the western edge of the centre, near Pont Édouard Daladier. From here, it's under 10 minutes' walk to the key sights.

Fast Facts

Currency Euro (€)

Language French

Free Wi-fi Widespread in cafes and bars.

Money ATMS are widespread and easy to use.

Tourist Information All three towns have centrally located tourist offices: Lyon's is in the centre of Presqu'île; Vienne's is just south of the town centre on the river; and Avignon's is in the heart of the old town.

Tarte aux pralines (tart topped with crushed sugar-coated almonds)

Bouchon Dining, Lyon

A bouchon might be a 'bottle stopper' or 'traffic jam' elsewhere in France, but in Lyon it's a small, friendly bistro that cooks up traditional cuisine using regional produce.

Bouchons originated in the first half of the 20th century when many large bourgeois families had to let go of their in-house cooks, who then set up their own restaurant businesses. The first of these *mères* (mothers) was Mère Guy, followed by Mère Filloux, Mère Brazier (under whom world-famous Lyonnais chef Paul Bocuse trained) and others.

Great For...

☑ **Don't Miss**

The informal, post-dinner history tours run by the gregarious owner at *bouchon* Le Musée (p256).

What to Drink

Kick-start your gastronomic experience with a *communard*, a blood-red aperitif of Beaujolais wine mixed with *crème de cassis* (blackcurrant liqueur), named after the supporters of the Paris Commune killed in 1871. When ordering wine, ask for a pot – a 46cL glass bottle adorned with an elastic band to prevent wine drips – of local

Bouchon

ELENA POMINOVA/SHUTTERSTOCK ©

Explore Ashore

From the cruise dock at Quai Claude Bernard, some of the *bouchons* are within easy walking distance. Otherwise, jump on the tram at the Quai Claude Bernard stop, which is very close to the port.

❶ Need to Know

Many *bouchons* are shut weekends; advance reservations are recommended. Many of the best *bouchons* are certified by Les Authentiques Bouchons Lyonnais – look for a metal plaque outside depicting traditional puppet Gnafron with glass of Beaujolais in hand.

Brouilly, Beaujolais, Côtes du Rhône or Mâcon.

Traditional Dishes

Start with *tablier de sapeur* ('fireman's apron'; breaded, fried tripe), *salade de cervelas* (salad of boiled pork sausage sometimes studded with pistachios or black truffle specks), or caviar de la Croix Rousse (lentils in creamy sauce). Hearty main dishes include *boudin blanc* (veal sausage), *boudin noir aux pommes* (blood sausage with apples), *quenelles* (feather-light flour, egg and cream dumplings) or *quenelles de brochet* (pike dumplings served in a creamy crayfish sauce). Die-hard *bouchon* aficionados can't get enough of *andouillette* (a seriously feisty sausage made from pigs' intestines), *gras double* (a

type of tripe) and *pieds de mouton/veau/couchon* (sheep/calf/pig trotters).

Cheese & Dessert

For the cheese course, choose between a bowl of *fromage blanc* (a cross between cream cheese and natural yoghurt); *cervelle de canut* (*fromage blanc* mixed with chives and garlic), which originated in Croix Rousse; or local St Marcellin ripened to gooey perfection.

Desserts are grandma-style: think *tarte aux pommes* (apple tart), or the Lyonnais classic *tarte aux pralines,* a brilliant rose-coloured confection made with crème fraiche and crushed sugar-coated almonds.

Dining Etiquette

Seldom do you get clean cutlery for each course, and mopping your plate with a chunk of bread is fine. In the most popular and traditional spots, you'll often find yourself sitting elbow-to-elbow with your fellow diners at a row of tightly wedged tables.

Basilique Notre Dame de Fourvière

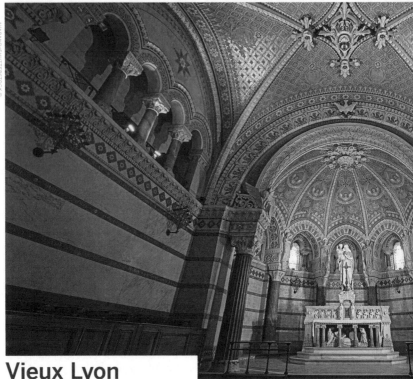

Vieux Lyon

Lyon's old town, with its cobbled lanes and medieval and Renaissance architecture, is a Unesco World Heritage Site. Its atmospheric web of streets divides into three quarters: St-Paul (north), St-Jean (middle) and St-Georges (south). Lovely old buildings line rue du Bœuf, rue St-Jean and rue des Trois Maries.

Great For...

☑ Don't Miss

A traditional puppet show at one of Lyon's most famous puppet theatres, Théâtre Le Guignol de Lyon (p257).

Look up to see gargoyles carved on window ledges along rue Juiverie, home to Lyon's Jewish community in the Middle Ages.

Cathédrale St-Jean-Baptiste

Lyon's partly Romanesque **cathedral** (www.cathedrale-lyon.fr; place St-Jean, 5e; ⊙cathedral 8.15am-7.45pm Mon-Fri, 8am-7pm Sat & Sun, treasury 9.30am-noon & 2-6pm Tue-Sat; MVieux Lyon) was built between the late 11th and early 16th centuries. Its Flamboyant Gothic façade (1480) portals are decorated with 280 square stone medallions. Inside, the highlight is the **astronomical clock**.

Musées Gadagne

Housed in a 16th-century mansion, this twin-themed **exhibition space** (🗷04 78 42 03 61; www.gadagne.musees.lyon.fr; 1 place du Petit Collège, 5e; adult/child €8/free, both

⚓ Explore Ashore

It's a very pleasant half-hour stroll from the dock to Vieux Lyon via the Presqu'île peninsula between the rivers. Otherwise, get the tram from Quai Claude Bernard by the dock to Guillotière. Change to the metro and head to the Vieux Lyon stop, at the southern end of the district. Allow 15 minutes. You can fill a day in this area, either side of lunch.

❶ Need to Know

Shop in style: art galleries, antiquarian and secondhand bookshops fill Vieux Lyon's pedestrian streets.

museums €9/free; ⊘11am-6.30pm Wed-Sun; Ⓜ Vieux Lyon) incorporates the excellent Musée d'Histoire de Lyon, chronicling the city's layout as its silk-weaving, cinema and transportation evolved, and Musée des Marionettes du Monde, which pays homage to iconic Guignol. A 4th-floor cafe adjoins 14th-century terraced gardens.

Le Petit Musée Fantastique de Guignol

The star of this tiny, two-room **museum** (☑04 78 37 01 67; www.le-petit-musee-fantas tique-de-guignol.boutiquecardelli.fr; 6 rue St-Jean, 5e; adult/child €5/3; ⊘10.30am-12.30pm & 2-6.30pm Tue-Sun, 2-6pm Mon; Ⓜ Vieux Lyon) is Guignol, the Lyonnais puppet famous for slapstick antics and political commentary. Ask staff to set up the English soundtrack on the cute, sensor-activated exhibits.

Fourvière

From Vieux Lyon, tree-shaded footpaths wind steeply uphill to Fourvière. The easiest way up is via the funicular, up the escalators from the Vieux Lyon metro station.

Over two millennia ago, the Romans built the city of Lugdunum on these slopes, crowned today by showy 19th-century **Basilique Notre Dame de Fourvière** (☑04 78 25 13 01; www.fourviere.org; place de Fourvière, 5e; rooftop tour adult/child €10/5; ⊘basilica 7am-7pm, tours 9am-12.30pm & 2-6pm Mon-Fri, 9am-12.30pm & 2-4.45pm Sat, 2-4.45pm Sun Apr-Nov; 🚠Fourvière). Nearby, the **Musée Gallo-Romain de Fourvière** (☑04 73 38 49 30; www.museegalloromain.grandlyon.com; 17 rue Cléberg, 5e; adult/child €4/free; ⊘11am-6pm Tue-Fri, from 10am Sat & Sun; 🚠Fourvière) hosts a wide-ranging collection of ancient artefacts found in the Rhône Valley as well as superb mosaics.

Lyon

Commanding a strategic spot at the confluence of the Rhône and the Saône Rivers, Lyon has been luring people ever since the Romans named it Lugdunum in 43 BC. Commercial, industrial and banking powerhouse for the past 500 years, Lyon is France's third-largest city, and offers today's urban explorers a wealth of enticing experiences.

◎ SIGHTS

Musée des Beaux-Arts   Museum
(📞04 72 10 17 40; www.mba-lyon.fr; 20 place des Terreaux, 1er; adult/child €8/free; 🕑10am-6pm Wed, Thu & Sat-Mon, 10.30am-6pm Fri; Ⓜ Hôtel de Ville) This stunning and eminently manage-able museum showcases France's finest collection of sculptures and paintings outside of Paris, from antiquity onwards. Highlights include works by Rodin, Monet and Picasso. Pick up a free audio guide and be sure to stop for a drink or meal on the delightful stone terrace off its cafe-restaurant or take time out in its tranquil cloister garden.

Musée des Confluences   Museum
(📞04 28 38 12 12; www.museedesconfluences. fr; 86 quai Perrache, 6e; adult/child €9/free; 🕑11am-7pm Tue, Wed & Fri, to 10pm Thu, 10am-7pm Sat & Sun; 🚊T1) This eye-catching building, designed by the Viennese firm Coop Himmelb(l)au, is the crowning glory of Lyon's newest neighbourhood, the Con-fluence, at Presqu'île's southern tip. Lying at the confluence of the Rhône and Saône Rivers, this ambitious science-and-humanities museum is housed in a futur-istic steel-and-glass transparent crystal. Its distorted structure is one of the city's iconic landmarks.

Centre d'Histoire de la Résistance et de la Déportation   Museum
(📞04 78 72 23 11; www.chrd.lyon.fr; 14 av Berthelot, 7e; adult/child €8/free; 🕑10am-6pm Wed-Sun; Ⓜ Perrache, Jean Macé) The WWII headquarters of Gestapo commander Klaus Barbie evokes Lyon's role as the

'Capital of the Resistance' through moving multimedia exhibits. The museum includes sound recordings of deportees and Re-sistance fighters, plus a varied collection of everyday objects associated with the Resistance (including the parachute Jean Moulin used to re-enter France in 1942).

👆 TOURS

Walking Tours   Walking
(📞04 72 77 69 69; www.visiterlyon.com/visites -guidees; adult/child from €12/8; 🕑by reserva-tion) The tourist office organises a variety of excellent tours through Vieux Lyon and Croix Rousse with local English-speaking guides. Book in advance (online, by phone or in person at the tourist office).

Cyclopolitain   Cycling
(📞04 78 30 35 90; www.visite-insolite-cyclopoli tain.com; tours 2 people €40-70; 🕑noon-5.30pm Tue-Fri, 10am-5.30pm Sat; Ⓜ Bellecour) Tiny and/or tired feet can rest aboard a cycle-taxi tour. Choose from four different itineraries, each running either one or two hours.

✖ EATING

Le Musée   Bouchon $$
(📞04 78 37 71 54; 2 rue des Forces, 2e; lunch mains €14, lunch menus €19-26, dinner menus €23-32; 🕑noon-1.30pm & 7.30-9.30pm Tue-Sat; Ⓜ Cordeliers) Housed in the stables of Lyon's former Hôtel de Ville, this delightful *bou-chon* serves a splendid array of meat-heavy Lyonnais classics, including a divine *poulet au vinaigre* (chicken cooked in vinegar). The daily changing *menu* features 10 appetisers and 10 main dishes, plus five scrumptious desserts, all served on cute china plates at long family-style tables.

Le Poêlon d'Or   Bouchon $$
(📞04 78 37 65 60; www.lepoelondor-restaurant. fr; 29 rue des Remparts d'Ainay, 2e; lunch menus €18-20, dinner menus €27-33; 🕑noon-2pm & 7.30-10pm Mon-Fri; Ⓜ Ampère-Victor Hugo) This upmarket *bouchon* is well known among local foodies, who recommend its superb *andouillette* (chitterlings) and pike dump-lings. Save room for the delicious chocolate mousse or the vanilla crème brûlée.

Cinq Mains — Neobistro $$

(📞04 37 57 30 52; www.facebook.com/cinqmains; 12 rue Monseigneur Lavarenne, 5e; menu lunch/dinner €19/33; ⏱noon-1.30pm & 7.30-9.30pm; Ⓜ Vieux Lyon) When young Lyonnais Grégory Cuilleron and his two friends opened this neobistro in early 2016, it was an instant hit. They're working wonders at this cool loft-like space with a mezzanine, serving up tantalising creations based on what they find at the market. A new generation of chefs, and a new spin for Lyonnais cuisine.

⭐ ENTERTAINMENT

Théâtre Le Guignol de Lyon — Puppet Theatre

(📞04 78 29 83 36; www.guignol-lyon.net; 2 rue Louis Carrand, 5e; adult/child €10/7.50; Ⓜ Vieux Lyon) One of Lyon's most famous puppet theatres, Théâtre Le Guignol de Lyon has a collection of about 300 puppets. As with many other puppet theatres, shows run just under an hour, and you'll be able to go backstage after the performance.

ℹ INFORMATION

The excellent-value **Lyon City Card** (www.lyoncitycard.com; 1/2/3 days adult €25/35/45, child €17/24/31) offers free admission to every Lyon museum, the roof of Basilique Notre Dame de Fourvière, guided city tours, Guignol puppet shows and river excursions (April to October), along with numerous other discounts. The card also includes unlimited citywide transport on buses, trams, the funicular and the metro.

Tourist Office (📞04 72 77 69 69; www.lyon-france.com; place Bellecour, 2e; ⏱9am-6pm; 📶; Ⓜ Bellecour) In the centre of Presqu'île.

ℹ GETTING AROUND

BICYCLE

Pick up a red-and-silver bike at one of the 300-odd bike stations throughout the city and drop it off at another with Lyon's **Vélo'v** (www.velov.grandlyon.com; 1st 30min free, next 30min €1, each subsequent 30min period €2) bike-rental scheme. Start by paying a one-time flat fee for

Local Food Markets

Lyon's famed indoor food market **Les Halles de Lyon Paul Bocuse** (📞04 78 62 39 33; www.hallespaulbocuse.lyon.fr; 102 cours Lafayette, 3e; ⏱7am-10.30pm Tue-Sat, to 4.30pm Sun; Ⓜ Part-Dieu) has more than 60 stalls selling their renowned wares. Pick up a round of impossibly runny St Marcellin from legendary cheesemonger Mère Richard, and a knobbly Jésus de Lyon from pork butcher Collette Sibilia. Or enjoy a sit-down lunch of local produce at the stalls, lip-smacking *coquillages* (shellfish) included.

Lyon has two main outdoor food markets: the **Marché de la Croix Rousse** (bd de la Croix Rousse, 1er; ⏱6am-1pm Tue-Sun; Ⓜ Croix Rousse) and the **Marché St-Antoine** (quai St-Antoine, 1er; ⏱6am-1pm Tue-Sun; Ⓜ Bellecour, Cordeliers). Each has more than 100 vendors.

Les Halles de Lyon Paul Bocuse
TRAVELSTOCK44/ALAMY STOCK PHOTO ©

a *carte courte durée* (short-duration card; €1.50 for 24 hours, €5 for seven days).

PUBLIC TRANSPORT

Buses, trams, a four-line metro and two funiculars linking Vieux Lyon to Fourvière and St-Just are operated by TCL (www.tcl.fr). Public transport runs from around 5am to midnight.

Tickets valid for all forms of public transport cost €1.90 (€16.90 for a *carnet* of 10) and are available from bus and tram drivers as well as machines. An all-day ticket costs €5.80. Time-stamp tickets on all forms of public transport.

Lyon

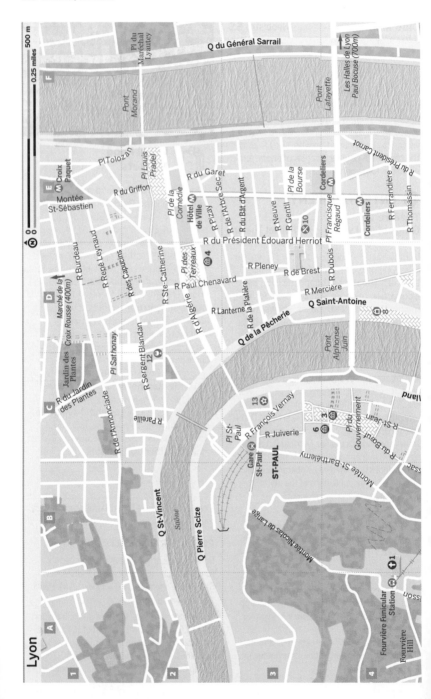

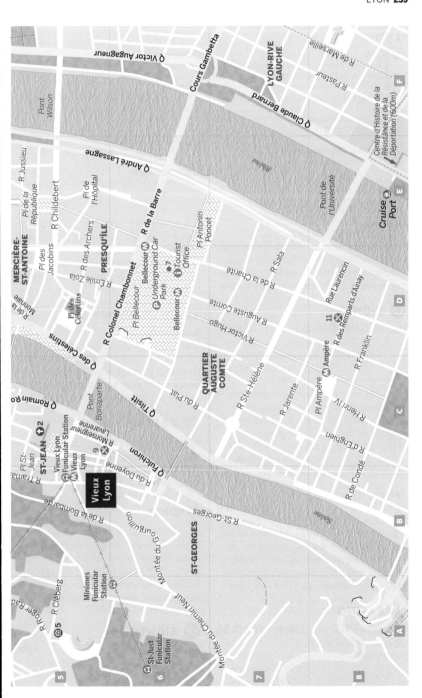

Lyon

Vienne

France's Gallo-Roman heritage is alive and well in this laid-back riverfront city, whose compact old quarter hides spectacular Roman ruins, including a temple and a theatre.

SIGHTS

Musée Gallo-Romain   Museum
(📞04 74 53 74 01; www.musees-gallo-romains.com; D502, St-Romain-en-Gal; adult/child €6/free; ⊙10am-6pm Tue-Sun) Across the Rhône from Vienne, the Musée Gallo-Romain highlights Vienne's historical importance, displaying several rooms full of dazzling mosaics and models of ancient Vienne, surrounded by the actual excavated remains of the Gallo-Roman city.

Pick up a free audio guide for in-depth coverage of the works on display.

Temple d'Auguste
et de Livie   Historic Site
(place Charles de Gaulle) **FREE** Best of all the Roman monuments in Vienne is this striking Roman temple right in the heart of the old town. Take a look at the superb Corinthian columns. It was built around 10 BC to honour Emperor Augustus and his wife, Livia.

EATING

L'Espace PH3   Modern French $$
(📞04 74 53 01 96; www.lapyramide.com; 14 bd Fernand Point; mains €23-24, lunch menu €24; ⊙noon-1.30pm & 7.30-9.30pm) Overseen by two-Michelin-starred chef Patrick Henrir-

oux, L'Espace PH3 offers an affordable gastronomic menu, serving a small selection of French classics with a creative twist. The lunch *menu* is an absolute steal. In summer, meals are served out on the superb garden terrace.

ⓘ INFORMATION

Tourist Office (📞04 74 53 70 10; www.vienne-tourisme.com; 2 cours Brillier; ⊙9am-noon & 1.30-6pm Tue-Sun, 10am-noon & 1.30-6pm Mon) This tourist office has details of museums and historical sites in the Viennois area. It also offers bike hire (€3/5 per half-/full day).

ⓘ GETTING AROUND

Vienne's town centre is compact and easily walkable, with everything within 10 to 15 minutes' walk time, including the Musée Gallo-Romain across the river.

Avignon

For 70-odd years of the early 1300s, the Provençal town of Avignon was the centre of the Roman Catholic world, and though its stint as the seat of papal power only lasted a few decades, it's been left with an impressive legacy of ecclesiastical architecture.

SIGHTS

Palais des Papes   Palace
(Papal Palace; 📞tickets 04 32 74 32 74; www.palais-des-papes.com; place du Palais; adult/

child €12/10, with Pont St-Bénézet €14.50/11.50; ⊙9am-8pm Jul, to 8.30pm Aug, shorter hours Sep-Jun) The largest Gothic palace ever built, the Palais des Papes was erected by Pope Clement V, who abandoned Rome in 1309 in the wake of violent disorder after his election. Its immense scale illustrates the medieval might of the Roman Catholic church.

Ringed by 3m-thick walls, its cavernous halls, chapels and antechambers are largely bare today – but tickets now include tablet 'Histopads' revealing virtual-reality representations of how the building would have looked in all its papal pomp.

Musée du Petit Palais   Museum

(🖉04 90 86 44 58; www.petit-palais.org; place du Palais; adult/child €6/free; ⊙10am-1pm & 2-6pm Wed-Mon) The archbishops' palace during the 14th and 15th centuries now houses outstanding collections of primitive, pre-Rennaissance, 13th- to 16th-century Italian religious paintings by artists including Botticelli, Carpaccio and Giovanni di Paolo – the most famous is Botticelli's *La Vierge et l'Enfant* (1470).

Pont St-Bénézet   Bridge

(🖉tickets 04 32 74 32 74; bd de la Ligne; adult/child 24hr ticket €5/4, with Palais des Papes €14.50/11.50; ⊙9am-8pm Jul, to 8.30pm Aug, shorter hours Sep-Jun) Legend says Pastor Bénézet (a former shepherd) had three visions urging him to build a bridge across the Rhône. Completed in 1185, the 900m-long bridge linked Avignon with Villeneuve-lès-Avignon. It was rebuilt several times before all but four of its 22 spans were washed away in the 1600s, leaving the far side marooned in the middle of the Rhône. There are fine (and free) views from Rocher des Doms park, Pont Édouard Daladier and Île de la Barthelasse's chemin des Berges.

🟢 ACTIVITIES & TOURS

Avignon Guided Tours   Tours

(🖉reservations 04 32 74 32 74; www.avignon-tourisme.com; 41 cours Jean Jaurès; tours from €16.50) The tourist office (p263) runs year-round themed, guided walks exploring the city's past, both the obvious (architecture, art, history) and the esoteric (a behind-the-scenes tour of the palace's secret corners, and a fun tour exploring

Palais des Papes

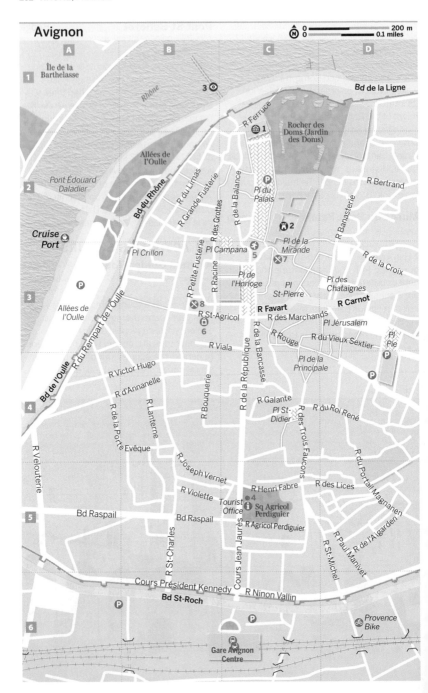

Avignon

Île de la Barthelasse

Rhône

Bd de la Ligne

3 ⊙

R Ferruce

Rocher des Doms (Jardin des Doms)

🏛 1

Allées de l'Oulle

Pont Édouard Daladier

Bd du Rhône

R du Limas

R Grande Fusterie

R des Grottes

R de la Balance

Pl du Palais

R Bertrand

R Banasterie

Cruise Port

Pl Crillon

🅿

Pl Campana

R Petite Fusterie

R Racine

Pl de l'Horloge

🏛 2

Pl de la Mirande

✝ 5

✕ 7

R de la Croix

Pl St-Pierre

Pl des Chataignes

Allées de l'Oulle

🅿

R du Rempart de l'Oulle

✕ 8

R St-Agricol

6

R Viala

R Favart

R des Marchands

R Rouge

R du Vieux Sextier

Pl Jérusalem

R Carnot

Pl Pie

🅿

Bd de l'Oulle

R Velouterie

R Victor Hugo

R d'Annanelle

R Lanterne

R Bouquerie

R de la République

R de la Bancasse

Pl de la Principale

🅿

R de la Porte Evêque

R Galante

Pl St-Didier

R des Trois Faucons

R du Roi René

R du Portail Magnanen

R Joseph Vernet

R Violette

Tourist Office

ℹ ● 4

R Henri Fabre

Sq Agricol Perdiguier

R des Lices

Bd Raspail

Bd Raspail

R St-Charles

R Agricol Perdiguier

Cours Jean Jaurès

R Paul Manivet

R St-Michel

R de l'Aigarden

Cours Président Kennedy

R Ninon Vallin

Bd St-Roch

🅿

🅿

🅿

Provence Bike

🚉 Gare Avignon Centre

Avignon

animals in papal art called 'The Popes and Their Pets'). Most tours are in French only – ask about English-language tours when you reserve, either in person or online.

Le Carré du Palais — Wine Tasting

(04 90 27 24 00; www.carredupalais.fr; 1 place du Palais) The historic Hôtel Calvet de la Palun building in central Avignon has been renovated into a wine centre promoting and serving Côtes du Rhône and Vallée du Rhône appellations. Stop in to get a taste of the local vintages.

🛍 SHOPPING

Oliviers & Co — Beauty, Food

(04 90 86 18 41; www.oliviers-co.com; 19 rue St-Agricol; ☺2-7pm Mon, 10am-7pm Tue-Sat) Fine olive oil and olive-oil-based products, such as soap, creams and biscuits.

✪ EATING

Restaurant L'Essentiel — French $$

(04 90 85 87 12; www.restaurantlessentiel. com; 2 rue Petite Fusterie; menus €32-46; ☺noon-2pm & 7-9.45pm Tue-Sat) In the top tier of Avignon's restaurants for many a year, this elegant restaurant remains (as its name suggests) as essential as ever. First there's the setting: a lovely, honey-stoned *hôtel particulier* (mansion) with a sweet courtyard garden. Then there's the food: rich, sophisticated French dining of the first order, replete with the requisite foams, veloutés and reductions.

Christian Etienne — French $$$

(04 90 86 16 50; www.christian-etienne.fr; 10 rue de Mons; lunch/dinner menus from €35/75;

☺noon-2pm & 7.30-10pm Tue-Sat) If it's the full-blown, fine-dining French experience you're after, then Monsieur Etienne's much-vaunted (and Michelin-starred) restaurant is the place to go. It's the real deal: truffles and foie gras galore, and the kind of multicourse *menus* that demand a second mortgage. It's a bit dated inside: go for the lovely, leafy terrace for fine views of the medieval building.

🛈 INFORMATION

Tourist Office (04 32 74 32 74; www. avignon-tourisme.com; 41 cours Jean Jaurès; ☺9am-6pm Mon-Sat, 10am-5pm Sun Apr-Oct, shorter hours Nov-Mar) Offers guided walking tours and information on other tours and activities, including boat trips on the River Rhône and wine-tasting trips to nearby vineyards.

🛈 GETTING AROUND

The main sights of Avignon are all within easy waking distance of each other.

Bus tickets (€1.30) are sold on board. Buses run from 7am till about 8pm. The main transfer points are Poste (main post office) and place Pie. For Villeneuve-lès-Avignon, take bus 5.

Vélopop (08 10 45 64 56; www.velopop.fr; per half-hour €0.50) Shared-bicycle service, with 17 stations around town. Membership is €1/5 per day/week.

Provence Bike (04 90 27 92 61; www. provence-bike.com; 7 av St-Ruf; bicycles per day/ week from €12/65, scooters €25/150; ☺9am-6.30pm Mon-Sat, plus 10am-1pm Sun Jul) Rents out city bikes, mountain bikes, scooters and motorcycles.

MAIN,
GERMANY

Main, Germany

Rising in Franconia and joining the Rhine near Mainz, the Main (pronounced 'mine') is the longest German-only river. From Bamberg to its confluence, it travels some 400km through locks and picturesque scenery, dotted with historic towns. Frankfurt's skyscrapers are quite a contrast to the picturesque towns that follow, though it too has a rather traditional and charming old town. Scenic Würzburg is renowned for its art, architecture and delicate wines. A disarmingly beautiful architectural masterpiece, Bamberg's entire Altstadt is a Unesco World Heritage Site.

With One Day in Frankfurt

With a day in Frankfurt, begin in the historic heart at the **Kaiserdom** (p270), visiting its museum and, if you're feeling active, climbing its tower. See more of medieval Frankfurt at the **Römerberg** (p270) and find a traditional tavern for lunch. Then spend the afternoon in the standout **Städel Museum** (p270).

Best Places for...

Gallery Städel Museum, Frankfurt am Main (p270)

Baroque Würzburg Residenz, Würzburg (p268)

Souvenirs Handwerkskunst am Römer, Frankfurt am Main (p271)

Pub Food **Klösterbräu, Bamberg** (p274)

Market Kleinmarkthalle, Frankfurt am Main (p271)

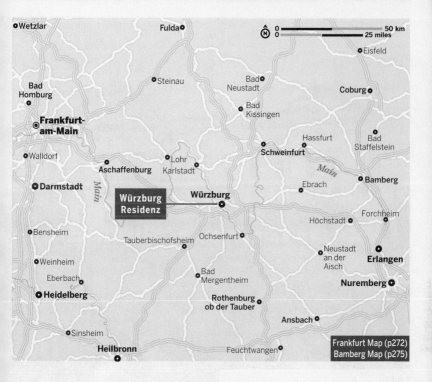

Getting from the Ports

Frankfurt The dock is a short walk from the old town near Untermainbrücke and five minutes from metro stations.

Würzburg Cruises dock at walkable Ludwigkai.

Bamberg Cruise ships dock at the harbour about 3km northwest of the centre, near where the Regnitz and Main meet. Shuttles meet arrivals. Buses run along Hafenstraße, but you'll require a change at the train station to get into the old centre: think half an hour.

Fast Facts

Currency Euro (€)

Language German

Free Wi-fi Most restaurants, bars and cafes have free wi-fi for customers; you may need to ask for the code.

Money ATMs are common and easy to use.

Tourist Information Each town has a centrally located tourist office: in the Altstadt in Bamberg's; on Marktplaz in Würzburg; and in the central square, Römerberg, in Frankfurt.

PAIRATH TAWIN/SHUTTERSTOCK ©

Würzburg Residenz

The vast Unesco-listed Residenz, built by 18th-century architect Balthasar Neumann as the home of the local prince-bishops, is one of Germany's most important and beautiful baroque palaces.

Great For...

☑ **Don't Miss**

The amazing zigzags of the Grand Staircase.

The structure was commissioned in 1720 by prince-bishop Johann Philipp Franz von Schönborn, who was unhappy with his old-fashioned digs up in Marienberg Fortress, and took almost 60 years to complete. Today the 360 rooms are home to government institutions, university faculties and a museum, but the grandest 40 have been restored for visitors to admire. The complex also houses collections of antiques, paintings and drawings in the **Martin-von-Wagner Museum** (no relation to Peter) and, handily, a winery in the atmospheric cellar, the **Staatlicher Hofkeller Würzburg**, that is open for tours (including tasting).

Explore Ashore

It's about a 10-minute walk from the quay at Ludwigkai to the old town, and another 10 minutes up the hill to the Residenz. Taxis and perhaps shuttles will be on hand also. There's no bus route to the Residenz itself. Allow two to three hours here to take a tour and stroll the gardens as well.

❶ Need to Know

www.residenz-wuerzburg.de; Balthasar-Neumann-Promenade; adult/child €7.50/free; ⏱9am-6pm Apr-Oct, 10am-4.30pm Nov-Mar, 45min English tours 11am & 3pm, plus 1.30pm & 4.30pm Apr-Oct

Treppenhaus

Top billing goes to the brilliant zigzagging Treppenhaus (Grand Staircase) lidded by what is still the world's largest fresco, a masterpiece by Giovanni Battista Tiepolo depicting allegories of the four then-known continents (Europe, Africa, America and Asia).

Noble Halls

Feast your eyes on the ice-white stucco-adorned **Weisser Saal** (White Hall), before entering the **Kaisersaal** (Imperial Hall), canopied by yet another impressive Tiepolo fresco. Other stunners include the gilded stucco **Spiegelkabinett** (Mirror Hall), covered with a unique mirror-like glass painted

with figural, floral and animal motifs (accessible by tour only).

In the residence's south wing, the **Hofkirche** (Court Church) is a Neumann and Tiepolo co-production. Its marble columns, gold leaf and profusion of angels match the Residenz in splendour and proportions.

Hofgarten

Entered via frilly wrought-iron gates, the Hofgarten (Court Garden; open until dusk, FREE) is a smooth blend of French- and English-style landscaping teeming with whimsical sculptures of children, mostly by court sculptor Peter Wagner. Concerts, festivals and special events take place here during the warmer months.

Frankfurt am Main

Glinting with glass, steel and concrete skyscrapers, Frankfurt-on-the-Main (pronounced 'mine') is unlike any other German city, a high-powered finance and business hub. Yet at its heart, Frankfurt is an unexpectedly traditional and charming city, with half-timbered buildings huddled in its quaint medieval Altstadt heart.

◉ SIGHTS

Städel Museum   Museum
(☎069-605 098; www.staedelmuseum.de; Schaumainkai 63; adult/child €16/14; ☺10am-7pm Tue, Wed, Sat & Sun, to 9pm Thu & Fri; ☗15/16 Otto-Hahn-Platz) Founded in 1815, this world-renowned art gallery has an outstanding collection of European art from masters including Dürer, Rembrandt, Rubens, Renoir, Picasso and Cézanne, dating from the Middle Ages to today. More contemporary works by artists including Francis Bacon and Gerhard Richter are showcased in a subterranean extension lit by circular skylights. Admission prices can vary according to temporary exhibitions. Queues can be lengthy, so save time by pre-booking tickets online.

Kaiserdom   Cathedral
(Imperial Frankfurt Cathedral; www.dom-frankfurt.de; Domplatz 1; tower adult/child €3/1.50; ☺church 9am-8pm Sun-Thu, from 1pm Fri, tower 9am-6pm Apr-Oct, 10am-5pm Nov-Apr; ⓤDom|Römer) Frankfurt's red-sandstone cathedral is dominated by a 95m-high Gothic tower, which can be climbed via 328 steps. Construction began in the 13th century; from 1356 to 1792, the Holy Roman Emperors were elected (and, after 1562, consecrated and crowned) in the *Wahlkapelle* at the end of the right aisle (look for the 'skull' altar). The cathedral was rebuilt both after an 1867 fire and after the bombings of 1944, which left it a burnt-out shell.

Römerberg   Square
(ⓤDom|Römer) The Römerberg is Frankfurt's old central square. Ornately gabled half-timbered buildings, reconstructed after WWII, give an idea of how beautiful the city's medieval core once was. In the square's centre is the **Gerechtigkeitsbrunnen** (Fountain of Justice).

Museum Judengasse   Museum
(www.museumjudengasse.de; Battonnstrasse 47; adult/child €6/free, multimedia guide €2; ☺10am-8pm Tue, to 6pm Wed-Sun; ⓤKonstablerwache) Most of Frankfurt's medieval Jewish ghetto – Europe's first, dating from 1460 – on narrow Judengasse (Jews' Street) was destroyed by a French bombardment in 1796, but you can get a sense of local Jewish life during the 15th to 18th centuries from the excavated remains of houses and ritual baths. Laws confining Frankfurt's Jews to the ghetto were repealed in 1811. Renovated in 2016, the museum here spotlights the former residents' interactions with Frankfurt's Christian residents, the city council and the emperor.

Museum für
Moderne Kunst   Museum
(MMK; Museum of Modern Art; ☎069-2123 0447; www.mmk-frankfurt.de; Domstrasse 10; adult/child €12/6, all three sites €16/8; ☺10am-6pm Tue & Thu-Sun, to 8pm Wed; ⓤDom|Römer) The outstanding Museum of Modern Art focuses on European and American art from the 1960s to the present, with frequent temporary exhibits. The permanent collection (not always on display) includes works by Roy Lichtenstein, Claes Oldenburg and Joseph Beuys. Free English-language tours on varying topics take place at 4pm every Saturday. The main premises are referred to as MMK1; there are another two exhibition spaces, MMK2 (in the TaunusTurm at Taunustor 1) and MMK3 (opposite MMK 1 at Domstrasse 3).

☞ TOURS

Tourist Office
Walking Tours   Walking
(www.frankfurt-tourismus.de; Römerberg 27; 1hr city tour €10.90, with Main Tower entry €16.90, 1½hr old town tour €12.90; ☺Mar-Dec; ⓤDom|Römer) Various walking tours of Frankfurt depart from the Römer tourist

Kleinmarkthalle

office, providing historical context for this hyper-modern city. Annual schedules are posted on the tourist office website, which also sells tickets.

🅐 SHOPPING

Handwerkskunst am Römer
Gifts & Souvenirs

(www.handwerkskunst-frankfurt.com; Braubach-strasse 39; ⏰10am-8pm Mon-Sat, from 11am Sun; ⓤDom|Römer) Exquisite handcrafted souvenirs at this long-established shop include traditional toy-soldier nutcrackers, adorable 'smokers' (incense burners) depicting peddlers, miners, organ-grinders and so on, cuckoo clocks, music boxes, tiny wooden figurines and Christmas decorations.

Frankfurter Fass
Food & Drinks

(www.frankfurter-fass.de; Töngesgasse 38; ⏰10am-6.30pm Mon-Fri, to 4pm Sat; ⓤHauptwache) Pick up *Apfelwein,* as well as apple brandy, regional wines, vinegars, oils, spirits, salts, mustard and other local delicacies like Frankfurt bonbons filled with cider liqueur, at this emporium.

🅧 EATING

Kleinmarkthalle
Market €

(www.kleinmarkthalle.de; Hasengasse 5-7; ⏰8am-6pm Mon-Fri, to 4pm Sat; ⓤDom|Römer) 🍴 Aromatic stalls inside this bustling traditional market hall sell artisan smoked sausages, cheeses, roasted nuts, breads, pretzels, loose-leaf teas, pastries, cakes and chocolates, along with fruit, vegetables, spices, fresh pasta, olives, meat, poultry and, downstairs, fish. It's unmissable for picnickers or self-caterers, or anyone wanting to experience Frankfurt life. The upper-level wine bar opens to a terrace.

Dauth-Schneider
German €€

(☎069-613 533; www.dauth-schneider.de; Neuer Wall 5; mains €8-13.50; ⏰11.30am-midnight; 🚆Lokalbahnhof) With a history stretching back to 1849 (the basement housed an apple winery), this convivial tavern is a wonderful place to sample both the local drop and classic regional specialities such as *Sulz Fleisch* (cold meat and jelly terrine), *Gekochte Haspel* (pickled pork knuckle) with sauerkraut, and various tasting

Frankfurt am Main

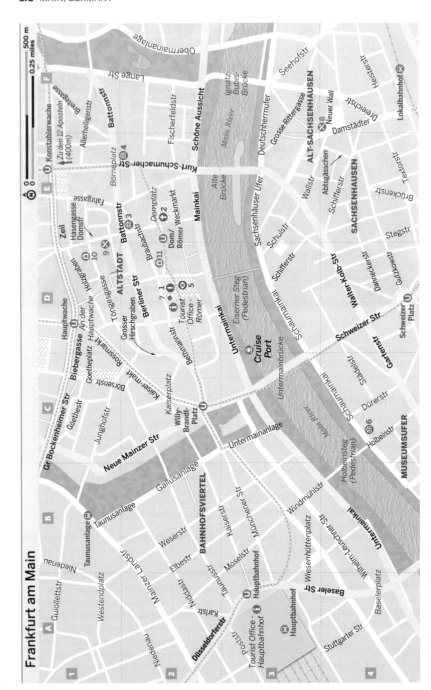

500 m
0.25 miles

Obermainanlage

Lange Str

Guiollettstr

Niedenau

Westendplatz

Niedenau

Taunusanlage

Gr Bockenheimer Str

Goethestr

Junghofstr

Westendplatz

Mainzer Landstr

Taunusanlage

Weserstr

Elbestr

Taunusstr

Niddastr

Karlstr

Gallusanlage

Kaiserstr

Moselstr

Münchener Str

BAHNHOFSVIERTEL

Neue Mainzer Str

Untermainanlage

Willy-Brandt-Platz

Kaiserplatz

Börsenstr

Biebergasse

Goetheplatz

Rossmarkt

An der Hauptwache

Hauptwache

Zeil

Hasengasse

Domstr

Grosser Hirschgraben

Tongesgasse

Holzgraben

ALTSTADT

Berliner Str

Braubachstr

Battonnstr

Domstr

Dom/Römer

Römer

Tourist Office - Römer

Bethmannstr

Kaiserplatz

Untermainkai

Untermainkai

Cruise Port

Eiserner Steg (Pedestrian)

Mainkai

Alte Brücke

Schöne Aussicht

Fischerfeldstr

Börneplatz

Kurt-Schumacher-Str

Fahrgasse

Allerheiligenstr

Breitegasse

Battonnstr

Konstablerwache

Zu den 12 Aposteln (400m)

Main River

Ignatz-Bubis-Brücke

Deutschherrnufer

Grosse Rittergasse

ALT-SACHSENHAUSEN

Neuer Wall

Damstädter

Dreieichstr

Seehofstr

Heisterstr

Lokalbahnhof

Textorstr

Brückenstr

SACHSENHAUSEN

Abtsgässchen

Schifferstr

Wallstr

Sachsenhäuser Ufer

Schulstr

Schifferstr

Schaumainkai

Schaumainkai

Walter-Kolb-Str

Schweizer Str

Schweizer Platz

Gartenstr

Dürerstr

Stegstr

Daneckerstr

Gutzkowstr

Main River

Holbeinsteg (Pedestrian)

Holbeinstr

MUSEUMSUFER

Städelstr

Untermainbrücke

Untermainanlage

Hauptbahnhof

Hauptbahnhof

Tourist Office - Hauptbahnhof

Poststr

Düsseldorferstr

Baseler Str

Baseler Str

Wiesenhüttenplatz

Wilhelm-Leuschner-Str

Windmühlstr

Untermainkai

Baselerplatz

Stuttgarter Str

Frankfurt am Main

platters. Tables fill the tree-shaded terrace in summer.

Zu den 12 Aposteln
German €€

(☎069-288 668; www.12aposteln-frankfurt.de; Rosenbergerstrasse 1; mains €9-24; ⊙11.30am-1am; Ⓤ Konstablerwache) Glowing with sepia-toned lamplight, the 12 Apostles has ground-floor and cellar dining rooms serving traditional German dishes: *Matjes* (herring) with sour cream, apple and fried onion; roast pork knuckle with pickled cabbage; Frankfurter schnitzel with *Grüne Sosse* (green sauce); and *Käsespätzle* (handmade cheese noodles with onions). It brews its own light and dark beers on the premises.

ℹ INFORMATION

Frankfurt's tourist office has two city branches:

Tourist Office – Hauptbahnhof (☎069-2123 8800; www.frankfurt-tourismus.de; Main Hall, Hauptbahnhof; ⊙8am-9pm Mon-Fri, 9am-6pm Sat & Sun; ℝ Hauptbahnhof) At the main train station.

Tourist Office – Römer (☎069-2123 8800; www.frankfurt-tourismus.de; Römerberg 27; ⊙9.30am-5.30pm Mon-Fri, to 4pm Sat & Sun; Ⓤ Dom|Römer) Smallish office in the central square.

ℹ GETTING AROUND

Frankfurt's excellent transport system, part of the RMV (Rhein-Main-Verkehrsverbund; www.rmv.de) network, integrates all bus, *Strassenbahn* (tram), S-Bahn (commuter rail) and U-Bahn (metro/subway) lines.

Tickets can be purchased at transit stops from *Fahrkartenautomaten* (ticket machines). Zone 50 encompasses most of Frankfurt. Machines accept euro coins and notes (up to €10 or €20) and chip-and-pin credit cards, which excludes many US-issued cards.

A *Tageskarte* (all-day ticket), valid from the start of service until 5am the next day, costs €5.35; a *Gruppentageskarte* (all-day group ticket), for up to five people is just €11.30 – a superb deal.

Cycling is a great way to get around Frankfurt, which is criss-crossed with designated bike lanes. **Next Bike** (☎030-6920 5046; www.nextbike.de; per 30min €1) has dozens of pick-up points throughout the city; register with a credit card, then use the app to get the lock code.

Würzburg

Straddling the Main River, scenic Würzburg is renowned for its art, architecture and delicate wines. The definite highlight is the Residenz, one of Germany's finest baroque buildings, though there's plenty more to see besides.

⊙ SIGHTS

Dom St Kilian
Church

(www.dom-wuerzburg.de; Domstrasse 40; ⊙8am-7pm Mon-Sat, to 8pm Sun) Würzburg's highly unusual cathedral has a Romanesque core that has been altered many times over the centuries. The elaborate stucco work of the chancel contrasts starkly with the bare whitewash of the austere Romanesque nave that is capped with a ceiling that wouldn't look out of place in a 1960s bus station. The whole mishmash creates quite an impression and is possibly Germany's oddest cathedral interior. The **Schönbornkapelle** by Balthasar Neumann returns a little baroque order to things.

EATING

Bürgerspital Weinstube
Franconian €€

(📞0931-352 880; www.buergerspital-wein stuben.de; Theaterstrasse 19; mains €7-25; ⏱10am-midnight) If you are going to eat out just once in Würzburg, the aromatic and cosy nooks of this labyrinthine medieval place probably provide the top local experience. Choose from a broad selection of Franconian wines (some of Germany's best) and wonderful regional dishes and snacks, including *Mostsuppe* (a tasty wine soup). Buy local whites in the adjoining wine shop.

 **INFORMATION**

Tourist Office (📞0931-372 398; www.wuerz burg.de; Marktplatz 9; ⏱10am-6pm Mon-Fri, to 3pm Sat, to 2pm Sun May-Oct, closed Sun & slightly shorter hours Nov-Apr) This efficient office within the attractive Falkenhaus can help with room reservations and tour bookings.

GETTING AROUND

Würzburg can be easily tackled on foot.

Bamberg

A disarmingly beautiful architectural masterpiece with an almost complete absence of modern eyesores, Bamberg's entire Altstadt is a Unesco World Heritage Site and one of Bavaria's unmissables.

SIGHTS

Bamberger Dom
Cathedral

(www.erzbistum-bamberg.de; Domplatz; ⏱9.30am-6pm Apr-Oct, to 5pm Nov-Mar) Beneath the quartet of spires, Bamberg's cathedral is packed with artistic treasures, most famously the slender equestrian statue of the **Bamberger Reiter** (Bamberg Horseman), whose true identity remains a mystery. It overlooks the tomb of cathedral founders, Emperor Heinrich II and his wife Kunigunde, splendidly carved by Tilmann Riemenschneider. The marble tomb of Clemens II in the west choir is the only papal burial site north of the Alps. Nearby,

the Virgin Mary altar by Veit Stoss also warrants closer inspection.

Altes Rathaus
Historic Building

(Old Town Hall; Obere Brücke; adult/child €6/5; ⏱10am-4.30pm Tue-Sun) Like a ship in dry dock, Bamberg's 1462 Old Town Hall was built on an artifical island in the Regnitz River, allegedly because the local bishop had refused to give the town's citizens any land for its construction. Inside you'll find the Sammlung Ludwig, a collection of precious porcelain, but even more enchanting are the richly detailed frescos adorning its facades – note the cherub's leg cheekily protruding from the eastern facade.

Klein Venedig
Area

(Little Venice; Fischerei) FREE A row of diminutive, half-timbered cottages once inhabited by fishermen and their families (hence the street's name meaning 'fishery') comprises Bamberg's Klein Venedig (Little Venice), which hems the Regnitz' east bank between Markusbrücke and Untere Brücke. The little homes balance on poles set right into the water and are fronted by tiny gardens and terraces, the river flowing sluggishly past just centimetres below ground level.

TOURS

BierSchmecker Tour
Walking

(www.bier.bamberg.info; adult €22.50) Possibly the most tempting tour of the amazingly varied offerings at the tourist office is the self-guided BierSchmecker Tour. The price includes entry to the Fränkisches Brauereimuseum (depending on the route taken), plus five beer vouchers valid in five pubs and breweries, an English information booklet, a route map and a souvenir stein. Not surprisingly, it can take all day to complete the route.

 EATING

Klosterbräu
Pub Food €

(Obere Mühlbrücke 1-3; mains €7-13; ⏱11.30am-10pm Mon-Sat, to 2pm Sun) This beautiful half-timbered brewery is Bamberg's oldest. It draws *Stammgäste* (regulars) and tourists alike who wash down filling slabs of

Bamberg

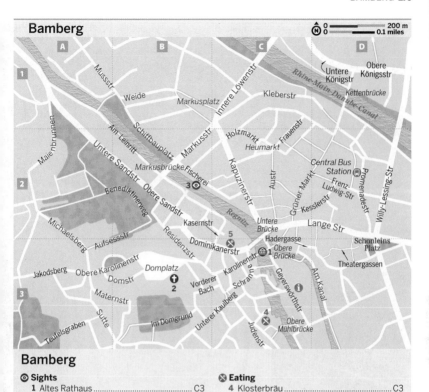

Bamberg

⊚ **Sights**
1 Altes Rathaus C3
2 Bamberger Dom B3
3 Klein Venedig... B2

⊗ **Eating**
4 Klosterbräu.. C3
5 Schlenkerla C3

meat and dumplings with its excellent range of ales in the unpretentious dining room.

Schlenkerla   German €

(☑0951-560 60; www.schlenkerla.de; Dominika-nerstrasse 6; mains €7-13; ⊙9.30am-11.30pm)
Beneath wooden beams as dark as the superb *Rauchbier* poured straight from oak barrels, locals and visitors gather around a large ceramic stove to dig into scrumptious Franconian fare at this legendary flower-festooned tavern. Staff pass beers through a tiny window in the entrance for those who just want to taste a beer but not sit.

 INFORMATION

Tourist Office (☑0951-297 6200; www.bamberg.info; Geyerswörthstrasse 5; ⊙9.30am-6pm Mon-Fri, to 4pm Sat, to 2.30pm Sun) Large

professional office with parking, toilets and a children's playground all nearby. Staff sell the Bambergcard (€14.90), valid for three days of free bus rides and free museum entry.

ⓘ GETTING AROUND

Cruise ships dock at the harbour about 3km northwest of the centre, near where the Regnitz and Main meet. Shuttles meet arrivals. Buses run along Hafenstraße, but you'll require a change at the train station to get into the old centre.

Several buses, including 901, 902 and 931, connect the train station with the **central bus station** (ZOB; Promenadestrasse), which has a handy 12-hour left-luggage facility. Bus 910 goes from the ZOB to Domplatz.

Once in the Aldstadt, sights are all within easily walkable distance of each other.

Church of the Saviour on the Spilled Blood (p226), St Petersburg

In Focus

Protest against Brexit, London

ANGYALOSI BEATA/SHUTTERSTOCK ©

Europe Today

These are challenging times for Europe. Economically, many countries are still struggling, while politically, pro- and anti- European Union (EU) forces are engaged in a titanic struggle. While some countries have backed candidates that favour a stronger, united Europe, others have gone for populists and nationalists, with a rise of far-right politics in the mix too.

State of the Union

Where Europe should be headed as a political entity remains a burning question for EU nations, especially those hostile to relinquishing further powers to the European Parliament. In 2016, a referendum in the UK over the issue saw voters opt by a slim majority for 'Brexit'; in other nations, hostility towards the EU appears to be growing, as the established political order seems to be dissolving. From the French *gilets jaunes* (yellow vests) protests that began in 2018, to rising Islamophobia and anti-Semitism across the region, it is a worrying time for both those in Brussels and those at the head of traditional political parties across the region.

Refugees

Hostility towards Muslims has been on the rise in the wake of the worst refugee crisis to hit Europe since the end of WWII. Since 2015, over three million refugees and migrants have arrived in the EU, the majority of them fleeing from war and terror in Syria and other troubled countries. Many of these cross the Mediterranean in boats, a perilous journey that has resulted in thousands of deaths from drowning as overloaded, unseaworthy vessels sink or capsize.

Government responses have ranged from some countries in the EU's Schengen Area closing previously open borders to Germany's acceptance of nearly two million asylum seekers in the past few years. Populist leaders have exploited the refugee crisis to stoke anti-immigration hostility in several countries, notably Italy, where far-right interior minister Matteo Salvini has made refugees a political target.

Greener Europe

On a brighter note, many European countries are stepping up efforts to combat climate change. Increasingly, high-speed rail services provide an eco-friendly alternative to short-haul flights, green spaces flourish in urban areas, bicycle-share schemes are becoming prevalent in cities and towns, and vehicle emissions are being reduced with more electric and hybrid engines and biofuels. Several countries and cities in the region have pledged to take diesel cars and vans off their roads in the near future.

Eurovision

Less seriously, every May Europe plops down on the sofa to enjoy the Eurovision Song Contest. This one-of-a-kind musical marathon has been screened every year since 1956, making it the longest-running television show of its kind. Created to symbolise Euro harmony, the contest has also developed into a reflection of Euro discord. Is the voting system rigged? Should acts sing in English or in their own language? Is that kitschy pop song some kind of coded political statement? Each country enters one song, and then votes for their favourites among the competitors. Inevitably, this leads to accusations of 'block voting' (neighbouring countries tending to vote for each other, for example). Confusingly, too, several non-European countries are allowed to enter. The host city, with a few exceptions, is in the winner country of the previous year, with cities competing domestically for the honour and associated tourism boost.

Stained-glass window depicting Charlemagne, Kölner Dom (p38)

History

Europe's history is a complex, often stormy story that could fill multiple libraries of dusty tomes. From Imperial Rome to the EU via medieval chivalry, the Renaissance, bitter religious feuds and two catastrophic world wars, this real-life 'Game of Thrones' has provoked chaos, coalitions, war, peace, treachery and heroism.

753 BC	447 BC	323 BC
According to legend, Rome is founded by Romulus and Remus. It eventually becomes an expansive empire that lasts over 1000 years.	Construction begins on the Parthenon, the principal temple on the Acropolis of Athens.	The death of Alexander the Great is a transition point between the Classical and Hellenistic eras of ancient Greek history.

Aachen Cathedral, Germany

The Franks

Following the decline of Rome, Rome's Eastern Empire in the Balkans carried on as Byzantium, with its capital in Constantinople, its size and influence ebbing and flowing until its final collapse in 1453.

Western Europe, however, regressed into what became known as the 'Dark Ages'. Robbed of the stability of *Pax Romana,* it became a fragmented mesh of migrating people and localised power struggles, settled and resettled by successive waves of Vandals, Goths, Huns and Slavs. Populations emptied from cities, Roman technological proficiency seemed to disappear off the face of the earth, and no single entity was able to fill the power vacuum until the rise of the Franks.

The Franks were a Germanic tribe that spread across Western Europe between the 3rd and 8th centuries restoring some 'light' to the prevailing 'darkness'. Maintaining a tentative love-hate relationship with the Romans in their early days, the Franks hung onto numerous watered-down Roman traditions after the empire fell, including a loyal adherence to the

AD 170	395	800
The Romans construct the Porta Nigra in Trier.	On the death of Emperor Theodosius I, the Roman Empire splits into western and eastern courts.	Charlemagne, King of the Franks and the so-called 'Father of Europe', is crowned first Holy Roman Emperor by Pope Leo III in Rome.

Christian faith. Frankish power reached its apex in the early 9th century with the ascension of Charlemagne as Holy Roman Emperor. Re-establishing Rome's long-lost imperial title, Charlemagne presided over the Frankish kingdom of Francia, aka the Carolingian Empire, with lands that comprised most of modern-day France and Germany. Crowned by Pope Leo III in Rome on Christmas Day 800, he headed a noble line of monarchs that lasted until 1806. Tranquillised by political stability and aided by Charlemagne's penchant for the liberal arts, Francia enjoyed a brief cultural flowering known as the Carolingian Renaissance that enthusiastically mined the culture of ancient Rome. Thanks to this mini cultural resurgence, Western European culture survived a potential Barbarian implosion and hung onto Latin as its binding language.

After Charlemagne's death in 814, the Frankish empire quickly descended into civil war and was split into opposing fiefdoms. The western half evolved into what we now know as France. The eastern half became the Holy Roman Empire, a loose confederation of kingdoms, duchies and free cities that paid tribute to the Holy Roman Emperor, an elected Catholic monarch crowned by the Pope and one of the most powerful and important rulers in Europe for much of the Middle Ages.

The Hundred Years' War

Anyone seeking a quick synopsis of the rough and tumble of the Middle Ages need look no further than the Hundred Years' War. Conjuring up images of crenellated castles, knights in armour and medieval codes of chivalry, this bitter amalgamation of battles and back-stabbing between England and France dragged on for five generations, from the early victories of English king Edward III in the 1330s, to the final capitulation of his great-great-grandson, Henry VI, nearly 120 years later.

Though protracted and complex, the pivotal issue in this century-long confrontation concerned the kingdom of France and who should rule it – the French House of Valois or the English House of Plantagenet.

Although Anglo-French relations had been deteriorating for decades by the early 14th century, things didn't officially turn warlike until French king Charles the Fair died without a male heir in 1328. Risking the ire of his cross-channel frenemies, Edward III, the French-speaking, half-Gallic English king, audaciously declared himself the rightful heir to the throne of France. He had a valid claim. As the grandson of French king Philip IV, Edward was the scion of an Anglo-French bloodline that went back nearly 300 years. England had been ruled by Francophone monarchs since 1066 when William of Normandy had defeated Saxon king Harold II at the Battle of Hastings and proceeded to seat himself on the English throne. More French land was added a century later when the English crown passed to Henry II, the son of a French count, whose coronation in 1154 put Anjou, Brittany and Aquitaine under English rule. By the late 12th century, England, through a combination of marriage, inheritance and war, ruled over half of France. Not surprisingly, the French weren't particularly enamoured with their interfering new neighbours, and when Edward

1054	**1347–51**	**1492**
After seven centuries of disagreement, the church suffers a schism between Catholicism and Eastern Orthodoxy.	The Black Death rages across Europe wiping out an estimated 45% to 50% of the continent's population.	Spain's Catholic monarchs conquer Granada, expel all Jews from Spanish lands, and dispatch Christopher Columbus to the Americas.

made his claim to the throne in 1337, the freshly installed French king Philip of Valois decided he wasn't going to take it lying down.

Thus began the Hundred Years' War, a long-winded medieval jousting tournament fought against a backdrop of seesawing fortunes and legendary battles, all of them waged on French soil.

The Avignon Papacy

For 67 years starting in 1309, the papacy was based in Avignon, France. This so-called 'Babylonian Captivity' began when French-born Pope Clement V refused to move to Rome. The court remained in France during the tenure of six further pontiffs until the reign of Gregory XI in 1376.

The Renaissance

If pressured to single out just one sweeping cultural movement that has affected Europe more than any other since the fall of the Roman Empire, most historians would cite the Renaissance.

First nurtured in Italy in the late 14th century, the Renaissance was an artistic and cultural movement that unapologetically tapped the philosophy and ideas of classical antiquity for inspiration. Revisiting the work of Greek and Roman scribes and builders, Italian 'Renaissance Men' such as writer Francesco Petrarch, architect Filippo Brunelleschi and painter Leonardo da Vinci styled themselves as budding humanists aiming to replace the tradition and dogma of the Middle Ages with self-expression and rational thought. Science and philosophy, which had been bogged down by religious orthodoxy for centuries, suddenly experienced a shot in the arm. The Renaissance ushered in an exciting new era of exploration and discovery that gradually spread all over Europe. Scientists looked up to the stars and carefully dissected the human body; artists rethought the rules of painting using realism, linear perspective and close studies of nature; architects dusted off building methods forgotten since Roman times to shape giant domes and elegant colonnades.

In a relatively short space of time, European civilisation made a giant intellectual leap forward. Developments were revolutionary and contagious, changing society forever. Michelangelo designed a spectacular new dome for St Peter's Basilica in Rome; Columbus, at the behest of the Spanish monarchy, set sail for the Americas; and the printing press, pioneered by Johannes Gutenberg in Germany, became the new means of mass communication. As the Renaissance flourished, leading to wider literacy and more critical thinking, it also inadvertently allowed space for the development of the next big sea-change – the Reformation.

The Reformation

In the callow years of the 16th century, an academic pamphlet written by a little-known German professor at Wittenberg University named Martin Luther prompted the biggest religious schism in European history. Luther's so-called *Ninety-Five Theses,* which he (perhaps) nailed provocatively to the door of Wittenberg's Schlosskirche in 1517, questioned

1517	1618–48	1756–63
Martin Luther's *95 Theses* ushers in the Reformation, a fundamental reorganisation of Christian institutions that leaves a bloody aftermath.	The Thirty Years' War, Europe's costliest, pitches Catholics against Protestants and Habsburgs against Bourbons.	The Seven Years' War becomes the first de facto global conflict with ramifications felt throughout Europe's colonies.

many of the long-held doctrines of the all-powerful Catholic clergy and ushered in what became known as the Reformation. The effects of the rupture were drastic and long-lasting. Over the next 130 years, a new 'protestant' religion gradually infiltrated Western Christianity as uppity European monarchs like England's Henry VIII broke ties with Rome and a series of bitter wars wracked and decimated much of the continent.

Luther's propositions were influenced, in part, by the spread of humanism and critical thinking prompted by the Renaissance. But they also threw light on a host of darker issues. Dissatisfaction with the papacy had been growing for decades with the fabulously wealthy Catholic Church increasingly derided as corrupt, intransigent and hopelessly out-of-touch with the common worshipper. Although Luther's initial beef had been with the church's granting of indulgences (the reduction of punishments for sins), he soon widened his philosophy to proffer more fundamental revisions. Luther and his reformist followers questioned the supremacy of the pope, were unenthusiastic about the veneration of Catholic saints, and pointedly disagreed with the literal interpretation of the Holy Eucharist. With equal vigour, they hailed the Bible rather than the clergy as the sole source of divine inspiration.

By the early 17th century, whole nation states were embroiled in the growing religious fissure, with England, Scandinavia and the Dutch Republic identifying as Protestant, and Spain and Italy remaining staunchly Catholic. In France, Huguenots (Protestant Calvinists) battled it out with Catholics for 36 years, with the latter finally coming out on top in 1598. The Holy Roman Empire remained religiously split down the middle, a division that sparked the opening shots of the Thirty Years' War.

The Thirty Years' War

Few people today could list the causes or adversaries in the Thirty Years' War (1618–48), yet this long and costly conflict remains one of the bloodiest in European history, usurped only by WWI and WWII in its casualty rate. The crux issue was religion and the main battleground was the Holy Roman Empire.

By the early 17th century, the loose confederation of duchies and kingdoms that inhabited modern-day Germany was split sharply along religious lines mapped out during the Reformation. Protestantism held sway in the north and east, while Catholicism dominated the southern and western states. When Catholic Holy Roman Emperor Ferdinand II took power in 1618, he began a policy of Protestant suppression throughout the empire, a provocative move that went explicitly against the religious freedoms that had been guaranteed by the Peace of Augsburg in 1555.

Angry about the blatant infringement of their religious rights, Protestants quickly revolted, starting in Bohemia where belligerent rebels ejected the emperor's imperial representatives in Prague and appointed their own king, Frederick V, an avowed Calvinist, as an alternative. It was the spark that lit the fuse. Moving to crush the Bohemian upstarts, Ferdinand sent troops to Prague in 1620 and defeated the bolshie Bohemians at the Battle of White Mountain. But for the Protestants the setback was only the end of the beginning. Other European

1789	**1815**	**1871**
The French Revolution overthrows the Bourbon monarchy and lays down the principals of liberty, equality and fraternity.	The Congress of Vienna ends the Napoleonic wars and redraws the map of Europe.	After over a decade of war between competing European powers, unification in both Italy and Germany is successful.

powers had been watching the gathering storm from the sidelines with an eye to settling their own political and religious scores. By the 1630s, Bohemia, allied with other Protestant German states, had enlisted the support of the Calvinist Dutch Republic, Lutheran Sweden and – somewhat bizarrely – the Catholic rulers of France, while Ferdinand and his Catholic cohorts cosied up to Habsburg Spain, who were already engaged in a separate squabble with the Dutch over the republic's audacious declaration of independence in 1581.

Viewed through a historical prism, the Thirty Years' War was a prolonged and horribly damaging conflict that laid to waste large parts of north-central Europe. In some regions, up to 50% of the population lost their lives either directly in combat, or from a moribund mixture of disease, famine and displacement. In many ways, the conflict marked the last sting in the tail of the Reformation. The ensuing treaties signed in 1648, known communally as the Peace of Westphalia, ended Europe's wars of religion that had raged for more than a century.

Jews in Central Europe

The first Jews arrived in central Europe with the conquering Romans, settling in important Roman cities. As non-Christians, Jews had a separate political status. Highly valued for their trade connections, they were granted various trading privileges in certain cities.

The First Crusade (1095–99) brought pogroms, usually against the will of local rulers and townspeople. Many Jews resisted, before committing suicide once their situation became hopeless. This, the *Kiddush ha-shem* (martyr's death), established a precedent of martyrdom that became a tenet of European Judaism in the Middle Ages.

In the 13th century, Jews were declared crown property by Frederick II, an act that afforded protection but exposed them to royal whim. Things deteriorated with the arrival of the plague in the mid-14th century, when Jews were persecuted and libellous notions circulated throughout the Christian population. The 'blood libel' accused Jews of using the blood of Christians in rituals.

Expulsions remained commonplace through the 15th century, with large numbers emigrating to Poland, where the Yiddish language developed. The Reformation (including a hostile Martin Luther) and the Thirty Years' War brought difficult times for Jewish populations, but by the 17th century they were again valued for their economic contacts.

By the late 19th century, Jews had equal status in most respects and central Europe had become a world centre of Jewish cultural and historical studies. There was a shift to large cities, such as Leipzig, Cologne, Vienna, Prague and Berlin, where a third of German Jews lived.

Central Europe became an important centre for Hebrew literature after Russian writers and academics fled the revolution of 1917. In Germany, the Weimar Republic brought emancipation for the 500,000-strong Jewish community, but by 1943 Adolf Hitler had declared Germany *Judenrein* (literally 'clean of Jews'). This ignored the hundreds of thousands of Eastern European Jews incarcerated on 'German' soil. Around six million Jews died in Europe as a direct result of Nazism.

1914–18	**1917**	**1939–45**
Colonial rivalry, rearmament and complex alliances push Europe into WWI following the assassination of Archduke Franz Ferdinand.	The Russian Revolution ushers in seven decades of communism in what was to become the Soviet Union.	Hitler invades Poland, dragging Europe into WWII, the costliest military conflict in history, and the breeding ground for the Holocaust.

Europe's Darkest Hours: 1914–45

When patriotic recruits in Britain, France, Austria, Russia and Germany joined up to fight in the summer of 1914, they assumed that Europe's little 'contretemps' over the Balkans would be over by Christmas. They couldn't have been more wrong.

Following the assassination of Archduke Franz Ferdinand in Sarajevo, Austria declared war on Serbia, activating a complex system of European alliances that had been built up over three decades. Germany dutifully backed Austria, Russia jumped to the defence of the Serbs and the French elected to support Russia, their long-standing partners in the 'Triple Entente'. When the Germans invaded Belgium in August 1914 hoping for a quick victory over the French, the British (the third member of the Triple Entente) sent their troops across the Channel to join the French army just in time to thwart a German advance on Paris in the Battle of the Marne.

Fatefully, the Marne was the war's first and last notable advance. In late 1914, the Allies (Britain, France, Russia and, later, Italy) and the Central Powers (Germany, Austria and the Ottoman Empire), evenly matched and led by a batch of stubborn generals, dug in for four years of what would become known as 'trench warfare', a military stalemate in which no side was able to gain the upper hand. Instead, the deadlocked armies took to butchering each other on an industrial scale. During the four-month Battle of the Somme, an estimated one million soldiers perished, around 26,000 of them on the first day.

Despite all its well-documented horrors, the 'war to end all wars' had a significant impact on technology. Aircraft and tanks were used in warfare for the first time, and submarines, field telephones and chemical weapons all played a key, often macabre, role. But it wasn't enough to break the deadlock. Instead, the war ground on and on, the impasse only broken when the Americans joined the conflict in 1917 on the side of the Allies. The Germans – already weakened by political problems at home and threatened by an army on the verge of mutiny – were increasingly outnumbered by their newly bolstered enemy. In November 1918 they reluctantly agreed to surrender. Yet, despite the military cessation, no Allied army ever set foot on German soil during WWI and German casualties remained significantly lower than British and French losses on the Western Front. It was thus surprising when the Germans were dictated harsh peace terms at the Treaty of Versailles in 1919, losing land, colonies and the lion's share of their military machine. Even more disastrously, the country was forced to admit 'war guilt' and pay massive reparations to the Allies for the next 13 years.

As any student of 20th-century history knows, WWI, and its failure to broker a fair and lasting peace, led directly to WWII. Thousands of German soldiers returned home in 1919 feeling humiliated and betrayed by their leaders. Looking around for a scapegoat, many, including a twice-decorated Austrian corporal called Adolf Hitler, began suggesting that Germany had been 'stabbed in the back' by the Communists and the Jews.

Reckless conspiracy theories coupled with the economic and political chaos that reparations helped ferment, gave birth to a frightening new form of nationalism in Italy and Germany reflected in Benito Mussolini's 'blackshirts' and Hitler's Nazi Party. By the early

1957	**1989**	**1991**
Six European countries, including France and Germany, sign the Treaty of Rome, a precursor to the EU.	The Fall of the Berlin Wall marks the end of the Cold War and the 'Iron Curtain' dividing Eastern and Western Europe.	The Dissolution of the Soviet Union leads to the formation of new independent states including Ukraine and Russia.

1930s, with the Nazis winning significant support at the ballot box, it had become clear that the bickering of WWI had never been truly resolved. It would take rearmament, political extremism, the death of six million Jews and another devastating war for Europe to disentangle itself from a web of distrust and deceit. And the next war would be the biggest and bloodiest the world had ever seen.

Learning to Live Together

After WWII ended in 1945 most of Europe lay in ruins, propped up by economic aid from the Americans (through the US$12 billion Marshall Plan) or the Soviet Union (through the concurrent Molotov Plan). Yet, following centuries of war, genocide, and petty squabbles between incestuous royal families, the continent appeared to have finally learned its lesson. Slowly but surely, Europe began to put its differences aside and work on forging long-term cooperation. However, there were some major kinks to be ironed out first. For 45 years after WWII, Europe was front line in the jittery Cold War, with the continent split in two by the infamous 'Iron Curtain', the Soviet-dominated Warsaw Pact countries in the east and American-led NATO guarding the west. Although the Cold War was not without its sporadic flare-ups, European governments, still haunted by the spectre of Hitler and the Holocaust, largely managed to keep their weaponry under wraps. Engaging in a shaky diplomacy, both sides elected to lob words rather shells over the Iron Curtain as the Soviets built a wall in Berlin and sent in tanks to snuff out popular rebellions in Hungary in 1956, Czechoslovakia in 1968 and Poland in 1981. But not even the big fish in the Kremlin could hold back the inevitable tide of history in 1989 when the Berlin Wall came tumbling down amid a wave of popular unrest and protest, most of it remarkably peaceful.

Pan-Europeanism had been around since the Roman times, but its early manifestations had usually been in the form of loosely organised empires united by force and dominated by a single land-grabbing power. From the outset, the EU was a far more democratic beast. Its antecedents lay in the European Coal and Steel Community (ECSC) set up in 1951 between France, Germany, Italy and the Benelux countries to discourage regional competition over natural resources. Largely a reaction to the rampant nationalism that had helped fuel WWII, the ECSC quickly morphed into the European Economic Community (EEC), a more cohesive customs union with ambitions to forge greater integration. As the community grew beyond its initial six members, extending to nine in 1973 and 12 by 1986, its remit expanded as well. In 1979, the first elections were held to a European Parliament; in 1985, the Schengen Agreement established open borders between member countries; and in 2002 monetary union came about with the introduction of the 'euro'. Renamed the European Union in 1992, the community had grown to accommodate 28 member-states by 2013, including most of the former Warsaw Pact countries. Though not without its prickly issues – including the UK's controversial pledge to secede from the EU in 2016 – the problems of the EU seem refreshingly minor compared with the plagues, revolutions and century-long wars that afflicted their European ancestors of yore.

1991–99	2002	2016
With Kosovo's declaration of independence in 2008, communist Yugoslavia becomes seven different countries.	Fifteen European countries adopt the euro as their official currency.	In a summer referendum, the UK controversially votes to leave the EU in a process known as Brexit.

Sculpture Hall, Musée du Louvre (p120), Paris

European Art

Millennia of European art has seen some artists seek to document the groundbreaking political events of their time, others reaffirm the prevailing religious doctrine and a small vanguard help push the envelope beyond the confines of their conformist contemporaries to create the next big thing, be it romanticism, naturalism, surrealism or the avant-garde.

Ancient Art

Art was a crucial part of everyday life for ancient civilisations: decorative objects were a sign of status and prestige, while statues were used to venerate and honour the dead, and monuments and temples were lavishly decorated in an attempt to appease the gods. You'll find sculptures and artefacts from early civilisations in all of Europe's top art museums, including the Louvre in Paris and the State Hermitage Museum in St Petersburg. Perhaps the most famous ancient artwork is the *Venus de Milo* in the Louvre, thought to have been created between 130 BC and 100 BC by the master sculptor Alexandros of Antioch.

Giotto & the Proto-Renaissance

Walk into an art gallery anywhere in Europe and it's not hard to discern which paintings hail from the Middle Ages. Medieval art was dominated by its overtly religious subject matter, a pious pastiche of two-dimensional human forms and zealous biblical scenes that paid little attention to the complexities of everyday life. The reason? Most of the art that was painted between Roman times and the Renaissance was commissioned by the all-powerful Catholic Church and designed to embellish the interiors of religious buildings. Iconic and spiritual in nature, its main purpose was to reinforce the prevailing Catholic doctrine. For over 500 years, few artists had the courage or audacity to break the mould. But as England and France took up arms in the Hundred Years' War and the Black Death raged indiscriminately across the continent, a skilful Italian draughtsman from Tuscany named Giotto di Bondone (1267–1337) began quietly pushing against the accepted conventions.

Exhibiting the spirit and style of the Renaissance 200 years before Leonardo da Vinci grafted a smile onto the face of the *Mona Lisa,* Giotto was an artist way ahead of his time. Born near Florence, the Italian master is said to have spent his early life working as a shepherd boy before being discovered by the eminent Tuscan painter Cimabue, who allegedly observed him etching naturalistic pictures of his sheep onto a rock. Taken under Cimabue's wing, Giotto quickly eclipsed the fame of his mentor. Despite working almost exclusively in the religious realm, he was one of the first painters to introduce the notion of perspective into European portrait-painting, giving his figures three-dimensional features and drawing them accurately from real life. In another break with tradition, Giotto added grace and humanity to the human form, endowing the faces of his subjects with a rich range of emotions from joy to despair.

Giotto remains one of the most groundbreaking and influential painters in the history of European art. His small but distinguished oeuvre both pre-empted and paved the way for the Renaissance.

Da Vinci & the High Renaissance

Rising in the wake of Giotto, the Renaissance, with its progressive ideas about humanism and individual expression, pushed the boundaries of painting and sculpture to a new level. Serving their apprenticeship in the late 1400s, Leonardo da Vinci, Michelangelo and Raphael emerged as the illustrious pathfinders of High Renaissance art. These three prodigious geniuses personified the central tenets of Renaissance art, a period that saw a rebirth of interest in classical antiquity, a reappreciation of ancient mythology and a noble quest to inject realism into art.

Using his vast scientific and anatomical knowledge, polymath Leonardo da Vinci (1452–1519) spearheaded numerous technical innovations, experimenting with light manipulation, linear perspective and the depiction of subtle emotions in the human face. He worked all of these elements into his enigmatic magnum opus, *Mona Lisa,* which has gone on to become one of the most famous (and valuable) paintings of all time and is now housed in the Louvre. Not to be outdone, Michelangelo (1475–1564) used his dynamic sculpting skills to create a wonderfully realistic study of strength and beauty in his statue of *David,* while Raphael (1483–1520) devoted his energy to fashioning a grandiose fresco, *The School of Athens,* in the Vatican. The painting is considered by many to be the greatest homage to classicism to come out of the Renaissance.

Mona Lisa

MURATART/SHUTTERSTOCK ©

★ Top European Artworks

Life of Christ & Life of the Virgin (Giotto, 1305) – Scrovegni Chapel, Padua

Mona Lisa (da Vinci, 1503–06), Musée du Louvre, Paris

The Night Watch (Rembrandt, 1642) – Rijksmuseum, Amsterdam

The Third of May 1808 (Goya, 1814) – Museo del Prado, Madrid

Velázquez & Baroque

Diego Velázquez (1599–1660), a Spanish painter from Seville, was a giant of 17th-century European art whose influence still resonates today. Sometimes called the greatest of the 'Old Masters' or the definitive artist's artist, Velázquez absorbed much of what had gone before him and heavily influenced a large part of what came next. Everyone from Goya, the French realists, the 19th-century impressionists and avant-garde modernists owe him a huge debt.

Usually classified as a baroque painter, Velázquez' early influences included the Italian artist Caravaggio, an early proponent of *chiaroscuro* (the contrast between light and shade in a painting), and the multi-talented Titian, a Venetian master celebrated for his deft use of colour.

Like Giotto, Velázquez was way ahead of most of his contemporaries. It took nearly 200 years for the art world to fully appreciate the genius of his sharp eye and fastidious attention to detail. Fellow Spaniard Goya borrowed liberally from Velázquez' unconventional approach to framing a painting – his 1801 portrait of Charles IV and his family is unashamedly modelled on Velázquez' *Las Meninas*. The 19th-century French artist Edouard Manet was another champion of Velázquez' light brushwork and pale-toned palate. Indeed, it was through Manet that Velázquez came to exert a profound influence on the emerging French impressionist movement. Later admirers of Velázquez included Salvador Dalí, Francis Bacon and Pablo Picasso.

Dutch Golden Age

While most of 17th-century Europe was caught up in the flamboyance and drama of baroque painting, the newly independent Dutch Republic was edging in a different direction. Religious topics barely figured in the detailed and graphically realistic paintings of the Dutch Golden Age (c 1600–1700). Instead, leading artists such as Vermeer and Hals turned their attention to secular matters, creating diminutive canvases rendered in vibrant oils that celebrated gritty day-to-day life. Landscapes, still life, maritime scenes, portraiture and genre painting were all popular collectables in the Dutch Republic, where the church was replaced by a prosperous class of merchants and entrepreneurs. Notwithstanding, certain baroque techniques, such as the way an artist depicted the interplay of light and shadow in a scene, still held sway.

There were so many jobbing artists in 17th-century Holland that painting workshops became like mini-factories and anyone of modest financial means clamoured to have an original canvas or two adorning their walls. The packed artistic field was led by Old Masters whose names still resound today: Rubens, Hals, Vermeer and the peerless Rembrandt Van Rijn.

Rembrandt (1606–69) is still considered to be one of the most illustrious artists of all time. Among the Golden Age painters, he was undoubtedly the most versatile and difficult to classify. A miller's son from Leiden, he excelled in landscapes and etchings, although he was equally adept at creating larger, more ambitious paintings. His most celebrated work, *The Night Watch,* is a colossal canvas that depicts over 30 detailed characters and makes dramatic use of light, shade and movement. However, Rembrandt's biggest legacy is probably his self-portraits (he painted well over 40 in his lifetime) that track his slow ageing process in minute, often unflattering detail.

The Louvre

The Musée du Louvre (p120) in Paris is the world's largest and most visited art museum, containing over 38,000 artworks and
receiving in excess of eight million annual visitors.

Goya & Romanticism

Emerging as a proverbial Beethoven of the art world in the 18th century, Francisco de Goya (1747–1828) acted as a bridge between two distinct eras. The Spanish romantic painter is sometimes referred to as the last of the Old Masters and the first of the more enlightened modernists. His vast body of work, which spanned over 60 years, from the 1760s to the 1820s, included cartoons, court paintings, documentary realism, macabre war prints, the first nonmythical nude in Western art, and the disturbing 'black paintings', which he etched directly onto the walls of his house when he was old, deaf (like Beethoven) and battling insanity.

Inspired by Goya, romanticism reached its peak in the mid-19th century when it became popular in Britain and France. Suddenly, clarity and dainty brushstrokes were out, and expressive colours and large heroic landscapes were in. British artists such as JMW Turner and John Constable became obsessed with the optical effects of the weather and its impact on light and colour. Their dark, stormy landscapes and blurry skies would act as an important precursor to the impressionist movement that followed. Eugène Delacroix (1798–1863), the leading French romantic of the era, preferred historical events and studies of North African culture over landscapes, but infused his work with lashings of energy and movement.

From Impressionism to Modernism

Although impressionism has its roots in romanticism and could claim antecedents going back as far as Velázquez, the movement was a radical departure from anything that had gone before. When the early impressionists, including the soon-to-be-famous Monet, Degas, Renoir, Sisley, Pissarro and Cézanne, debuted their work at an exhibition in a photo studio in Paris in April 1874, they were met with bafflement and derision rather than polite applause. Stunned by such a bold artistic leap, many traditionalists weren't yet ready to ponder the subtleties of Degas' nudes or Monet's blurry sunsets.

Tearing up the erstwhile artistic rule book, these precocious French painters were proposing a revolutionary new approach to art. Experimenting with different painting techniques, the impressionists used delicate brushstrokes, dynamic colour contrasts and clever ways of capturing light to enliven their work. Above all, they were solidly anchored in the present. Monet and his contemporaries purposely eschewed trite treatments of mythology and religion to paint solely from personal observation, often setting up their easels *en plein air* rather than in a traditional studio. Favoured subjects included the newly built railways, crowded Parisian cafes, ballet dancers and placid river scenes. Attempting to emulate the emerging photographic technology, artists sought to capture fleeting moments in their paintings in the same way a camera would.

As impressionism grew more palatable and entered the mainstream, some of its adherents – led initially by Paul Cézanne – began pushing the envelope further to create more abstract works. The new style, dubbed post-impressionism, peaked in the mid-1880s and was characterised by the intricate pointillism of Pissarro, the swirling colours of Dutch master Van Gogh, and the vivid primitivism of Paul Gauguin, whose paintings of island life in the South Pacific seemed exotic to his mainly European audience.

Gauguin was a heavy influence on Pablo Picasso (1881–1973), the most famous artist of the 20th century, who practically wrote his own art history, weaving his way through a smorgasbord of stylistic shifts from his Blue Period to his Rose Period and from cubism to surrealism. Seminal works included the proto-cubist *Les Demoiselles d'Avignon* and the potent anti-war statement, *Guernica*. Picasso drew on multiple sources for his inspiration, tracking back as far as pre-Roman Iberian sculpture for artistic ideas. In turn, he inspired a whole generation of new artists to branch out and ruthlessly experiment. By the advent of modernism in the late 19th century, Europe was no longer just exporting artistic ideas, it was importing them as well. Its ever-evolving art scene had never been so fickle and fragmented.

From Fauvism to Conceptual Art

The upheavals of the 20th century inspired many new artistic movements. The fauvists were fascinated by colour, typified by Henri Matisse (1869–1954), while the cubists, such as Georges Braque (1882–1963) and Picasso, broke their work down into abstract forms, taking inspiration from everything from primitive art to psychoanalysis. The dadaists and surrealists took these ideas to their illogical extreme, exploring dreams and the subconscious: key figures include René Magritte (1898–1967) from Belgium, Max Ernst (1891–1976) from Germany, and Joan Miró (1893–1983) and Salvador Dalí (1904–89) from Spain. Conceptual art, which stresses the importance of the idea behind a work rather than purely its aesthetic value, also got its start in the early 20th century, with the works of Marcel Duchamp (1887–1968) having a seminal influence on the movement.

Modern & Contemporary Art

After 1945, abstract art became a mainstay of the European scene, with key figures such as Joseph Beuys (1921–86) and Anselm Kiefer (1945–) from Germany and the Dutch-American Willem de Kooning (1904–97). The late 20th century and 21st century to date have introduced many more artistic movements: abstract expressionism, neoplasticism, minimalism, formalism and pop art, to name a few.

Singer Building (p216), St Petersurg

SVETLANASF/SHUTTERSTOCK ©

European Architecture

Architecture has long been a unifying force in European culture, with differing styles ebbing and flowing with the onward march of history. Some styles have reacted to technological advances, others have mirrored changing tastes in art, music or literature. Classicism stands out as an overriding theme; adding spice are the more flamboyant Gothic, baroque and art nouveau styles.

Classicism: Setting a Blueprint

Classical architecture began with the ancient Greeks but was later copied and developed by the Romans, who spread it liberally around their burgeoning empire, making it the first truly pan-European architectural movement.

Classicism emphasised symmetry, proportion and order. Although the building techniques of classicism were largely forgotten in the Middle Ages, the style was avidly revived during the Renaissance. It made another reappearance in the mid-18th century with interest spiked by the rediscovery and excavation of well-preserved Roman ruins such as Pompeii. Never totally out of vogue, the style is still appreciated today through the New Classical movement.

294 IN FOCUS EUROPEAN ARCHITECTURE

Sturdy Romanesque

After the fall of the Roman Empire, European architecture went through a period of frag-
mentation, lacking any continent-wide 'glue' to hold it together. Instead, specific regions
began to nurture their own individual styles in isolation. Islamic geometry held sway in
Spain. Byzantine classicism dominated the east, and Carolingian churches dotted the skyline in central Europe. It wasn't until the emergence of Romanesque that Europe regained
some architectural commonality. Romanesque first appeared in Italy and France in the
10th century. Its subsequent spread across the continent led it to become the first truly
pan-European architectural style since the sack of Rome. Not surprisingly, ancient Rome
was an overriding influence for Romanesque builders. Not only did they revive Roman
building techniques lost during the Dark Ages, they also revisited Roman style icons, like
the simple but sturdy semicircular arch.

While Romanesque varied from country to country and evolved gradually over the two
centuries it was in vogue (c 1000–1200), there are certain binding threads that make a
classic Romanesque building easy to identify. Sturdiness and scale were all-important.
Romanesque churches, monasteries and castles had thick, muscular walls punctuated
with small windows and chunky arched doors. A second motif was the pared-back decoration. Embellishment in early medieval constructions was relatively austere, especially
when compared to the later ornamentation of Gothic and baroque. One notable exception
was the use of arcades – rows of diminutive arches held up by mini-columns – that were
typically built across the facades of churches, often to dramatic effect. More than anything,
Romanesque architecture was built to last. And last it did. All over Europe, copious castles
and churches stand as testament to the skill and work ethic of their medieval makers.

Gothic Stands Tall

The grandiose, elegant, yet wonderfully flamboyant Gothic building style originated in
France in the late 12th century and is most closely associated with religious buildings,
particularly the lavish cathedrals that appeared all over Europe between 1200 and 1450.

Starting around 1200, new construction techniques allowed architects to build larger
and higher. Reinforced by stronger ceilings and giant exterior buttresses, churches in the
High Middle Ages were able to support thinner walls, more elegant facades and bigger
windows, which were subsequently filled with a mosaic of stained glass. The dark, chunky,
slightly uncouth edifices of Romanesque were usurped by the light, spacious and
unashamedly decorative buildings of Gothic.

The defining feature of Gothic architecture is the pointed arch, a sharp contrast to the
smooth rounded arches that characterised Romanesque buildings and would reappear
during the Renaissance. Other typical Gothic concepts were the ribbed vault (a dome-like
ceiling vault criss-crossed by diagonal 'ribs') and the flying buttress (an exterior support
that served both decorative and load-bearing purposes).

The Gothic penchant for stained glass reached its zenith in ornate 'rose windows'
(often set above the main church doors) that refracted colourful light into bright interiors.
Doorways were extravagantly decorated with statues of pious saints, while exteriors were
punctuated by leering gargoyles that often doubled up as drainage outlets. Usually taking
decades or more to build, Gothic cathedrals became the skyscrapers of the medieval
world with ambitious architects adding ever taller towers and spires to express the indomi-
table power of the Catholic Church.

The Renaissance: A Roman Rebirth

Just as it had done for art, the Renaissance marked the rebirth of classicism in architecture, prompting an enthusiastic reappreciation of the aesthetic glories of ancient Greece and Rome. Its story starts with a personality, Filippo Brunelleschi (1377–1446), an Italian goldsmith turned architect from Florence, who developed the technique of linear perspective in art before turning his attention to designing buildings. A typical 'Renaissance Man', it was Brunelleschi who engineered the magnificent dome on the Duomo in Florence (the largest dome of its kind since Rome's Pantheon had been built 1300 years earlier), inspired by his deep-rooted mathematical knowledge and healthy appreciation for all things Roman. Several years earlier, Brunelleschi and his friend, the sculptor Donatello, had travelled to Rome to study the ancient ruins and both had come away mightily impressed.

> ### Tallest Buildings
> Between 1311 and 1884, the tallest building in the world was always a Gothic cathedral, with the title passing between cathedrals in Lincoln, Stralsund, Beauvais, Strasbourg, Hamburg, Rouen and Cologne, respectively.

While Brunelleschi solved many of the technological problems that had impeded architectural development in medieval Europe (he even designed his own construction machines), the overall style of Renaissance buildings borrowed heavily from later cultural innovators such as Leonardo da Vinci and Michelangelo. Building-wise, this meant symmetrical facades, elegant pillars, simple semicircular arches and an overall sense of proportion. In France, grand chateaux such as those built in the Loire Valley mixed Renaissance elegance with recognisable Gothic undertones. Domes became popular additions to Renaissance churches. Although the Renaissance began in Florence in the late 14th century, it gradually spread throughout Western Europe, though making less of an impact in the east.

Baroque Goes Berserk

Architectural tastes move in cycles with sober periods often alternating with more flamboyant interludes. Baroque sits squarely in the latter camp, an intense post-Renaissance style that's synonymous with ornamentation and extravagance, a modus operandi that was also colourfully replicated in painting, music and literature.

The baroque movement originated in Italy in the late 17th century before spreading to France, Eastern Europe and Spain. Most graphically displayed in churches and palaces, it was closely associated with the Counter-Reformation, the era in which the Catholic Church began pushing against a rising tide of Protestantism. Anathema to Puritans and Calvinists, baroque wasn't championed so enthusiastically in Protestant northern Europe.

While showy baroque draughtsmen never jettisoned Renaissance ideas completely, their approach to architecture came from an entirely different angle. Buildings were viewed as 'sculptures' to be carved rather than 'boxes' to be filled. Prominent baroque features included intricate ceiling frescoes, gilded church altars, lifelike statues and ostentatious facades.

Rejecting the sobriety of classicism, baroque put curves, undulations and movement into the architectural vocabulary. Typical churches were embellished with twisted columns and violin-shaped curves both inside and out. Inspired by emerging baroque painters like Caravaggio, architects tried to capture the dramatic interplay of light and shadow in their structures using windows, recesses and screens to theatrical effect. Unlike Renaissance buildings, decoration was no longer placed strategically around discreet interiors, but swarmed all over the place.

The baroque style wasn't confined to churches: it was also enthusiastically applied to urban mansions and rural stately homes. The Palace of Versailles is a pre-eminent and rather lavish example. By the end of the 18th century, baroque flamboyance went into overdrive with the evolution of rococo (sometimes known as late-baroque), an even more ostentatious style characterised by its spectacular amalgamation of mirrors, marble, gold and stucco.

Towards Modernism: Beaux Arts, Art Nouveau & Art Deco

After the lurid exclamation mark of rococo, European architecture became more fragmented and capricious with trends coming and going quickly, sometimes within the space of a decade. For a short period starting in the 1830s, Europe returned briefly to classical order (with some restrained ornamentation) in a new style known as beaux arts. An academic idea born at a leading arts academy in Paris, beaux arts was essentially neoclassicism with a few embellishments, its flat roofs and arched windows contributing to the kind of grandiose buildings that wouldn't have looked out of place in ancient Greece. Though well represented in Paris (and lapped up in the rapidly expanding United States), beaux arts didn't make a huge impression on the rest of Europe.

Far more popular continent-wide was the gracefully curvaceous style of art nouveau, which drew inspiration from the 19th-century British Arts and Crafts Movement and the Gothic-loving pre-Raphaelite painters, who dismissed the standardisation of classicism in favour of more naturalistic medieval forms. Art nouveau took different names in different countries but reached its apogee in Spain, where it was known as *modernisme*. Inspired by a handful of talented Catalan architects led by Antoni Gaudí, Spanish *modernisme* was whimsical, highly decorative and closely associated with nature. Characterised by its flowing natural curves and undulations, it made beautiful decorative features of windows, benches, chimneys and even door handles. Asymmetrical *modernisme* buildings often had an otherworldly, fairy-tale quality that departed radically from anything that had gone before. In Italy art nouveau was known as *Stile Liberty* (after the British Department Store), while in Germany, Austria and the Nordic countries it was called *Jugendstil*.

Two decades after art nouveau came another short-lived wave. Art deco was an elegant, functional yet thoroughly modern architectural style whose origin can be pinned to an exact time and place – Paris 1925, at the International Exposition for Arts Décoratifs. Drawing from cubism, futurism and primitive African art, this flashy new genre promoted lavish, yet streamlined buildings with sweeping curves and exuberant sun-burst motifs. Historically, art deco acted as a more ornate precursor to modernism. Its legacy was stamped all over Europe in German theatres, Spanish cinemas, London's famous Underground train stations and even in a few religious buildings.

Bratwurst, Sauerkraut and Pretzel

GEORGE DOLGIKH/SHUTTERSTOCK ©

Food & Drink

Europe is united by its passion for eating and drinking with gusto. Every country has unique flavours, incorporating olive oils and sun-ripened vegetables in the hot south, rich cream and butter in cooler areas, delicate river and lake fish, and meat from fertile mountains and pastures. Each country has its own tipples, too, spanning renowned wines, beers and feistier firewater.

France

Each French region has its distinctive dishes. Broadly, the hot south favours dishes based on olive oil, garlic and tomatoes, while the cooler north tends towards root vegetables, earthy flavours and creamy or buttery sauces. The French are famously unfussy about which bits of the animal they eat – kidney, liver, cheek and tongue are as much of a delicacy as a fillet steak or a prime rib. Bouillabaisse, a saffron-scented fish stew, is a signature southern dish. It is served with spicy rouille sauce, Gruyère cheese and croutons. The Alps are the place to try fondue: hunks of toasted bread dipped into cheese sauces. Brittany and Normandy are big on seafood, especially mussels and oysters. Central France prides itself on its hearty cuisine, including foie gras (goose liver), bœuf bourguignon (beef cooked in red wine), *confit de canard* (duck cooked in preserved fat) and black truffles.

Sweet Treats

From pralines to puddings, Europe specialises in foods that are sweet, sticky and sinful. Germans and Austrians have a particularly sweet tooth – treats include *Salzburger nockerl* (a fluffy soufflé) and *Schwarzwälder kirschtorte* (Black Forest cherry cake), plus many types of *Apfeltasche* (apple pastry) and *Strudel* (filled filo pastry).

But it's the French who have really turned dessert into a fine art. Stroll past the window of any *boulangerie* (bakery) or patisserie and you'll be assaulted by temptations, from creamy *éclairs* (filled choux buns) and crunchy *macarons* (meringue-based biscuits with a ganache filling) to fluffy *madeleines* (shell-shaped sponge cakes) and wicked *gâteaux* (cakes). Go on – you know you want to.

France is Europe's biggest wine producer. The principal regions are Alsace, Bordeaux, Burgundy, Languedoc, the Loire and the Rhône, all of which produce reds, whites and rosés. Then, of course, there's Champagne – home to the world's favourite bubbly, aged in centuries-old cellars beneath Reims and Épernay.

Germany, Austria & Switzerland

The Germanic nations are all about big flavours and big portions. *Wurst* (sausage) comes in hundreds of forms, and is often served with sauerkraut (fermented cabbage). The most common types of wurst include *Weisswurst* (veal sausage), *Currywurst* (sliced sausage topped with ketchup and curry powder) and bratwurst. Served countrywide, bratwurst is made from minced pork, veal and spices, and is cooked in different ways: boiled in beer, baked with apples and cabbage, stewed in a casserole, grilled or barbecued.

Austria's signature dish is *Wiener Schnitzel* (breaded veal cutlet), but schnitzel in general (usually featuring pork) is also popular in Germany. Other popular mains include *Rippenspeer* (spare ribs), *Rotwurst* (black pudding), *Rostbrätl* (grilled meat) and *Putenbrust* (turkey breast). Potatoes are served as *Bratkartoffeln* (fried), *Kartoffelpüree* (mashed), Swiss-style *rösti* (grated then fried) or *pommes frites* (French fries).

The Swiss are known for their love of fondue and the similar dish, *raclette* (melted cheese with potatoes).

Beer is the national beverage. Pils is the crisp pilsner Germany is famous for, which is often slightly bitter. *Weizenbier* is made with wheat instead of barley malt and is served in a tall, 500mL glass. *Helles Bier* means light beer, while *dunkles Bier* is dark beer. Germany is principally known for white wines – inexpensive, light and intensely fruity. The Rhine and Moselle Valleys are the largest wine-growing regions.

German Wine

There are 13 official wine-growing areas in Germany, the best being the Mosel-Saar-Ruwer region. It boasts some of the world's steepest vineyards, where the predominantly Riesling grapes are still hand-picked. Slate soil on the hillsides gives the wines a flinty taste. Chalkier riverside soils are planted with the Elbling grape, an ancient Roman variety.

East of the Moselle, the Nahe region produces fragrant, fruity and full-bodied wines using Müller-Thurgau and Silvaner grapes, as well as Riesling.

Riesling grapes are also the mainstay in Rheingau and Mittelrhein (Middle Rhine), two other highly respected wine-growing pockets. Rheinhessen, south of Rheingau, is responsible for Liebfraumilch, but also some top Rieslings.

Other wine regions include Ahr, Pfalz (both in Rhineland-Palatinate), Hessische Bergstrasse (Hesse), Baden (Baden-Württemberg), Würzburg (Bavaria) and Elbtal (Saxony).

The Württemberg region, around Stuttgart, produces some of the country's best reds, while Saxony-Anhalt's Saale-Unstrut region is home to Rotkäppchen (Little Red Riding Hood) sparkling wine, a former GDR brand that's been a big hit in the new Germany.

Czech Republic

Like many nations in Eastern Europe, Czech cuisine revolves around meat, potatoes and root vegetables, dished up in stews, goulashes and casseroles. *Pečená kachna* (roast duck) is the quintessential Czech restaurant dish, while *klobása* (sausage) is a common beer snack. A common side dish is *knedliky,* boiled dumplings made from wheat or potato flour.

The Czechs have a big beer culture, with some of Europe's best *pivo* (beer), usually lager style. The Moravian region is the up-and-coming area for Czech wines.

Portugal

The Portuguese take pride in simple but flavourful dishes honed to perfection over the centuries. Bread remains integral to every meal, and it even turns up in some main courses. Be on the lookout for *açorda* (bread stew, often served with shellfish), *migas* (bread pieces prepared as a side dish) and *ensopados* (stews with toasted or deep-fried bread). Seafood stews are superb, particularly *caldeirada,* which is a mix of fish and shellfish in a rich broth, not unlike a bouillabaisse. *Bacalhau* (dried salt-cod) is bound up in myth, history and tradition, and is excellent in baked dishes. Classic meat dishes include *porco preto* (sweet 'black' pork), *cabrito assado* (roast kid) and *arroz de pato* (duck risotto).

Portuguese wines are also well worth sampling, particularly fortified port and reds from the Douro valley and *alvarinho* and *vinho verde* (crisp, semi-sparkling wine) from the Minho.

Hungary

Hungary boasts Eastern Europe's finest cuisine. It's very meaty, that's true, but big on flavour. Try one of the staples such as paprika-laced *pörkölt* (a stew not unlike what we call goulash) or *gulyás* (or *gulyásleves*), a thick beef soup cooked with onions and potatoes. And don't overlook specialities such as *libamaj* (goose liver prepared in an infinite number of ways) and *halászlé,* a rich fish soup.

Hungarians love their wine and take it seriously. In summer, spritzers (or wine coolers; red or white wine mixed with mineral water) are consumed in large quantities.

Sausage Country

In the Middle Ages, German peasants found a way to package and disguise animals' less appetising bits and the humble *Wurst* (sausage) was born. Today, it's a noble and highly respected element of German cuisine, with strict rules determining varietal authenticity. In some cases, as with the finger-sized Nuremberg sausage, regulations even ensure offal no longer enters the equation.

There are more than 1500 sausage types, all commonly served with bread and a sweet *(süss)* or spicy *(scharf)* mustard *(Senf)*. The availability of sausages differs regionally. A *Thüringer* is long, thin and spiced; *Blutwurst* is blood sausage; *Leberwurst* is liver sausage and *Knackwurst* is lightly tickled with garlic. Saxony has brain sausage *(Bregenwurst)* and Bavaria sells the white, rubbery *Weisswurst*. Hamburg, Berlin and the Ruhrgebiet all claim to have invented the takeaway *Currywurst*.

Vegetarians & Vegans

Though things are improving and vegan restaurants are popping up fast, vegetarians will have a tough time in some parts of Europe where eating meat is still the norm and fish is often seen as a vegetarian option. However, you'll usually find something meat-free on most menus, though there may not be much choice. Vegans will have an even tougher time – cheese, cream and milk are integral ingredients in most European cuisines. Vegetable-based starters, tapas, meze, pastas, side dishes and salads are good options for a meat-free meal. Shopping for yourself in markets is an ideal way of trying local flavours without having to compromise your principles.

Serbia

Serbia's cuisine is a fusion of Turkish, Hungarian and Mediterranean influences that zing the palate and fill the stomach; it's generally fresh, organic and affordable. While grilled meats, *paprika* (capsicum), beans and cabbage are ubiquitous, there are distinct differences between regional menus, depending on historical influences. All cities, towns and larger villages have *restorani* (restaurants), *pekare* (bakeries) and *roštilj* (barbecue) joints; *kafane* (taverns) often serve meals in addition to booze.

Russia

The Russian food scene has made a giant leap towards cutting-edge modernity in the past decade, particularly in large cities, where international culinary mainstream trends mix with the unique cuisines of the Caucasus and Central Asia. In addition, there's been a powerful movement to reinvent traditional Russian gastronomy. Bans on EU-produced foodstuffs have resulted in the proliferation of locavore places – creative chefs play with products from all over the country, which boasts a vast diversity of climates and landscapes. The tapestry of peoples and cultures along the Volga River yields several specialities, such as the Finno-Ugric clear dumpling soup called *sup s klyutskami*. The *kasylyk* (dried-horsemeat sausage) and *zur balish* (meat pie) are both from Tatarstan, where *chek chek* (honey-drenched macaroni-shaped pieces of fried dough) are an essential part of any celebration.

Ukraine

When it comes to food, Ukraine is the land of abundance, with distinct regional variations. In western Ukraine, gastronomy leans towards Central Europe. Local versions of polenta *(banosh)* and goulash *(bograch)* are especially popular. Central Ukraine is where you'll find traditional Ukrainian cuisine at its best, with *borsch* (beetroot soup), *vareniki* (dumplings) and *halushky* (pasta cubes) as main staples. Odesa and southern Ukraine have a cuisine of their own – heavy on vegetables, stews and Black Sea fish.

View over Porto (p190), Portugal

JOYFULL/SHUTTERSTOCK ©

Survival Guide

Directory A–Z

Accessible Travel

Cobbled medieval streets, 'classic' hotels, congested inner cities and underground subway systems make Europe a tricky destination for people with mobility issues. However, the train facilities are good and some destinations boast new tram services or lifts to platforms.

Download Lonely Planet's free Accessible Travel guide from http://lptravel. to/AccessibleTravel. The following websites can help with specific details.

Accessible Europe (www.accessibleurope.com) Specialist European tours with van transport.

Mobility International Schweiz (www.mis-ch.ch) Good site (only partly in English) listing 'barrier-free' destinations in Switzerland and abroad, plus wheelchair-accessible hotels in Switzerland.

Mobility International USA (www.miusa.org) Publishes guides and advises travellers with disabilities on mobility issues.

Society for Accessible Travel & Hospitality (SATH; www.sath.org) Reams of information for travellers with disabilities.

Electricity

Most of Europe (including Russia) uses the 'europlug' with two round pins. Switzerland uses a third round pin in a way that the two-pin plug usually – but not always – fits. Buy an adapter before leaving home; those on sale in Europe generally go the other way, but ones for visitors to Europe are also available – airports are always a good place to buy them.

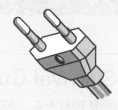

Type C
220V/50Hz

Climate

Paris

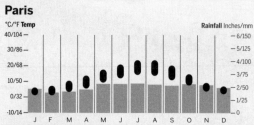

St Petersburg

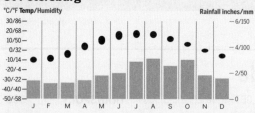

Vienna

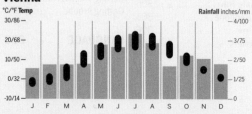

Type F
230V/50Hz

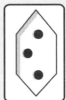

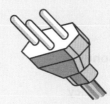

Type J
230V/50Hz

Entry & Exit Formalities

Visas

o Citizens of the US, Canada, Australia, New Zealand and the UK need only a valid passport to enter nearly all countries in Europe, including the entire EU.

o Russia requires most visitors to have a prearranged visa before arrival and even an 'invitation' from (or booking with) a tour operator or hotel. It's simpler and safer to obtain these visas before leaving home. Citizens of South American countries, South Africa and many states of the former USSR can travel visa-free to Russia.

o Australians and New Zealanders need a visa for the Ukraine. Citizens of the EU, USA and Canada do not.

o Transit visas are usually cheaper than tourist or business visas, but they allow only a very short stay (one to five days) and can be difficult to extend.

o All visas have a 'use-by' date and you'll be refused entry afterwards. In some cases it's easier to get visas as you go along rather than arranging them all beforehand. Carry spare passport photos (you may need from one to four every time you apply for a visa).

o Consulates are generally open weekday mornings. If there's both an embassy and a consulate, you want the consulate.

o Because regulations can change, double-check with the relevant embassy or consulate before travelling.

Customs

The EU has a two-tier customs system: one for goods bought duty-free to import to or export from the EU, and one for goods bought in another EU country where taxes and duties have already been paid.

o When entering or leaving the EU, you are allowed to carry duty-free 200 cigarettes, 50 cigars or 250g of tobacco; 2L of still wine plus 1L of spirits over 22% alcohol or another 4L of wine (sparkling or otherwise); for other goods (eg coffee, perfume, electronics) up to €430 (air/sea entry) or €300 (land entry).

o When travelling from one EU country to another, the duty-paid limits are 800 cigarettes, 200 cigars, 1kg of tobacco, 10L of spirits, 20L of fortified wine, 90L of wine (of which not more than 60L is sparkling) and 110L of beer.

o Non-EU countries often have different regulations and many countries forbid the export of antiquities and cultural treasures.

Health

Good healthcare is readily available in Western Europe, and for minor illnesses, pharmacists can give valuable advice and sell over-the-counter medication. They can also advise if you need specialised help and point you in the right direction. The standard of dental care is usually good.

While the situation in Eastern Europe is improving since the EU accession of many countries, quality medical care is not always readily available outside major cities. Embassies, consulates and five-star hotels can usually recommend doctors or clinics.

Condoms are widely available in Europe, however emergency contraception may not be, so take the necessary precautions.

It is unwise to travel anywhere in the world without travel insurance. A good policy should include comprehensive health insurance including medical care and emergency evacuation. If you are engaging in hazardous sports, you may need to pay for extra cover.

If you're an EU citizen or a citizen of Iceland, Liechtenstein, Norway or Switzerland, the free EHIC (European Health Insurance Card) covers you for most medical care in 32 European countries, including maternity care and care for chronic illnesses such as diabetes (though not for emergency repatriation). However, you will normally have to pay for medicine bought from pharmacies, even if prescribed, and perhaps for some tests and procedures. The EHIC does not cover private medical consultations and treatment out of your home country; this includes nearly all dentists, and some of the better clinics and surgeries. With Brexit negotiations

ongoing as of early 2019, it is unclear how the EHIC health card will be affected for British citizens. Check www.nhs.uk for updates.

Non-EU citizens should find out if there is a reciprocal arrangement for free medical care between their country and the countries they are visiting.

Internet Access

All European river cruises offer wi-fi access and this is increasingly free, though you may have to pay for better speeds.

Internet access varies enormously across Europe. In most places you'll be able to find wi-fi (also called WLAN in some countries), although whether it's free varies greatly. Internet cafes are increasingly rare but not impossible to find.

Access is generally straightforward, although a few tips are in order. If you can't find the @ symbol on a keyboard, try AltGr + 2, or AltGr + Q. Watch out for German and some Balkans keyboards, which reverse the Z and the Y positions. Using a French keyboard is an art unto itself.

Where necessary in relevant countries, click on the language prompt in the bottom right-hand corner of the screen or hit Ctrl + Shift to switch between the Cyrillic and Latin alphabets.

LGBT+ Travellers

Across Western Europe you'll find very liberal attitudes towards homosexuality. The Netherlands, Belgium and Spain were the first three countries in the world to legalise same-sex marriage in 2001, 2003 and 2005, respectively.

Eastern Europe, and in particular Russia, tends to be far less progressive. Outside the big cities, attitudes become more conservative and discretion is advised.

Money

Currency

The euro, used in Germany, Austria, France and Portugal, is made up of 100 cents. Notes come in denominations of €5, €10, €20, €50, €100, €200 and €500, though any notes above €50 are rarely used on a daily basis. Coins come in 1c, 2c, 5c, 10c, 20c, 50c, €1 and €2.

Hungary uses the forint (Ft), the Czech Republic the Koruna česká (Kč, or Czech crown), Russia the rouble (R), Serbia the Serbian dinar (RSD) and Switzerland the Swiss Franc (Sfr).

Taxes & Refunds

When non-EU residents spend more than a certain amount (around €175, but amounts vary from country to country) they can usually reclaim any sales tax when leaving the country.

Making a tax-back claim is straightforward. First make sure the shop offers duty-free sales (often a sign will be displayed reading 'Tax-Free Shopping'). When making your purchase, ask the shop attendant for a tax-refund voucher, filled in with the correct amount and the date. This can be used to claim a refund directly at international airports, or stamped at ferry ports or border crossings and mailed back for a refund.

Tipping

● Tipping isn't such a big deal in Europe as it is, say, in North America.

● In restaurants, between 10% to 12% is common in central Europe, although a service charge may already be added to the bill, in which case you don't tip. Small change suffices in Portugal.

● Tipping isn't usual in bars, though you could leave small change for table service.

● Round taxi fares up.

Safe Travel

Travelling in Europe is usually very safe. With comprehensive healthcare, political stability and generally low crime rates, you'd be

unlucky to encounter any serious problems.

● There was a spike in terrorist attacks in Europe between 2015 and 2017; countries affected included France and Germany. Keep an eye on the news and always check your home country travel advice before embarking on a trip.

● With Ukraine in the news for all the wrong reasons, safety is a major concern for travellers these days. But although crime is on the rise, Ukraine remains a rather safe European destination, unless you venture into the war zone, which accounts for a tiny part of the country's territory in the far east.

● Pickpockets operate in some larger cities. Be particularly aware in public squares and on crowded public transport where backpacks are best worn on the front.

Telephone

If your mobile phone is European, it's often perfectly feasible to use it on roaming throughout the continent. If you're coming from outside Europe, it's usually worth buying a prepaid local SIM in one European country. Even if you're not staying in Europe long, it's more cost-effective for travellers visiting from outside Europe to purchase a prepaid local SIM. In several countries

you need your passport to buy a SIM card. Roaming charges within the EU have been abolished, so buying a SIM card in one country and using it in another won't be costly.

In order to use other SIM cards in your phone, you'll need to have your handset unlocked by your home provider. Even if your phone is locked, you can use apps such as Whatsapp to send free text messages internationally wherever you have wi-fi access or Skype to make free international calls whenever you're online.

Europe uses the GSM 900 network, which also covers Australia and New Zealand, but is not compatible with the North American GSM 1900 or the totally different system in Japan and South Korea. If you have a GSM phone, check with your service provider about using it in Europe. You'll need international roaming, but this is usually free to enable.

Important Phone Numbers

The number ☎112 can be dialled free for emergencies in all EU states.

Russia Police ☎102, ambulance ☎103

Serbia Police ☎192, ambulance ☎194

Time

Nearly all of Europe, but not Russia, observes daylight saving time on synchronised dates in late March (clocks go forward an hour) and late October (clocks go back an hour). The European Parliament proposed to scrap daylight savings time in 2018, but the proposal has yet to be approved by the EU.

Portugal GMT

Central Europe GMT plus one hour

Eastern Europe GMT plus two hours

Russia GMT plus three hours

Toilets

Many public toilets require a small fee either deposited in a box or given to the attendant. Sit-down toilets are the rule in the vast majority of places, though squat toilets can very occasionally be found in rural areas.

Public-toilet provision is changeable from city to city. If you can't find one, simply drop into a hotel or restaurant and ask to use theirs, or make a nominal purchase at a cafe.

Transport

Getting There & Away

Europe is one of the world's major destinations, sporting many of its busiest airports with routes fanning out to the far corners of the globe. More adventurous travellers can enter from Asia on some epic long-distance train routes. Numerous ferries jockey across the Mediterranean between Europe and Africa.

Flights, cars and tours can be booked online at www.lonelyplanet.com/bookings.

Air

Regardless of your ultimate destination, it's sometimes better to pick a recognised transport 'hub' as your initial port of entry, where high traffic volumes help keep prices down. The busiest, and therefore most obvious, airports are London, Frankfurt, Paris and Rome. Most of these gateway cities are well serviced by low-cost carriers that fly to other parts of Europe.

Long-haul airfares to Eastern Europe are rarely a bargain; you're usually better flying to a Western European hub and taking an onward budget-airline flight or train. The main hubs in Eastern Europe are Budapest, Moscow and Prague.

Main European airports:

o Schiphol Airport, Amsterdam (www.schiphol.nl)

o Frankfurt Airport, Frankfurt (www.frankfurt-airport.com)

o Heathrow Airport, London (www.heathrow.com)

o Barajas Airport, Madrid (www.aeropuertomadrid-barajas.com)

o Aéroport de Charles de Gaulle, Paris (www.easycdg.com)

o Leonardo da Vinci Airport, Rome (www.adr.it)

Low-Cost Carriers

Low-cost carriers have revolutionised European transport. Over longer distances, airlines sometimes offer the cheapest transport connections, although flying is environmentally costly and often less comfortable than going by train and bus. Most budget airlines have a similar pricing system – namely, that ticket prices rise with the number of seats sold on each flight, so book as early as possible to get a decent fare.

Some low-cost carriers – Ryanair being the prime example – have made a habit of flying to smaller, less convenient airports on the outskirts of their destination city, or even to the airports of nearby cities, so check the exact location of the departure and arrival airports before you book.

Many flights also leave at the crack of dawn or arrive inconveniently late at night.

Departure and other taxes (including booking fees, checked-baggage fees and other surcharges) soon add up and are included in the final price by the end of the online booking process – usually a lot more than you were hoping to pay – but with careful choosing and advance booking you can get excellent deals.

Getting Around

European towns and cities have excellent local transport systems, often encompassing trams as well as buses and metro/subway/underground-rail networks.

Most travellers will find areas of interest in European cities can be easily traversed by foot or bicycle.

Bus

Domestic buses provide a viable alternative to trains in most countries; they are usually slightly cheaper and somewhat slower. Buses are generally best for short hops, such as getting around cities and reaching remote villages, and they are often the only option in mountainous regions.

Train

Comfortable, frequent and reliable, trains are *the* way to get around Europe. France,

Climate Change & Travel

Every form of transport that relies on carbon-based fuel generates CO_2, the main cause of human-induced climate change. Modern travel is dependent on aeroplanes, which might use less fuel per kilometre per person than most cars but travel much greater distances. The altitude at which aircraft emit gases (including CO_2) and particles also contributes to their climate change impact. Many websites offer 'carbon calculators' that allow people to estimate the carbon emissions generated by their journey and, for those who wish to do so, to offset the impact of the greenhouse gases emitted with contributions to portfolios of climate-friendly initiatives throughout the world. Lonely Planet offsets the carbon footprint of all staff and author travel.

Germany, the Low Countries and Switzerland score highly in quality and quantity of railways.

● Many state railways have interactive websites publishing their timetables and fares, including www.bahn.de (Germany) and www.sbb.ch (Switzerland), both of which have pages in English. Eurail (www.eurail.com) links to 28 European train companies.

● Man in Seat 61 (www.seat61.com) is comprehensive, while the US-based-Budget Europe Travel Service (www.budgeteuropetravel.com) can also help with tips.

● European trains sometimes split en route to service two destinations, so even if you're on the right train, make sure you're also in the correct carriage.

● A train journey to almost every station in Europe can be booked via www.voyages-sncf.com.

Taxi

Taxis in Europe are metered and rates are usually high. There might also be surcharges for things such as luggage, time of day, pick-up location and extra passengers.

Bike

It is easy to hire bikes throughout most of Europe. Many Western European train stations have bike-rental counters.

A growing number of European cities have bike-sharing schemes where you can casually borrow a bike from a docking station for short hops around the city for a small cost. Most schemes have daily rates, although you usually need a credit card as deposit.

Language

Don't let the language barrier get in the way of your travel experience. This section offers basic phrases and pronunciation guides to help you negotiate your way around Europe. Note that in our pronunciation guides, the stressed syllables in words are indicated with italics.

To enhance your trip with a phrasebook (covering all of these languages in much greater detail), visit **lonelyplanet.com**.

Czech

Hello.	*Ahoj.*	*uh·*hoy
Goodbye.		
Na shledanou.	*nuh·*skhle·duh·noh	
Yes.	*Ano.*	*uh·*no
No.	*Ne.*	ne
Please.	*Prosím.*	*pro·*seem
Thank you.	*Děkuji.*	*dye·*ku·yi
Excuse me.	*Promiňte.*	*pro·*min'·te
Help!	*Pomoc!*	*po·*mots

Do you speak English?
Mluvíte anglicky?   *mlu·*vee·te *uhn·*glits·ki
I don't understand.
Nerozumím.   ne·ro·zu·*meem*
Where's (the toilet)?
Kde je (záchod)?   gde ye (*za·*khod)
I'm lost.
Zabloudil/   *zuh·*bloh·dyil/
Zabloudila jsem. (m/f)   *zuh·*bloh·dyi·luh ysem

French

Hello.	*Bonjour.*	bon·zhoor
Goodbye.	*Au revoir.*	o·rer·vwa
Yes.	*Oui.*	wee
No.	*Non.*	noh
Please.	*S'il vous plaît.*	seel voo play
Thank you.	*Merci.*	mair·see
Excuse me.		
Excusez-moi.	ek·skew·zay·mwa	
Help!	*Au secours!*	o skoor

Do you speak English?
Parlez-vous anglais?   par·lay·voo ong·glay
I don't understand.
Je ne comprends pas.   zher ner kom·pron pa
Where's (the toilet)?
Où sont   oo son
(les toilettes)?   (lay twa·let)
I'm lost.
Je suis perdu(e). (m/f)   zhe swee·pair·dew

German

Hello.	*Guten Tag.*	*goo·*ten taak
Goodbye.		
Auf Wiedersehen.	owf *vee·*der·zey·en	
Yes.	*Ja.*	yaa
No.	*Nein.*	nain
Please.	*Bitte.*	*bi·*te
Thank you.	*Danke.*	*dang·*ke
Excuse me.		
Entschuldigung.	ent·*shul·*di·gung	
Help!	*Hilfe!*	*hil·*fe

Do you speak English?
Sprechen Sie Englisch?   *shpre·*khen zee *eng·*lish
I don't understand.
Ich verstehe nicht.   ikh fer·*shtey·*e nikht
Where's (the toilet)?
Wo ist   vaw ist
(die Toilette)?   (dee to·a·*le·*te)
I'm lost.
Ich habe mich verirrt.   ikh *haa·*be mikh fer·*irt*

Hungarian

Hello.	*Szervusz.* (sg)	*ser·*vus
Goodbye.	*Viszlát.*	*vis* lat
Yes.	*Igen.*	*i* gen
No.	*Nem.*	nem
Thank you.	*Köszönöm.*	*keu* seu neum
Excuse me.	*Elnézést kérek.*	*el·*nay zaysht *kay* rek
Help!	*Segítség!*	*she·*geet·shayg

Do you speak English?
Beszél angolul? (pol)   be·sayl *on·*gaw·lul
Beszélsz angolul? (inf)   be·sayls *on·*gaw·lul

I don't understand.
Nem értem.   nem *ayr*·tem
Where are the toilets?
Hol a véce?   hawl o *vay*·tse
I'm lost.
Eltévedtem.   el·tay·ved·tem

Portuguese

Hello.	*Olá.*	o·*laa*
Goodbye.	*Adeus.*	a·de·*oosh*
Yes.	*Sim.*	seeng
No.	*Não.*	nowng
Please.	*Por favor.*	poor fa *vor*
Thank you.	*Obrigado.* (m)	o·bree·*gaa*·doo
	Obrigada. (f)	o·bree·*gaa*·da
Excuse me.	*Faz favor.*	faash fa·*vor*
Help!	*Socorro!*	soo·*ko*·rroo

Do you speak English?
Fala inglês?   faa·la eeng·*glesh*
I don't understand.
Não entendo.   nowng eng·*teng*·doo
Where are the toilets?
Onde é a casa de   ong·de e a *kaa*·za de
banho?   ba·nyoo
I'm lost.
Estou perdido.   shtoh per·*dee*·doo (m)
Estou perdida.   shtoh per·*dee*·da (f)

Russian

Hello.	Здравствуйте.	*zdrast*·vuyt·ye
Goodbye.	До свидания.	da svee·*dan*·ya
Yes.	Да.	da
No.	Нет.	nyet
Please.	Пожалуйста.	pa·*zhal*·sta
Thank you.	Спасибо.	spa·*see*·ba
Excuse me./	Извините,	eez·vee·*neet*·ye
Sorry.	пожалуйста.	pa·*zhal*·sta
Help!	Помогите!	pa·ma·*gee*·tye

Do you speak English?
Вы говорите   vi ga·va·*reet*·ye
по-английски?   pa·an·*glee*·skee
I don't understand.
Я не понимаю.   ya nye pa·nee·*ma*·yu
Where are the toilets?
Где здесь туалет?   gdye zdyes' tu·al·*yet*

I'm lost.
Я потерялся/   ya pa·teer·*yal*·sa/
потерялась. (m/f)   pa·teer·*ya*·las

Serbian

Hello.	*Zdravo.*	*zdra*·vo
Goodbye.	*Zbogom.*	*zbo*·gom
Yes.	*Da.*	da
No.	*Ne.*	ne
Please.	*Molim.*	*mo*·lim
Thank you.	*Hvala.*	*hva*·la
Excuse me.	*Oprostite.*	o·*pro*·sti·te
Help!	*Upomoć!*	u·po·moch

Do you speak English?
Govorite/Govoriš li   go·vo·ri·te/go·vo·rish
engleski? (pol/inf)   li *en*·gle·ski
I don't understand.
Ja ne razumijem.   ya ne ra·*zu*·mi·yem
Where are the toilets?
Gdje se nalaze   gdye se *na*·la·ze
toaleti?   to·a·*le*·ti
I'm lost.
Izgubio/Izgubila   iz·*gu*·bi·o/iz·*gu*·bi·la
sam se. (m/f)   sam se

Ukranian

Hello.	Добрий день.	*do*·bry den'
Goodbye.	До побачення.	do po·*ba*·chen·nya
Yes.	Так.	tak
No.	Ні.	ni
Please.	Прошу.	*pro*·shu
Thank you.	Дякую.	*dya*·ku·yu
Excuse me.	Вибачте.	*vy*·bach·te
Help!	Допоможіть!	do·po·mo·*zhit'*

Do you speak English?
Ви розмовляєте   vy roz·mow·*lya*·ye·te
англійською   an·*hliys'*·ko·yu
мовою?   *mo*·vo·yu
I don't understand.
Я не розумію.   ya ne ro·zu·*mi*·yu
Where are the toilets?
Де туалети?   de tu·a·le·ti
I'm lost.
Я заблукав/   ya za·blu·*kaw*/
заблукала. (m/f)   za·blu·*ka*·la (m/f)

Behind the Scenes

Acknowledgements

Cover photograph: Cochem Castle, Moselle Valley, Germany; Calle Montes/ Getty Images ©

Climate map data adapted from Peel MC, Finlayson BL & McMahon TA (2007) 'Updated World Map of the Köppen-Geiger Climate Classification', Hydrology and Earth System Sciences, 11, 163344.

Illustrations pp122–3, 206–7 and 214–5 by Javier Zarracina.

This Book

This 1st edition of Lonely Planet's *Cruise Ports European Rivers* guidebook was researched and written by Andy Symington, Mark Baker, Oliver Berry, Kerry Christiani, Gregor Clark, Marc Di Duca, Steve Fallon, Damian Harper, Catherine Le Nevez, Kevin Raub, Leonid Ragozin, Andrea Schulte-Peevers, Simon Richmond, Brendan Sainsbury, Regis St Louis, Benedict Walker and Nicola Williams.

This guidebook was produced by the following:

Destination Editors Jennifer Carey, Dan Fahey, Gemma Graham, Niamh O'Brien, Tom Stainer, Branislava Vladisavljevic

Senior Product Editor Sandie Kestell

Product Editor Shona Gray

Senior Cartographer Mark Griffiths

Book Designer Virginia Moreno

Assisting Editors Judith Bamber, Imogen Bannister, Michelle Bennett, Nigel Chin, Katie Connolly, Jacqueline Danam, Melanie Dankel, Emma Gibbs, Kellie Langdon, Alison Morris, Rosie Nicholson, Lorna Parkes, Susan Paterson, Monique Perrin, Sarah Reid, Fionnuala Twomey, Simon Williamson

Cover Researcher Naomi Parker

Thanks to Brooke Giacomin, Sandra Henriques Gajjar, Evan Godt, Kate Mathews, Kirsten Rawlings, Alison Ridgway

Send Us Your Feedback

We love to hear from travellers – your comments keep us on our toes and help make our books better. Our well-travelled team reads every word on what you loved or loathed about this book. Although we cannot reply individually to postal submissions, we always guarantee that your feedback goes straight to the appropriate authors, in time for the next edition. Each person who sends us information is thanked in the next edition, the most useful submissions are rewarded with a selection of digital PDF chapters.

Visit lonelyplanet.com/contact to submit your updates and suggestions or to ask for help. Our award-winning website also features inspirational travel stories, news and discussions.

Note: We may edit, reproduce and incorporate your comments in Lonely Planet products such as guidebooks, websites and digital products, so let us know if you don't want your comments reproduced or your name acknowledged. For a copy of our privacy policy visit lonelyplanet.com/privacy.

A – Z
Index

Symbols & Map Key

Look for these symbols to quickly identify listings:

- ◉ Sights
- ✪ Activities
- ⊜ Courses
- ◐ Tours
- ✪ Festivals & Events
- ✪ Eating
- ✪ Drinking
- ✪ Entertainment
- 🔒 Shopping
- ℹ Information & Transport

These symbols and abbreviations give vital information for each listing:

🌱 Sustainable or green recommendation

FREE No payment required

- ☏ Telephone number
- ☺ Opening hours
- P Parking
- ⊗ Nonsmoking
- ✳ Air-conditioning
- @ Internet access
- 🛜 Wi-fi access
- 🏊 Swimming pool

- 🚌 Bus
- ⛴ Ferry
- 🚋 Tram
- 🚆 Train
- 📋 English-language menu
- 🥗 Vegetarian selection
- 👪 Family-friendly

Find your best experiences with these Great For... icons.

 Art & Culture

 Beaches

 Budget

Cafe/Coffee

Cycling

Detour

Drinking

Entertainment

Events

Family Travel

 Food & Drink

 History

 Local Life

 Nature & Wildlife

 Photo Op

 Scenery

 Shopping

 Short Trip

Sport

Walking

Winter Travel

Sights

- Beach
- Bird Sanctuary
- Buddhist
- Castle/Palace
- Christian
- Confucian
- Hindu
- Islamic
- Jain
- Jewish
- Monument
- Museum/Gallery/ Historic Building
- Ruin
- Shinto
- Sikh
- Taoist
- Winery/Vineyard
- Zoo/Wildlife Sanctuary
- Other Sight

Points of Interest

- Bodysurfing
- Camping
- Cafe
- Canoeing/Kayaking
- Course/Tour
- Diving
- Drinking & Nightlife
- Eating
- Entertainment
- Sento Hot Baths/ Onsen
- Shopping
- Skiing
- Sleeping
- Snorkelling
- Surfing
- Swimming/Pool
- Walking
- Windsurfing
- Other Activity

Information

- Bank
- Embassy/Consulate
- Hospital/Medical
- Internet
- Police
- Post Office
- Telephone
- Toilet
- Tourist Information
- Other Information

Geographic

- Beach
- Gate
- Hut/Shelter
- Lighthouse
- Lookout
- Mountain/Volcano
- Oasis
- Park
- Pass
- Picnic Area
- Waterfall

Transport

- Airport
- BART station
- Border crossing
- Boston T station
- Bus
- Cable car/Funicular
- Cycling
- Ferry
- Metro/MRT station
- Monorail
- Parking
- Petrol station
- Subway/S-Bahn/ Skytrain station
- Taxi
- Train station/Railway
- Tram
- Underground/ U-Bahn station
- Other Transport

Simon Richmond

Journalist and photographer Simon Richmond has specialised as a travel writer since the early 1990s and first worked for Lonely Planet in 1999 on their Central Asia guide. He's long since stopped counting the number of guidebooks he's researched and written for the company, but countries covered include Australia, China, Greece, India, Indonesia, Iran, Poland, Japan, Malaysia, Mongolia, Myanmar (Burma), Russia, Singapore, South Africa, South Korea, Turkey and the USA. For Lonely Planet's website he's penned features on topics from the world's best swimming pools to the joys of Urban Sketching – follow him on Instagram (simonrichmond) to see some of his photos and sketches.

Brendan Sainsbury

Born and raised in the UK in a town that never merits a mention in any guidebook (Andover, Hampshire), Brendan spent the holidays of his youth caravanning in the English Lake District and didn't leave Blighty until he was 19. Making up for lost time, he's since squeezed 70 countries into a sometimes precarious existence as a writer and professional vagabond. When not scribbling research notes, Brendan likes partaking in ridiculous 'endurance' races, strumming old Clash songs on the guitar, and experiencing the pain and occasional pleasures of following Southampton Football Club.

Andrea Schulte-Peevers

Born and raised in Germany and educated in London and at UCLA, Andrea has travelled the distance to the moon and back in her visits to some 75 countries. She has earned her living as a professional travel writer for over two decades and authored or contributed to nearly 100 Lonely Planet titles as well as to newspapers, magazines and websites around the world. She also works as a travel consultant, translator and editor. Andrea's destination expertise is especially strong when it comes to Germany, Dubai and the UAE, Crete and the Caribbean Islands. She makes her home in Berlin.

Regis St Louis

Regis grew up in a small town in the American Midwest – the kind of place that fuels big dreams of travel – and he developed an early fascination with foreign dialects and world cultures. He spent his formative years learning Russian and a handful of Romance languages, which served him well on journeys across much of the globe. Regis has contributed to more than 50 Lonely Planet titles, covering destinations across six continents. His travels have taken him from the mountains of Kamchatka to remote island villages in Melanesia, and to many grand urban landscapes. When not on the road, he lives in New Orleans. Follow him on Instagram @regisstlouis.

Benedict Walker

A beach baby from Newcastle, Australia, Ben turned 40 in 2017 and decided to start a new life in Leipzig, Germany. Writing for LP was a childhood dream, and he has since covered big chunks of Australia, Canada, Germany, Japan, USA, Switzerland, Sweden and Japan for Lonely Planet guides. Come along for the ride, on Instagram @wordsandjourneys.

Nicola Williams

Border-hopping is way of life for British writer, runner, foodie, art aficionado and mum-of-three Nicola Williams who has lived in a French village on the southern side of Lake Geneva for more than a decade. Nicola has authored more than 50 guidebooks on Paris, Provence, Rome, Tuscany, France, Italy and Switzerland for Lonely Planet and covers France as a destination expert for the *Telegraph*. She also writes for the *Independent*, *Guardian*, lonelyplanet.com, *Lonely Planet Magazine*, *French Magazine*, *Cool Camping France* and others. Catch her on the road on Twitter and Instagram at @tripalong.

Kerry Christiani

Kerry is an award-winning travel writer, photographer and Lonely Planet author, specialising in Central and Southern Europe. Based in Wales, she has authored/co-authored more than a dozen Lonely Planet titles. An adventure addict, she loves mountains, cold places and true wilderness. She features her latest work at https://its-a-small-world.com and tweets @kerrychristiani.

Gregor Clark

Gregor Clark is a US-based writer whose love of foreign languages and curiosity about what's around the next bend have taken him to dozens of countries on five continents. Since 2000, Gregor has regularly contributed to Lonely Planet guides, with a focus on Europe and the Americas. Titles include *Italy*, *France*, *Brazil*, *Costa Rica*, *Argentina*, *Portugal*, *Switzerland*, *Mexico*, *South America on a Shoestring*, *Montreal & Quebec City*, *France Trips*, *New England Trips*, cycling guides to Italy and California and coffee-table pictorials such as *Food Trails*, *The USA Book* and *The LP Guide to the Middle of Nowhere*.

Marc Di Duca

A travel author for over a decade, Marc has worked for Lonely Planet in Siberia, Slovakia, Bavaria, England, Ukraine, Austria, Poland, Croatia, Portugal, Madeira and on the Trans-Siberian Railway, as well as writing and updating tens of other guides for other publishers. When not on the road, Marc lives near Mariánské Lázně in the Czech Republic with his wife and two sons.

Steve Fallon

A native of Boston, Massachusetts, Steve graduated from Georgetown University with a Bachelor of Science in modern languages. After working for several years for a daily US newspaper and earning a master's degree in journalism, he landed up in Hong Kong, where he lived for over a dozen years, working for a variety of media and running his own travel bookshop. Steve lived in Budapest for three years before moving to London in 1994. He has written or contributed to more than 100 Lonely Planet titles. Steve is a qualified London Blue Badge Tourist Guide. Visit his website on www.steveslondon.com.

Damian Harper

Damian has been writing for Lonely Planet for over two decades, contributing to titles as diverse as China, Beijing, Shanghai, Vietnam, Thailand, Ireland, London, Mallorca, Malaysia, Singapore & Brunei, Hong Kong, China's Southwest and the UK. A seasoned guidebook writer, Damian has penned articles for numerous newspapers and magazines, including *The Guardian* and *The Daily Telegraph*, and currently makes Surrey, England, his home. Follow Damian on Instagram (@damian.harper).

Catherine Le Nevez

Catherine's wanderlust kicked in when she roadtripped across Europe from her Parisian base aged four, and she's been hitting the road at every opportunity since, travelling to some 60 countries and completing her Doctorate of Creative Arts in Writing, Masters in Professional Writing, and postgrad qualifications in Editing and Publishing along the way. Over the past decade-and-a-half she's written scores of Lonely Planet guides and articles covering Paris, France, Europe and far beyond. Topping Catherine's list of travel tips is to travel without any expectations.

Leonid Ragozin

Leonid Ragozin studied beach dynamics at the Moscow State University, but for want of decent beaches in Russia, he switched to journalism and spent 12 years voyaging through different parts of the BBC, with a break for a four-year stint as a foreign correspondent for the Russian Newsweek. Leonid is currently a freelance journalist focusing largely on the conflict between Russia and Ukraine (both his Lonely Planet destinations), which prompted him to leave Moscow and find a new home in Rīga.

Kevin Raub

Atlanta native Kevin Raub started his career as a music journalist in New York, working for *Men's Journal* and *Rolling Stone* magazines. He ditched the rock 'n' roll lifestyle for travel writing and has written more than 70 Lonely Planet guides, focused mainly on Brazil, Chile, Colombia, USA, India, the Caribbean and Portugal. Raub also contributes to a variety of travel magazines in both the USA and UK. Along the way, the self-confessed hophead is in constant search of wildly high IBUs in local beers. Follow him on Twitter and Instagram (@RaubOnTheRoad).

Our Story

A beat-up old car, a few dollars in the pocket and a sense of adventure. In 1972 that's all Tony and Maureen Wheeler needed for the trip of a lifetime – across Europe and Asia overland to Australia. It took several months, and at the end – broke but inspired – they sat at their kitchen table writing and stapling together their first travel guide, *Across Asia on the Cheap*. Within a week they'd sold 1500 copies. Lonely Planet was born.

Today, Lonely Planet has offices in Franklin, London, Melbourne, Oakland, Dublin, Beijing and Delhi, with more than 600 staff and writers. We share Tony's belief that 'a great guidebook should do three things: inform, educate and amuse'.

Our Writers

Andy Symington

Andy has written or worked on more than a hundred books and other updates for Lonely Planet (especially in Europe and Latin America) and other publishing companies, and has published articles on numerous subjects for a variety of newspapers, magazines and websites. He part-owns and operates a rock bar, has written a novel and is currently working on several fiction and non-fiction writing projects. Andy, from Australia, moved to Northern Spain many years ago. When he's not off with a backpack in some far-flung corner of the world, he can probably be found watching the tragically poor local football team or tasting local wines after a long walk in the nearby mountains.

Mark Baker

Mark Baker is a freelance travel writer with a penchant for offbeat stories and forgotten places. He's originally from the United States, but now makes his home in the Czech capital, Prague. He writes mainly on Eastern and Central Europe for Lonely Planet as well as other leading travel publishers, but finds real satisfaction in digging up stories in places that are too remote or quirky for the guides. Prior to becoming an author, he worked as a journalist for The Economist, Bloomberg News and Radio Free Europe, among other organisations. Instagram & Twitter: @markbakerprague.

Oliver Berry

Oliver Berry is a writer and photographer from Cornwall. He has worked for Lonely Planet for more than a decade, covering destinations from Cornwall to the Cook Islands, and has worked on more than 30 guidebooks. He is also a regular contributor to many newspapers and magazines, including Lonely Planet Traveller. His writing has won several awards, including The Guardian Young Travel Writer of the Year and the TNT Magazine People's Choice Award. His latest work is published at www.oliverberry.com.

← More Writers ←

STAY IN TOUCH LONELYPLANET.COM/CONTACT

AUSTRALIA The Malt Store, Level 3, 551 Swanston St, Carlton, Victoria 3053
☏ 03 8379 8000,
fax 03 8379 8111

IRELAND Digital Depot, Roe Lane (off Thomas St), Digital Hub, Dublin 8, D08 TCV4, Ireland

USA 124 Linden Street, Oakland, CA 94607
☏ 510 250 6400,
toll free 800 275 8555,
fax 510 893 8572

UK 240 Blackfriars Road, London SE1 8NW
☏ 020 3771 5100,
fax 020 3771 5101

 twitter.com/ lonelyplanet

 facebook.com/ lonelyplanet

 instagram.com/ lonelyplanet

 youtube.com/ lonelyplanet

 lonelyplanet.com/ newsletter